Politik und Gesellschaft des Nahen Ostens

Reihe herausgegeben von
Martin Beck, Odense, Dänemark
Cilja Harders, Berlin, Deutschland
Annette Jünemann, Hamburg, Deutschland
Rachid Ouaissa, Marburg, Deutschland
Stephan Stetter, Neubiberg, Deutschland

Die Reihe beschäftigt sich mit aktuellen Entwicklungen und Umbrüchen in Nordafrika, dem Nahen Osten, der Golfregion und darüber hinaus. Die politischen, sozialen und ökonomischen Dynamiken in der Region sind von hoher globaler Bedeutung und sie strahlen intensiv auf Europa aus. Die Reihe behandelt die gesamte Bandbreite soziopolitischer Themen in der Region: Veränderungen in Konfliktmustern und Kooperationsbeziehungen in Folge der Arabischen Revolten 2010/11 wie etwa Euro-Arabische und Euro-Mediterrane Beziehungen oder den Nahostkonflikt. Auf nationaler Ebene geht es um Themen wie Reform, Transformation und Autoritarismus, Islam und Islamismus, soziale Bewegungen, Geschlechterverhältnisse aber auch energie- und umweltpolitische Fragen, Migrationsdynamiken oder neue Entwicklungen in der Politischen Ökonomie. Der Schwerpunkt liegt auf innovativen politikwissenschaftlichen Werken, die die gesamte theoretische Breite des Faches abdecken. Eingang finden aber auch Beiträge aus anderen sozialwissenschaftlichen Disziplinen, die relevante politische Zusammenhänge behandeln.

This book series focuses on key developments in the Middle East and North Africa as well as the Gulf and beyond. The regions' political, economic and social dynamics are of high global significance, not the least for Europe. The book series covers the whole range of the ongoing transformations in the region, such as new developments in regional conflict and cooperation after the uprisings of 2010/2011 including Euro-Arab and Euro-Mediterranean relations, or the Israeli-Palestinian conflict. On a (trans) national level, volumes in the series look at authoritarianism and reform, social movements, gender dynamics, Islam and Islamism, political economy, migration, as well as energy and environmental issues. The series focuses on innovative work in all sub-disciplines of political science and other social sciences disciplines that address political developments in the Middle East.

Dr. Martin Beck ist Professor für gegenwartsbezogene Nahost-Studien an der University of Southern Denmark in Odense, Dänemark.

Dr. Cilja Harders ist Professorin für Politikwissenschaft und Leiterin der „Arbeitsstelle Politik im Maghreb, Mashreq, Golf" am Otto-Suhr-Institut für Politikwissenschaft der Freien Universität Berlin, Deutschland.

Dr. Annette Jünemann ist Professorin für Politikwissenschaft am Institut für Internationale Politik der Helmut-Schmidt-Universität Hamburg, Universität der Bundeswehr Hamburg, Deutschland.

Dr. Rachid Ouaissa ist Professor für Politik des Nahen und Mittleren Ostens am Centrum für Nah- und Mittelost-Studien der Philipps-Universität Marburg, Deutschland.

Dr. Stephan Stetter ist Professor für Internationale Politik und Konfliktforschung an der Universität der Bundeswehr München, Deutschland.

Weitere Bände in der Reihe http://www.springer.com/series/12508

Anna Antonakis

Renegotiating Gender and the State in Tunisia between 2011 and 2014

Power, Positionality, and the Public Sphere

With a foreword by Prof. Dr. Cilja Harders

Springer VS

Anna Antonakis
Berlin, Germany

Dissertation Freie Universität Berlin, 2018

ISSN 2626-224X   ISSN 2626-2258   (electronic)
Politik und Gesellschaft des Nahen Ostens
ISBN 978-3-658-25638-8   ISBN 978-3-658-25639-5   (eBook)
https://doi.org/10.1007/978-3-658-25639-5

Library of Congress Control Number: 2019933865

Springer VS

This Springer VS imprint is published by the registered company Springer Fachmedien Wiesbaden
GmbH part of Springer Nature
The registered company address is: Abraham-Lincoln-Str. 46, 65189 Wiesbaden, Germany

In memory of Sofiane Chourabi, journalist and friend.
And Noura Borsali, feminist historian, who was so kind as to participate in this
study.

Foreword Cilja Harders

Tunisia's transformation is often taken to be model for a peaceful, negotiated transition from dictatorship to democracy, the last and only hope of the "Arab Spring" which all too soon turned into an "Arab winter". Since 2011, women's rights have been a highly visible, controversial and highly mobilizing issue in Tunisia – again leading to the perception, that the Tunisian transition is an outstanding example of emancipatory gender politics in a conservative context. This is not entirely wrong, claims Anna Antonakis, but it is definitely not the full story of the transformation. What is more, these narratives do not do justice to the struggles of women and the many shortcomings and pitfalls of a transition processes.

In this highly accessible and rich book, Anna Antonakis creates a multivocal assemblage of feminist and women's discourses and practices in the turbulent times since 2011. She successfully deconstructs those academic and public narratives, which depict the political dynamics in Tunisia between 2011 and 2014 as a simple ideological struggle between "secularists" and "islamists". Instead, she shows how, among others, women's rights and the state feminist legacy are used by actors of transformation and actors of restauration. Gender issues were indeed an arena and a battle field in the Tunisian transformation. But, as Anna Antonakis shows, the smoke of these battles tends to marginalize many other grievances, which drove the revolution. First and foremost, these concern structural marginalization of the "hinterland", socio-economic issues and a non-declared class-struggle.

In her innovative conceptual framework, Anna Antonakis infuses the quite Eurocentric concepts of the public sphere with a thorough analysis of power structures. Among others, she proposes the compelling concept of "dissembled secularism" in order to understand the highly ambivalent features of state feminism under Bourgiba and Ben Ali. This legacy fed into the production of a "stable patriarchal regime of consensus", which marks the Tunisian political system today. This system is based on an elite-centered politics of ideological polarization as driving force of the transformation process. In this polarization women's right's narratives were used time and again in order to accentuate ideological difference at least on a discursive level, while on the ground, secularists and islamists tend to share rather conservative gender perceptions. As a result, voices arguing for fundamental changes of the existing gender-regime were sidelined. At the same time, issues of class, inequality and marginalization were silenced by both camps and women's rights activism was caught between a rock and a hard place in many of the struggles, Antonakis looks at.

This exciting, insightful and thoroughly thought-through book offers a critical and nuanced evaluation of the impact of feminist action on the gender regime of post-revolutionary Tunisia. Tunisian feminists, Antonakis argues, brought indeed substantial changes to a hitherto very limited and controlled public sphere. Still, the differences between the pre-revolutionary and the post-revolutionary gender system are smaller than most women activists would have hoped for.

Berlin, November 2018   Cilja Harders

Acknowledgements

The thoughts, ideas and support of many people laid the groundwork for this research: I have encountered most interesting scholars, political practitioners and activists from different disciplines. These encounters and exchanges have all shaped, in one way or another, the outcome of this study. This book is based on the research I conducted in the frame of my PhD project, that I started in 2013 and defended in June 2017 at the Otto-Suhr-Institute of the Freie Universität Berlin. My deepest gratitude goes to my two academic supervisors Prof. Cilja Harders and Prof. Carola Richter, who have supported and guided this research over the years with their helpful comments and trust, encouraging me to seek independent, emancipatory scholarship, as well as opening up a new horizon of inquiry.

This research would not have been possible without the PhD scholarship by the Heinrich Böll Foundation and the support I received as a doctoral fellow at the SWP Berlin from 2013 to 2016 in the frame of the project "Elite Change and new Social Mobilization in the Arab World". I want to thank the whole research group for extraordinary discussions we had on the developments of the region. A special thank you to Dr. Muriel Asseburg, for her support and illuminating remarks and feedbacks helping me to seek critical scholarship of high quality and Dr. Isabelle Werenfels for her most valuable comments.

I'm thankful for new perspectives I gathered on my research in the frame of the DAAD network "Gender. Culture and Transformation in Tunisia," lead by Dr. Steffie Hobuß, Moez Maataoui and Ina Loch and the whole research group of the DAAD project "Maghreb in Transition", especially Dr. Amir Hamid.

I'm deeply indebted to all the interview partners and participants in Tunisia: Thank you for taking your time to answer my questions and your faith in me for conducting this research. I can only name a few of those friends and collegues who assisted and supported me in seeking critical knowledge production on and in Tunisia and introduced me to new localities: Azyz Amami, Ghofrane Heraghi, Samir Israel, Olfa Jelassi, Moudhafer Labidi and Slim Magr, Khouloud Mahdhaoui, as well as Chouikha Abdelhak. I also had the opportunity to visit various organizations and associations in Tunisia. I'm grateful to the Association Tunisienne des Femmes Démocrates for opening its doors to me in Tunis and in Kairouan. Furthermore, I thank the association Femme et Citoyenneté for welcoming me into their office in El Kef.

I'd like to especially thank Dr. Imad Alsoos, Prof. Natalie Fenton, Dr. Shir Hever, Sarah Mersch and Mareike Transfeld for their insightful comments on chapters of earlier drafts. For their wonderful help in editing and proofreading this book, I thank Jade Frisch, Tom Kaina and Jamie Zulauf. I thank the editors of this series and Sabine Schöller for their assistance in finishing this manuscript and the publication of this book.

Last but not least, I thank my partner and my friends, especially Atiaf Alwazir, Alina Bongk, May ElMahdi, Kathrin Schug as well as my parents Apostolos and Mechthilde Antonakis, for their unconditional support in all my endeavors.

Anna Antonakis,

Berlin, December 2018

Preface

In the year 2011, a "revolutionary spirit" contesting established neoliberal economic and hegemonic norms took grip of the world. In 2010 and 2011, men and women in the streets of Tunisia chanted the call for change expressed in the slogan "Work, Freedom and National Dignity!" *("Choghl, hourria, karama watanya!")* (Azouzi, 2013, p. 22), inspiring a global uprising in 2011. The demands were communicated under various oppressive conditions in wider national and international public spheres in demonstrations and blockades, poems and posts. Their struggle included different demands: social and economic justice, freedom of expression and the elimination of arbitrary state practices and corruption. But specifically, the uprisings in Tunisia and other countries across the region have – at least initially – carried the hope for a "revolution of women" and a renewal of the gendered social contract (Wahba, 2016, p. 67) as well.

This revolutionary spirit addressing inequalities went far beyond the narrative of the "Arab Spring" that originated in Tunisia but seemed to include the 99% of different parts of the world. Today, it appears that right-wing and fascist ideologies and conservative backlashes have channeled and co-opted resentments and have been garnished with racist and sexist ideologies. On the other hand, we are witnessing an increasing feminist awakening, expressed in states' foreign policy agendas or self-mediated practices by women.

Before and after the uprisings, negotiations around women's rights have been an instrument to mark the boundaries between secular and religious political camps, obscuring the actual struggles over state power. (Charrad, 2008, p. 111; Gray, 2011, p. 285; Marks, 2013, p. 224, Khalil, 2014, p. 196). However, scholars in these fields have not yet fully traced the different processes allowing gender to become a purely discursive marker for cultural-political differentiations in the public sphere. While this essential literature has exposed the centrality of gender in its instrumental function for nation building, power politics and (popular) mobilizations, it often remains focused on capitals and negotiations around legislation and institutions only.

The question of how the mere subject of feminism is negotiated in media industries, political institutions but also in everyday interactions and self-mediated practices online has not been addressed. Because of this, we lack understanding on global anti-feminist mobilization and its rise in popularity in recent years. I expect this research to contribute to further understanding on the restoration of authoritarian structures and conservative backlashes by exploring emancipatory and inclusive negotiations around gender in different publics and their geopolitical implications.

I started developing this study in 2012, building on two distinct research endeavors. In 2009, I undertook field research in Tunis on the situation of secular feminist organizations under authoritarian rule. I sought to combine this interest in feminist activism with my research on the dynamics of online and offline mobilizations during the "revolutionary period" from December 20th, 2010 until the ousting of Zine el-Abidine Ben Ali on January 14th, 2011. I argued that counterpublics created online could break the information monopoly of the hegemonic authoritarian publics sphere in Tunisia. Still euphoric about the role of social media in the process and the newly gained freedom of expression, I planned to critically investigate the use of social media by women in particular to enlarge their space of activism and break taboo issues in feminist publics. Even though I was aware of digital divides, that is the unequal access to Internet infrastructure, I soon discovered that an investigation of only online participatory practices of women's activists would rely on the core assumption of a modernist democratization paradigm incorporating a technological optimism. I see the danger of glossing over the actual power struggles taking place in the country that were de facto determining the aims and interests of the activists.

My previous research in Tunisia before the uprisings in 2009 was both the empirical and thus conceptual inception of this project. The change I experienced from a highly controlled public where even speaking the name of the president was problematic to new vocal expressions of the many has furthermore sensitized me to state feminist politics as a powerful instrument for domestic and foreign politics alike, because women's rights in Tunisia have often been singled out and exploited to "whitewash" the regime's control over the public sphere.

In the research perspective proposed here, "positionality", amongst others, aims to shed light on the producer of knowledge and does so with regards to gender relations in different societies. Becoming aware of my own privilege and bias throughout the project, in its conceptualization, the interview situations, as well as the writing process, was certainly not easy. I had received a three-year research grant from HBS enabling me to do this project. I'm aware that Tunisian feminists and scholars do not have this privilege. Along that line, I claim that we are lacking an "outsider's perspective" that would give new insights to identity struggles and political co-optations within the feminist movement in Western societies. In times of patriarchal and misogynist backlashes, true transnational feminist solidarity becomes more crucial than ever. In this context, it was very helpful to read Angela Davis' chapter on her visit to Egypt and the response of Egyptian feminist scholar Sara Salem on the possibilities of transnational feminist solidarity (Salem, 2013). Furthermore, I'm thankful to the numerous commentators and friends who pointed out problematic issues on different levels of this study.

In the course of this study, I temporarily acquired a position in the German public sphere from which I could analyze the situation of the policy process that was still ongoing in Tunisia and acquired symbolic power which is "constructed as the power to define how the social world is and should legitimately be ordered" (Bourdieu, 1995, p. 38). I believe that conscious usage of the resources and knowledge matter and are worthy of scrutiny. Here, the idea of "intellectual activism" that has been laid out by Patricia Hill Collins becomes crucial, and bears the empowering idea that everybody is able to make a change and shift power relations with their own means:

"As people push against, step away from, and shift the terms of their participation in power relations, the shape of power relations changes for everyone. Like individual subjectivity, resistance strategies and power are always multiple and in constant states of change" (Collins, 2000, p. 275).

Table of Content

Part I: Empirical and Theoretical Introduction:
The Public Sphere from a Post-colonial Perspective

1   Introduction 1
1.1   Preliminary Note on the Conceptual Approach 1
1.2   The Process of Constructing Knowledge 7
    1.2.1   Studying Gender and Women's Participation in the Age of
          Political Contestation in Tunisia 7
    1.2.2   Who is Speaking? Interviews Conducted for this Study 8
1.3   Research Objective and Structure of the Study 11

2   Positionalities, Modernity and the Public Sphere 15
2.1   Tunisia's Modelization and Regional Exceptionalism 16
2.2   Western Publics: What Are We Reproducing Here? 19
2.3   "Talking About a Revolution" from Different Positionalities................. 22
2.4   Conclusion: Applying Intersectionality 25

3   Constructing an Empirically Grounded Framework 29
3.1   Public Sphere(s) and Counterpublics..30
    3.1.1   The Public Sphere: Empirical and Theoretical Starting-Point 30
    3.1.2   Operationalization and Critique 32
    3.1.3   (Feminist) Counterpublics 35
3.2   Defining Publics within Matrices of Domination 37
    3.2.1   Power and the Three Dimensions of the Public Sphere 38
    3.2.2   The Hegemonic Domain of Power 41
    3.2.3   Typology of Counterpublics Within the Matrix of Domination .. 43

4   The Nation State Within the Matrix of Domination 49
4.1   State Institutions Regulating the Public Sphere...................................... 50
    4.1.1   The Nation-State and Marginalized Localities............................. 52
    4.1.2   Gender and Nation... 53
4.2   State Feminism as a Post-Colonial Hegemonic Legacy 54
    4.2.1   State Feminism Manifesting the Modern Subject of Feminism... 55

4.2.2   State Feminism and "Dissembled Secularism" 58
4.3. Conclusion: State Feminism in Relation to Authoritarianism 59

5   Detecting the Matrix of Domination: A Historical Perspective 61
5.1   French Colonial Rule and Reformist Counterpublics 62
5.2   Post-Colonial Patriarchal Regimes:
       Exploiting "Dissembled Secularism" 67
       5.2.1   Bourguiba and the Nationalist Project of Modernity 67
       5.2.2   Ben Ali's Regime: A Public Sphere between Liberalization,
               Privatization and Repression 75
5.3   Conclusion: A Hegemonic Public Sphere in Post-Colonial Tunisia 83

6   Counterpublic Resistance under Ben Ali's Rule 85
6.1   Feminist Counterpublics emerging in the 1980's 85
6.2   The 18th October Movement of 2005 91
6.3   Counterpublics Against Internet Censorship 93

7   Challenging the Matrix of Domination 97
7.1   The Uprisings in Gafsa 2008/2009 97
7.2   The Uprisings in 2010/2011 102
7.3   Menzel Bouzayane and the Kasbah Square Moment 106

**Part II: Analyzing Negotiations of Gender in Different
           Dimensions of the Public Sphere in Tunisia (2011-2014)**

8   The Structural Dimension of the Public Sphere: 115
8.1   Redefining Legislations for Gendered Inclusivity 116
       8.1.1   Negotiations within HIROR: The Women's Electoral Quota.... 117
       8.1.2   Institutionalizing a Pluralist Public Sphere? 120
       8.1.3   Elections for the Constitutional Assembly 121
8.2   Renegotiating the Constitution 125
       8.2.1   Whose Feminist Frameworks? 126
       8.2.2   CEDAW-Trouble and the Limits of State Feminism 135
8.3   Elections and a New "Patriarchal Bargain" 138
       8.3.1   The Constitution of 2014: Manifesting a Paradox 140
       8.3.2   The Negotiations Around the Electoral Quota in 2014 144
       8.3.3   Elections of 2014: The "Vote Utile"- Campaign Revitalizing
               Bourguibism 146
8.4   Conclusion: Renegotiating Gendered Institutions 149

9   The Representational Dimension of the Public Sphere 151
9.1   Who Is In? Media Representation of and by Women............................ 153
        9.1.1   The "Classical Media": Persisting Underrepresentations 154
        9.1.2   Counterpublics Online: Multifaceted Visibilities....................... 161
9.2   What Is On? Discussing the "False Problems"?..................................... 165
        9.2.1   Polygamie.. 167
        9.2.2   The Inheritance Legislation... 168
        9.2.3   Femen and Amina Sboui 171
9.3   Counterthematizations: "Let's Talk About the Real Issues"................ 177
        9.3.1   Gender and Labor.. 177
        9.3.2   Gender and Locality 181
        9.3.3   Gender and Health.. 184
9.4   Conclusion: Gender on the Mediatized Battlefield 186

10   The Interactional Dimension of the Public Sphere 189
10.1   Shaping Negotiations of Gender on the Ground.................................... 190
        10.1.1   Political Instrumentalizations and Foreign Funding 191
        10.1.2   Extremism and Radicalizations 195
        10.1.3   The Police and Gender Based Violence 199
10.2   Decolonizing and Localizing Feminist Terminologies and Practices... 205
        10.2.1   Unveiling Authoritarian Terminologies 205
        10.2.2   Reviewing the "Subject of Feminism".. 208
        10.2.3   The Family and Community as "Site of Transformation":
                     Deconstructing 'Naturalized Hierarchies'.................................... 214
10.3   Conclusion: Encountering (Violent) Excertion of Influence................ 217

11   Conclusion...219
11.1   About the Exploitation of Gender Politics... 219
11.2   Changes and Persistency the Public Sphere.............. 220
        11.2.1   Interdependencies: Political Institutions and Media 221
        11.2.2   Challenging Patriarchy, Decolonizing Feminism 223
11.3   Hidden Hegemonies: The Matrix of Domination 2.0 225

**12   Outlook: Negotiating Homosexualities in Tunisia: Inclusions and
          Exploitations in the Hegemonic Public Sphere after 2014** 229

References 233

List of Illustrations

Table 1: Gendered Adaption of the Public Sphere Model by Peter Dahlgren and Classification of the Empirical Material to the Conceptual Framework...p. 48f.

Chart 1: Presentation of Female Politicians in selected national Mass Media before, during and after the elections 2011.......................p.155

Chart 2: Media Coverage Accorded to Gender Issues in % ....p. 156

List of Abbreviations[1]

AFTURD	Association de la Femme Tunisienne pour la Recherche et le Développement, Association of Tunisian Women for Research and Development
ANC	Assemblée Nationale Constituante, National Constituent Assembly
ATFD	Association Tunisienne des Femmes Démocrates, Tunisian Association of Democratic Women
CAWTAR	Center of Arab Women for Training and Research
CEDAW	Convention on the Elimination against All Discrimination against Women
CPR	Congrès pour la République, Congress for the Republic
CREDIF	Centre de Recherches, d'Etudes, de Documentation et d'Information sur la Femme, Centre for Research, Studies, Documentation and Information on Women
CSP	Code du Statut Personnel, Personal Status Code
FSN	Front du Salut National, National Salvation Front
HIROR	Haute Instance pour la Réalisation des Objectifs de la Revolution, des Réformes Politiques et de la Transition Démocratique, Higher Commission for the Fulfillment of Revolutionary Goals, Political Reform, and Democratic Transition
IRIE	Instance Régionale Indépendante pour les Elections, the Independent Regional Authority for Elections
ISIE	Instance Supérieure Indépendante pour les Elections, the Independent High Authority for Elections
LGBT	Lesbian, Gay, Bisexual and Transgender
LTDH	Ligue Tunisienne des Droits de l'Homme, Tunisian Human Rights League
MENA	Middle East and North Africa
MIT	Mouvement Islamiste Tunisienne, The Movement of Islamic Tendency
PDP	Parti Démocratique Progressiste, Democratic Progressive Party

---

1 In this study, mainly French acronyms will be employed.

POCT	Party Ouvrier Communiste Tunisien, Communist Worker's Party
RCD	Rassemblement Constitutionelle Démocratique, Democratic Constitutional Rally
UDC	Union des Diplômés Chômeurs, Union of Unemployed Academics
UGET	Union Générale des Etudiants Tunisiens, General Union of Students of Tunisia
UGTT	Union Générale Tunisienne de Travail, Tunisian General Labor Union
UPL	Union Patriotique Libre, Free Patriotic Union's Party, al-Itihad al-Watany al-Hurr
UTICA	Union Tunisienne de l'Industrie, du Commerce et de l'Artisanat, The Tunisian Confederation of Industry, Trade and Handcraft
UWAW	Uprisings of Women in the Arab World
WSIS	World Summit on the Information Society

Note on Language, Transliteration and Citation

Throughout this book, I have adopted a simplified transliteration scheme. Where there exists a common English or French spelling of proper names – most notably in the case of party or city names like Ennahda or ElKef – I have opted for the most commonly used spelling.

In the following, quotes from the interviews will be highlighted by indentations; they have been translated into English by the author. Original quotes from the interviews over one line, will have a separate, indented paragraph, to highlight the respondents' contribution to this book. All other quotes from literature over four lines will be indented and petit.

Part I
Empirical and Theoretical Introduction:
The Public Sphere from a Post-colonial Perspective

1 Introduction

1.1 Preliminary Note on the Conceptual Approach

On June 1, 2016, the statue of Habib Bourguiba, Tunisia's first president after the country's independence in 1956, was inaugurated in the city center of Tunis. He is depicted on his horse, overlooking the avenue of his name, behind him what has become the town's and countries' landmark: The clock at the round square that was renamed "Place of the 14th of January" in commemoration of Ben Ali's escape to Saudi Arabia. After 24 years of dictatorial rule under President Ben Ali, the inauguration marks the re-appearance of a specific type of political leader. In this study, I refer to Habib Bourguiba as an "organic intellectual." This statesman has been associated with a unique Tunisian way of governing, the so-called "Bourguibism", that has been assumed to be "assigned to the dustbins of history" (Sadiki, 2008, p.110) under Ben Ali's regime. It is associated with state feminism and constructed as "secular." Bourguiba was widely understood to be the liberator of the nation and – at the same time - the liberator of women. Four years after people gathered in the Avenue Bourguiba and chanted the famous slogan "degage!" ("Go away!") directed at President Ben Ali in front of the Ministry of the Interior, *Bourguibism* re-appears in form of his statue right in front of the same Ministry overlooking that very boulevard. I claim that the publicly manifested re-appearance of Bourguiba marks the end point of a historical period for the Mediterranean country.

The re-installation of a statue of the country's first ruler in such a central space at the end of a "transformation period" seems puzzling. Habib Bourguiba's

© Springer Fachmedien Wiesbaden GmbH, part of Springer Nature 2019
A. Antonakis, *Renegotiating Gender and the State in Tunisia between 2011 and 2014*, Politik und Gesellschaft des Nahen Ostens,
https://doi.org/10.1007/978-3-658-25639-5_1

statue appears to be the unifier of a unity government that marks old-new stabilities since 2015 and includes the Islamic party Ennahda, Nidaa Tounes, and new liberal parties such as the Free Patriotic Union's Party (al-Ittihad al-Watany al-Hurr, Union Patriotique Libre, UPL). By contrast, the Popular Front (al-Jabhah al-Sha`biyyah, Front Populaire), a left party coalition founded in 2012, is excluded from the government. In the process that lead to this political constellation, I argue gender negotiations played a crucial role for shaping parties' ideologies, as well as political polarization and paving the way for a patriarchal consensus. Based on a multi-modal qualitative methodology, this research shows how women's rights have been a central space of negotiation to re-vitalize Bourguibism [i.e. state-feminism] at the expense of new pluralist female voices that couldn't find representation in the process and engages with the restoration of a hegemonic understanding of feminism.

In this book, I aim to draw a more holistic picture of re-negotiations of gender in political transformations through an empirically grounded analysis in post-revolutionary Tunisia. I expose the comprehensive mechanisms underlying political polarizations in different publics. The case is unique, as it constitutes a state at a surprising historical juncture leading to structural shifts in the public sphere. Using an interdisciplinary approach, conjugating intersectional theory and (counter) public sphere theory, I conceptualize feminist and female resistance in counterpublics against patriarchal hegemonic publics through multiple modalities. From the case study and according to the elaborated framework, I ask: What are challenges of feminist actors "bargaining at the center of power" in political institutions? Departing from the argument that representation of femininities and masculinities in popular media is essential to assess negotiations of gender: What and who are the themes and actors in this transformational process? By contrast, what intersectional oppressions remain underrepresented in the public sphere and how are they addressed (gender in relation to health, race, locality, and class)? What different forms of participation in (digital) counterpublics can be distinguished and how are they encumbered by "architectures of control" (Deibert et al, 2010)? Finally, is a Tunisian feminist generation, defined by global digital cultures, emerging?

This study is exploratory and draws from first hand data collection and extensive fieldwork in Tunisia. My body of data comprises over 30 transcriptions of explorative and guided interviews conducted between 2013 and 2016 on respective views on the transformation in Tunisia, dominant feminism(s) and changing perceptions of different media outlets and platforms. Research participants came from different localities in order to break the capital bias and included "hypervisible" bloggers such as Lina Ben Mheni, politicians and "ordinary" (h)activists in order to uncover their "situated knowledge" (Haraway, 1988) and to detect the manifold structural barriers to emancipatory politics. I conducted document analyses to expose changes at the institutional dimension of the public sphere. Furthermore, I relied on official sources in Arabic and French to trace compositions of institutional bodies. I interpreted quantitative media monitoring by NGOs and watchdog initiatives on women's representation in popular media. Besides literature by the Frankfurter School in German, I critically engage with the existing scholarship in English and French.

On a general note, feminism constitutes a contested concept and is debated in media, academia and activism in different regional contexts. Women take ambiguous stances towards it, depending on different racial and class experiences (Aronson, 2003, p. 904)[2]. In the Western scholarly debate, the concept of post-feminism has been discussed since the 1980s to point to a young generation of women who benefit from extensive opportunities for political, economic and social participation and therefore would not need to claim further political rights. Tunisian feminists have to defend themselves against the same argument. Nevertheless, women's stances towards "feminism" are very much influenced by the national context in which different feminist movements develop. In post-revolutionary Tunisia, state feminist practices associated with an authoritarian legacy come into focus. I claim that feminist counterpublics are then essentially engaging in demarcating their struggle from a former state project. It can be argued that the subject of feminism is to be re-invented as an essential part of gender renegotiation. This idea builds on Judith Butler's understanding of a feminist critique: "It is not enough to inquire into how women might become more fully represented in language and politics. Feminist critique ought also to understand how the category of 'women', the subject of feminism, is produced and restrained by the very structures of power through which emancipation is sought" (Butler, 1990, p. 2). Intersectionality encompasses the triangulation process between the collection and interpretation of the empirical data, the methodological approach and the theoretical concepts. I define feminist renegotiation as a communicative and participatory act aiming to add new or challenge hegemonic ideas that are powerfully manifested in the different dimensions of the public sphere.

This study goes "beyond the moment" (Lim, 2011) of the uprisings, and will investigate how gender relations were contested during the period commonly framed as "transformation", exploited and renegotiated in multiple forms in the public sphere. I target two major areas of study: Firstly, I explore the impacts of state feminist practices and ideology in post-colonial societies in constructing the "subject of feminism" and shed light on the articulation of resistance towards it. I hereby seek to divulge emancipatory renegotiations of feminism that unveil

---

2 Most of this research has been conducted before the global hashtag #metoo publicly multiplied the experience of women with sexism, encompassing a collective, structural level. The sharing of stories could be regarded as the common denominator of feminism. The reception of the hashtag lead to a new debate on feminism and the position of (women in the society that reached feuilletons and Twitter but also workspaces, communities and family circles.

historical codifications of women's rights in the modernist nationalist frame-work. Empirically, this study engages with different processes of gender negoti-ations in the public sphere as part of a transformative trajectory triggered by the uprisings in 2010/2011 in Tunisia. In this study, I employ the term of "women" and "woman". However, queer theory has pointed out the social and biological construction of these categories and paved the way for more visibility of Trans*people. This troubling of categories is often reflected in innovative scrip-tures such as "womyn" or women*.

Secondly, I aim to provide further understanding of the restoration of author-itarian structures and conservative backlashes within national and global com-munication infrastructure dominated by national political elites and popular cul-tural industries. I argue that an instrumentalization of gender, set within an en-tertainment and populist frame and articulated in various forms in the public sphere can be observed not only in Tunisia but also in Europe and the United States in legislations, media representations and interactions in public space.

Political scientist and analyst Amel Boubakeur qualifies the political oppo-sition between the Islamic Ennahda party and the "secular"[3] party Nidaa Tounes that appeared on the scene in 2012 as a "bargained competition". Rather than representing competing adversaries, they initiated a "pacted transition." She con-tinues that "the two blocs have increasingly monopolized the political arena, and the revolutionaries' demands for change and participation have been re-chan-neled into a reductive form of pluralism that ostensibly pits Islamists against representatives of the old regime" (Boubakeur, 2015, p. 5). This ideological competition, however, glossed over the actual agreements in terms of economic programs and would not challenge the neo-liberal direction of Tunisia's econ-omy that had led to the crisis in the first place. On this basis, a unity government including both camps was formed in 2015. From this perspective, Fabio Merone concludes there is a "middle class compromise upon which the new Tunisia is being constructed" (Merone, 2015, p. 79). Taking this as a point of departure, I will demonstrate that gender politics bear great explanatory potential for the in-stallation of this stable patriarchal regime of consensus that I will later frame as a "historical bloc."

The period between the uprisings and the first presidential and parliamentary elections in 2014 was not marked by competition of political programs but by ideological debates between national elites and party leaders. Rather than the socio-economic divide, it was ideological polarization that stood out in the pub-lic sphere as driving force of the political processes. By drawing on two different theoretical approaches, intersectionality and (counter) public sphere theory, this

---

3 Find the definition of the term "secular" as a political program in the post-colonial context that does indeed employ religion and its relation to state feminism under 4.2.1. (Boubakeur, 2015, p. 18).

study will analyze how gender politics have historically played into and instrumentally shaped this dynamic after the uprisings. Public sphere theory allows me to point to small and structural changes in a post-revolutionary, multifaceted context. It provides a new approach to studying states and societies in transformation without losing sight of structural oppression that classical transformation theories are often lacking.

I will elaborate the model on the basis of the three dimensions of the public sphere expounded by Peter Dahlgren, who represents one of the most cited scholars in the field of media and communication (Car, 2011, p. 123). He distinguishes the structural, representational and interactional dimensions of the public sphere (Dahlgren, 2005, p. 148). The first is concerned with legislations, the second refers to media output and the last to interactional publics constituted by different associations or networks[4]. However, most of public sphere theory, and Dahlgren's model presents no exception here, does not consider structural power relations that constitute inclusionary and exclusionary processes to the public sphere, nor do they explain the assertiveness of certain ideologies and their historic development in regulating access to institutions, organizations and resources that are central to participation in public spheres. My contribution to this theoretical debate is to integrate power structures from an intersectional paradigm. I mainly rely on the work of sociologist Patricia Hill Collins, who is considered a leading scholar in intersectional theory and her discussion of domains of power. She developed the model of the Matrix of Domination (Collins, 2000, p. 84) understood as interlocking structures of oppression within a historically defined national context. Ideology, in this work, refers to "a body of ideas reflecting the interests of a particular social group" (Collins, 2000, p. 299).

Within the intersectional perspective, I will critically revisit and integrate the concepts of counterpublics into Dahlgren's model, situating them on the different dimensions of public sphere to show the various forms of feminist contestations. The term of "negotiation" is reflected in the definition of the public sphere as constituted by "a constellation of communicative spaces in society that permit the circulation of information, ideas, debates— ideally in an unfettered manner—and also the formation of political will (i.e., public opinion)" (Dahlgren, 2005, p. 148). I define renegotiation as a communicative and participatory act aiming to add new or challenge existing hegemonic ideas powerfully manifested in institutional settings, social relations or everyday practices defining the public sphere. My understanding of participation is closely related to Lubna Skalli's framing of communication in her conceptualization of different media, that women employ to renegotiate their position: "[C]ommunications refer to different mediums –traditional, personal, modern and technological- that women use strategically and efficiently to organize, mobilize and produce alternative forms

---

4   I outline a discussion of the model in more detail in Chapter 3.

of knowledge that advance their struggle" (Skalli, 2006, p. 37).

In order to tackle the three dimensions of the public sphere, this study explores changes in national and international women's right's legislations and asks: What are the outcomes of the institutional renegotiation process in terms of (concrete) policies adopted under the respective governments in Tunisia? What were the challenges and perceptions of the feminist counterpublics "bargaining at the center of power"? Secondly, departing from the argument that representation of women in media outputs is essential to assess negotiations of gender, I investigate: Around what themes has gender been renegotiated and by whom in this transformational process? By contrast, what intersectional oppressions remain underrepresented in the public sphere and how do counterpublics attempt to address them? Finally, and importantly, I want to shed light on the processes of everyday negotiations and new feminist counterpublics that regrouped after 2011: What different forms of participation in counterpublics can be distinguished that emerged with the liberalization of the public sphere in January 2011 and what are their priorities in activism and challenges? Is a post-state feminist paradigm emerging?

Hence I claim that expressions of negotiations are found in a wide spectrum of participatory practices in counterpublics, which I understand as spaces of resistance on various levels: from "bodily comportment"[5] encompassing, for example, public women's rights demonstrations and the topless protest of Femen, to the creation of media outlets and feminist online networks such as the transregional Facebook group "The uprisings of Women in the Arab World", to lobbying and participating in political institutions renegotiating national and international women's rights codifications such as the constitution or the Convention on the Elimination of all forms of Discrimination against Women (CEDAW). I argue that all these forms of participation potentially contribute to the redefinition of norms and hegemonic ideologies challenging the patriarchal Matrix of Domination. I combined several modes of data collection to do justice to the multi-leveled processes under study: While a wide range of forms of participation is under scrutiny, this study does not claim to be exhaustive. I first conducted five explorative interviews in 2013 to assess the issues that require in-depth analysis. As well as numerous expert interviews and informal talks, I also conducted over thirty semi-structured qualitative interviews in different cities of Tunisia in 2014 to shed light on publics in different geographical localities. Document analysis and review of secondary sources from feminist writers and quantitative studies in media monitoring complete the body of data.

---

5   The term refers to non-verbal acts of resistance that can challenge established orders in a space by the mere presence of the female body. I define "bodily comportment" as an act of political participation in 3.2.3.

1.2   The Process of Constructing Knowledge

1.2.1 Studying Gender and Women's Participation in the Age of Political Contestation in Tunisia

Scholarship and policy analysis on "gender in transformation" on Middle Eastern and North African countries is primary focused on institutional debates and the negotiation of rights. However, this approach has been criticized from activist and academic perspectives for focusing on the institutional level only, hereby often ignoring the struggles of activists beyond political negotiations at the capital.

In light of this critique, Andrea Khalil's and Lilia Labidi's work offers an interdisciplinary approach to look at gender negotiations beyond political and legislative debates and has broadened the scope of actors. Andrea Khalil, a postcolonial and gender studies scholar focusing on Tunisia complements her analysis on gendered political institutions in transition by including media representations. She concludes that a state feminist ideology has –periodically- been challenged by different women's activisms after the uprisings. In 2014, however, she warns that "[t]he restoration of the foundational principles of the Tunisian state and Third World nationalist discourse signaled the persistence of a gender paradox where Tunisian women's social struggles coexisted within the male- gendered politics" (Khalil, 2014, p. 186).

Lilia Labidi, psychologist and sociologist employs a gender-sensitive lens to analyze the political processes in Tunisia from different perspectives. Her positionality has allowed her to delve deep into gender negotiations after the uprisings as she was involved herself as a minister of women affairs in Tunisia in 2011. She investigates the political process and the role women played in it (Labidi L., 2015). Additionally, she examined and recognized the role of women's artistic productions in literature (Labidi L., 2016a) and investigates political and ethical positions of female artists (Labidi L., 2014). Last but not least, she draws from her training as a psychologist to investigate issues of gender, oppression and mental health in her work on female suicides in Tunisia (Labidi L., 2016b, p. 122). Her works give distinguished insights into the complexity and the non-linear dynamics on the renegotiation of gender in post-revolutionary Tunisia. However, this involves broadening the scope of actors under investigation from politicians or established women's rights activists to include artists and "ordinary" women.

In Tunisian feminist scholarship, the instrumentalization of women's rights as a democratic *façade* was discussed mainly in international publications. It was more so identified as support for the authoritarian regime and a part of political bargaining between the ruling party and other forces in society. Feminist Tunisian scholar Amel Grami outlined this relation clearly in 2008:

"Many scholars point out that the state has an instrumentalist approach toward women, gender, and the family: Policies and laws that strengthen the position of the state itself are the ones that will be enacted. Women's lack of political power, results in their plight being taken lightly by decisionmakers and their rights being used as political commodities to be traded and exchanged between male leaders of various political groups" (Grami, 2008, p. 359).

Grami is not directly referring to Bourguiba or president Ben Ali, furthermore, she employs the more neutral formulation of "many scholars" to point to what I refer to as "state feminism" in its instrumental authoritarian dimension. There are important parallels in scholarship on Tunisia and Egypt in the transition period with regards to the return of authoritarian politics. Feminist scholars Nicolas Pratt and Nadje Al-Ali have both analyzed similar developments for the Egyptian context whereby political polarization and restorations of old authoritarian rule could be re-established, threatening achievements by women's rights activists (Pratt, 2016). Al Ali states that "women and gender are key to both revolutionary and counter-revolutionary processes and developments and not marginal to them" (Al-Ali, 2012). She specifically points to the use and instrumentalization of gender in the post-uprising period in Egypt, where "ironically, but again not surprisingly, we can see that women and gender issues are taking center stage in the old regimes' attempts to hold on to power and privilege, and in the violent backlash and counter-revolutionary processes we have been witnessing recently" (Al-Ali, 2012, p. 28).

This study can provide further understanding and give empirical evidence from the Tunisian context to confirm and elaborate on the claims made by Pratt and Al-Ali for Egypt and Andrea Khalil for Tunisia on the centrality of gender for revolutionary and counter-revolutionary processes and an increasing authoritarianism since 2013, departing from the same observations of a gender paradox. I hold that the conceptual framework of Matrices of Domination combined with public sphere theory can deepen our understanding of this paradox by shedding light on the restoration of the hegemonic understanding of feminism.

1.2.2 Who is Speaking? Interviews Conducted for this Study

I have previously argued that in order to increase our understanding of conservative rollbacks in Tunisia and elsewhere, we need to assess the different arenas where gender is negotiated first. I aim to build on this approach by integrating journalists, autonomous women's rights activists as well as members of feminist NGOs from different localities. The "situated knowledge" of the participants[6] as

---

6   The terms "participant," "respondent" or "interviewee" will be employed synonymously.

conceptualized by Donna Haraway (Haraway, 1988) shapes the outcome of this research. While some participants preferred to remain anonymous, others explicitly wanted to be mentioned by name.

My body of data is composed by transcriptions of explorative interviews conducted in 2013 and guided interviews, conducted in 2014. The analytical separation of "expert" and "activist" interview is simply helpful to work with my data, even though both can give insights and assessments concerning developments of an inclusive transformation process. Adding to that, many background and informal talks and participatory observations I made during the revolutionary protests of the Kasbah II in Tunis and conferences have influenced this research. The qualitative interviews were additionally taken into account in the more historical Chapters V -VII, to shed light on "blind spots" in existing literature dealing with Tunisia's history of women's rights.

In the following, I present a broad categorization of my interview partners covering engagements targeting different dimensions of the public sphere:
a) Members of Feminist Associations: The main type of participation represented in the sample is institutionalized women's activism. It appears as the most "visible" form of women's political participation in the public sphere that is actively promoting change in gender relations.
b) Members of Development Associations: This participation was often referred to as the only possible way for (young) women to engage in political processes, especially outside of the capital. In the sample, it refers to social and economic development projects but also to the enhancement of technical infrastructure.
c) Members of "semi-institutionalized" networks: Refers to participation beyond legal frames. It is thus defined by a regular exchange between people whose members may change but consist of a core group of activists. One example is the Facebook group "The uprisings of Women in the Arab World." This type of participation is related to the forms of organization that correspond to more project-driven forms of organization, usually associated with Internet-mediated communication.
d) Members of Parties: The sample includes participation in parties of the left spectrum and the opposition only. Actors of other parties arranging the political process such as Ennahda and Nidaa Tounes in particular, might have blurred the conceptual purpose of this research. Participation would then not be situated in a conflictual relationship with hegemonic structures in the society.
e) Journalists in Mass Media: In order to get insights into the gendered production of the representational dimension of the public sphere, interviews with female journalists provide an understanding of possible negotiation processes.
f) Feminist Writers and Scholars: These participants provide insights into

institutions, such as the interim government and the CREDIF[7]and reflect the scholarly discussion in gender studies in Tunisia.

g) Bloggers: With the uprisings in the region, these actors gained prominence in scholarship and media representation. Primarily, they have been and are still vocal about human rights violations and freedom of information. They create their own media content and have acquired a considerable influence on the representational dimension of the public sphere by the number of their followers and networks.

h) Autonomous Activists: Some participants would claim to be "autonomous activist" in the interviews. Often, they have had bad experiences within the NGO sector and decided to refrain from (internationally funded) civil society engagement. Hence, they have strong ties to other established civil society organizations, but have decided to turn towards project-based activism and do not define their activism within any of the categories above.

Including voices of activists who are not situated at the capital was pivotal for this study. In order to open new fields of knowledge, I focused on cities situated at the center of the country in structurally underdeveloped regions to look for participants. However, other categories of oppression are not easily mirrored by the sample: For instance, the sample covered different categories of sexualities without pre-defining this category in this study.

The three research dimensions, presenting the findings of the interviews in the second half of this book correspond broadly to the structure of the interview guide: It was developed in the fall of 2013, after a first round of exploratory interviews and included open ended questions. In order to assure a "participatory, community-based approach" (Hornig Priest, 2010, p. 196) we started from everyday life experiences (Flick, 2006, p. 18). The interviews revolved around four major themes: (Views on) Political Transformation, Participation and Activism, Feminist Themes and Positionings and media use and perception.

I combined the coding methods and the qualitative content analysis that I have employed within a multi-step analysis. The elaborated theoretical framework helped to generalize the thematic blocs discussed and structure the findings. The full transcriptions of the interviews brought about a raw material of 400 pages of text. Having verbatim transcriptions, you are "less likely to run the risk of 'amalgamation' in your raw data" (Wengraf, 2001, p. 320). Finally, the interview text is interpreted in its local and historical context. Hence, in the analysis, all citations indicate the locality and the month of the interview. The deduced codes and assigned text contents structure the narrative that is thus embedded in historically unfolding events.

---

7   The CREDIF is the « Centre for Research, Studies, Documentation and Information on Women ». It was created in 1990.

1.3   Research Objective and Structure of the Study

On the one hand, this research aims to contribute to critical feminist scholarship by unpacking the Tunisian transformation process[8] and investigating the way gender was exploited for political campaigning through highlighting ideological issues. In the analysis of the development of women's rights, focus on the political dynamics behind them is often lost. On the other hand, I aim to contribute to the scholarship by exploring different initiatives to renegotiate gender manifested in institutional settings, social relations, everyday practices and hegemonic norms defining the public sphere. The communication infrastructure forms the "nervous system of the social organism" (Kelly & Etling, 2008, p.23) that is shaped by national and international developments in politics and technology. I wish to emphasize social and geographical positionalities playing into the range of participatory practices, priorities and interests in this negotiation process. The liberalization of the public sphere has certainly led to the creation of various feminist counterpublics. This study looks at the different dimensions more specifically where these counterpublic interventions appear. It gives insights on how activists create and participate in feminist counterpublics and which ones could exert political influence to shape the outcomes of the transformation process.

Within the developed approach, I aim to understand the complex and intersecting gendered dynamics with regards to three dimensions of the public sphere in Tunisia between 2011 and 2014: first, institutional change with special regards to family and women's rights codifications; second, the role of mass and many-to-many media in producing themes and reproducing ideologies reaffixed to the bodies of women; and third, reactions and regrouping of women's activists and the formation of feminist ideas challenging the old gender order. The historical time frame for the processes under study is set between January 14th 2011 (Ousting of the former president Ben Ali) and the first parliamentary and presidential elections in 2014 (respectively in October, and first and second rounds of the presidential elections in November and December) leading to the unity government under president Béji Caïd Essebsi that I regard as the outcome of a patriarchal middle class consensus. In the following, I present the original research questions for this study. They originate from previous studies I carried out in 2010 and 2011 on the dynamics of the uprisings; against the background of unfolding empirical events in Tunisia in 2012 and from the explorative interviews I conducted in 2013 with feminist activists and journalists in Tunis. It is thus anchored in empirical observations rather than theoretical ones.

---

8   For a discussion on the terminology of transformation and revolution and the positioning of this work, see 2.3. "Talking about a revolution".

To approach the issues under study, my argument proceeds as follows: For the sake of clarity, I feel it necessary to commence the first part with an outline of epistemological and methodological reflections guiding this research in chapter 2. Exploring the connections between epistemology, Positionality and the Public Sphere, I situate this research in a specific context of knowledge production and expose challenges with regards to the "modelization" of the Tunisian case and its "regional exceptionalism" in Western publics, drawing from post-colonial perspectives. Women's rights will be situated in this narrative in particular. A more detailed discussion of intersectionality as a methodology and theory is introduced as an approach that can address these challenges.

Drawing from this discussion, I go on to present my theoretical approach in chapter 3: "Constructing an Empirically Grounded Theoretical Framework". I have previously given a preliminary note on my conceptual framework that will be elaborated in depth in this chapter. Taking into account the time and space context in which the public sphere is constructed, I engage public sphere theory and the underlying tension between an idealistic democratic concept and an analytical instrument. I argue that the "Matrix of Domination" limits, censors and defines how gender, class and other structures of oppression are renegotiated in the public sphere. My theoretical argument departs from the assumption that the boundaries of the public sphere are not fixed but change in historical and local contexts. Counterpublics are defined as a vibrant mosaic whose boundaries are set within a Matrix of Domination and underlie historical junctures. This will help to differentiate the needs and aims of women's participation in counterpublics and, most importantly, offers an explanation of the different resources and structures of oppression experienced by women. In 3.2.3., I position the counterpublics within the three dimensions of the public sphere.

Chapter 4 exposes the theoretical discussion of the state from a feminist political science perspective and discusses it with regards to public sphere theory: I define the state with regards to the public sphere and the hegemonic domain of power according to three dimensions: Firstly, by defining it, as a main actor in constructing legislative and cohesive boundaries of the public sphere. Second, drawing from intracategorical intersectional inquiry, I lay out how the nation state produced marginalized localities and emphasis the category of locality for the analysis of the Matrix of Domination in the specific Tunisian context. Thirdly, I present the state according to Yuval Davis' theorization on gender and nation. In the following section, I elaborate on the last dimension of the state, which I regard as incorporated in state feminism. Relying on scholarly research that exposes how state feminism in Tunisia has excluded poor, working class and rural women, I go on to define state feminism as part of the hegemonic domain of power.

In order to approach the case, Chapter 5 charts a historical overview for the Tunisian context, which is essential to contextualize the "Matrix of Domination", as Patricia Hill Collins has defined it, for a specific "social location" and within a historic specificity. Unlike many other studies on Gender and Tunisia, I want to specifically highlight the period of the 1930s and provide a more comprehensive account of the post-colonial period, especially with regards to the contested concept of "modernity", which is central to the discussion of feminisms in the region. Habib Bourguiba's implementation of the modern nation state is under close scrutiny here: I argue how a "dissembled secularism" served as an important pillar of the hegemonic domain of power to legitimize the modern state in the regimes of Bourguiba and Ben Ali. This historical perspective is crucial for the overall argument illustrating how the Matrix of Domination, expressed in different domains of power, has shaped, set limitations upon and determined how gender is being renegotiated in hegemonic publics in Tunisia today.

Chapter 6 sheds light on three different counterpublics that gained new momentum after 2011. I first show the articulation of autonomous feminist counterpublics departing from the space "Tahar Hadad" in the 1980s. Then, I discuss the 18th of October movement as an inter-ideological counterpublic laying important grounds for the formation of the "Troika government" in 2011. Counterpublics constituted online around the theme of freedom of expression and against censorship are outlined in a third place to also contextualize the dominant narrative of the "Facebook revolution". Departing from the epistemological reflections of "talking about a revolution", I will shed light on the narrative of the uprisings in Gafsa and Redeyef as a starting point of the uprisings in 2010 from the perspective of shifting public spheres in Chapter VII. I briefly lay out the uprisings of 2008, starting in Gafsa, and of 2010/2011, that started in Sidi Bouzid. My concern here is not what others have already treated in depth, i.e. reviewing the historical chronology of the uprisings by looking at different actors and dynamics of mobilization, but to go beyond the moment of the uprisings.

In the second part of the study, comprising chapters 8, 9 and 10, I employ Peter Dahlgren's model to structure the analysis of this work into discussions of the structural, representational and interactional dimension of the public sphere. I will point out the changes in the structural dimension of the Tunisian public sphere in chapter 8. The development of political institutions directly impacting gendered dimensions of the public will be examined. The bargain around women's emancipation on the institutional level will be essentially exemplified with the quota in electoral party lists, the elections and the national constitution and international women's rights frameworks. On the other hand, the reception of the institutional developments by women whose positionalities didn't allow them to access this dimension will be integrated as well.

Here, the issue of representation becomes crucial, which leads me to the second part and the representational dimension of public sphere, as laid out in chapter 9. As a first step, I look at the hegemonic public sphere by raising the questions of who is speaking and what they are speaking about. I go on to present the "hot topics" I identified as token for the renegotiation of gender arguing that they feed into ideological camp buildings, namely polygamy, the inheritance laws and Femen, an international feminist network promoting topless protest. These debates are juxtaposed to counterpublics advancing subjects of intersectional nature that actually bear the potential to disentangle feminist approaches from presumed ideological and political implications and redefine it in a frame of socio-economic justice: gender and labor, gender and locality and gender and health. In this context, the potential of information and communication technologies to build counterpublics at the representational dimension of the public sphere trying to redefine the subjects of feminism will be explored.

Chapter 10 recites the analysis of the interactional dimension of the public sphere with regards to challenges, space as a resource and decolonization strategies. I present three challenges for feminist participation interfering in and regulating their space of participation: The first is related to material resources and (international) political instrumentalization coupled with foreign funding reproducing the same patterns of an exclusive feminism. The second is derived from extremism and radicalization of a youth excluded from the modern nation state in marginalized localities and thirdly, I discuss the relation of the police and gender based violence. In the last section, I address decolonization processes by revolutionary feminist counterpublics. I recount how women of different positionalities seek to introduce change in their subordinated position by unmasking the "subject of feminism" and overcoming the limiting positions the concept of feminism offers them through the redefinition of terminologies and concepts, acknowledging differences among women, deconstructing naturalized hierarchies within the family and lastly, localizing feminist concepts.

In the Conclusion, chapter 11, I resume my main argument whereby the hegemonic domain of power could continue to perpetuate the three dimensions of the public sphere. However, this ideology is challenged by what I have determined as the "young" revolutionary feminist counterpublics: Four dimensions of this feminism will be summarized in their generational, (non-) ideological, methodological dimensions, and, as the fourth dimension, referring to the methods employed for raising awareness and networking online leads me to conclude on the Matrix of Domination 2.0 in a digitalized environment. Finally, "renegotiating homosexualities" reviews developments in 2015 in Tunisia that were not part of the period under investigation but represent an important empirical evolution of my argument.

2 Positionalities, Modernity and the Public Sphere

This chapter's purpose is to explore and outline the connections between epistemology, positionality and the public sphere. Drawing on Gayatri Chakravorty Spivac, Nikita Dhawan argues that "'epistemic change' at both ends of postcoloniality, is the heart of the project of decolonization" (Dhawan, 2013, p. 160; Spivak, 2007, 137). While this chapter deals with my positionality within processes of knowledge construction in a Western (German) public, unraveling the hegemonic discourses I speak to, chapter XI conveys ways of decolonization challenging the hegemonic scriptures that reach deep in the communities and even families of the activists that participated in this study.

"Positionality" goes back to the feminist philosopher Lina Alcoff, who concludes: "Who is speaking to whom turns out to be as important for meaning and truth as what is said; in fact what is said turns out to change according to who is speaking and who is listening" (Alcoff, 1992, p. 9). The concept is fruitful for epistemological discussion that includes the analytical bias and perspective of the researcher as a resource on its own. Furthermore, I argue positionality bears explanatory potential in the study of social change when investigating the priorities and possibilities of participation. With regards to the politics of knowledge, two major processes appear of particular importance to me in this study: first, the potential of translating knowledge and concepts for decolonization processes, second, the dimension of the political instrumentalization of knowledge.

Gender and gender studies are, as Samia Mehrez affirms, a travelling concept whose translational history should be reiterated. She states that:

"The history of the concept of gender in the Arab context is a history of cross-cultural communication and translation of knowledge. It is also a history of relations of power at a specific historical juncture, between civilizations within that exchange" (Mehrez, 2007, p. 109).

Looking at gender and its conceptual renegotiations in its various forms after the uprisings of 2010/2011 also incorporates an investigation of power relations between the two sides of the Mediterranean.

Mehrez shows how the Arabic word "jins" (جنس) emerged literally from the original word "genus". Its various meanings in the Arabic language range from *kind* to *class* and *race*, incorporating, I hold, an intersectional perspective. "Renegotiation", placed at the heart of this analysis, also entails translational politics

© Springer Fachmedien Wiesbaden GmbH, part of Springer Nature 2019
A. Antonakis, *Renegotiating Gender and the State in Tunisia between 2011 and 2014*, Politik und Gesellschaft des Nahen Ostens,
https://doi.org/10.1007/978-3-658-25639-5_2

that, as will be seen, prompt the original concept to re-appear and aspire to de-colonize it by counter-hegemonic practice. This is where the potential to redefine traditional norms and revolutionize gender relations is situated. Judith Butler elucidates that it is "only by passing through unsettled and deauthorized modes of knowledge", that the "matrix of oppression" can be questioned. In this sense, translation "stages an encounter with the epistemic limits of any given discourse, drawing the discourse into a crisis from which it cannot emerge through any strategy that seeks to assimilate and contain difference" (Butler, 2013, p. 12 f.). This study aims to shed light on the "unsettled and deauthorized" modes and spaces of knowledge creation that I seek to analyze within the popular theory of public spheres.

In the following, I will engage the relationship between the particular knowledge production on Tunisia and gender within the tension of "modeliza-tion", set within the frame of post-colonial modernity. Offering a reflection on the meta-discourse will clarify the premises of my argument and the need to develop critical approaches in the context of the uprisings in 2010/2011.

2.1   Tunisia's Modelization and Regional Exceptionalism

The reflection on epistemological positions for this study departs from the con-cepts of modelization and regional exceptionalism of Tunisia. While traditionally praised as an "economic miracle" and for its progressive and pro-Western women's rights, it became the "Birthplace of the Arab Spring" and an exception in its democratic transformation after 2011. In the period under study, Tunisia was (again) discussed as a "model" for "the region" in national and international politics, academia and media. This image is nourished by external and internal actors alike: After the Tunisian elections in 2014, US President Barack Obama referred to Tunisia as a model for the region (Grodsky, 2016, p. 202). Tunisian scholar Khadija Arfaoui states: "If democracy succeeds in Tunisia, then it is bound to have a positive impact on the rest of the Arab world; if it fails, it is likely that it will succeed nowhere else" (Arfaoui, 2016, p. 226).

The modelization of the country reached a peak when the so called "Quartet initiative", consisting of the strong Tunisian General Labor Union (Union Gé-nérale Tunisienne du Travail UGTT), the Tunisian Confederation of Industry, Trade and Handcraft (Union Tunisienne de l'Industrie, du Commerce et de l'Ar-tisanat UTICA), the Tunisian League for Human Rights (Ligue Tunisienne des Droits de l'Homme LTDH) and the Bar Association, was honored with the No-bel Peace Prize in October 2015.

There are three issues I see emerging with regards to the modelization of Tunisia. The first bears a relational argument, wherein a country is stylized as a "model" with regards to a specific region in a geo-political context. Tunisia is supposed to stand out as "exceptionally" modern – but exceptionalism is always defined in relation to "another" which is therein explicitly or implicitly devalued.

It is constructed around a region less defined in geographical and more in supposedly cultural terms, as the "Arab World": Even though Tunisia gave the African continent its name through its Roman name "Africa" (including parts of present-day Algeria), knowledge production and analysis of Tunisia is rarely undertaken in the framework of African studies. Its exceptionalism is usually positioned within the region of "Middle East and North Africa" or the "Arab World," excavating Tunisia from its African context. The construction of the MENA countries and a division of Africa into "Northern" and "Sub-Saharan" parts has been criticized in literature and can be regarded as the result of "political scholarship," as Nigerian feminist scholar Molara Ogundipe-Leslie has outlined (Ogundipe-Leslie, 1994, p. 217). African countries such as Cambodia, Uganda or Cote d'Ivoire witnessed uprisings in 2011 where "the disenfranchised have begun to re-assert their dignity" (Manji, 2012, p. 2), but were excluded from the narrative of the "Arab Spring".

Secondly, the modelization entails the articulation of rights and values that attach the model to a predefined value system and employs an essentialist understanding of "culture" (Yuval-Davis, 1997, p.41). Tunisia has indeed introduced more democratic processes and institutions in comparison to before 2011, such as the elections in 2011 and 2014. The new constitution that was publically debated for almost three years stands out as an example for procedural democracy. Charrad and Zargough praise the process in which women's rights codifications were debated in the public sphere[9] as initiating a shift from "politics from above" to "politics from below" (Charrad & Zarrugh, 2014, 232). The new constitution was celebrated in national and international publics for having syncretized oppositional value systems. At the same time, it is a "modern" document as it includes the right to work or the right to water.

Tunisian exceptionalism draws primarily from its progressive women's rights codification; a pattern that re-appeared in the period under study.[10] Saunders (2003) identifies gender justice and highly developed technologies as a part of the modernization paradigm, besides widespread literacy and education, tolerance and democracy (40 ff. quoted in Dhawan, 2007, p.55).

The Family Status Law (Code du Statut Personnel, CSP), introduced in 1957, is considered to be the most progressive women's rights codification in the "Arab World" (Charrad, 2008). In 2001, Jerry Sorkin, a "Middle East specialist"

---

9   I have analyzed the debate around Article 28 of the first draft of the constitution in Tunisia in section 7.2.1.

10 For example the article published by the UN office for Human Rights is entitled: "Tunisian transition a model for the region and beyond" (High Commissioner of Human Rights, 2015).

trained in international business, published a piece in the Middle East Quarterly that clarifies the relationship between what I call "Tunisia's exceptionalism" and women's rights. His argument is strikingly similar to the discourses concerning Tunisia in the years 2011-2015, where "progressiveness", pro-Western foreign policy and women's rights are weaved together: "Tunisia has struck what appears to be a balance between a pro-Western vision and its identity as an Arab country. The result is that Tunisian society reflects a progressiveness that equals, if not exceeds, that of any other Arab country. The growing importance and respect for women is evident (…) and in family matters women have equal rights, at least in theory (but also increasingly in practice), when it comes to family planning, divorce, and freedom of travel" (Sorkin, 2001). In this context, Roula Seghaier points out however, that the topic of the legalization of sex work in Tunisia (since 1942) has barely been addressed in contexts of showing Tunisia's exceptionalism as it is considered "not respectable enough for local academia"[11] (Seghaier, 2018).

US Gender studies scholar Doris Gray sees this progressive women rights codification and the oppression of Islamists who were "successfully portrayed within and outside Tunisia as akin to terrorists, were either in jail or in exile" (Gray, 2012, p. 286) as the two main pillars for Western support of the authoritarian regime in Tunisia (ibd.).

Thirdly, from the perspective of revolutionary Tunisians, the country was far from the model it was celebrated for. The "culture of consensus" associated with a modern procedural democracy has left behind a disfranchised youth. It is this very principle of consensus, appearing here as a structuring element of the political transformation in Tunisia, that has been criticized by philosophers Laclau and Mouffe. They stress that, for democratic politics, it is "vital to acknowledge that any form of consensus is the result of a hegemonic articulation and that it always has an 'outside' that impedes its full realization (Laclau, Mouffe, 2014, p. xviii). This study's primary concern is to trace the function of women's rights for consensual politics and investigate its relation to hegemonic articulations of the state.

Modelizations easily gloss over de facto existent discontents within the population with regards to the persistence of socio-economic injustice, but also the application of democratic institutions, and the lack of reform of the Tunisian state institutions, notably the Ministry of the Interior (Sayigh, 2016). Faith in a democratic system has waned considerably in Tunisia over the period under study. According to PEW polls, in 2013, a majority of 63% of those surveyed agreed that "democracy is preferable to other kinds of government." The per-

---

11 See for a discussion on the interventions of Sex Workers to demand their right after 2011, chapter 9.3.1 on Gender and Labor

centage dropped to 48% one year later. In 2014, those favoring a "stable government, even without democracy" outnumbered those preferring "democracy, even with political instability", as the preferred political system (PEW-Report, 2014). While the methodology and questions of these polls can certainly be criticized, they reflect public attitudes of the time - that the democratic institutions put in place would not sufficiently represent the major demands and hopes associated with the uprisings. First and foremost, these were socio-economic transformation[12] and eradication of corruption and arbitrary state practice. The last two demands were addressed mainly to the Ministry of Interior: Namely, the famous "Degage!" at the Avenue Bourguiba was chanted in front of the latter, not a presidential palace or the prime minister's office. However, to this day, it still enjoys great autonomy in Tunisia (Sayigh, 2016; Silva, 2013, p. 4).

Despite the problems I identified with regards to Tunisian exceptionalism, I would like to point out that young feminist counterpublics socialized in a digitalized, networked environment can capitalize on the spaces it offers and consciously navigate the pitfalls of modelization by bringing in subversive, postcolonial critiques and attempt to induce emancipatory change within their own society. In the following, I attempt to embed this research deeper in the context of knowledge production, critically reflecting on my own positionality.

2.2   Western Publics: What Are We Reproducing Here?

At the beginning of 2014, I found myself confronted with Western publics and their obsession with women's bodies, pushing me to reflect on my own focus of analysis in my study. Laying out this self-reflexivity from a Western positionality serves to expose the patterns in the construction of gendered images of the Tunisian nation in its post-colonial context.[13] My affiliation with a German policy think tank increased the visibility of my research beyond academic and activist publics. My positionality gave me a privileged access to public spheres and the validation of political processes. I received requests to comment upon the constitutional process in Tunisia, which was mainly framed as "successful" in German mass media. From the privileged role of an "expert," I became aware of

---

12 For an interpretation in a global perspective, see Grodsky's comparative study on revolutionary movements in Germany, Georgia, South Africa, Poland and Egypt. He claims that democracy has become since World War II the only "convenient instrument for revolution," while they are in fact much more on economic rights (Grodsky, 2016, p.2f.).

13 Against this background, it would have been interesting to systematically analyze the reception in the hegemonic domain of power in Saudi Arabia or Qatar to investigate the different mechanisms for the construction of the Tunisian « exceptionalism » from the perspective of the Gulf countries.

the interaction between different public spheres and their codes of content. Keeping it short, simple and not too academic made me aware of the effects of media reductionist logic. The challenge of replying to journalists, who only have a restricted number of characters for their pieces, challenged me but also revealed at least two important aspects that helped me to gain a deeper understanding of the complicated nature of this research, my positionality and the centrality of gender in public knowledge creation on political processes in the so-called Arab world.

First, in German media discourse, the struggle for women's rights in Tunisia lacked important historical contextualization: it was rarely stated that women's rights organizations were rather lobbying for the *status quo* than for the elaboration of existing rights. A debate that would consider the development of women's rights codifications since colonial rule and a critical assessment of state feminist practices did not take place. Western media representations tended to over-emphasize the role women played in the uprisings as an innovation in and of itself, ignoring their active participation in various fields in the past. In the first place, scholars, activists and researchers, myself included, felt the obligation to recall women's achievements over the years in order to contextualize their involvement in the current developments.

This resonates with Al-Ali's observations of the depictions of women in the uprisings and calls for an active usage of the knowledge of women's movements to encounter this discourse: "In light of Western media representations (…) we should clarify: for decades they had been active members in trade unions, political opposition parties and more informal networks and organizations that were all instrumental in the recent political developments" (Al-Ali, 2012, p. 27). Writing, diversifying and remembering this history was considered a priority for many of the Tunisian activists and scholars I spoke to over the course of this research. It represents a strategy to counteract narratives eradicating the achievements, debates and production of knowledge in Tunisia.

The second aspect arose by virtue of the journalists' fixation on questions of women's rights that would determine how "democratic" the country had become. Once more, gender politics became an identity marker for a "good" and a "bad" post-revolutionary development. From a post-colonial theory perspective, the theme of gender and development has been analyzed as an "alibi" for renewed intervention of the West, covering economic and geopolitical interests (Dhawan, 2009; p. 55). Gender studies scholar Huma Ahmed-Ghosh entangles political and academic power plays, impacting, I claim, the epistemological grounds of my endeavor:

"[T]he debate about women's rights becomes complex because it is ridden with not just global and local politics, and numerous interpretations of Islam, but also by competing feminisms and masculinities, academic power plays, and colonial and post-colonial analysis" (Ahmed-Ghosh, 2008, p. 100f.).

My drive to talk about social justice stems from a conviction that gender justice and socio-economic justice can only be developed at the same time[14]. In the context of the Western publics, however, there was little or no room to critically reflect upon those relations, mainly because gender is understood as a one-dimensional category and is negotiated within political institutions as women's rights, only. When interrogated about the "success" of the Tunisian transformation, I usually start by examining the economic conditions of the country highlighting demands for social justice which has been continually articulated in various contexts since 2011. I stressed that concerns for the majority of the people were even exacerbated due to an economic crisis and that despite more freedom of expression, the revolutionary demands have not been met.[15] Unfortunately, clarifying the link between gender politics and the dangers of the persisting marginalization of certain regions demands time, so I was interrupted with the words: "Yes, but tell us about 'women's rights' that have 'now' been achieved."

These experiences pushed me to again critically revisit my own research focusing on gender at the heart of social changes. The work of feminist thinkers such as Donna Haraway resonate with this phenomenon very well, especially regarding my own positioning when: "Gender is a field of structured and structuring difference, in which the tones of extreme localization, of the intimately personal and individualized body, vibrate in the same field of with global, high-tension emissions" (Haraway, 1988, p. 588).

In the context of the post-9/11 Afghan intervention, Lila Abu-Lughod addresses the difficulties in speaking to US media outlets on gender in Afghan society. For Abu-Lughod this incorporated a dilemma: "Why did this not please me, a scholar who has devoted more than 20 years of her life on the subject?" (Abu-Lughod, 2002). Her answer resonates very much with my own experiences: "Instead of political and historical explanations, experts were being asked to give religio-cultural ones, instead of questions that might lead to the exploration of global interconnections, we were offered ones that worked to artificially divide the world into separate spheres—recreating an imaginative geography of West versus East, us versus Muslims, cultures in which First Ladies give speeches versus others where women shuffle around silently in burqas" (Abu-Lughold, 2002, p. 784).

---

14 I discussed these intersections in the interviews I conducted with Tunisian activists that will be presented later in the analytical chapter.
15 See (in German) my argument not to idealize Tunisia and take into consideration the socio-economic factors I have repeated over the years: "The Goals of the Protests Have Not Been Met" http://www.zeit.de/politik/ausland/2015-10/friedensnobelpreis-internationales-dialog-quartett-tunesien-kritik "The Disappointment for Young People is Huge"- http://www.srf.ch/news/international/die-enttaeuschung-bei-jungen-menschen-ist-gross.

Similarly, Maya Mikdashi's piece "The uprisings will be gendered", points to the narrow focus of analysis of international actors with regards to gender. She regroups the modes of framing gender in the context of the uprisings into three loose themes: first, discussion of women and sexual minorities, second, in context of the fear of Islamists, and third, the use of gendered and sexualized violence in context of protests (Mikdashi, 2012). She raises the important question that grounds this study's epistemology, referring to the power dynamics at stake when employing and using the category of gender for analysis:

"What power dynamics and hegemonic discourses are being reproduced with every selective deployment of 'gender' in the media and in every syllabus on 'politics' or 'citizenship' that includes one or two weeks (yay!) about 'women' or 'gender?'" (Mikdashi, 2012).

Detecting and uncovering the deep politization of knowledge production is a pivotal aim of this study. The intersectional approach, which will be outlined hereafter, constitutes an ideal instrument to confront the current episteme and "draw the discourse into a crisis" (Butler, 2013, p. 12 f.). In the following, I will look at the terminology of "revolution" and show its various meanings in the context of the Tunisian 2010/2011 uprisings that can be related to different positionalities as well.

2.3   "Talking About a Revolution"[16] from Different Positionalities

When investigating processes that are still ongoing, researchers become part of the narratives that are in the process of construction: in this context, the terminology of "revolution" with regards to the uprisings in Tunisia 2010 needs some contextualization. The term "Revolution of Dignity" ("thawrat el karama"), hinting towards the objective of the uprisings, is commonly used in Arabophone discourse (Azouzi, 2013, p. 17), whereas the term "Revolution of Jasmine", until today, was mainly employed by Western outlets (see for example (Janier, 2016) in *Le Monde Diplomatique*.[17] The origin of the term remains ambiguous: Tunisian journalist Zied el-Hani most probably coined the term during the 2011 uprisings,[18] but this version is challenged by Akram Belkaid and other Tunisian journalists and historians, claiming the word had been used in the Tunisian press to designate Ben Ali's coup against Bourguiba (Belkaïd, 2012).

In this study, I will not use the term "Revolution of Jasmine" for the following three main reasons that reveal broader issues that this study engages with: Firstly, it hides the atrocities and violence of the days that activists experienced

---

16 In reference to the song by Chapman, Tracy (1988).
17 For an analysis of the term "Jasmine Revolution" and the slogan "Ben Ali, degage!," as "discursive events," see (Azouzi, 2013).
18 See his blogpost entitled ثورة الياسمي, from 13 January 2011:http://journaliste-tunisien-110.blogspot.de/2011/01/blog-post_13.html (Journaliste Tunisien 30/10, 2011).

in the streets, creating the image of a "peaceful uprising" and glossing over the involvement of the security apparatus in killings, torture and harassment of protesters and opposition. Secondly, the flower of Jasmine doesn't necessary represent the whole country but rather evokes associations of the bourgeois suburbs of Tunis, like Sidi Bousaid [not to confuse with Sidi Bouzid, at the center of the country] or ElMarsa, where the flower can be found in neatly-kept gardens. Thirdly, under authoritarian rule, it was employed in campaigns to attract tourists, exploiting the image of a clean and peaceful country. The previous marketization of the flower under authoritarian rule should be kept in mind when producing and reproducing terminology. French political scientists Geisser and Ayari hold that the term expresses a "touristic neo-orientalism" (Ayari M. G., 2011) and propose the "Revolution of the *Nouzouh*" ("Prickly Pear"[19]), instead, hereby referring to the pejorative that people from the center of the country are given in contrast to the *Belids*, the urban Tunisian class. While their proposition addresses the urban-rural divide between the *Sahel* (the coastal region) and the *Dakhe* (the "interior" region), it is also problematic: Again, the focus is shifted away from the objective ("dignity") of the uprisings to the Tunisian actors (*Nouzouh* versus *Belids*) and thus misses the opportunity to engage with global dependencies and inequalities that caused the call for dignity from "marginalized localities" in the first place.[20]

The date of departure is another distinctive factor when "talking about the revolution." In the local narrative of Sidi Bouzid, for example, the day of the self-immolation of Mohamed Bouazizi on December 17th is regarded as the starting point of the revolution, which is still ongoing, whereas the narrative in the capital sees the 14th of January, the day of Ben Ali's departure, as the day of the revolution, hereby emphasizing an end, rather than a starting point of a revolutionary process. These different views translate into distinct memory cultures: While the main square at Avenue Bourguiba in Tunis has been renamed "Place of the 14th of January", the Youth center in Sidi Bouzid, is called "Space of 17th of December". [21] Another narrative, which I will present in more detail, relates the uprisings of 2010 to the protests that swept the miner basin in Gafsa in 2008 (see Chapter 7.1).

Tunisian scholars, such as Dorra Ben Alaya, have tried to grasp the developments in their countries by reiterating the narratives of the "revolution" on social media. Ben Alaya approaches the term as a "constructed object," measures the developing meaning appointed to it in two different time periods and finds:

"In February 2011, respondents seemed focused on trying to understand 'what happened' and on creating the revolution as a represented object. In June 2011, the respondents are concerned with

---

19 This resistant plant grows in the arid regions of the center of the country.
20 For a discussion on marginalized localities within the post-colonial state, see chapter 4.1.
21 For further investigation, it would be interesting to explore these different narratives and their impact on memory culture manifested in different localities in different regions of Tunisia.

the assignment of meaning and specific value to the object. This is done through a favorable definition of identity referents for some, and through questioning the merits of the revolution and a revival
of the necessary despotism idea for others" (Ben Alaya, 2013, p. 16).
Ben Alaya broadly distinguishes the adherents to these two viewpoints as "revolution enthusiasts" and "pessimists". Interestingly, the pessimists had the idea
of an "undeserved democracy" and a reactive prejudice of "necessary despotism" (Ben Alaya, 2013, p. 2.15). While her analysis focuses on social media
communication and the time shortly after the uprisings, I decided to conduct
interviews with activists "offline" to explore different judgments and values, priorities and experiences in the transformational process. By shifting the focus to
behind the screens, I argue that positionalities in terms of gender, class and locality can appear and have explanatory potential for the negotiation of "meaning" inherent in the "revolution" as described by Ben Alaya.

Depending on their positionality in society with regards to gender, class, educational degrees, religion and/or locality, citizens experienced the uprisings and
the following period of political transformation very differently. These experiences, I argue, translate into various engagements and disengagements with the
process. For many of the interviewed activists[22], the revolutionary process has
not come to an end yet. Speaking of a "transformation" is then perceived as an
external concept, forcibly applied on social realities. Some of these actors have
rejected the use of the terms transition and transformation overall, referring to
the current period as a "revolutionary phase" instead, considering that their demands, a structural change of the political, economic and cultural condition, have
not been met. Pointing out the underlying global socio-economic dependencies
of the capitalist system, Firoze Manji finds in 2011: "What we have witnessed
in Tunisia and Egypt is but only Act 1 Scene 1 of a long struggle that may take
many decades to reach a transformative conclusion" (Manji, 2012, p. 8).

This study's aim is not to discern whether the uprisings in Tunisia can be
understood as a "revolution" according to different theoretical schools, nor to
evaluate benchmarks of a transformation as in classical transformation theories.
Rather, it is "curious about the webs of differential positioning" (Haraway, 1988,
p. 590). The knowledge I want to create is based on the analysis of subjective
accounts constituted by power structures; gender and locality in particular. I examine the formation of counterpublics by women of various backgrounds by re-
constructing the strategies and methods they use in their activism. Drawing from
intersectional theory and methodology (Crenshaw, 2001; Hooks, 2011), the analysis is sensitive to different forms of structural oppression. While "[s]ituated
knowledges are about communities not about isolated individuals," the accounts

---

22 "Activist" can be considered a disputed concept. I employ the term here in a very broad sense,
with regards to those who actively participate in formal and informal political ways in movements, associations and parties. Furthermore, it designates citizen-journalists and bloggers, who
write from the position to bring about change.

act as "halting voices into a collective subject position" (Haraway, 1988, p. 590). This approach is about joining particular views, collecting different stories from the field to find a satisfyingly comprehensive account of the process of the transformation period and the particular renegotiation of gender. I will now discuss the fundamentals of intersectionality with special regards to its epistemic critique to approach the methodological framing of this study in more detail.

2.4   Conclusion: Intersectionality Guiding the Research

I have previously laid out some epistemological and methodological challenges in the study of changing gender relations from a privileged position of knowledge creation. In order not to reproduce the process of modelization rooted in post-colonial dependencies outlined above, I rely on the intersectional approach, constituting the overall bracket that respectively informs the epistemological ground, the construction of the theoretical framework, methodological stances and the methods applied for data recovery. In the following, I will outline how intersectionality speaks to each of these parts. I argue that this approach encourages reflection on how the research should be conducted within an anti-positivist[23] paradigm and engages the researchers with the epistemological issues and political positioning. After explicating the historical background to the academic concept, I will elaborate on its application, exhibiting methodological considerations and changes in conceptualizations in the course of this project.

Embedded in a struggle for civil rights in the 1970s and 1980s in the United States, the concept stems from empirical, activist grounds[24]. The collection "All women are white, all blacks are male but some of us are brave" (Hull, Scott, & Smith, 1982) assembles writings from Black feminists and can be regarded as a major reference which urges the priority and necessity to shed light on the experiences of Black women in a White institutional system. In her article from 1977, Smith points to the ignorance of everybody not affected by the situated knowledge of Black (lesbian) women:

"For whites, this specialized lack of knowledge is inextricably connected to their not knowing in any concrete or politically transforming way that Black women of any description dwell in this plate. Black women's existence, experience, and culture and the brutally complex systems of oppression which shape these are in the 'real world' of white and/or male consciousness beneath consideration, invisible, unknown" (Smith, 1982, p. 156).

Before, it was mainly White women who could access positions of power, for instance in academia, to contribute to dominant discourses. While feminist theory discussed worldwide oppressive patriarchal structures, claiming universal

---

23 For an elaborated distinction between positivism and constructivism see (Flick, 2006, p.69f.).

24 Earlier writings on the particular experiences of Black women, dating back centuries, have not been taken into account by wider (academic) publics so far.

knowledge, it was not systematically taken into consideration how other forms of oppression such as race, class and other categories determining subordinated positions affect women's experiences differently. On the other hand, critical theories of racial discrimination often lack(ed) a gendered perspective that takes the specific oppressions and life experiences of black women and women of color into account which Kimberlé Crenshaw criticizes as a "single-axis framework" setting forth only a "subset of a much more complex phenomenon. (…) Because the intersectional experience is greater than the sum of racism and sexism" (Crenshaw K. , 1989, p. 140).

While intersectionality was developed mainly from the position of Black[25] US scholars, their argument can be translated to other contexts as well. Patricia Hill Collins, whose model of the Matrix of Domination is significant for building the framework for my analysis of gender renegotiations, suggests:

"Recall that Black feminist thought views Black women's struggles as part of a wider struggle for human dignity and social justice. When coupled with the Black feminist epistemological tenet that dialogue remains central to assessing knowledge claims, the domains-of-power argument presented here should serve to stimulate dialogues about empowerment" (Collins, 2000, p. 276).

In order to understand and write about empowerment in a post-colonial context, an assessment of power structures is crucial. It also incorporates a serious reflection in how far "empowerment" remains embedded in hegemonic discourse, and what were the historical pre-conditions leading to global inequalities (Dhawan, 2009, p.54).

Patricia Hill Collins calls for an introduction of "Black feminist thoughts" into academia to oppose the domination of White theories (Collins, 1998). As a consequence, (White) concepts of feminism have been called into question. This paradigm has been framed as the "third wave of feminism" in Rebecca Walker's 1992 essay "Becoming the Third Wave" (Walker, 1992). It highlighted not only differences in realities between men and women but also differences *among* women. By pointing out the radical differences between women and problematizing the "assumption that 'women' denotes a common identity" (Butler, 1990, p. 4), theoreticians like Judith Butler challenge any universalizing notions of what it means to be a "woman". The tension between universalism and particularism is particularly played out in the negotiation of women's rights and has been addressed by scholars from different angles (Voorhoeve, 2015, p. 2; Mohanty, 1984, p. 337).

From my standpoint, intersectional methodology constitutes a key principle guiding the study of our social realities and is therefore particularly interesting for scholars that tend to implement bottom-up approaches in social science. The focus of projects in early stages can be re-shifted or enlarged when integrating

---

25 "Black" and "White" are capitalized in order to reflect the social constructivism of race as an "invented category". It "refers alternately to a set of ideas, practices and people" (Collins, 2004, p. 310).

an intersectional perspective. This is due to the imperfectness and openness of the theory (Davis, 2008, p. 77). While in the earlier stage of this research I wanted to focus on feminist organizations in the capital of Tunis; over the course of the project I increased my scope of investigation. I realized that talking to women's rights activists only in the capital would give a biased perspective on the question of how gender is being renegotiated in Tunisia. |Over the course of the study, the category of "locality" was highlighted.

My role as a Western researcher was more accentuated through the decision to not only work with women in Tunis with whom I've had established networks and friendships with since 2009, but to also go to fields in more oppressive contexts in terms of infrastructure, violence and poverty. As a result, the "serious ethical danger" (Ferguson, 1998, p. 95) faced by Western researchers who are working in countries in the Global South in particular became more crucial. At the same time, feminist scholar Donna Haraway warns of the danger of "romanticizing and/or appropriating the vision of the less powerful while claiming to see from their perspective" (Haraway, 1988, p. 584). Departing from the understanding that "giving voice to the oppressed" is an "expression of intersectionality" (Marx Ferree & Choo, 2010, p. 131), enlarging the scope of my interview sample was certainly an important methodological decision. Talking about feminisms with women from different localities, experiences and classes and the way they perceived change in Tunisia allowed to uncover the hegemonic dimension of feminism for the Tunisian context.

Last, but not least, I hold that intersectional perspectives are fruitful with regards to debates of technology and social change. This supports the thesis that social media is closely related to power politics and should be analyzed in close relation to it. It offers a new perspective on exclusion mechanisms with regards to access to ICTs and unequal distribution of knowledge and information. When studying the use of social media for creating spaces for activism, I call for deploying qualitative methods and *shift the focus behind the screens,* centering the actors using and coding social media and their specific constituencies, instead of relying on the new diverse quantitative data sets only. This is in accordance with the perspectives provided by Carola Richter and Hanan Badr calling for more "people centered analysis of social media" (Richter & Badr, 2016, p. 11).

In this chapter, I spoke about the broader issue of knowledge creation in a specific historical and geographical context by means of positionality and the public sphere and outlined its importance with regards to the subject of analysis. After having introduced intersectionality as an epistemological and methodological basis that can be read as an answer to the questions addressed, I will now go on to the conceptualization of the empirically driven theoretical framework and the application of the intersectional position in the next chapter.

3 Constructing an Empirically Grounded Framework

The reconstitution of state and societal relations in light of the development of new Information and Communication Technologies (ICTs) (Raupp, 2011, p. 75) have increased the popularity of public sphere approaches. In relation to the events, which unfolded in 2010/2011, scholars engaged with the concept in relation to new media (Shirky, 2011; Ben Moussa, 2013; Faris, 2013;), the transformation of media systems (Webb, 2014) and social movements (see the Special Issue of Mediterranean Politics, Asseburg & Wimmen, 2015).

I hold that working with public sphere theory allows the implementation of a more holistic approach to explain political and social dynamics and shed light on a complex web of changing and stagnating power relations in societies, including institutional politics and politics of resistance towards them, the entanglement of global media and the state as well as changing relations between citizens and the government. Public sphere theory takes media into account with regards to at least three fields of inquiry corresponding to this research objective: the powerful constituencies of mass media in polarizing and/or pluralizing societies, the mobilization of racist, sexist and other oppressive discourses within it and access and usage of media by marginalized actors in a digitalized environment. The (global) uprisings of 2010/2011 have led to more interdisciplinary collaborations between communication studies and political science. Political science studies mainly employ them in relation to participation and democracy. Communication studies, on the other hand, are more concerned with the construction of publics, examining media (and the arrival of ICTs) as a vehicle in their formation. Public sphere is, if anything, more empirically grounded in the methodologies of the later discipline, while theorizations on the public sphere in political science all too often remain abstract and offer little to no methodological solutions.

© Springer Fachmedien Wiesbaden GmbH, part of Springer Nature 2019
A. Antonakis, *Renegotiating Gender and the State in Tunisia between 2011 and 2014*, Politik und Gesellschaft des Nahen Ostens,
https://doi.org/10.1007/978-3-658-25639-5_3

3.1   The Public Sphere(s) and Counterpublics

In this first theoretical section, I will outline and revisit some major discussions in public sphere theory: The relation between the public sphere and space and the definition of the public sphere as dominant in the Habermasian tradition of the "discursive model". I then move on to discuss the implicit tensions of the public sphere between a normative model and an analytical concept. In a second step, I look at conceptualizations of counterpublics and define the particularities of feminist counterpublics opposing patriarchal structures of oppression. Finally, I exhibit the model of three dimensions of the public sphere by Pater Dahlgren in order to operationalize the public sphere as an empirical and analytical starting point. Drawing on the discussion of intersectional theory, I outline my major points of critique of the public sphere and counterpublic sphere framework alike to set the stage for the conceptual contribution of this study by bringing together intersectional theory, public sphere theory and the study of societies in transformations.

3.1.1 The Public Sphere: Empirical and Theoretical Starting-Point

Western theorization on the relation between the public sphere and democratic theory can be traced back to ancient Greek times, when the *agora,* the market place of cities like Athens, constituted the central space of democratic practices (Raupp, 2011, p. 76). Citizenship was constructed based on the ability to participate in public face-to-face debates on the common good in the space of the *polis*. This relation between space, debate and decision-making for the community laid the groundwork for democracy theories, which declare the public sphere as "central to political life" (Benhabib, 1992, p. 74). However, women, migrants who were born outside of the polis and slaves were excluded from the process. Consequently, sexism, xenophobia and racism and/or tribalism remain understudied in traditional scholarship on Greek democracy.[26] A "non-exclusive public sphere" has been considered a "conceptual impossibility" by thinkers of "radical democracy" Ernesto Laclau and Chantal Mouffe (Laclau, Mouffe, 2014; xvii).

The "discursive model" of the public sphere that this study focuses on is represented by Jürgen Habermas, taking salons in European cities as point of departure. The question of whether the theory of public spheres can be applied in other (authoritarian) contexts has been debated extensively in the literature (Ayish,

---

26 Newer research on gender in Greek antiquity, however, investigates specific educational and athletic rights of women in Sparta (o'Pye, 2012, p.10), a more militarized polis.

2008; Lynch, 2006; Eickelman, 1999). In the African context, public sphere theory has been critically examined by Tarik Dahou as an *aporia* in the frame of African sociological studies (Dahou, 2005). Arguing from their respective regional contexts, their work expresses a "critical attitude" that has barely been recognized in Western theorization.

Habermas' definition of the public sphere (*die Öffentlichkeit* – in singular) as a "network for the communication of opinions and standpoints" generating public opinion (Habermas, 1992, p. 436) remains the starting point for the core of theories in the field. By placing the practice of political reasoning, defined as discussion and consensus-building at the heart of his analysis, Habermas' approach has opened the way to a broadened understanding of political participation towards a more "inclusively understood concept of discursive will formation (…) which emphasizes the determination of norms of action through the practical debate of all affected by them" (Benhabib, 1992, p. 86). In this context, the Tunisian transformation process has been regarded as a model for procedural democracy that supports inclusive structures for building political institutions in which all actors involved aim to reach a consensus for the good of all Tunisians.

Before I continue in this line of critique in 3.1.2., I find it important to highlight the distinction between the "public sphere" and "space" as a local physical place as laid out in ancient conceptions. Social change can be explained by shifting relations between the two: my argument relates not only to the "square moments", when citizens occupied public space together in the uprisings of 2010/2011 but also with regards to finding and creating safe spaces to discuss long term strategies of change in a post-revolutionary society. The tent cities that were built up in Tunis at the *Kasbah* square, or *Tahrir* squares in Tunis, Cairo and in Sanaa, to name just a few, illustrate this renegotiation of the public sphere over space. The days when men and women of different classes and political orientation occupied space together, while sleeping in mixed tents, walking side by side in the marches, were considered as exceptional experiences. In Yemen, "women's participation challenged cultural taboos" (Alwazir, 2012). However, these public manifestations of citizens' unity across gender were quickly politicized (Alwazir, 2012) and women were pushed back from the public space to so-called private spheres through different counterrevolutionary means as described by scholars and activists Dina Whaba or Atiaf Alwazir alike (Alwazir, 2012, Wahba, 2016, p. 61).

The recognition of pluralism and legitimate, different interests and lifestyles within societies makes the assumption of one public sphere appear anachronistic. In this context, Fraser raises the question of whether the assumption of a single public sphere is an expression of domination or a utopian ideal.

3.1.2 Operationalization and Critique

Scholars have further operationalized the concept of the "public sphere" in order to make it more applicable for empirical analysis. In this study, I will focus on the framework offered by Peter Dahlgren as a more descriptive starting point. He distinguishes the public sphere into three dimensions according to structures, representation and interaction. I will present it in more detail hereafter and point out its shortcomings from an intersectional, post-colonial perspective afterwards.

The first dimension is concerned with the institutional features that structure the public sphere. Most importantly, this includes the analysis of political legislations or mass media organizations with regards to finance, control and ownership. This dimension incorporates "society's political institutions, which serve as a sort of 'political ecology' for the media and set boundaries for the nature of the information and forms of expression that circulate" (Dahlgren, 2005, p. 149). I claim that women's rights can be framed as part of this dimension as well. Codification of political and economic rights, as well as regulations regarding the family structures regulate access and the content that circulates.

The relations between media ownership and political affiliations constitute another important object of study here. Research shows that in authoritarian contexts such as Egypt, private and public media alike are often organized in clan or family structures (Richter & Badr, 2016). In recent years, models of public funding of media by citizens, as has been common in European countries, have come under more fierce attack, especially from right-wing actors for spreading too libertarian an agenda in terms of gender roles and the representation of sexual orientations and identities. The ecology of the public sphere deeply influences the "content that circulates" and public will-formation. At the same time, four of the eight wealthiest people in the world are CEOs of companies fostering innovation in ICTs: Microsoft, Amazon, Oracle and Facebook (Oxfam, 2017). With the growing monopoly of Internet businesses such as Google or Facebook, used by millions of people, the ecology of internet communication becomes increasingly monopolized.

The second dimension in Dahlgren's model is concerned with the "output of the media," including mass media and alternative media. This representational dimension of the public sphere can be read as the content of media that is distributed in different communicative forms – via radio, TV, print or the Internet. Habermas (2006) has argued that this output is essentially defined by the neoliberal structures underlying them: "The intrusion of the functional imperatives of the market economy into the 'internal logic' of the production and presentation of messages that leads to [...] [i]ssues of political discourse becom[ing] assimilated into and absorbed by the modes and contents of entertainment. Besides personalization, the dramatization of events, the simplification of complex matters, and the vivid polarization of conflicts promotes civic privatism and a mood of anti-politics" (Habermas, 2006:27; quoted in Fenton, p.66). Habermas establishes here the relation between "privatism" and "anti-politics" that I will take up later.

In authoritarian states, the representational dimension can be regulated by different means of oppression and censorship, ranging from police surveillance in the streets to blocking websites online. Propagandistic and biased reporting and a general lack of diversity in journalistic and media practices maintain a legitimizing discourse for the political system in power. In this context, the representational dimension of the public sphere can be regarded as a reflection of the norms and interests of those holding power over the structural dimension of the public sphere.

Finally, the conceptualization of the interactional dimension relies on the idea that a public sphere cannot consist of an audience or recipients only. Here, Dahlgren brings in a normative understanding of "democracy" when stating: "it is imperative not to lose sight of the classic idea that democracy resides, ultimately, with citizens who engage in talk with each other" (Dahlgren, 2005, p. 149). This is where deliberations on opinions, ideologies and values are situated. Dahlgren differentiates interaction into two elements. The first is the communicative "processes of making sense, interpreting, and using the output". This can be regarded as the interaction of the citizens with the media. Second, he frames interactions between citizens themselves, which can include anything from two-person conversations to large meetings, as the interactional dimension of the public sphere. With the second element of the interactional dimension of publics, Dahlgren bridges the gap between everyday-life and public action. It corresponds to the public sphere of "salons" in the 17th and 18th century that Jürgen Habermas takes as a point of departure for his theorization. The creation and engagement of associations, networks and NGOs can be discussed as participation at the interactional dimension. In communication studies, this third dimension incorporates new means of peer-to-peer communication, focusing on "the ways users interact with the media and with each other in particular online sites and spaces" (Löblich & Musiani, 2014, p. 352).

However, the framework is problematic in at least three points. My critique here departs from the intersectional theory perspective and relates to more general reviews of public sphere theory as expressed by political theoretician Natalie Fenton (Fenton, 2016) and Ernesto Laclau and Chantal Mouffe (Laclau, Mouffe, 2014): First, Dahlgren does not include a discussion of power structures, such as patriarchal, racist or classist and their intersections that determine the structural dimension of the public sphere in the first place. There is little explanation of the background of the structural dimension of the public sphere in a global economy perspective. In his earlier work, he hints at the constituent elements that construct the structural dimension of the public sphere: "structural elements from the broader arrangement of society includes social stratification, power alignments and not least the State" (Dahlgren, 1995, p. 11). A discussion of these "power alignments" with reference to the model is missing. While he recognizes the emancipatory potential of media for struggles around class, gender or race, he limits it to a modernist understanding in which "emancipation needs a moral vision", referring to the European Enlightenment (Dahlgren, 1995, p. 118). His argument is embedded in a Eurocentric view, implying a modernist understanding of emancipation that would lead to democracy in pre-defined European terms.

This exemplifies how the theory is captured by the liberal democracy of Western developed nations, as scholar Natalie Fenton argues. The implicit normative standards whereby more interaction would lead to more pluralism and this would automatically be translated into political power and influence are upheld, while underlying power structures in a society, causing, for example, unequal distribution of wealth and access to information, are ignored. Especially with regards to the processes under study, Fenton's warning becomes crucial: "Pluralism, as a value and set of practices, poses no threat to the neoliberal discourses that can be seen as a powerful and largely successful attempt to reshape the direction of travel of the political for a whole generation" (Fenton, 2016, p. 79).

Secondly, given the unequal distribution of power and resources in societies worldwide, a mutual conflictual relationship between the dimensions can be assumed. For critical empirical investigations, patterns structuring the relations between the three dimensions could be identified. This discussion becomes even more crucial when exploring changes and shifts *between* and *within* those different dimensions and when analyzing their reconstitution in times of political turmoil or revolutions.

A third argument derives from feminist theory. This perspective highlights the importance of investigating who can participate in which dimension of the public sphere and pointing to the social inequalities defining the constitution of the public sphere and counterpublics. The very concept of the public sphere is problematic as it implicitly assumes a "private" realm. In the quote above, Habermas makes the relation between privatism and de-politization explicit. Nancy Fraser develops her concept of "subaltern counterpublics" through a review of Habermas' understanding of the bourgeois public sphere, pointing out Habermas' implicit assumptions, which are not supported by realities on the ground nor, more specifically, by women's realities (Fraser, 1992). Her major critique concerns his non–recognition of power structures affecting the subject in a given society that limit and regulate their ability to participate in the public sphere. By pointing to the inequalities that exist in any society, she leads the way to critical examinations of participation processes. Who is able to speak in which publics and why?

Fraser and other feminist scholars have been critically reviewing the dichotomy of private and public spheres (Pratt, 2016; Ghannam, 2002, p. 88; Abu-Lughod, 1998, p. vii; Fraser, 1992; p.73). The renegotiation of the private and public boundaries also constitutes an important pillar of feminist emancipatory politics. Nancy Fraser has defined the terms of "private" and "public" as "cultural classifications and rhetorical labels" (Fraser, 1992, p. 73). According to Fraser this constitutes a "center of the rhetoric of privacy that has historically been used to restrict the universe of legitimate public contestation" (ibd.). Her argument can be related to feminist struggles worldwide, which are characterized by the attempt to deconstruct the division between private and public by emphasizing the political dimension of "private issues" such as violence against women or domestic abuse.

3.1.3 (Feminist) Counterpublics

In public sphere scholarship, the question of "what constitutes a counterpublic" has been discussed extensively (Downey & Fenton, 2003, p. 195). Theorizations on counterpublics are mainly defined *ex negativo* and refer to forms of organization and communication of actors that remain outside of hegemonic public spheres. Various authors find different explanations: Some point to their specific interests and experiences (Wimmer, 2007, p. 162 f.), because they "challenge the dominant public sphere" (Downey & Fenton, 2003, p. 193) or because they are "holding a marginal position within the political field in terms of their social, material, and political resources" (Spiegel, 2010, p. 323). In this regard, the concept of counterpublics can only be understood in relation to "hegemonic public spheres" which are, from a political and economic point of view, more powerful.[27] Fraser understands "counterpublic" as essential for critical theory and for democratic practice and defines them as „parallel discursive arenas where members of subordinated social groups invent and circulate counter-discourses, which in turn permit them to formulate oppositional interpretations of their identities, interests, and needs" (Fraser, 1992, p. 67).

Furthermore, Feminist counterpublics are, by definition, situated in "a conflictual relationship with the dominant public sphere as it aims to challenge the hegemonic, sexist gender discourses" (Minic, 2014, p. 136). This conflict though lies at the heart of democratic practice because "Counterpublic spheres engage constantly in struggles over meaning and experiment with and rehearse forms of democratic recovery" (Fenton, 2016, p. 58).

---

27 The argument for applying a multi-level approach when investigating public spheres in transformation is elaborated further in chapter 4.

"Counter-publics" have been criticized for an antagonistic understanding of realities, where the "hegemonic" and the "counterpublics" do not correspond to the complexities of realities. The strict separation ignores mobility and fluctuation between the publics. From the perspective of "radical and plural democracy", Mouffa and Laclau argue in favor of defending antagonistic relationships that seem to have disappeared with the advent of the information society and the process of globalization: While the importance of pluralism is recognized, they claim that a "profound transformation of the existing relations of power" would "require the creation of new political frontiers, not their disappearance" (Laclau, Mouffe, p. xv).

I share their concern that in refraining from the concepts of "counter", marking a clear antagonism, existing social divisions would be glossed over. This does not imply that the relations are always structured in the same way. While feminist counterpublics exist in every society, as patriarchy remains a dominant oppressive structure worldwide, the formulation of the "conflictual relationship" can thus vary from social stigmatizations or ridiculing to endangering women's physical well-being. The concept of counterpublics highlights the acts of resistance to patriarchy in their diversity. Also, the relation is not fixed, "but voices become more or less hegemonic in their offered interpretation of the world" (Yuval-Davis, 2011, p. 105). In the study of transformation processes, it is pivotal to investigate *what* circumstances make them "more or less hegemonic". Through this approach, the function of gender debates in the Tunisian transformation can be exhibited, uncovering state feminism as a hegemonic ideology in the Tunisian case.

Fraser's functional understanding facilitates empirical inquiry when she points out that:

"On the one hand they function as *spaces of withdrawal and regroupment*, they also function as bases and training grounds for *agitational* activities directed *toward wider publics*. It is precisely in the dialectic between these two functions that emancipatory potential relies" (Fraser, 1992, p. 124; emphasis added).

She introduces the idea of their "dual character" on the function of autonomous space for regroupment on the one hand, and the understatement of influencing the wider public sphere on the other hand. A dialectic relation is at the heart of emancipatory politics.

In light of the theoretical framework and empirical investigation, however, it is noteworthy that Fraser does not provide a differentiation of counterpublics which could lead to a closer examination of their constitutions from within, focusing instead on the actor's perspective. When, in her definition, listing "women, workers, peoples of color, and gays and lesbians" as examples of subordinated social groups constituting counterpublics, the categories employed fail to take into consideration the intersecting power relations that are, in my opinion, essential for analyzing the constitution of counterpublics. She fails to consider the specific struggles and "regroupment processes" in their intersections: under which category would women of color organize in this perspective? Women from rural backgrounds? Or LGBTs from working class backgrounds? Here, my empirical findings have shown that the realities are not that simple. Realities on the ground speak for much more differentiated mechanisms in the constitution of counterpublics. Women can actually face a dilemma of where to organize or prioritize their activism. Furthermore, the conflictual relation to the hegemonic public sphere may vary in its traits. The intersectional lens can help to provide further understanding of what constitutes oppressions and overcome the limitations of Fraser's theorization.[28] Positionality, defined through the intersection of class, race, gender and other categories manifesting oppression, defines interests and resources for participation in counterpublics.

3.2   Defining Publics within Matrices of Domination

Integrating and linking the descriptive model of dimensions of public spheres on the one hand, and the analytical approach on Matrices of Domination on the other hand is intended to explain first, how the structural, representational and interactional, dimensions are constituted, shaped, expressed and penetrated by the domains of power. Secondly, it can explain particular "regroupment processes" in counterpublics beyond mono-dimensional explanations emphasizing the relation between counterpublics and the hegemonic public sphere within the matrix of oppression. Thirdly, it also helps to investigate reciprocal dynamics between domains of power and the constitution of feminist counterpublics in contexts of political turmoil and transformation and sheds light on multifaceted strategies of resistance.

---

28 Nancy Fraser has certainly contributed to critical public spheres theory, especially with regards to conceptualizations of counterpublics, and more recently with her work on transnational public spheres (Fraser, 2014), where it could be argued that she is attempting to reach out to post-colonial approaches. Nevertheless, she fails to reflect on her own positionality as a White feminist and to credit scholars having worked on intersectional theory over the last thirty years. With regards to the relation between feminism and capitalism, Fraser notes in a highly discussed essay that "the movement for women's liberation has become entangled in a dangerous liaison with neoliberal efforts to build a free-market society" and gives different arguments on how "feminism has contributed to neoliberal ethos" (Fraser, 2013). In their reply entitled: "the White feminist fatigue syndrome", Bhandar and Ferreira da Silva point out how Fraser is reproducing White feminist patronage by employing the term "feminism" (in singular) for the critical thoughts of White feminist only. They show by contrast, how Black feminists have over the years and repeatedly formulated "critiques of capitalist forms of property, exchange, paid and unpaid labor, along with culturally embedded and structural forms of patriarchal violence (Bhandar & Ferreira da Silva, 2013)."

3.2.1 Power and the Three Dimensions of the Public Sphere

When combining intersectional theory with theorizations of public and counter-public spheres in this empirically driven study, "complex interactions between structures of power and oppression and interconnected aspects of individual and group identity and social location" (Grace, 2014, p. 1) must be taken into consideration. The "Matrix of Domination" by Patricia Hill Collins contains two elements: it

"has (1) a particular arrangement of intersecting systems of oppression, e.g., race, social class, gender, sexuality, citizenship status, ethnicity and age; and (2) a particular organization of its domains of power, e.g., structural, disciplinary, hegemonic, and interpersonal" (Collins, 2000, p. 299).

Collins distinguishes two different understandings of power: the first consists of the "dialectical relationship linking oppression and activism" (Collins, 2000, p. 274). This means that the more oppressed group has the biggest interest in getting into a conflictual relationship with the group that oppresses it in a given society. It synthesizes the idea that fierce oppression will create resistance. Collins defines power "as an intangible entity that circulates within a particular Matrix of Domination and to which individuals stand in varying relationships. These approaches emphasize how individual subjectivity frames human actions within a Matrix of Domination" (Collins, 2000, p. 274). Instead of individual subjectivity, I introduced the term of "positionality" earlier and linked it to the public sphere.

For empirical investigations, Collins's differentiation of power into four domains should be our employed for further operationalization and to revisit the public sphere model. As the epistemological and methodological starting points of public sphere theory and intersectional approaches are very different, each domain of power has to be examined carefully and integrated into the three dimensions of the public sphere in order to avoid imprudent assumptions of parallels.

The Structural Domain of Power

The structural dimension of power relates to legislation and the organization of citizenship. Here, Collins names "legal system, labor markets, schools, the housing industry, banking, insurance, the news media, and other social institutions" that have "historically disadvantaged Black women in the US" as "interlocking social institutions" (Collins, 2000, p. 277). In order to drastically change these historically developed and wide-scale domains of power, the social institutions need to be fundamentally changed. A revolution can be the beginning of an empowerment process, which benefits those at the bottom of the Matrix of Domination. In national uprisings, revolution and turmoil, institutional arrangements such as law texts or press codes are challenged, and police forces are violently opposed. When social institutions are then renegotiated under new banners, for example by including formerly marginalized actors in dialogues and decision making, the disciplinary domain of power can still be in place and influential from inside the institutions. [29]

The Disciplinary Domain of Power

The disciplinary domain of power refers to "a way of ruling that relies on bureaucratic hierarchies and techniques of surveillance". It hereby „manages power relations" (Collins, 2000, p. 280). Rather than "simple" mechanisms of inclusion or exclusion, this domain of power incorporates mechanisms of controlling. Collins sees disciplinary domain manifest in the modern large and impersonal bureaucratic apparatus of States. For example, in representational democracy, the electoral code set the legislative frame of inclusions and exclusions for active franchise. Once inside the institution, or "strong public," different mechanisms of legislations and non-written rules become powerful. Collins exemplifies this relation within the academic system (Collins, 2000, p. 282f.).

The Hegemonic Domain of Power

The hegemonic domain of power in Hill Collins's conceptualization of the Matrix of Domination is concerned with ideologies, culture and consciousness. In the second part of this study (Chapters 6-8), the hegemonic domain of power comes under closer scrutiny because it has been central in constructing and controlling the three dimensions of the public sphere: I argue that it structured the debates on the women's rights codifications, influenced media representation of women and gender topics and penetrates the interactional dimension of the public sphere in various ways. The effects of the hegemonic domain of power range

---

29 One episode during my fieldwork illustrated this relation very well: when looking at the Tunisian case, the electoral code was allowing all citizens over 18 years to be elected, but once the parliamentarians were established, they were confronted with the disciplinary domain of power. I interviewed Adnen Hajji, who was one of the main organizers of the uprisings in Redeyef and Gafsa in 2008, just after his official election for Parliament in October 2014. On my way to the interview meeting point at the office of the local union in Redeyef, a young construction worker who knew that I was going to see the new representative in parliament of the town, spontaneously called out: "Let's hope he will not forget us, once he is in Tunis." In my opinion, this manifested the awareness of the domain of disciplinary control that would hamper the possibilities to act for those who come from the margins and enter positions of authority.

from influences on materialistic aspects like the funding of associations, to hierarchies within families. The empirical evidence supports Patricia Hill Collins's
claim that it is a central link to legitimize the Matrix of Domination: "By manip-
ulating ideology and culture, the hegemonic domain acts as a link between social
institutions (structural domain), their organizational practices (disciplinary domain), and the level of everyday social interaction (interpersonal domain)"
(Collins, 2000, p. 284). As hegemony is a central concept for the definition of
counterpublics, I will discuss it separately hereafter.

The Interpersonal Domain of Power

Finally, the interpersonal domain of power "functions through routinized, day-
to-day practices of how people treat one another (e.g., micro-level of social organization)" (Collins, 2000, p. 287) and constitutes "discriminatory practices of
everyday lived experiences that because they are so routine typically go unno-
ticed or remain unidentified" (Collins, 2000, p. 299). Thus, Collins notes how
these assaults and micro-aggressions can be encountered by a number of different, often creative and subversive strategies. Producing knowledge about these
practices and making this knowledge accessible via reports, videos, personalized
accounts or other forms of communication entering the representational dimension of the public sphere can help to raise awareness and can constitute a powerful way to negotiate change. The interpersonal domain of power penetrates
arenas of participation situated at the structural dimension of the public sphere,
meaning that women working in parliaments are not free from experiencing sexism structuring everyday encounters. Drawing from this analytical framework
relating institutional changes and everyday practices can reveal the gaps between
theory and practices in gender politics. Gender based quota regulations allow for
the inclusion of women, but do not automatically translate into changes of behavior. They also neglect intersectional understandings of inclusion and varieties
of other forms of discrimination that women of color or lower-class backgrounds
experience. A focus on the institutional mechanism of inclusion and exclusion
and quantitative approaches to representation often cannot grasp the persistence
of the interpersonal domain of power.
    Following up on Laclau and Mouffe, I argue that it is only through transfor-
mation in all four domains of power that sustainable change can occur. Otherwise, the continued discriminatory practices can continue to persist, while public
attention becomes a structuring element of who continues to be affected. Struggles against oppression are not equally represented in the public sphere. In chapter II, I laid out how the negotiation of oppressive gender relations can especially
be exploited for racist and conservative agendas. In order to understand these

relations in more detail, following up on Laclau and Mouffe's and Collin's distinction, I will discuss hegemony as a central category for political analysis.

3.2.2 The Hegemonic Domain of Power

While the relation between the structural and the interpersonal domains of power follow a similar level of analysis as the structural and interactional dimensions of the public sphere, the incorporation of the other dimensions – "representational" on the one hand and "disciplinary and hegemonic" on the other hand – provide the conceptual starting point for theory-modeling and a response to the critique of public sphere theory outlined above. A discussion of "hegemony" will provide further explanations of the constituencies of the three dimensions of the public sphere and define the situation of counterpublics more clearly.

Hill Collins' definition of the hegemonic domain of power as "a critical site for not fending off hegemonic ideas from dominant culture, but in crafting counter-hegemonic knowledge that fosters changed consciousness" can be related to the broader theorizations of cultures in Gramscian and Foucaultian discourse analysis. The relations between hegemony and articulations against it are not fixed. When studying public spheres in political transformations, analyzing hegemony provides deeper understanding of these multifaceted processes. I very much agree with Pamela Beth Radcliff, a historian who explores the participation of ordinary men and women in the democratic transformation in Spain in the 1970s. She introduces a contextualized and inconsistent understanding of hegemony:

"Since hegemony is always incomplete, it implies a constant 'war of positions' or at least negotiation, which leaves room both for resistance and counter-hegemonic attacks (…) Since hegemony is always in flux, it oscillates between periods of stability and crisis that provide more or less space for opposition" (Beth Radcliff, 1996, p. 4).

Antonio Gramsci's theory on "cultural hegemony," which has since been adapted to international communication theory as well (Thussu, 2010), can be related to the hegemonic domain of power in Collins' understanding. In this perspective, the dominant social group in a society has the capacity to exercise intellectual and moral direction over the society at large. A "common sense" is built through ideological control of cultural production and distribution (Gramsci, 1971). The ruling class can exercise "social authority" over subordinated classes without using methods of coercion, but rather through "the exercise of a special kind of power, the power to frame alternatives and contain opportunities, to win and shape consent" (Clarke, Hall, Jefferson & Roberts, 1975, p. 102). While the ecology of the media determines the degree of influence in and inclusion of the media content, the latter represents structuring images, debates and arguments to reach consensus. In international communication studies, hegemony is used to explain the political function of the mass media in propagating and maintaining dominant ideologies. Even in national contexts with relative press freedom and without direct control of journalists, mass media still operate within the logic of dominant ideologies, merely representing the interests of an "elite" positioned within the mass media sector, the government officials or leading positions in the economy. The concepts of hegemony and public spheres were intertwined in political communication theory by the "hegemonic model of communication" which argues that "the elite in society decide what ideas dominate in the public sphere" (Lilleker, 2006, p. 128). Counter-hegemonic expressions, organized in counterpublics, always incorporate a critique of the establishment. It is important to keep in mind, that this critique can be formulated from right-wing, fascist standpoints and emancipatory, progressive standpoints alike. Warf and Grimes, for example, define counter-hegemony in the context of Internet communication as "varied messages from groups and individuals who refuse to take existing ideologies and politics as normal, natural, or necessary, typically swimming against the tide of public opinion" (Warf & Grimes, 1997, p. 260).

Struggles over this hegemonic domain of power appear on the representational dimension of the public sphere. Patricia Hill Collins herself points out the importance of mass media for the spreading of racist, nationalist, classist or sexist ideologies through manipulation and placement of images when she writes that "an increasingly important dimension of why hegemonic ideologies concerning race, class, gender, sexuality, and nation remain so deeply entrenched lies, in part, in the growing sophistication of mass media in regulating intersecting oppressions" (Collins, 2000, p. 284).

For the Tunisian context, a plurality of gender roles and diversified feminist understandings that would not only recur on the modernization paradigm can then be regarded as attempts to break with hegemonic gender representations, that have assumed a "universal structuring function" (Laclau, Mouffe, 2014, p. xi). The modernization discourse and politization of women's rights by foreign governments have been stated in the literature as a major challenge for states undergoing times of war, crisis and transformation (Hays-Mitchell & Irvine, 2012, p. 6), and will be closer investigated in Chapter IX. After the uprisings, a "renegotiation" of the hegemonic power and the particular element of "feminism" as linked to a modernist understanding can be observed. With the liberalization of the public sphere, new spheres to come to terms with state feminism or to "kill it," as the young Tunisian journalist Ons Bouali wrote in the spring of 2011, would open up (Bouali, 2011). From a philosophical point of view, Tunisian scholar Soumaya Mestiri advances the need to "decolonize feminism" in Tunisia (Mestiri S. , 2016, p. 82). "Killing" and "decolonizing" state feminism mirror a hegemonic struggle and the aim of Tunisian activists and writers to disentangle gender politics from political camps and ideologies.

3.2.3 Typology of Counterpublics Within the Matrix of Domination

In the following, I attempt to embed and characterize counterpublics with regards to the three dimensions of the public sphere that they tackle. Hypothetically, counterpublics exist along the three dimensions of public spheres. I claim that the interpersonal domain of power, expressed in the discriminatory practices of everyday life predefines the "regroupment process," where individuals come together and join a counterpublic, as laid out by Nancy Fraser. The specific experience of women defined by intersecting structures of oppression expressed at the interactional dimension of the public sphere defines their priorities and interests in counterpublic participation. My aim is to conceptually grasp these different positions with regards to the Matrix of Domination with the separation of the formation of *women's and feminist counterpublics* on the one hand and *women in counterpublics* on the other hand. When referring to "women in counterpublics," I take into consideration the female activists who do not organize around their gender but for example around their locality or class to challenge the Matrix of Domination. Reasons for this that hamper coalition building between counterpublics will be presented in the analysis. While the whole Matrix of Domination is ubiquitous, this domain of power relates to everyday interactions and realities. The structural domain of power determines their resources, enabling or limiting their participation in the structural, representational or interactional dimension of the public sphere.

It is important to remember that since the 1970s, political participation theory has constantly broadened its scope, from a very limited understanding of what can be understood as political participation in democratic countries (e.g., elections) to more varied forms such as demonstrations, sit-ins, and so on. Feminist scholars put this new approach forward aiming to make women's participation visible. Political scientist Cilja Harders employs a broadened concept of participation and links it to a "state analysis from below:

"Political participation includes informal, individual, hidden, illegal, and 'nonpolitical' actions and networks, as well as organized, public collective actions inside and outside of institutionalized frameworks. State analysis from below pays special attention to how class, race, ethnicity, and gender structure access to and use of specific resource flows and participation patterns" (Harders, 2015, p. 149).

In relation to Harders' understanding of participation that entails an analysis of structures of oppression, I have outlined the relation between positionality, resources and priorities for participation. After the uprisings in Tunisia, counterpublic action expressing multifaceted interests can then be translated into a variety of forms, from local neighborhood meetings to advocacy and lobbying of current legislation and constitutional debates affecting the institutional dimension of the public sphere for women, to the translocal, digitally constituted counterpublics which bring women from different countries together around a common purpose. In the following I will clarify these different negotiation processes by situating them within the three dimensions of the public sphere. To reiterate, I defined renegotiation as a communicative and participatory act aiming to add or challenge ideas manifested in institutional settings, social relations or everyday practices defining the public sphere.

Counterpublics at the Structural Dimension of the Public Sphere

Counterpublics situated at the structural dimension of the public sphere aim to change national and international institutions and the ecology of the media in order to achieve more rights and representation. In Tunisia, I argue that feminist associations that can look back to a longer history of counterpublic resistance were able to tackle these institutions by different means of lobbying. Moreover, these feminists could actively negotiate the codification of women's rights in interim political institutions such as the Higher Commission for the Fulfillment of Revolutionary Goals, Political Reform, and Democratic Transition" (HIROR) and the Independent High Authority for Elections (ISIE). They participated directly in changing the institutions defining the structural domain of power of the matrix of oppression. Besides this important access, the pressure to remain autonomous within this dimension of the public sphere is very high: I rely here on Collins' argument where the purpose of the disciplinary domain of power is to support the hegemonic domain of power. This implies that bureaucratic practices play in favor of a patriarchal system. Women who gain access to negotiate the structural dimension of the public sphere are usually confronted with the disciplinary and hegemonic domain of power.

There are many examples alongside the Tunisian one of women involved in taking up political roles in "strong publics" being confronted with stigmatization, ridicule and other personal attacks. Therefore, I argue that counterpublics at the structural level of the public sphere must have more resources and other privileges, in terms of funding or education, at their disposal. They are at the forefront of the war on positions that can translate into more sustainable institutions.

Counterpublics at the Representational Dimension of the Public Sphere

The "model of women's media action" developed by Byerly & Ross (2006, p. 124ff.) can help to distinguish different forms of counterpublics situated at the representational dimension of the public sphere. The authors have theorized about feminist media participation based on the experiences of the international women's movement. In their typology, they distinguish four paths, illustrating mechanisms for women's media activism. It incorporates counterpublics in their "factual dimension," which understands counterpublics as both alternative media (in particular, feminist media spaces created online) and counterthematization (Wimmer, 2007, p. 158).

The first "politics to media" describes feminist activists who use media as an important element of their work i.e. in spreading knowledge and integrating feminist views and standpoints via the mass media to a wider society to gain legitimacy and support. The second path, "media professions to politics," refers to women who are already positioned in the media sector as professional journalists or editors and actively use this position to place and promote feminist themes "from within" the media system. The third path, "advocate change agents," includes strategies of putting pressure on the media system to improve gender equality by giving guidelines or by issuing reports on gender and media. Chinese feminist media scholar Bu Wei writes: "Their concerns and goals focus on changing the media and shifting the agenda in media reports" (Wei, 2008, p. 321). The last path identified in the model is 'women's media enterprises', and refers to the independent, often small, media outlets created by feminists themselves and who produce their own knowledge and disseminate it via their proper media with the maximum of control. Counterpublics engaging with the representational dimension of the public sphere then oppose the hegemonic domain of power by circulating and sharing knowledges, images and ideas to ultimately "construct new knowledge" (Collins, 2000, p. 286). In light of increasing digitalization, I wonder whether typologies can actually grasp the very diverse ways women and counterpublics employ media to their ends.

From an intersectional perspective, exposing stereotypical images can be one dimension of critical feminist media scholarship[30] that shall be included in the model of feminist media action. In the academic field, scholars have highlighted the limited body of research on the relation of media and gender relations in developing countries (Ben Salem M. , 2010). Feminist scholars have developed an "Arab feminist media research" perspective. According to media scholar Salam Al-Mahadin from the University of Amman, this scholarship is concerned

---

30 Researching these questions would require a distinct methodology and methods that would allow for qualitative content analysis, focusing solely on media output and the representational dimension of the public sphere.

with "the political, social and economic agenda which shapes both Arab and Western media choice in ways that delimit a certain type of Arab woman and attempt to 'discursively condition' the reader/viewer to accept her as a certain norm" (Al-Mahadin, 2011, p. 7). I would frame the conceptual engagement with these issues as another path of feminist media action tackling academic publics.

Counterpublics at the Interactional Dimension of the Public Sphere

After the uprisings, many women's organizations were founded in a variety of local contexts that I frame as counterpublics constituting themselves against patriarchal domination. For example, the two associations "Victory of the Rural Woman" (Victoire de la Femme Rural, VFR) from Sidi Bouzid and "Woman and Citizenship" (Femme et Citoyenneté, FEC) from ElKef were both created after the uprisings. While the former places a differently positioned woman (singular) at the center and claims her "victory", the latter employs citizenship as a central concept of their work. Other organizations reveal the attempt to localize the advancements of women's rights and establish counterpublics from a local positionality, such as the "Association Rayhana for the Woman of Jendouba" (Rayhana pour la Femme de Jendouba) and the "Association Femmes Rurales Jendouba" (founded in 2013). Others do not claim a specifically decentralized approach, such as "Voix de Eve" (Eve's Voice), founded in 2012 in Regueb (Governorate of Sidi Bouzid) or the association "Elle" from Kasserine. There are also other organizations organized around both gender and religious identity, such as "Tunisiat", while not explicitly stating their religiosity in the name of the association. The association "M'nmety" (My Dream) founded by Black Tunisians addresses intersecting structures of sexism and racism in Tunisia. While not having an explicit gender approach, most of their members as well as the president, Saâdia Mosbahare, are Black Tunisian women. They take up a primary role in challenging the image of the hegemonic White Tunisian citizen.

I found it of particular importance to include the element of "bodily comportment" alongside NGOs that I frame as counterpublics at the interactional dimension of the public sphere. Here, the body becomes the medium and the message challenging hegemony (Kraidy, 2013). Resistance then literally involves *everybody*, independent of resources. Annelies Moors argues for a "politics of presence," which takes into account not only the rational mode of communication, as in the Habermasian ideal, but one that would also "allow for the inclusion of other forms of critical expression and non-verbal modes of communication. Such forms and styles of participation may include, for instance, bodily comportment, appearance, styles (...)" (Moors, 2006, p. 120). "Bodily comportment" challenges a hegemonic order in the public sphere. Judith Butler and others have recently theorized on the "vulnerability and resistance" of bodies in the public space:

"What I am suggesting is that it is not this or that body that is bound up in a network of relations, but that the body, despite its clear boundaries or perhaps precisely by virtue of those very boundaries is defined by the relations that make its own life and action possible" (Butler, 2015, p. 130).

"Loitering" refers to "hanging out" in public space, an action with important gendered implications. The hegemonic discourse expects women to stay at home or enter public space for specific purposes. It has been regarded as radical feminist dissent to challenge the dominant public sphere (Phadke, Ranade, & Khan, 2009). The sanctions inflicted by state authorities or community members of body-centered communication vary greatly according to the positionalities of women. On example of radical bodily comportment is Amina Sboui's topless protests that infiltrated national and international publics.

The development of Web 2.0 technologies has enabled a whole generation of young women to take an active part in creating and disseminating knowledge in counterpublics. Youth sociologist Anita Harris contents that the technologies enable the creation of public selves:

"I suggest that need to take seriously young women's styles of technology-enabled social and political engagement, as they represent new directions in activism, the construction of new participatory communities, and the development of new kinds of public selves" (Harris, 2008, p. 482).

In recent years, online feminist counterpublics have come under close scrutiny. Elsewhere I have analyzed in more detail the formation of feminist hashtags in different countries (Antonakis, 2015b). The accounts of masses of women and men sharing experiences of everyday life in a patriarchal environment regrouped around a hashtag on Twitter can constitute the beginning of wider transformations. The step to communicate about one's own life experiences online is then an attempt to reset the boundaries between what is considered private and not in the interest of the general public. As Vivienne and Burgess (2012, p. 362) state: "This sharing of personal stories in public spaces in pursuit of social change is an example of 'everyday activism." Most recently, the hashtag #metoo has led to the exclusion of formerly powerful individuals, such as producer Harvey Weinstein, from the public sphere.

Still, I find it imperative to not lose sight of the positionality from which they communicate and clarify which dimension of the public sphere can be tackled. Nevertheless, these analyses have to be seen against the background of the digital divides that are still prevalent and the neoliberal paradigm within which the mass media operates.[31] In order to give an overview over the theoretical steps I have taken, the following table summarizes my conclusions by presenting the general model, its adaption within the Matrix of Domination and finally the way

---

31 See for a further discussion of the sensationalist logic of the mass media departing from a Habermasian critique, chapter 8.

I'm planning to adapt the model to the empirical realities in Tunisia and the related subjects. The framework shall illustrate how public sphere can be utilized within an emancipatory research when pointing to concrete practices of multi-faceted negotiations.

Operationaliza-tion	Structural Dimension of the Public Sphere	Representational Dimension of the Public Sphere	Interactional Dimension of the Public Sphere
General model of the public sphere after Dahlgren (2005)	Institutions owning and regulating the Media Sector and freedom of expression Ecology of the media	Output of the media	Communication between two and more citizens Making sense of the media output
Adaption within the Matrix of Domination	National and Supranational political institutions codifying women's and minority rights and regulating their access to the public sphere via various political and economic resources Gender distribution within the media as owners and producers	Women as subject of the media: Quantity and diversity of women's representation in mass media, Plurality of gender roles, Subjects related to gender negotiations, Feminist media projects	Communication between two and more citizens emphasizing their positionality Gendered regroupments Making sense of the media output
Application: Counterpublics in Tunisia between 2011-2014	Feminist associations participating in interim bodies with legislative function (HIROR, ISIE) negotiating electoral laws, the constitution of 2014, CEDAW, the family Code (CSP) Complementarity and National Women's Day 2012 and 2013	Coverage of Femen and Amina Sboui Online Counterpublics Reports and data collected and published by feminist NGOs	Local women's and feminist NGOs and associations and local, spontaneous networks Revolutionary corporeal practices Demonstrations and occupation of space by female workforce

Table 1 Gendered Adaption of the Public Sphere Model by Peter Dahlgren and Classification of the Empirical Material to the Conceptual Framework

4 The Nation State Within the Matrix of Domination

In this chapter, I argue that the analysis of transformation should incorporate both the national context and its local specific scriptures of power and resistance without losing sight of international developments in the ecology of media systems (see also Antonakis, 2018, p. 138) as well as realms considered "private". In my distinction of the state and the regime, I take Robert Fishman's work on South European state transitions in the 1980s as a starting point. He summarizes: "Regimes are more permanent forms of political organization than specific governments, but they are typically less permanent than the state" (Fishman, 1990, p. 428). Furthermore, I consider the nation-state an "imagined community" or a "fiction" that would imply that the boundaries of the nation and the boundaries of the state correspond (Yuval-Davis, 1997, p. 11). The state is thus not seen here as an autonomous actor: drawing from research on the state from anthropological perspectives, I rather seek to understand, "how the state comes into being, how 'it' is differentiated from other institutional forms and what effects this construction has on the operation and diffusion of power throughout society" (Sharma & Gupta, 2006, p. 8). This approach blends into the matrix of domination.

Despite processes of globalization and digitalization, state institutions remain a pivotal field of analysis in the construction of the public sphere within Matrices of Domination. Given that a public sphere is constructed by legislation and (state owned) mass media in particular, I would claim that when speaking of "one" public sphere, we refer to a predefined national territory whose institutions convey a specific hegemonic ideology. This approach emphasizes the exploration of negotiations of gender in a national context and a specific time period. Furthermore, the theoretical approach of the public sphere permits integration of a transnational perspective. The theoretical debate on the transnational research dimension will be introduced when delving into the empirical context mainly with regards to three objects of study: transnational institutions to improve women's rights, such as the CEDAW, transnational activist networks and the communication infrastructures they rely on, such as Facebook, and finally foreign funding of feminist counterpublics and therefore the transnational flow of

© Springer Fachmedien Wiesbaden GmbH, part of Springer Nature 2019
A. Antonakis, *Renegotiating Gender and the State in Tunisia between 2011 and 2014*, Politik und Gesellschaft des Nahen Ostens,
https://doi.org/10.1007/978-3-658-25639-5_4

capital to support "women's empowerment".[32]

Theorization on the relation between the family and the state forms an important part of feminist and intersectional literature. In "It's All in the Family: Interconnections of Gender, Race and Nation" (1998), Collins argues that the hierarchies which construct a society are "naturalized" within the family. In a mutual process, the family reproduces the patriarchal norms of the state. I frame the family as a site of transformation in chapter 10.2.3, exhibiting attempts by feminist actors to address these hierarchies.

4.1   State Institutions Regulating the Public Sphere

State institutions are present in all three dimensions of the public sphere by regulating and providing communicative infrastructure, offering public media services and promoting or restricting freedom of press and freedom of expression. I understand the state and its institutions as gatekeepers opening and closing the field of the public sphere. I follow Jürgen Habermas's definition - "state authority [referring in particular to the permanent administration and standing army] is so to speak the executor of the political public sphere, not part of it" (Habermas, 1964, p. 51), but I do not regard it – especially in times of increased digitalization and globalization – as the only executor. In their gendered study on digital censorship in Malaysia, Heike Jensen et. al. explain that "gender and sexuality within the framework of the nation-state is essential for understanding the morality debates that have increasingly come to dominate discussions about internet governance and digital censorship and surveillance (Jensen, sm Kee, Venkiteswaran, & Randhawa, 2012, p. 67). However, it would be wrong to assume that it is the only agent to censor and limit gendered access to the public sphere; they frame "norms, markets and architectures" as other important fields of inquiry (ibd.).

The regime's gatekeeper function can be situated at two distinct domains of power: Firstly, the structural domain of power entailing the state institutions and political arenas, such as parliaments with legislative function, but also state mass media. As a regulator of citizenship, for instance, through women's rights codification, state institutions open and close gendered public arenas. Secondly, Max

---

32 In this context, Yuval-Davis states that "not enough recognition is given to the role of diaspora communities in contemporary nationalist struggles." Tunisians who lived in a "political exile, who aimed to go back the moment the political situation changes" (Yuval-Davis, 1997, p.18). While I wouldn't put much emphasis on a typology of diapora communities, it can be stated that the Tunisian public sphere post-2011 has indeed been constructed by many of them, some more visible (Rached Ghannouchi, Moncef Marzouki, Hechmi Hamdi, Slim Riahi) others less so (consultants, businessmen, journalists).

Weber states "the state is the only human *Gemeinschaft* which lays claim to the monopoly on the legitimated use of physical force" within a given territory(Weber M. , 1919, p. 10), hereby essentially controlling the disciplinary domain of power.

While a new range of possibilities has opened up to engage in counterhegemonic action, these are also closed down in a constant and ongoing struggle (Downey & Fenton, 2003, p. 200). Counterpublics have been described as independent from the state and autonomous in the sense that no political system can take advantage of them or use them for its legitimation (Scheuch, 2003). Empirically, this distinction is not easily maintained: the concern of instrumentalization and co-optation of feminist counterpublics by state actors, especially the regime and parties, was raised repeatedly in the interviews. It has been stressed that no formation of local counterpublics can actually function outside of "existing industrial–commercial public spheres, especially electronic publicity" (Downey & Fenton, 2003, p. 193).

In authoritarian regimes, such as Tunisia prior to January 14[t] 2011, the government was omnipresent in the public sphere. The ideal of Habermas, where the public sphere should be accessible for everybody; a space where citizens come together to discuss issues that are not their private interest, didn't exist. However, it is in this context that one could speak of a single hegemonic public sphere, because the emergence of counterpublics was almost impossible due to the repression of all forms of communication enforced by different methods.[33] Political debate was confined to an exclusive "elite circle" and a plurality of opinions was lacking(Remili, 2011, p. 12). This situation certainly changed after 2011, but the entanglement of the state and public and private media companies persisted: there are several examples to illustrate the strong relations between political and media actors dominating the structural dimension of the public sphere. Hechmi Hamdi, a businessman and media entrepreneur, opened his satellite TV channel *Almoustaquilla* ("the Independent") in 1999 from London and became active in politics when launching the Party of Progressive Conservatives (PPC) as part of the larger movement "Popular Petition for Freedom, Justice and Development" (Pétition Populaire pour la liberté, la justice et le développement), renamed in 2013 "the current of love" (le courant d'amour, or Tayar el-Mahaba). This party gained 26 seats in the elections of 2011 and two seats in 2014. Hamdi presented his candidature for presidency in 2014 and came fourth in the first round with 5.75% of the votes.

The party "Free Patriotic Union" (Union Patriotique Libre, UPL) headed by the businessperson Slim Riahi is another case in point. He founded the political party in January 2011 while holding a powerful position within media ecologies. He established the media channels *Ettounsiya Al-Oula*, *Ettounsiya Sport* and

---

33 For a more detailed analysis, see chapter 5.2.

Ettounsiya News. Furthermore, he became the president of the football club "Club Africain." Presenting his candidacy for the presidential election in 2014, he gained 5.55% of the votes, placing him only slightly behind Hamdi.[34] The rise and powerful resistance of media moguls despite political transformations have been described in transformation studies of the societies of the former Soviet Union (Dyczok & Gaman-Golutvina, 2009). The Tunisian case appears comparable, where most media outlets remained in the hands of the former "secular" elites (Labidi, 2012).

4.1.1 The Nation-State and Marginalized Localities

I regard the centralized nation state as a main actor producing marginalized localities through the distribution of material resources and "cultural heritage." Locality can be reframed as a geographical scale through which structures of oppression operate in Tunisia's matrix of domination. As Cilja Harders and others have pointed out, the local has to be included analytically and valued when studying societies in transformation. The local is defined by Harders in a critical transformation perspective as "political space, which is both a testing and contesting ground for changing state-society relations and thus deserves the closest scrutiny" (Harders, 2013, p. 113).

Patricia Hill Collins introduces "local realities" as a prism of the Matrix of Domination: "Thus, regardless of how any given matrix is actually organized either across time or from society to society, the concept of a Matrix of Domination encapsulates the universality of intersecting oppressions as organized through diverse local realities" (Collins, 2000, p. 228). Locality constitutes an environment that shapes everyday experiences and in which structural discriminations are manifested and played out. Harders operates with the concept of political "scales" which may be fruitfully combined with the dimensions of the public sphere and the definition of counterpublics within them. Both have a relational connection to the centers of power, which change according to subjective positions and political actions on "inter-scale politics beyond the center" (Bouziane, Harders, & Hoffmann, 2013, p. 3).

The disparities between the coastal areas, referred to as the *Sahel,* in opposition to the *Dakhel,* incorporating the territories of the Center, West and the South of the country, mirror decades of structural unequal distributions of wealth in the

---

34 At the time of writing, the link which directs to the election results of the first round was not accessible on the official homepage of the Independent High Authority for Elections anymore, it only provides data for the second round (http://www.isie.tn/resultats/resultats-presidentielles/). As a secondary source, see for example: „Tunisie : L'ISIE annonce les résultats définitifs du 1er tour des présidentielles"(2014).

country. Different indicators express this marginalization of regions: Data from the statistical national institute shows the unequal migration flows in the country, with the region of "Grand Tunis" standing out as receiving a surplus of people. This is closely linked to socio-economic structures such as the repartition of private and public investments (Szakal, 2016) and expressed in much higher unemployment and a maternal mortality rate three times higher than in the rest of the country, mirroring the absence of doctors and lack of health services (Mestiri, 2016). Furthermore, I will argue later that it affects and intersects with (gendered) outcomes of differences in economic resources, mobilities and everyday life conditions manifested in local space. The analytical framework presented here thus models the category of geographical locality as an important dimension to encompass the Matrix of Domination in Tunisia. In the course of the transformation, the state has even been recognized as responsible for the systematic oppression of regions:

The Dignity and Truth Commission constitutes the main body for transitional justice in Tunisia. The institution can be regarded as a major outcome of the protests of 2010/2011: It answers to such core demands as to tackle the corruption of the regime and decades of arbitrary state violence. The legislation determining the competences of the Truth and Dignity Commission allows citizens (and civil society organizations) to deposit a dossier in the name of their region as well. Represented by the Tunisian Forum for Economic and Social Rights, Kasserine, as one of the poorest regions of the country, claimed to be accredited the status of "victim region" in 2015. This concept has been introduced for the first time in any process of transitional justice in an Arab country (Sbouai 2015). The initiative succeeded and consequently, the planned and systematic marginalization by the state is recognized (see also Antonakis & Chennaoui, 2018).

4.1.2 Gender and Nation

Scholars worldwide have investigated the relation between gender and nationalism in different contexts[35] and a good share is concerned with post-colonial states. In this context, the policy field of gender politics has been singled out as highly symbolic when renegotiating the new arrangements of power within the nation. Myra Marx Ferree understands the arrangements and power relations within the state, the family and corporations as "gender regime", operating in a

---

35 The online research forum *H-Nationalism* provides a space dedicated to "Gender and Nationalism Studies" in an attempt to shed light on feminist scholarship on nations and nationalism that remains ignored by the mainstream in academic knowledge production, touching upon a core field of political science studies: https://networks.h-net.org/node/3911/pages/125881/gender-and-nationalism-studies

particular time and place and distinguishes it from the "gender order," comprising the totality of gender regimes.

Most importantly for this study, the field of gender politics has been identified as a "near universal instrument in the process of cultural othering", thus being placed at the heart of identity politics (Spiegel, 2010, p. 21; Yuval-Davis, 47). Yuval-Davis distinguishes three different categories to analyze the construction of the nation through a gendered lens: origin, culture and citizenship (Yuval-Davis, 1997, p. 21). The first relates to biological reproduction of the nation by its citizens. Questions of reproductive health come into focus here. Secondly, with regards to cultural reproduction and gender relations, she discusses women as "symbolic guardians" and as an "embodiment of the collectivity." Yuval-Davis makes this relation specific arguing that "discourse and struggles around the issues of 'women's emancipation' or 'women following tradition' (as have been expressed in various campaigns for and against women's veiling, voting, education and employment) have been at the center of most modernist and anti-nationalist struggles" (Yuval-Davis, 1997, p. 23). The image of "the modern Tunisian Woman" conjured by nationalists in the liberation struggles was employed to identify the new Nation after 1956. Tunisia's "exceptionalism" hereby departs from a similar essentialist understanding of "culture" in its construction and re-negotiation process of the nation after 2011, when "symbols, ways of behavior and artifacts (…) unproblematically constitute cultures of specific national and ethnic collectivities" (Yuval-Davis, 1997, p.41). I claim that the theoretical framework enables a more differentiated view on these cultural "struggles" that can be located in different dimensions of the public sphere and attempt to demark themselves from these fixations, bringing in differentiations and positionalities. Thirdly, she distinguishes the national with regards to citizenship that she defines as a "criterion for membership in the national collectivity" (Yuval-Davis, 1997, p. 23). The last dimension is of particular relevance when discussing newer concepts of "homonationalism" that I can only sketch out briefly in the conclusion of this book. Building on the third point and against the background of Yuval Davis' theorization on the mutual construction of gender and nation (Yuval-Davis, 1997, p. 4), I will now look at state feminism as a legacy constructing nation-state hegemony in Tunisia.

4.2 State Feminism as a Post-Colonial Hegemonic Legacy

I will first give a short definition of state feminism and then look at state feminism from two perspectives: First, set within the intersectional paradigm, this investigation can also contribute to the discussion on state feminist legacies, which engage with the issue of representation in demanding rights based on the identity category of "women." Judith Butler, who links it to the core challenge of feminist identity politics, has most prominently outlined this issue: "The subject of feminism is itself a discursive formation and effect of a given version of representational politics. And the feminist subject turns out to be discursively constituted by the very political system it is supposed to facilitate its emancipation" (Butler, 1990, p. 2). In this context, I engage with arguments that address the exclusive nature of state feminist programs that have promoted and been to the advantage of "the modern Tunisian woman" as white, middle class and secular.

Second, I frame state feminism as an "authoritarian legacy" (Voorhoeve, 2015) that is linked to Tunisia's exceptionalism and *dissembled secularism*. As a pillar of the hegemonic domain of power legitimizing the post-colonial Tunisian nation state, it contributed to justifying oppression against Islamic actors claiming state power. I conceptualize state feminism as a specific form to reproduce the hegemonic domain of power legitimizing the Matrix of Domination and as deeply marked by French colonialism: These relations have been theorized most prominently in post-colonial feminist studies (Dhawan & Castro, 2005; Yuval-Davis, 1997).

A nuanced approach represented by feminist scholar Lila Abu-Lughold regards the state feminist programs in post-colonial societies as "regulatory and emancipatory" at the same time (Deb, 2012, p. 2). In the frame of this study, women of different positionalities have embraced and recognized the emancipatory dimension of women's rights. For instance, they challenged the "regulatory" dimension of state feminism and the oppressive structures it reproduced.

4.2.1 State Feminism Manifesting the Modern Subject of Feminism

The complex relation between modernity, women's rights and post-colonial legacy is concisely articulated by Daouad: "Every time that the colonizer said clearly that the women are the pivot of the modernization, that they have to be acquired by them so that the Maghreb societies develop, the Maghreb women will pay it with a regression" (Daoud, 1993, p. 11, *translated by author*). The instrumental character of gender politics, exposing political dynamics over hegemony and state power, came to light. Murphy (2003) employs the term "state feminism" for the Tunisian context and Brand ascertains: "In Tunisia a clear program on and for women has long been an explicit part of state policy" (Brand, 1998, p. 102).

The journalist Ons Bouali writes in March 2011: "There is no need to recall the monumental progress installed by the feminism of Habib Bourguiba and his contemporaries, but, more than half a century later, state feminism has to die"

(Bouali, 2011, *translated by author*). While not contesting women's rights implemented in 1957 *per se*, she nevertheless pointed critically to restricting ideologies of Tunisian state feminism and a "hypocrite celebration" of the Tunisian exceptionalism that I would like to investigate more closely. From the perspective of the matrix of domination, the exclusion mechanisms of state feminist programs based on categories such as race, locality and religion come into focus. Moghadam opened the debate on the benefits of state feminist programs in contrast to customary laws:

> "[r]evolutions and legal reforms in the Middle East accorded women a wider range of rights and opportunities than had been the case under customary or Islamic laws, gave them access to the public space and public sphere, and helped change perceptions and attitudes within at *least some sections of the population*" (Moghadam, 2004, p. 18 f., emphasis added).

More recent scholarship engages in a closer examination of these "sections" and points to the intersections of the modernist programs with class in Morocco, Egypt and Tunisia (Hafez, 2014; Marks, 2013; Khalil, 2014). Hafez addresses a cultural and ideological class divide in the Egyptian context which was implemented in the second half of the twentieth century:

> "While the middle and upper classes turned away from harem life to adopt Western cultural social norms for a handle on progress and financial opportunity, the lower classes maintained a strong hold on their Islamic faith and now clung to Ottoman forms of gender segregation that had previously been of no particular importance to them, as a form of 'Islamic life'" (Hafez, 2014, p. 180).

This reading however, runs the risk of homogenization that assumes a causal relation between class and religion. However, it shows how opposition towards "modernity" and its pillars was often formulated through religious discourse. In Tunisia, religious women wearing the veil were not only marginalized by state-feminist practices, such as the ban of the headscarf in the public sphere, but also by counterpublics opposing the authoritarian regime.

On the other hand, Errazzouki investigates the perspective of work ing-class women in Morocco by highlighting the relation between neo-liberal reform and state-feminist ideology characterized as a "smokescreen." The needs of working-class women have not been taken into account in the creation of concrete policies (Errazzouki, 2014, p. 262). Mervat Hatem points to class and urban/rural inequalities of modernist (state feminist) projects and Khalil summarizes how state feminism was employed in Tunisia to maintain the regional and classist system:

> "A continued rural/urban, poor/elite class divide inherited from the postcolonial regimes produces a split between Tunisians of the two socio-political classes. The gendered aspect of this class divide was manifest in Ben Ali's state-feminism that was radically slanted in favor of urban and power-privileged women and advanced a policy that neglected rural and poor Tunisian women" (Khalil, 2014, p. 198).

While state feminism was "slanted" in favor of middle- and upper-class urban women, it should not be overlooked that the emancipation and integration of "rural women" was declared a benchmark by the ministry of women at the time. It was proclaimed at the international UN women's conference in Beijing in 1995, and also part of the 10th national strategic action plan. In the national policy document, the empowerment of rural women was situated primarily within a development discourse and in order to improve basic infrastructure in the regions.[36] The lip service in international publics is important with regards to my overall argument: It showcases the regime's aspiration of representing gender politics to international public spheres, independent of the actual policies pursued.

At the institutional level, a "solidarity fund" was set up to support women of rural backgrounds, but in reality, the ministry had only a small budget and lacked the professionalism to tackle the proclaimed tasks (Khalil, 2014, p. 64). The former minister of women's affairs, Laila Labidi, recounted that the person in charge of the dossier on "rural women" in the agricultural ministry lacked a high school degree and refused to organize field trips (Khalil, 2014, p. 63). Most of the work on supporting of women in rural areas was confined to the state feminist organization "National Union of the Tunisian Woman" (Union National de la Femme Tunisienne, UNFT). During her time in office in 2011, Lilia Labidi had tried to shed light on the budgets spent and attempted to organize an audit to integrate the state feminist institution of the UNFT to the ministry of women's affairs during the interim government without success (Interview Lilia Labidi, 2016, p. 2 and 6). In this context, the "promotion of rural woman" can be regarded as a discursive strategy of the nation state, whose interest may be in attracting foreign development funds rather than carrying out a committed action plan. The portraying of "the modern Tunisian woman" as white, secular, urban and middle-class constituted a priority. The representation blends into the broader program of the modern nation state with a liberal economic program

The collection "Remaking Women: Feminism and Modernity in the Middle East," edited by anthropologist and gender studies scholar Lila Abu-Lughod in 1998, brings together different perspectives from post-colonial scholars, pushing for new "thinking about the implications for women of the projects of modernity" (Abu-Lughod, 1998, pp. vii-x). The authors oppose and challenge the dichotomy where women's domesticity would be a sign of backwardness while entering the public sphere would be related to modernity. I have pointed already to the instrumentalization of the public appearance of women in Tunisian policies. The "Modern Tunisian Woman" figured as the public face of the authori-

---

36 The electronic version of the entire speech from Néziha Zarrouk, ministry of women, at the time has been prepared at the Fourth World Conference on Women (UN, 1995). Rural women have been accorded a place of choice in this overall strategy, both in the programs directly aimed at developing their skills, and in the many projects designed to improve general living conditions in rural areas." The portal "femmes.tn" which can be regarded as the online medium for state feminist dissimulation (the website was taken down by the time of writing): http://www.femmes.tn/fr/index.php?option=com_content&task=view&id=34&Itemid=53&limit=1&limitstart=3

tarian state. To elude the public eye, which was entirely controlled by the authoritarian regimes could also mean to find spaces of resistance within the family. Secondly, Abu-Lughod expresses the authors' suspicion about the "way modernity is so easily equated with the progress, emancipation, and empowerment of women" and reflects critically on the state programs relating to fields of education, health or family which imply "hidden forms of discipline and control" (Abu-Lughod, 1998, p. viii). This is what we can grasp with Collins' idea of the disciplinary domain of power articulated through the state feminist program. In the next section, in that perspective, I will show how it has systematically disadvantaged women from different regions and lower classes, while at the same time providing education and reproductive rights for all. Chapter V then explores the state feminist politics of Bourguiba and Ben Ali in more detail.

4.2.2 State Feminism and "Dissembled Secularism"

Moroccan sociologist Fatima Mernissi examines the relationship between anticolonial, nationalist struggles and the development of the situation of women in the world. She distinguishes two legacies of the conflict over women's position in society: "Since Western colonizers took over the paternalistic defense of Muslim women's lot, any changes in their conditions were seen as concessions to the colonizer. (…) 2. The question of women's liberation has been viewed almost exclusively as a religious problem" (Mernissi, 1975, p. 7f.). Monica Marks analyzes Tunisia's promotion of women's rights as means of state control over religious freedom "as a function of shifting political objectives and threats" (Marks, 2013, p. 226). Propaganda defending women's rights has helped to disguise human rights abuses and to suppress Islamic resistance movements. Bourguiba's Neo-Destour party and Ben Ali's Democratic Constitutional Rally (*Tajammuʻad-Dusturi ad-Dimuqrāṭi,* Rassemblement Constitutionelle Démocratique, RCD) were the dominant parties in a practically one-party state. Later on, the campaign against political opposition of the Mouvement de la Tendance Islamic or the Ennahda party was facilitated by portraying the Islamic party as an oppressive force threatening gender equality and Tunisian Exceptionalism with regards to women's rights in the region. The Islamic party challenged the one-party system in the 1980s.

It has been argued that this struggle over state power is reflected in a binary terminology that is employed by national and international observers and academics as well. Tunisian society is hereby divided into "Islamists" and "seculars." As Voorhoeve writes: "This binary is at least partly a legacy of the authoritarian regimes; it is a pillar of anti-Islamist state propaganda which divided society along the lines of good ('progressive' and feminist secularists) and evil ('backwards' and misogynist Islamists)" (Voorhoeve, 2015, p. 3). This doesn't mean, however, that these regimes didn't reproduce patriarchal power structures even in the aftermath of 2011. Andrea Khalil analyzes the state's brand of "modern secularism" as an "ideology that was used to gain and maintain power" (Khalil, 2014, p. 186). One powerful expression of this ideology is mobilization against the "Islamist threat" as taking back women's rights.

Amel Boubakeur points to the historical construction of the term secular and distinguishes it from "secularist":

> "The term *secular* refers to the political narrative that Tunisian post-colonial regimes used to legitimize their authoritarianism vis-à-vis the alleged threat of Islamism. It does not, however, mean that these forces avoided using Islam as a political resource. In contrast, 'secularist' refers to Tunisian leftist parties that officially demand that religion remain in the personal realm (Boubakeur, 2015, p. 18).

In order to clarify the terminology of "secular" as a narrative that capitalized on religion to maintain power, I find it helpful to introduce the concept of *dissembled secularism*, which constitutes an important pillar of the modernist hegemonic domain of power. State feminism hereby also contributed to the cultural reproduction of the nation.

4.3 Conclusion: State Feminism in Relation to Authoritarianism

The theoretical framework can advocate for reading state feminism as an authoritarian legacy, which has produced deep cracks in feminist movements and identification with feminism up until today. The two perspectives on state feminism presented here can be employed to expose the patriarchal power structures of secular regimes and reveal a "dissembled secularism" that I frame as a pillar of the hegemonic domain of power organizing and legitimizing the Matrix of Domination and the opening and closing opportunities to engage in power negotiations in counterpublics in the Tunisian context. In light of the theoretical argument, renegotiating gender in post-revolutionary Tunisia then implies a renegotiation of state feminism.

For now, I have laid out the epistemological, methodological and theoretical positions grounding this research. I argued how the Matrix of Domination limits, censors and defines how gender, class and other structures of oppression are (re-) negotiated in the public sphere through four domains of power. I claim that each of the dimensions are interwoven and perpetuated by the historically-developed organization of power in national and also international contexts. In part two of this study, specific challenges around the hegemonic and the disciplinary domain of power are explored, which are both neglected in classical public sphere models.

5 Detecting the Matrix of Domination: A Historical Perspective

In this chapter, I contextualize the "Matrix of Domination" and its organization of power. Patricia Hill Collins defines it in a specific "social location" and historic specificity "in which social groups are embedded and which they aim to influence" (Collins, 2000, p. 228). In this chapter, I relate the historical analysis to the claims outlined in the previous chapter, where I framed state feminism as a pillar of the hegemonic domain of power. Detecting the structuring element that is essential for hegemonic representations of gender politics and feminism provides a deeper understanding of the negotiations taking place in the period between 2011 and 2014 in Tunisia. In this context, Fraser proposes: "a critical-historical approach that seeks to locate normative standards and emancipatory political possibilities precisely within the historically unfolding constellation" (Fraser, 2014, p. 10). I understand the communicative context that determines and defines the construction of public spheres and sites of resistance within them as essential when walking the thin line between an empirical and theoretical approach to grasp the different renegotiation processes under investigation.

I will look at three phases that preceded the transition period: I want to specifically highlight the period of the 1930s and provide a more comprehensive account of the colonial period, especially with regards to the contested concept of "modernity," which is central to the discussion of feminism in the region (Abu-Lughod, 1998, p. v). In a second step, the period of Bourguiba's regime (1956 -1987) and the regime of Ben Ali (1987 – 2011) will be investigated: Firstly, I will pinpoint the developments and changes in gender policies expressing a "gender regime" according to the definition of (Marx Ferree, 2012, p. 9). I will emphasize structural developments in the public sphere in relation to the hegemonic domain of power, e.g. the ideologies expressed.

© Springer Fachmedien Wiesbaden GmbH, part of Springer Nature 2019
A. Antonakis, *Renegotiating Gender and the State in Tunisia between 2011 and 2014*, Politik und Gesellschaft des Nahen Ostens,
https://doi.org/10.1007/978-3-658-25639-5_5

5.1   French Colonial Rule and Reformist Counterpublics

This subchapter focuses on colonial Tunisia, which has been framed as a "protectorate", which can be regarded as a euphemism for "colony".[37] Tunisian scholars specializing in gender studies, such as Noura Borsali or Dalenda Larguèche, are trying to shed light on the herstory that took place before the rule of president Habib Bourguiba in pursuit of keeping the heritage of the women's movements and female resistance diversified.

The personage of the *Amazigh* queen Kahena represents one female figure whose action is inscribed in the collective memory of many feminists of the region. She was fighting against Arabic-Islamic rule in the 7th century in North Africa and organized the resistance against their colonial rule around Carthage (Yousif, 2002, p. 75). Interestingly enough, these female figures were revitalized in discussions on Facebook after the uprisings. In the context of Tunisian knowledge creation on Facebook, the "Tunisian woman" is constructed as a fighter, opposing Arab colonialism renegotiating an "Arab" versus "Amazigh" or "Carthagian" ethnic identity of the Tunisians:

> "The affirmation of a 'non-Arab' identity advanced by inscriptions in the lines of a Berberian (ElKahena) or Carthaginian and a glorious past (Queen Dido, the Punic ports, Hannibal…) is inherent in several publications. These claims have to be related to the affirmations of an authentic 'Tunisianity', sometimes in opposition to an assimilation to the rest of the Arab World" (ben Alaya, 2014, p. 30).

I see the pattern of a "Tunisian exceptionalism" that is also conveyed through the female figure of Dido and Kahena repeated here.

Another entry point to shed light on renegotiations of gender before the age of modernization is presented by feminist historian Noura Borsali, whose aim is to "[r]e-habilitate and re-valorize the role being played by the Tunisian women in the liberation struggles and also in demanding their rights" (Borsali, 2012, p. 13 – *translated by the author*). She claims that her research serves to challenge the idea that women's rights in Tunisia were "served on a silver platter" by the first president Habib Bourguiba. Rather, a class of intellectuals has been favoring the full education of girls since the middle of the 19th century (Borsali, 2012, p. 29f). Ahmed Bin Dhiaf (1804- 1874), a consultant and official in the Beylical government at the time, engaged with issues of women's emancipation and stressed the role of professional and religious education for girls.[38] In a similar

---

37 For a discussion of the "diplomatic choice" to employ the term protectorate during a time of competing imperialist interests, see (Cohen, 1971, p.3).

38 Bechir Tlili translated his 1856 handwritten document "Epistle on Women" (*Risalah fi al-mar'a*) to French in 1973. The letter is a response to the French rulers and mirrors a traditional conservative position. However, in his politics, he was considered a reformer. This double positioning with regards to the colonizers and to their own project of society can also be stated for later president Habib Bourguiba.

vein, the grand vizier and prime minister under Sadok Bey,[39] Khereiddine Pacha (1822/1823 - 1890) stressed the need for both professional and religious education. Kheireddine Pacha, for instance, "forcefully asked in 1877 for a new status for women while emphasizing the need for girls to go to school and get educated." He also defended women's emancipation despite criticism (Zlitni & Touati, 2012, p. 47).

Besides these early philosophers and politicians of the 19th century, other intellectuals have paved the way for a specific Tunisian understanding of gender equality by introducing a reformist view on religious grounds such as Mohamed Fadhel Ben Achour and Mohamed Tahar Ben Achour, the contested director of the Zeitouna mosque in the 1950s. The scholar Tahar Haddad (1899-1935) is certainly the most prominent representative. He published his reformist ideas on gender politics in his 1930 book "Our Women in the *Sharia* and Society," laying the ground for a Tunisian feminist understanding of society. Haddad remains an important figurehead for feminists today (Ben Said Cherni, 1986, p. 9) and can be considered the more important 'intellectual father' of Tunisian feminism. Though he completed his education at the Zeitouna-mosque in Tunis and worked as a notary, he was close to the labor union movement, believing in total gender equality (Skandrani, 2012). The influential Zeitouna University of Tunis, the legitimate religious institution observing and commenting on the developments in the Tunisian state from a religious perspective, enjoyed a high level of legitimacy at the time. In advocating for the expansion of women's rights, Haddad based his argument on the Koran. In his writings he creates a symbiosis of the fight for worker's rights, religious arguments and gender equality with syndicalism and feminist ideas intersecting in this tradition (Haddad, 1978).

Historian Claude Liauzu points out the restricted public that these reformists, who I would consider "traditional intellectuals,"[40] could reach. They were under

---

39 "Bey" was the title for a governor under Ottoman rule. In the historical literature on Tunisia, two phases are distinguished: The first period is set from 1574 - 1705 and defines the time of Ottoman control, when the Beys were officially nominated and sent from Istanbul. The second from 1705 until independence (the French colonizers kept the Beycal system) marks the "Hussayinid period": Named after Bey Hussayn whose reign ended in 1705. Successors were directly drawn from Husayn's descendants (Chomiak & Parks, 2016, p. 985).

40 The notion of "intellectual" can be discussed within Gramsci's theory. Gramsci distinguishes the intellectual into two groups: Firstly, there are the "traditional" professional intellectuals, literary, scientific and so on, whose "position in the interstices of society has a certain inter-class aura about it, but derives ultimately from past and present class relations and conceals an attachment to various historical class formations. Secondly, there are the "organic" intellectuals, the thinking and organizing element of a particular fundamental social class. These organic intellectuals are distinguished less by their profession, which may be any job characteristic of their class, than by their function in directing the ideas and aspirations of the class to which they organically belong." (Editor's note in: Gramsci, 1971, p.3)

pressure from two sides: on one hand from fellow scholars of Zeitouna University,[41] "the circle of the prisoners of the tradition" (Liauzu, 2004, p. 26) who didn't agree with this reformist religious line, and on the other hand by a younger, secular, nationalist elite.

This latter elite, however, which would later be at the forefront of the liberation struggles with the Neo-Destour party, emanated from an educational institution anchored in French colonialism: In 1875, French colonizers established the bilingual *collège Sadiqi* in order to institutionalize a French-Arab education system, demarcating itself from the 'French only' institutions of the Tunisian protectorate on the one hand, and the Arabic schools on the other hand. It is important to note that students of this institution usually pursued their higher degrees in France (Hermassi, 1994, p. 64).

Tunisian historian and Islamic studies scholar Abdellatif Hermassi has analyzed these two centers of education –sadiqi and zeitouna- as "counter-models" illustrating the "split in the elites" of the country, introduced by the educational policies of the colonizers. Furthermore, he argues that the separation of the Destour and Neo-Destour party in the frame of the congress of Ksar Hellal held in 1934 constitutes an illustration of the two competing education systems, which had produced two distinct groups of elites, now represented in two different parties (Hermassi, 1994, p. 63). The later president and founder of the Neo-Destour party Habib Bourguiba as well as the later president and founder of Nidaa Tounes party, Béji Caïd Essebsi are both alumni of the *Sadiqiyya* system.[42] Against the background of the latest developments in the country, the unity government of Ennahda and Nidaa Tounes of 2015 appears to have united the traditional elite of the Zeitouna with the neo-destourian elite.

Shedding light on counter-narratives sidelined by hegemonic ideologies reproduced in academic publics is one way to engage in a more diversified study on feminism in Tunisia. In a similar vein, commodification of gender in concrete legislations, nowadays highlighted as "progressive", can be analyzed. For instance, Dalenda Largèche sheds light on the abolishment of polygamy that was already established in the city of Kairouan with the *"Kairouani Sadaq"* (the marriage contract of Kairouan) dating back to the 8th Century, forbidding men to take a second wife (Larguèche, 2011). This proves that the abolition of polygamy

---

41 The (institutional) history of this university illustrates an interesting struggle over knowledge production in the public sphere and deserves closer scrutiny. Starting as a *Madressa* in the year of 737, the Zeitouna mosque is considered the oldest educational institution in the Arab World according to the historian Hassan Hosni Abdelwaheb. In 1956, Bourguiba separated the university from the Mosque. The university was finally reorganized as a faculty for Sharia and theology studies and integrated to the University of Tunis in 1961 (Camau & Geisser, 2004, p.86 f.).

42 The actual President Béji Caid Essebsi proclaims: "Sadiki, where I received my diploma, was a school in the large sense of the term, a school of patriotism and culture. We, the Sadikians, were all bilingual, of French and Arabic culture" (Essebsi, 2004, p. 178).

has indeed existed in Tunisian society before Bourguiba's nationalist state project and the introduction of the family code.

When investigating counterpublics situated at the representational dimension of the public sphere before national independence, a feminist identity linked to religious categories can be explored. The periodical magazine *Leila* can be considered a pioneer publication from a feminist counterpublic. It was published for over five years from 1936 and was then transformed into a weekly newspaper published from 1940-1941. It was founded by Ahmed Zarrouk and published in French, illustrating its audience and authors to be part of an urban elite, which is also expressed by its price of five francs (Bendana, 2007). In the articles, issues of external influence on the independent women's movement were discussed critically, as well as feminism, literature and culture (Labidi L. , 2007). In 1939, however, Lilia Labidi states that the magazine took a more "overt political character, with articles such as 'Leila, your Muslim sisters are in prison!', 'The Tunisian woman and public life' and 'Women in the arts and politics' (Labidi L. , 2016, p. 199). Tunisian-American scholar Nadja Mamelouk has analyzed the publication in detail, concluding that the publishers constructed the image of a "New Muslim Woman" in opposition to colonial feminist discourses as part of a national ideology (Mamelouk, 2008, p. ii). Indeed, it can be stated that under colonial rule, Tunisian Muslim women were among the first to engage in female counterpublics and pushed for more representation in the public sphere, hereby challenging the hegemonic identity of the new modern Tunisian woman as installed by the colonial system.

This development of modern Muslim feminist thoughts is reflected as well in the first organization founded by women to defend women's rights, the "Tunisian Muslim Women's organization," created in 1936 by B'chira Ben Mrad during the colonial rule and officially recognized in 1951. The association lobbied for equal access to education for boys and girls (Dwyer, 1997) and collected money for students pursuing their studies in France. Furthermore, they published their ideas in the magazine "Chams al Islam" (Sun of Islam) created by B'chira Mrad's father (Labidi L., 2016, p. 200). They were soon to be oppressed by the nationalist project, when women's organizations were increasingly put under the control of the regime marking the introduction of state feminism. Habib Bourguiba closed it down when he became president. A feminist counterpublic that would take up a religious identity category would have threatened his hegemonic state project. Ironically enough, he himself profited from the support of the Tunisian Muslim Women's Organization for his studies abroad.

Another major women's organization was the Union of Women of Tunisia (Union des Femmes de Tunisie UFT), founded in 1944 by women from the Communist Party (Parti Communist Tunisienne, PCT), it established a strong connection between women's rights and a socialist cast. It was mostly French

women married to Tunisian men from the socialist party who were the origina-
tors of the union, hereby taking up a privileged role in the matrix of domination
installed by colonialism. Brand states that, for the UFT, due to its European background: "Its numerous activities notwithstanding, its presence and work remained marginal due to the class background and ethnicity of its founders"
(Brand, 1998, p. 203). The Union of Women of Tunisia would later be absorbed
by the National Union of the Tunisian Woman (Union Nationale de la Femme
Tunisienne, UNFT), which will become the major state feminist institution. I
argue that the change in name reflects a larger shift in claims of state representation: as "women of Tunisia" become "the Tunisian woman" (*al Mara'a Al Tunisia*), the female identity is bound to a national identity and doesn't allow for a
pluralistic interpretation. I will explore the notion of "the Tunisian woman" in
more detail and in the context of my interviews later on.

Besides these examples of "classical" women's participation in the public
sphere through organizations and media, gender renegotiations have also been
triggered by individual women's bodily acts in the interactional dimension of the
public sphere. Lilia Labidi recalls the "Discussion on the condition of women
and on the veil" that expanded in the 1920s, leading to the "veil debate" from
1924-1929 (Borsali, 2006, p. 26). Manoubia Ouertani, an unmarried sewing
teacher at the nuns' school publicly removed her veil in 1924 during a speech
she was giving on the condition of women at an event organized by French so-
cialists in Tunisia (Labidi L. , 2016, p. 196). The conference was entitled "For
or against the feminism of countries of the occident in countries of the orient."
Besides Ouertani, Najet Ben Othman, and Habiba Menchari used the act of public unveiling to proclaim the liberalization of women. They hereby impacted the
representational dimension of public sphere pushing the "veil debate". The acts
were criticized by Tunisian nationalists, theologians and French colonizers alike
(Zlitni & Touati, 2012). Five years later, a second intervention of Manoubia
Ouertani in the form of a conference, again at the socialist club "Essor", on "The
Muslim Woman of tomorrow: For or against the veil" sparked further debates in
French and Arabophone publics. In this context, lawyer and journalist Habib
Bourguiba wrote an article entitled 'Le voile' (The veil), in which "he sharply
criticized the French socialist organizers of these events, for at the time he saw
the veil as an organic part of Tunisian identity" (Labidi L. , 2016, p. 197). This
important historical document reveals that his modernist, secular understanding
of feminism was constructed only "*a posteriori*", after Tunisian independence
(Bessis, 2004, p. 103). Furthermore, the opposing positions of statesman Bourguiba illustrate the power of gender in the cultural production of national hegemony, that he was fully aware of and capable of exploiting.

In reviewing the first phase of negotiations of gender, I have found two competing centers of knowledge creation forming different types of intellectuals: the
more traditional intellectuals of the Zeitouna mosque and the alumni from the

French Arabic School Sadiki, created by the French colonialists. Two presidents, Habib Bourguiba and Béji Caïd Essebsi, are *Sadikians* and architects of the respectively post-colonial and post-revolutionary Tunisia in 1956 and 2011, demonstrating the persisting postcolonial hegemonic domain of power. I will now look at the construction of this hegemonic legacy in more detail.

5.2   Post-Colonial Regimes Exploiting "Dissembled Secularism"

5.2.1 Bourguiba and the Nationalist Project of Modernity

Besides early writings and legislation that I have briefly outlined, Tunisia's progressive legislation in the field of gender policies is mainly credited to the "enlightened despot" Habib Bourguiba (Chabbi, 2011). Bourguiba's legacy illustrates how nation building and gender politics are deeply interwoven and produce a hegemonic ideology permeating the construction of the public sphere. In this regard, state feminism can be framed as an ideology, from which other pioneers in women's rights, such as Tahar Haddad, have been systematically excluded.

Habib Bourguiba, head of the Neo-Destour party[43] became the first president of Tunisia after the end of colonial French rule. He had united the country in the liberation struggle and established a strong nationalism, inspired by nationalist projects in Turkey or Egypt (Moghadam V. , 2004). In Tunisia, the question of whether its progressive status in family laws can be credited to state-led reforms only or also to the role of revolutionary women's mobilizations during anti-colonial rule is still being debated. While Western researchers such as (Brand, 1998) tend to see the progressive status of women as the result of top-down state policies, journalists and scholars attempt to introduce a more nuanced analysis. They see the progressive rights of women not only as the result of a top-down policy but emphasize the participation of women in anti-colonial struggles and earlier feminist movements that cleared the way for Bourguibist feminism. The instrumentalizations of the policy fields by the president in order to preserve his strong position, however, has been claimed by Western and Tunisian scholars alike. Noura Borsali stresses how Bourguiba presented himself as the father of the progressive Family Code (Personal Status Code, or in its French abbreviation: CSP) and also as the father of the nation (Borsali, 2008).

---

43 The Neo-Destour party was renamed the Destourian Socialist Party (PSD) in 1964. The traditional Destour party's influence diminished considerably after the split into the Destour and neo-Destour party already in 1934 and hustled to survive until the beginnings of the 1960s (Guerfali, 2005).

In 1956, shortly after independence, a committee of experts drafted the new constitution and passed the Personal Status Law (Code du Statut Personnel, Tunisia.)[44] Noticeably, gender regulations and women's rights were developed almost simultaneously with the first new national institutions. However, the elections for the first Constituent assembly were only reserved for men according to the electoral code of 6th January 1956. Nora Borsali's work gives insights into the election period that took place on 25th March 1956. She evokes the contested debates inside the newly elected Constituent Assembly on political equality between men and women on July 17th of the same year, when discussing the preamble of the first constitution (Borsali, 2008, p. 31 ff).

Without a doubt, the president can be closely connected to this new legislation, which gave women progressive rights.[45] Unlike in Turkey, where Mustafa Kemal Atatürk realized a reformist project of the state and society between 1924-1938, fully secularizing the public sphere, Bourguiba didn't want to break completely away from an Islamic project and establish a secular state. The principle of *Itjdihad*[46] became an important characteristic of *Bourguibism* (Bessis, 1999, p. 3).

In 1957, women were given full citizenship rights including the right to actively and passively vote.[47] The law granting polygamy was abolished throughout the country and the act made punishable by law. Men and women received the right to divorce one another, and the age of marriage was put up to 17 years, and only by consent of the woman. Also in terms of parenthood, the rights of mothers were strengthened: In the case of the father's death, mothers were able to be responsible for childcare exclusively without appointing a male custodian, and the right of adoption was introduced. One important bastion of discriminatory state practice remains until this day – the inheritance laws that were still inspired by Sharia law, codifying a woman's share of the inheritance as half of that of the man's (Brand, 1998, p. 208 ff; Bessis, 1999, p. 7). I will come back

---

44 In 1947, Cheikh Med Abdelaziz Djait had already charged a commission in his function as minister of justice to elaborate a Muslim family law that should harmonize the Maleki and Hanafi school of thoughts (Borsali, 2012, p. 30). One of his successors, Amhed Mestiri, minister of justice in the first cabinet of Bourguiba and one of the main figures in elaborating the CSP, explains in his book published in 2011 how this code, including the 769 Articles, was found in the archives of the ministry of Justice in 1956, but that it was judged not capable to meet the modern exigencies of the Tunisian society "without explicitly infringing the koranic text" (Mestiri, Ahmed, quoted in (Borsali, 2012, p. 31).

45 In my interviews, it was claimed that Bourguiba came to observe the work of the committee every day.

46 *Itjdihad* is an Islamic legal term referring to independent reasoning and entails negotiation and application of the Koran and the sayings of prophet Mohammed on actual socio-political contexts.

47 This parity didn't include the right for women to be elected president– a legal discrimination that was re-discussed during the drafting process of the new constitution after the uprisings 2011. In 2014, Kalthoum Kannouw was the first woman to present candidature for presidency in Tunisia.

to this legislation in chapters 8 and 9, because it constitutes a pivotal issue in the debate of gender politics in the public sphere after the uprisings.

In the context of "top-down" policies affecting women's lives (Moghadam V. M., 2014), these reforms regarding gender, taking place on a structural level, can be considered as opening up the public sphere for women. This is particularly true for women whose options of choice were broadened and whose resources would allow aspiring for more independent lives. However, the CSP as an efficient instrument for implementing gender justice for all Tunisians was debated extensively within the feminist counterpublics in Tunisia around the circle of Tahar Haddad (Marzouki, 1993, p. 242). In 1992, Tunisian feminist scholar Daghhough found out that 34% of Tunisian women did not know the CSP at all (Darghouth Medimegh, 1992, p. 65).

The reason why Bourguiba didn't establish a secular regime and laicism, keeping any religious argumentation out of the family code, is still under debate today. Religious motives were certainly an important element in the constitution of the national ideology and – from the perspective of the matrices of domination – a structuring principle for the hegemonic domain of power. Some advance arguments relate to Bourguiba's *"Realpolitik"*. In this context, it has been emphasized that in the anti-colonial struggles, Bourguiba enabled "creative application of Islamic symbols and institutions" (Marks, 2013, p. 227) in order to form a common cause with Salah Ben Youssef, representing the more conservative and religious movement of the interior regions. In order to construct a united front against colonial rule, Bourguiba and his followers merged with "the Youssefistes", despite their disagreement: One of their political disputes was over the procedures of the anti-colonial struggle. While Youssef wanted an immediate departure of the French from Tunisian territory, Bourguiba opted for a "politique des étapes" (Entelis, 2004, p. 230). Furthermore, the Youssefistes were more inclined to pan-Arabism, while the Bourguibists emphasized a Tunisian "exceptionalism", representing a nation-state, rather than a regional political project.

When the French realized that Tunisian independence was inevitable, they backed Bourguiba, originally from the *Sahel* (representing the coastal areas) and Tunisia's more educated middle and upper class (Marks, 2013, p. 230). Here, the nation-states role in defining the category of locality structuring the matrix of domination becomes clear.[48] On the other hand, the Youssefistes, who had a stronghold in the South and the island of Djerba, were oppressed and eliminated from the political scene after independence[49], as Bourguiba was afraid that they could challenge his political hegemony (Sadiki, 2008, p.118). Furthermore,

---

48 For the conceptual discussion on the "marginalized localities," see chapter 4.1.2.
49 Ben Youssef himself was shot dead in Germany in 1961, where he had been living in exile.

Bourguiba could rely on the support of the National Labor Union UGTT, that he guaranteed to be presided over by his close allies (Entelis, 2004, p. 230).

Another argument in the debate on Bourguiba's instrumentalization of religion is based on his published declarations of 1929 following the debate of the veil, where he states: "The role of the elite is not to impose its lifestyle, risking to become entirely detached from the masses that it is charged to guide" (quoted in: Liauzu, 2004; p. 24, translated by author). He can hereby be considered the more "organic" intellectual, educated within the specific French-Arab system of the *Sadyqiyya* and appealing in his political discourse to the "masses" and the "people," in opposition to the "traditional intellectuals" of the *Zeitouna* and other more conservative and aristocratic nationalists that constituted the Destour party. In this regard, he strategically employed Islamic virtue within his modernist project. Crucially, it is against this background, that the proclaimed "secularism" was "used to gain and maintain power" (Khalil, 2014, p. 186). In context of the regime's *Realpolitik*, upholding hegemony, I propose to conceptualize it as a dissembled secularism.

The Impact of National Educational Reforms on Local Publics

Besides these direct implications for women's increased access and mobility to and within different dimensions of the public sphere by granting family and political rights, there were also indirect effects that led to restructurings of the interactional dimension of the public sphere for the future generation. One of the most important fields is that of educational policy: Bourguiba also introduced an obligatory school system all over the country for boys and girls in mixed schools. Children had to go to school until the age of 14 (Charrad M. , 2008).

These reforms in the field of education had deep impacts on societal power structures at the local level, not only in more urban spaces but also in rural areas: The modernization project didn't only have a gendered outcome but impacted tribal and kinship structures. Hereby, the reformist family code, "reflected a nuclear ideal of the family [and] resulted from the victorious leadership's efforts to undermine its political rivals among Islamic clerics and patriarchally organized kinship groupings in rural areas" (Charrad M. , 2008, p. 112). Charrad's analysis shows that Habib Bourguiba could ensure his power via his gender and education politics by breaking the local structures that would have challenged his nationalist project.

The anthropological historical study by Nadia Abu-Zahra brings to light how these reforms affected girls' lives in rural areas in multiple ways. They would now not only go to school and profit from education but would transgress tribal boundaries when walking to public schools. Gendered and tribal power structures were challenged, because children of different tribes and areas were coming together on their way to school, crisscrossing formally tribe-segregated spaces (Abu-Zahra, 1992/1993, p. 70). Abu-Zahra describes the diminishing process of power structures that were prevalent on the community level in the town of Sidi Ameur in the Tunisian Sahel region, not far from the city Monastir. She places great importance on the free education of girls and boys in challenging the privileges of the formerly wealthy and powerful families, in this specific local space, the *Zawya* group. Adapting these observations to the proposed theoretical framework, Abu-Zahra illustrates the interdependence of top-down policies and slow changes emerging at the interactional dimension that challenge the hegemonic and interpersonal domains of power. It is by the politics of presence of both genders of different tribes that the public sphere changed and pre-modern tribally-defined societal organizations, or *assabyia*, broke up.[50]

The Tunisian Woman in Singular: Creating Hegemonic Images

The authoritarian nature of gender politics established by Bourguiba becomes evident when looking at the uniformed landscapes of feminist organizations. In 1956, the field of women's and feminist organizations was increasingly monopolized: The National Union of Tunisian Women (Union Nationale des Femmes Tunisiennes, UNFT) was the only feminist institution that Bourguiba would allow to exist and provide financial support (Marzouki, 1993, p. 83). Consequently, the Union of Tunisian Women (UFT) and the other women's organizations faced the "dilemma" of choosing whether to integrate into the UNFT or stay separate, facing possible oppression after the national liberation struggles (Brand, 1998, p. 203).

The UNFT incorporated the official state feminist institution by assuming "the traditional female roles of feeding and clothing the needy and inculcating hygiene, nutrition and morality to the children of the new modern state" (Ben Youssef Zayzafoon, 2005, p. 124). Furthermore, the UNFT was the executing institution of "modernizing" women of rural backgrounds (Interview Lilia Labidi, p.3.). Feminist scholar Lamia Ben Youssef Zayzafoon argues that its main purpose was to "prevent the revolutions within the family," initiated by the CSP by stressing the moral responsibilities, derived from Islamic virtues, of "the Modern Tunisian woman" for the family and the nation. Hereby, the UNFT created female "national subjects" that are "responsible rather than liberated" (ibd.) Her argument demonstrates how state feminism, incorporated within the hege-

---

50 For a discussion of different *assabyya* systems (solidarity, or "social glue") and their transformations in Tunisia see (Sadiki, 2008, p. 115, ff).

monic domain of power, remained thus deeply patriarchal, where women's bodies and lifestyles were policed within a modernist paradigm supporting the ruling elite.

Additionally, the UNFT became a sort of a career-furthering instrument that "women tended to join for reasons related to ambition (...) A typical UNFT member was a woman of the middle-class or more modest means" (Brand, 1998, p. 205). This shows how, besides the deconstruction of tribal structures, social (upwards-)mobility was established in the name of modern nationalism. The UNFT was later on presided by the "first Woman" Leila Ben Ali, who became the symbol of the oppressive nature of state feminism. It was only in 1983 that Habib Bourguiba allowed for the establishment of a ministry of women's affairs following pressure from feminists who didn't want to recognize the UNFT as a proper governmental representative of the feminist cause (Interview Lilia Labidi, via Skype, September 2016, p. 3 f.). According to Labidi, the ministry of women's affairs was finally set up in order to increase control over the emerging autonomous feminist counterpublics of the 1980s.[51] Until today, the ministry and the UNFT are two parallel institutional structures within the state, which can get into a "conflictual relation with each other."

In this period of almost two decades, or approximately one generation after the introduction of the CSP, the role of women in positions of power has been discussed more openly and claimed by feminists at the representational dimension of the public sphere. In 1983, the President Bourguiba decided to designate two female ministers: Prof. Dr. Souad Yacoubi, who was first Secretary of State and the Minister of Health. Fatiha Mzali, the wife of Prime Minister Mohamed Mzali, who was formerly the president of the UNFT became the Minister of Women's Affairs, the first person to occupy the new function. The feminist and women's minister in the interim cabinet of 2011, Lilia Labidi points to a double structure maintained by the choices in *personalia*:

> "What is interesting is that Fatiha Mzali, who was at the UNFT, became women's minister while maintaining the two separate structures, she didn't integrate the structures form the UNFT to the ministry" (Lilia Labidi, via Skype, September 2016).

By keeping this structure under Mzali's authority, they remained closely tied to the statesman Bourguiba, who could *de facto* expand his control over feminist formal structures in the country.

Besides the establishment and reform of institutions, Bourguiba also presented himself as the "liberator of women" via publicly displayed symbolic

---

51 For a more detailed analysis of the development of feminist counterpublics from the space of "Tahar Hadad" in Tunis's media, see chapter 6.1.

means. He hereby anchored hegemonic ideologies in the representational dimension of the public sphere. His most famous stages in this regard are those when meeting with women and unveiling them, taking off their traditional white (cream) long *Sefsari.* These actions have been widely mediated via photos and videos.[52] That he now qualifies the veil as a *"miserable chiffon,"* where he had previously defined it as a traditional symbol of Tunisian identity under colonial rule, reveals his instrumentalization of both women and tradition (Bessis, 2004, p. 103; 108). These symbolic actions of unveiling in the public sphere by the first president remain collectively anchored in the feminist narrative. I argue that by those means he established a close link between himself and women's liberation struggles but limited it to a secular interpretation.[53] Though Bourguiba 'symbolically encouraged' women to take off their veil after independence, the headscarf has been formally banned from public schools by Decree No. 108 since 18 September 1981 (Ben Salem M. , 2010). This development can be regarded as re-translating and enforcing the ideology of "the modern Tunisian woman" by exploiting the structural dimension of the public sphere regulating the exclusion of women designated as "others" from state institutions.

The (Economic) Reproduction of the Nation: Family Planning policies

The reforms undertaken in family planning under Bourguiba constitute another axis of the "modernization" of the state and illustration of state feminism. In Collins's understanding: "Family planning comprises a constellation of options, ranging from coercion to choice, from permanence to reversibility regarding reproduction of actual populations (Collins, 1998, p. 75)." Yuval-Davis regards "reproductive rights as touchstone of feminist politics" (Yuval-Davis, 1997, p. 22) and sets it within the analysis of the biological reproduction of the nation. In light of the modernist project, I argue that it cannot be disentangled from economic factors that seem to be under-theorized in Yuval-Davis' discussion of gender and nation. The same is true for educational and labor politics. A workforce composed by men and women would lead Tunisia to more economic growth, so

---

52 See, for example, this original footage from the 1950s, where you see Bourguiba midst a group of women, unveiling them and then, in a paternalistic gesture, tapping their cheeks, no matter the age of the women (at 2:30): https://www.youtube.com/watch?v=Rx6N4CzE3_s.

53 He expressed his "secular" politics also by other means: In 1960, he drank a glass of orange juice in front of TV cameras during the Ramadan fast, provoking the more traditional parts of the society. At the same time, he defended his gesture based on religious arguments.

the image of women had to go beyond representations of motherhood and include images of workers and even soldiers to serve the nation.[54]

Tunisia can be considered a worldwide pioneer in abortion rights:[55] In 1965, abortion was legalized for women who already had five children or more and the full right to abortion was introduced in 1973 (United Nations Population Fund, 2010). Not only was abortion legally allowed without the need to give reasons, but it was also ensured that women of all classes could undergo the procedure free of charge in a professional, medical environment. Female contraception was also introduced early: Birth control pills have been available in pharmacies since 1960, and their price was government-subsidized (Soubai, 2012). The National Office for Family and Population (l'Office Nationale de la Famille et de la Population; ONFP) is still in charge of distributing contraceptives and is accessible all over the country.

According to women's health scholar Angel Foster, Tunisia remained a "global leader in reproductive health and rights" (Foster, 2012, p. 153) by introducing medication giving women more sexual freedoms. For instance, in 2001, Tunisia became the first country in the Arab world to register a dedicated emergency contraceptive pill (ECP) (Foster, 2012, p. 154). A French mediction by HRA Pharma is available directly from pharmacists without prescription at a government regulated price (as of 2013, according to the International Consortium for Emergency Contraception). The idea of being "pro-choice", leaving decision-making concerning their own bodies to women themselves and facilitating this by providing equal access to health care is a feminist argument. The accessibility of medical infrastructure for biological reproduction constitutes at the same time an important mechanism to control birth rates that Abu-Lughold described as "novel forms of discipline and regulation" (Abu-Lughod, 1998, p. vii) exercised by the state.

Reproduction policies illustrate the ambiguous character of state feminism. Bourguiba understood a lower birth rate as a tool to modernize the country. Population growth rates dropped significantly after the introduction of the new family policies: from 4.6% in 1966 to 3.6% within six years in 1973 (Daoud, 1993, p. 58) and decreased constantly. In 2012, Tunisian women gave birth to 2.1 children on average (Soubaï, 2012). Besides the introduction of more individual

---

54 Women have been allowed to serve in the military since 1956, but since 2003, the service has been obligatory for men and women from the age of 18 by the age of 20. In practice, only 25-30% of the population did their national service and they were mostly men (Borel, 2002). While the current law does not exclude women from national duties, Minister of Defense, Farhat Horchani, re-launched a debate on explicitly including men and women in the military in May 2016. He argued that the increased security threats and the fight against terrorism required more forces in the army (TempsReel, 2016).

55 For example, France introduced the right to abortion two years after Tunisia.

freedom, the reforms can also be read as an efficient method to regulate population size.

5.2.2 Ben Ali's Regime: A Public Sphere between Liberalization, Privatization and Repression

The legacy of Bourguiba's regime posed challenges for his successor: Growing resistance against the nationalist state project and the Neo-Destour on the one hand, and social contestations alimented by the neoliberal economic choices within the modern state paradigm on the other, empowered a movement of Islamic tendencies. The rise in bread prices in 1984 that was imposed by the IMF lead to the so called "bread riots" that were violently oppressed. The movement was inspired by the Iranian Revolution of 1978 that could regroup different parts of society, including intellectuals, syndicalist and Marxist movements who chose Islam as their language of protest (Hermassi, 1994, p. 79).

Geisser and Camau argue that it was Bourguiba's repression against the increasingly politicized Islamic opposition that would be the biggest threat to his nationalist project. His fear of the Islamists heralded the decline of his power: In order to safeguard his regime, whose hegemonic modernist ideology was threatened, he confined it to an increasingly professionalized security apparatus of which he eventually lost control. The Tunisian regime shifted from an authoritarian state to a "police state" (Camau & Geisser, 2004, p. 17 f.).

In 1987, Bourguiba was ousted by Zine Abdel Ben Ali, a man with a background in police and military security in charge of controlling and monitoring the Islamist scene. Contrary to his precursor, he didn't come from the *Sadiqyya* school system but rather from a career in the security and intelligence sector: He was trained at the French Military School and the US Army School at Fort Bliss, Texas (Al-Amin, 2012, p. 46). He can be considered a politician that could capitalize more on the disciplinary domain of power, the means of surveillance and direct control, than the hegemonic domain of power and the manipulation of ideologies. Bourguiba appointed him Minister of Interior in 1984 to fight the Islamist opposition in the country and he eventually assumed the position of prime minister in October 1987. In a "*medical coup d'Etat*" on 7 November 1987, Ben Ali declared the former president as being too sick for official government positions and took power in a bloodless coup. In light of the elaborated theoretical framework, the regime change between Habib Bourguiba and Ben Ali could be understood as how the disciplinary domain of power, controlling the public sphere by means of surveillance and bureaucracy in order to maintain legitimacy and fight counterpublics, became indispensable and ultimately out of control of the president, whose hegemony has been seriously challenged with the rise of the Islamists.

The Economic "Miracle"

After his *coup* against Bourguiba, President Ben Ali renamed the Neo-Destour party the Democratic Constitutional Rally (Rassemblement Constitutionelle Démocratique, RCD) in 1988 and pursued the politics of "Change" *("tahawwul")*: He reopened the public sphere for political participation and opted for a policy of "pacification" with opposition groups, especially the Islamist movement (Brand, 1998; Lamloum, 2002). Furthermore, he implemented a policy of market liberalization that initially had a slow start in the 1970s but increased in its effectiveness since 1986 with the introduction of structural adjustment programs (SAP) aiming to install internal and external equality by means of state interventions (Bellin, 2002; Khiari, 2004). These reforms have led to considerable success in international terms and laid the groundwork for Tunisian economic exceptionalism, outlined in chapter II: Tunisia has repeatedly been pointed out as a "model" by the International Monetary Fund (Bond, 2012). In 2007, Tunisia was ranked the "most competitive country of Africa", the 30th competitive country in the world and the first of the African continent in the global competitiveness report (Schwab, 2007, p. XVII).[56]

Scholars, departing from Marxist and Gramscian theory, have critically investigated the Tunisian "economic miracle" after implementation of the SAP and point to the increasing political dominance of the regime that could unfold by introducing liberal market reforms (Tsourapas, 2013, p. 23). The Tunisian economy was characterized by a clientelism in which all public economic procedures, from requesting state scholarships for studies to the opening of small- and large-scale businesses (taxis, cafés, companies), demanded an authorization issued by mediators of the ruling RCD party (Allal A. , 2016, p. 18). The journalist Halimi summarizes the paradoxical nature of the party for *le Monde Diplomatique*: "The RCD was all at the same time: economically liberal, politically police and [a] member of the socialist international" (Halimi, 2011).

Ironically enough, the World Bank, one of the major drivers behind the SAP in the 1980s, published a report on the relation between private business and state regulations under the RCD regime in 2014. It acknowledges, how privatization led to the monopolization of economic power of a political elite: "The Ben

---

56 While the underlying methodology of these reports can be criticized, their fields of investigation incorporate different dimensions: institutions, infrastructure, macroeconomics, health and primary education, higher education and training, market efficiency, technological readiness, business sophistication and innovation (Schwab, 2007, p. XiV).

Ali clan abused entry regulation for private gain at the expense of reduced competition" (Freund, Nucifora, & Rijkers, 2014). Besides this blatant proof of the failures in their own approach, no official review of the SAP has been discussed in this context. Scholar Firoze Manji concludes from the SAP programs that have been introduced "across the African continent" how "the most serious consequence of these policies was not the reversal of the many gains of independence, but the erosion of the ability of citizens to control their own destinies (Manji, 2012, p. 4)."

In the context of India, where similar projects of liberal reform have been implemented, Kumari states that "on the whole, the advantages of a liberalized economy and globalization have accrued more to women of the higher strata of society rather than those from the lower rang" (Kumari, 2010, p. 199). The economic state-led reforms and the clientelist system installed by Ben Ali and his party had gendered outcomes from which mostly women from the middle and upper class could profit.

Ben Ali's *Tahawwul*

In assessing the period of *tahawwul,* within the research area of ideological negotiations, Laurie Brand's book "Women, the State and Political Liberalization" (Brand, 1998), provides interesting insights from a comparative perspective. She explores the impact of women's rights organizations during the periods of political reforms in the MENA region. In this time period, secular and Islamic opposition were granted permission to (re-)appear in the public sphere, for example, via media outlets and NGOs (Non-Governmental Organizations). In Ben Ali's "national pact" of 1988, which was signed by oppositional movements such as the MTI on the anniversary of his coming to power (November 7th), he emphasizes *Itjdihad* as an important pillar of national jurisprudence and the basis of the CSP and Islam as "a source of inspiration and pride" (quoted in: McCarthy, 2014, p. 742; Daoud, 1993). Calculating a re-appearance of Islamic forces that would struggle for state power, this declaration can be read as "the beginning of new Islamization of state discourse" (Brand, 1998, p. 192), where Ben Ali tried to co-opt Islamic ideology to maintain hegemonic power in the authoritarian state. He hereby ensured maintenance of his sway over religious publics, and control of the "symbolic border guards" that were important in the sections of society, outside of the capital and the coastal areas.

Ben Ali hereby continued and exacerbated the politics of Habib Bourguiba. Contrary to the former, he presented himself more openly as "the guarantor of both religion and modernity". The paradox of the system of dissembled secularism installed by Bourguiba became more articulated. The strategy employed relates to Yuval-Davis' argument on the cultural construction of the modern nation:

"Because often the hegemony of the modern nation state in the post-colonial world has been limited and mostly confined to urban centers and the upper class, the use of cultural and religious traditions as symbolic border guards has enabled, to a large extent the continued co-existence of the 'modern' center with the pre-modern sections of society" (Yuval-Davis, 1997, p. 61).

Employing religious rhetoric allowed Ben Ali to co-opt it and eliminate the subversive potential of religion for political opposition.

Although not formally institutionalized, the "The Movement of Islamic Tendency" (Mouvement de la Tendance Islamique, MTI), founded in 1981 participated in Ben Ali's national pact of 1989, where it acknowledged the Code du Statut Personnel. In order to participate in the elections and to keep to the current legislation, the MIT had to renounce any religious connotations in their name. They subsequently choose the name of Ennahda ("Renaissance") and applied for a license in 1989 (Ayari M. B., 2012, p. 64). The famous quote accredited to party leader Rached Ghannouchi: "I trust in God and Ben Ali" (Daoud, 1993, p. 105), does much to nourish the rumors of a "secret pact" that had been concluded with the national security forces (Lamloum, 2002, p. 105).[57]

This short and selective opening of the public sphere, allowing for more counterpublic activities in forms of media and political organizations resulted in a first *epreuve de force* between secularist feminist ideologies and Islamic ideas that Brand describes as "a polemical exchange" (Brand, 1998, p. 192). With the perceived Islamist threat in the 1980s and the government's publicly affirmed will to negotiate with Islamic actors, condemning the oppressive politics of his successor Bourguiba, civil society actors united to defend their individual rights. Women's rights activists mobilized against a possible backlash. There are various accounts of a hostile climate towards women, when Ennahda attacked Tunisia's secularism and started to challenge the CSP, despite the fact they had accepted this institution a year before (Borsali, 2012; Brand, 1998, p. 194 f.). It is also within this time period, that the most prominent and influential feminist civil society organization, the Tunisian Association of Democratic Women (Association Tunisienne des Femmes Démocrates, ATFD) was able to obtain an official permit (Interview with N. Borsali, 2009). On the one hand, the "politics of change," initiated by Ben Ali the structural dimension of the public sphere became more flexible to integrate counterpublics. On the other hand, the fear of the

---

57 Geisser elaborates on the secret negotiations between the exiled Ennahda members and the Ben Ali administrations, where intelligence, especially before the international information summit, was exchanged with the prospect of a middle or long term retour to the political scene. Against this background he states that Ennahda had never excluded the option of legally operating under authoritarian rule (Geisser & Gobe, 2005-2006).

"Islamization" of society after Ben Ali had given religious actors a short time of relative freedom pushed civil society for better institutionalization.

The more liberal politics towards Islamic actors changed drastically after members of the officially unrecognized movement Ennahda performed very well when running on independent lists during the 1989 elections. They received up to 30% of the votes in some areas of the country, including the capital (Brand, 1998, p. 195), representing a danger for the state's authoritarian one-party system. In his speech on November 7th, 1990, Ben Ali proclaimed that the state holds the power over defining the "national consensus" and "the only defender of Islam in Tunisia." He clarified that the state would not accept any camp opposing it. Hereby, he assured himself control over the hegemonic domain of power incorporating both secularism and the political Islam.[58] The crackdown on opposition parties was soon to follow: Members of Ennahda were imprisoned and mosques placed under heightened surveillance and control protocols. After a short period marked by hope for liberalization and pluralism, the Islamist movement was again highly oppressed by Ben Ali's regime. Between 1991 and 1994, the Ennahda movement was completely "exterminated on Tunisian soil," its members either in prison or pushed into exile and the party activities were criminalized[59] (Ayari M. B., 2012, p. 64). In the new wave of authoritarianism, both Islamist and human rights activists from a left and secularist political spectrum were oppressed and feared their integrity.

Besides these repressive policies, Ben Ali strengthened women's rights mainly in terms of economic independence and parenting by reforming the family code CSP in 1992. Among those reforms, proclaimed on National Women's Day, 13th August, were: 1) A mother's consent must be obtained for the wedding contract of a daughter who is still a minor; 2) Married girls who are still legal minors have the right to manage their own private life and affairs; 3) Creation of a fund to guarantee payment of child support and alimony to divorced women and their children (Belhaj, 2010, p. 5). Further amendments in 2008 granted women the right to receive the conjugal residence in cases of divorce: if the couple has children of a lower age, imprisoned mothers invoke the right of an extended prison cell to take care of their young children (Belhaj, 2010, p. 5). In terms of the legislative manifestation of women's rights, it can be stated that the state feminist program under the presidents Bourguiba and his successor Ben Ali was continuously strengthening the rights of women in different spheres, from family and workspaces to prison.

---

58 A "legal opposition," constituted by the parties PDP, FDLT et Ettajdid, was thus granted some structural power but was under high surveillance and served the cosmetic purpose of pluralism under the *de facto* unique party system (Lamloum, 2002, p.103).

59 In this context, the role of women within the Ennahda movement, who had relatively more possibilities of participation and their network building during times of the imprisonment of their husbands remains understudied.

Over the course of this historical review, I have shown how reforms for women's rights went hand-in-hand with the repressive policies and associated human rights abuses by the regime. With regards to Yuval-Davis's distinction, state feminist policies encapsulate and manage all three dimensions of the construction of the nation: the biologist dimension, the cultural dimension and the dimension of citizenship rights embodied in a nationalist program. In the following, I will present how the representational dimension of the public sphere was controlled and managed by the regimes in order to uphold their hegemonic ideology.

The Representational Dimension of the Public Sphere

This section's purpose is to present the main features of the representational dimension of the public sphere under the authoritarian regime to give a descriptive point of departure for the negotiation processes during the period under study. I will point out the government's role as a gatekeeper and regulator of the public sphere by specifically looking at the "controlled liberalization" introduced by Ben Ali by the beginning of the 1990s. The entanglement of mass media ownership that I have previously discussed with regards to the relationship between the regime and the public sphere will be highlighted and historically grounded.

Overall, the representational dimension of the public sphere was manipulated, through different means, serving the purpose of legitimizing the power of the respective regimes of Bourguiba and Ben Ali. The government took a potent role in what I have described as the regulator of the public sphere. The various policies enacted by the former Tunisian leaders can be accorded to the disciplinary domain of power. The classical media landscape and the overall "ecology of the media" was strictly controlled by the two regimes. Print publications of any sort had to be approved by the Ministry of Communication leading to a "media desert" (Khechana, 2009, p. 102). Hereby, I will analyze the developments of this policy with regards to the classical media and online publics.

Habib Bourguiba restricted the public sphere based upon discriminatory press codes, a centralized media system and the persecution of journalists of any persuasion challenging the state's information policy (Khechana, 2009, p. 99). One example being the confiscation of Tunisia's first independent weekly magazine, *El Rai* ("the opinion"), in 1977, which was shut down after only one month of existence. Khekhana goes on to describe that because of a general deprivation of material resources, independent media was practically impossible to sustain. State TV and radio were required to follow the official information policies of the regime. Bourguiba employed the mass media for political campaigning while other political parties, which for instance in 1981 was only one opposition party, had no access to the state-owned media (Sadiki, 2008, p.120).

With Ben Ali taking power in 1987, cautious liberalization tendencies defined by decentralization and de-monopolization policies within the structural dimension of the public sphere can be observed (Smati, 2009). With a reform of the radio code in 1990, implementing a separation of radio and TV, authorities were supposed to clear the way towards more pluralism in the media. This reform, however, amounted to little more than a superficial change, rather than a substantial structural reform: The presidents of the broadcasting corporations were still appointed by the government, consequently remaining under its tough control procedures.

Further de-monopolization of the audio-visual media landscape was initiated by the privatization of radio and TV under Ben Ali in 2003. However, the welcoming of this policy by "The Association of Tunisian Journalists" (l'Association des Journalistes Tunisiens, AJT)[60], that had de facto become a "political cell of the RCD party since the 1990s," (Syndicat National des Journalistes Tunisiennes, 2009) made it clear that the new private companies were underpinning the hegemonic domain of power in the public sphere because of clientelism. Thus, the policy only constructed a façade of pluralism, as I will detail hereafter.

The process of privatization did not run independently from the regime, rather, the media sector was treated as another economic branch that was under the control of the president. Only Ben Ali's closest family circle and the "Trabelsi Clan," the family of his wife Leila Ben Ali, were accorded the privilege of opening media outlets: In 2008, radio Zeitouna, which had a religious outlook, was launched by Sakher el-Matri, step-son of the president, while Shams FM, founded in 2010, was headed by his daughter Cyrine Ben Ali Mabrouk. (Erdle, 2010, p. 145). Private outlets were mainly focused on entertainment. Hannibal's news journal, for example, was very short and lasted only seven minutes, mainly covering the presidential activities (Smati, 2009, p. 91).

Ben Ali used all kinds of media outlets to strengthen his position during electoral campaigns within the representational dimension of the public sphere.[61] A report published by International Media Support in 2004 shows that 77% of the

---

60 The AJT was founded in 1962 and had its "golden times" of resistance in the 1970s and 1980s, before becoming increasingly coopted. The National Syndicate of the Tunisian Journalists (Syndicat Nationale des Journalistes Tunisiens, SNJT) was created in 2008 to replace the dysfunctional structure of the AJT and create a veritable counterpublic. However, they faced oppressive politics, co-optations and severe financial constraints. Some insights into their situation can be found in an appeal, entitled "The National Syndicate of Tunisian Journalists: Chronic of a programmed conspiracy," clarifying that the RCD had taken over *de facto control* of the syndicate in 2009. It was published in the online-magazine Nawaat that was censored in Tunisia: https://nawaat.org/portail/2009/08/16/syndicat-national-des-journalistes-tunisiens-chronique-dune-conspiration-programmee/ (Syndicat National des Journalistes Tunisiens, 2009).

61 To my knowledge, there are no media monitoring data available covering the election periods during Bourguiba's regime: In four presidential elections, his party Neo-detour and Socialist Detour Party gained almost 100% without competition.

audio-visual media content covered the president's RCD party, while print media showed an even more uniform picture with 92% of their coverage focusing on the president and his party. This made political campaigning almost impossible for the opposition with two out of three challengers publicly encouraging their followers to vote for Ben Ali (Khechana, 2009, p. 101).

Public debates, like TV panels, were "*faux débats*" (Khechana, 2009, p. 100), serving only to maintain the preponderant position of the unity party regime, illustrating its hegemonic power in the public sphere. The audio-visual landscape was "transmitting an anachronistic discourse, where the *langue de bois* and uniform thinking were appropriate" (Khechana, 2009, p. 100). This relation is also illustrated by the name of the first national TV channel, Tunis 7, referring to the date of Ben Ali's coming to power on November 7th. This examination for the Tunisian context is consistent with the overall analysis on the transformation of the media systems by privatization in the region by Carola Richter and Hanan Badr:

> "However, the real outcome of the privatization of media markets in most of the Arab countries has been an even stronger influence by the ruling political regimes. Major media outlets like TV channels were often outsourced to the hands of loyal business elites or simply newly founded by family members of the rulers" (Richter & Badr, 2016, p. 10).

The findings from the perspective of communication studies bring us back to the argument that privatization allowing for the establishment of more media outlets and hereby inducing change at the structural dimension of the public sphere does not necessarily foster pluralism, as long as the same mechanisms of control, encapsulated within the disciplinary and hegemonic domain of power, are still in place.

Counterpublic media tackling the representational dimension of the public sphere, challenging the uniform state policies, would be oppressed, regardless of their underlying ideology. The newspaper *el-Fajr* ("dawn"), founded by members of the Ennahda movement, and the radical leftist *el-Badil* ("alternative") were only able to release a few publications in early 1990 before being forbidden in 1991 and their principle directors being imprisoned (Khechana, 2009, p. 99). The satellite TV channel *El Hiwar el Tounsi* ("Tunisian Dialogue")[62], founded by the left opposition figure and businessman Tahar Ben Hassin, and the oppositional journal El Mawqif ("The Position"), published by the Democratic Progressive Party (Ḥizb ad-Dimuqraṭi at-Taqaddumi, Partie Démocratique Progressiste, PDP), constitute considerable exceptions and became a bastion for the more secularist opposition.

The arrival of satellite TV channels led to an internationalization of the media landscape, and for the first time, Tunisians had the opportunity to verify and

---

62 See more on the role of the TV channel el Hiwar el Tounsi, which had to change its broadcast frequencies several times, as a counterpublic media during the uprisings in 2008 in Gafsa in chapter 6.1.

compare information. These developments marked a shift in the relations of the dimension of the public sphere, as the structural dimension of the media was no longer totally controlled by the regime. In a first attempt to limit the effects of this change, the government tried to pass a draconian law in parliament, limiting access to those media by deciding who would be allowed to install a private satellite dish. The government soon gave up on the law as it became clear that this technology would be too hard to control (Smati, 2009, p. 94). With these technological developments, for the first time in history, the information monopoly of the state was broken, and satellite TV became an important news source for Tunisians, especially on national issues. For instance, national TV did not cover the terror attack claimed by Al-Qaida on the El-Ghiriba synagogue in Djerba in 2002 at first, so the Tunisian people had to rely on international news channels to discover what was happening in their own country.

Analysts emphasize the role of the Qatari news channel Al-Jazeera in giving the Tunisian opposition, such as young activists, ex-ministers of Bourguiba or members of associations and labor unions, a platform (Khechana, 2009, p. 103). Nevertheless, the development of this transnational public sphere was still restricted, as journalists and editors working for Al-Jazeera were not free to work in Tunisia and invited participants were often banned from travelling to Al-Jazeera studios in Qatar or elsewhere. With its alternative flows of information and financial independence, Al-Jazeera has been able to implement a counterpublic stretching across and linking the representational dimension of public spheres transregionally. Hence, further investigation here does not fall under the purview of this study, which is primarily concerned with the negotiations of gender in counterpublics *within* the Tunisian public sphere.

5.3   Conclusion: A Hegemonic Public Sphere in Post-Colonial Tunisia

Building on the theoretical framework, I have demonstrated in this chapter how the modernist anti-colonial nationalist project of Bourguiba and its continuation under President Ben Ali was of an authoritarian nature. For this, state-feminist practices, perpetuating all dimensions of the public sphere, constituted an important pillar. While Bourguiba and his neo-Destour party lead the country to independence, modernist and Western values continued to be inscribed in the hegemonic domain of power. However, they were coupled with religious rhetoric, and continuing Sharia law, a state ideology that I framed as "dissembled secularism". Ben Ali expedited on it by "Islamizing the state discourse" positioning himself as the (one and only) protector of religious values and secularism alike.

I hold that state-feminism can be conceptualized as an oppressive structure within the hegemonic domain of power: Following up on existing scholarship, I have framed it as an ideology, legitimizing the oppression of oppositional groups, mainly of the Islamist camp, yet constituted as a "smokescreen" (Errazzouki, 2014, p. 262) to de-legitimize counterpublics. One argument to discredit counterpublics defending women's rights as human rights was that they shouldn't ask for more, as they "already have everything."

The creation of counterpublics was made almost impossible by the regime's complete control over the three dimensions of the public sphere. This control entailed threatening and imprisoning journalists who were critical of the hegemonic ideology legitimizing the state; forbidding alternative media outlets, associations and parties; repressive policies regarding access to the internet; and last but not least a self-censorship system imposed by civil authorities. The resulting "information desert" ensured an authoritarian legacy of the Bourguiba and Ben Ali regimes. Most organizations and spaces, including the media and academia were controlled and/or co-opted by state-feminist politics. This came at the expense of a deeper debate about the relation of women's rights and religion, and the balance and relations of different individual rights and freedoms.

6 Counterpublic Resistance under Ben Ali's Rule

This chapter sheds light on counterpublics that were created despite the authoritarian politics and elaborated censorship system put in place in Tunisia. I do not claim to give an exhaustive account of the multiple attempts to create (feminist) counterpublics under the authoritarian regimes throughout Tunisia's history.63 Rather, my analysis centers on three distinct counterpublics. They present different dimensions for preparing the ground for the uprisings of 2010/2011 and the renegotiation of gender in the public sphere once the authoritarian state started to lose its grip on power. They are all mostly located at the capital; records on oppositional publics "beyond the center" are very difficult to find, mirroring the largely urban-centered research approach in scholarship on Tunisia. The 2008 uprisings in Gafsa constitute a small exception here.

The first section examines feminist autonomous counterpublics that emerged in the 1980s, their institutionalization and representation. The second section looks more closely at the regroupment of the 18th October movement, created during the World Summit on the Information Society (WSIS) in 2005, beyond party lines. I will particularly point out the agreements taken on gender politics within this counterpublic. Finally, I will present counterpublics that have been formed against Tunisian internet censorship for free speech, relying on information and communication technologies.

6.1 Feminist Counterpublics emerging in the 1980's

The Tunisian Association of Democratic Women (Association Tunisienne des Femmes Démocrates, ATFD) and the Association of Tunisian Women for Research and Development (Association des Femmes Tunisiennes pour la Recher-

---

63 For a detailed overview on the formation of oppositional political parties and associations during the time of Ben Ali, see (Geisser & Gobe, 2005-2006), who states that opposition (in the capital) remained restricted to around one hundred individuals. This small circle, in which "everybody knows everybody," was also referred to in the interviews I conducted.

© Springer Fachmedien Wiesbaden GmbH, part of Springer Nature 2019
A. Antonakis, *Renegotiating Gender and the State in Tunisia between 2011 and 2014*, Politik und Gesellschaft des Nahen Ostens,
https://doi.org/10.1007/978-3-658-25639-5_6

che et le Développement, AFTURD) rose out of the counterpublic of the Independent Tunisian Feminist Movement (Mouvement Féministe Tunisienne Indépendant, MFTI) of the 1980s. Both were able to institutionalize in the period of Ben Ali's politics of *tahawwul* and in the rise of political Islam described earlier (Daoud, 1993; Labidi L., 2007).

This feminist autonomous women's organization ATFD, founded in 1989 in Tunis by a network of feminist activists had exchanged ideas and discussed theoretical approaches in the context of the cultural club Tahar Haddad by the end of the 1970s[64]. The club situated in the *medina,* the old town of Tunis was the only cultural club run by a woman at the time (Dwyer, 1997, p. 480). The decision to adopt the name of the reformist thinker of the 1930s can be seen as a broader effort to revitalize the history of women's movements and theorizations of gender and nation that were effaced by the dominant narrative of Bourguiba's modernist project. Media projects and political projects alike defining the autonomous movement of the 1980s originate here, forming a sort of Tahar Hahdad counterpublic.

Laila Labidi qualifies the members of the club as "A group of several dozen women from the new national bourgeoisie - some of them political independents, others from various leftist movements, using a variety of points of reference," that came together in this "most emblematic of women's spaces in Tunisia" (Labidi L. , 2007, p. 9). The ideas circulating within this feminist counterpublic were inspired by socialist sentiments (Dwyer, 1997, p. 482).

The ATFD is, especially today, seen as a political player, or a "ministry". However, combatting patriarchal violence at the interactional dimension of the public sphere was and continues to be a fundamental aim of the association. They create "center d'écoutes," women's shelters for women, giving medical, psychological and legal advice for female victims of violence. In this context, the ATFD can rely on advanced expertise as a resource, with some of its 150 – 200 members having professional backgrounds in fields such as advocacy and psychoanalysis.

While they assisted women in demanding their rights in concrete cases and created a space of regroupment, they also orientated their activism towards wider publics more generally: speaking out for the rights of all citizens and respect for human rights. Their feminist struggle, including the interpersonal domain of power by working with victims and survivors, was linked to a struggle for democracy, pluralism and social justice, targeting the structural domain of power

---

64 I have elsewhere analyzed the ATFD as a "mobilized public" that could successfully participate in the constitutional process as their struggles could easily be framed within the political polarizations that characterized the second and third phases of the "transformation" (Antonakis, 2015a).

as well. Alliances were built between agencies of the Tunisian League for Human Rights (LTDH), such as the International Federation for Human Rights or the women's section of UGTT (labor union). Even critics of the ATFD that would consider them as too *bourgeois* or out of touch with the actual economic problems of society admit their integrity under Ben Ali's rule.

While the ATFD was officially recognized under Ben Ali's regime, its freedom of action and mobility was restricted. These restrictions took the form of observation and intimidation of their members, and even control over their meetings. In a study I conducted on autonomous feminist actors in 2009/2010, the instrumentalization of state politics on one hand, and the Islamist project on the other hand were stressed. A member of the ATFD whom I met in 2010 explains the relation to the state-feminist institution UNFT:

> "We encountered a lot of resistance to work with the government and everything related to the party in power, the UNFT[65], for instance. We worked with them for the preparation of Beijing 1995 [the fourth UN conference on the status of women,[66] organized by the women's commission; note from the author], we had a Tunisian network called "network Rihanna," and we have seen to what point it is hard to work with them. Autonomy is a fundamental principle, autonomy with regards to the government as well. (But) since then, we practically don't work together anymore" (A.J. Tunis, November 2010).

Her account is typical for the struggle of women's rights counterpublics not to get co-opted by the state's hegemonic gender politics (Al-Ali, 2012, p. 30). In defending secular rights, feminist organizations found themselves in the position of being easily co-opted by state-feminist politics and used as a tool to repress conservative or Islamist thinking. At the same time, defending women's rights as human rights put them in the position of having to defend the citizen rights of Islamists and Islamic regroupments. Even though vehemently opposed to the Islamist project, the Islamic movement has been regarded as a more or less "legitimate" political force in Tunisia, backed by an important part of society.

This dilemma of women's rights activism trapped somehow between the authoritarian state and the Islamic movements becomes evident in the next quote by the same member:

> "For the feminists, there was a lot of resistance towards the Islamists. We consider the Islamist project as contradictory to women's interests, even though we are for the freedom of the Islamists. We are not necessarily

---

65 For an analysis of the UNFT and its place in the modernist state program, see chapter 5.2.1.
66 The entire speech by Néziha Zarrouk, Minister of Women affairs at the time, can be found here: http://www.un.org/esa/gopher-data/conf/fwcw/conf/gov/950905171419.txt. The speech reproduces much of the official state feminist ideas: The modernist project by Ben Ali is presented as an exceptional model and the strategies to improve women's rights, especially with regards to the need to improve the situation of rural women and migrant women.

against their right for an active life and to form associations. At a certain
moment, we supported their demands for their political prisoners and all
of this. But to work together from there has caused us many problems,
within civil society as well" (A.J. Tunis, November 2010).

The question of the legitimacy of an Islamist opposition was certainly debated
within the feminist counterpublics and I hold that it is wrong to assume that
opinions were homogenous on this issue. Especially within the ATFD, which
considers itself a pluralistic association, different opinions and approaches by
the members can be distinguished. Within feminist counterpublics, critique of
Islamist counterpublics was not necessarily structured around culturalism and
essentialist arguments, but addressed socio-economic inequalities constituting
the Matrix of Domination: "Their [radical Islamists'] big forces, so the women
say, are that they canalize social frustrations and it's these [structures] that have
to be attacked in order to reduce their audience" (Charrad M. , 2001, p. 126).

The stance of secularist women towards the persecution, imprisonment and
torture of Islamists under Ben Ali, impacts upon questions of transitional justice
today. While there are records of the imprisonment and prosecutions of secular
women's rights activists, violations towards female Islamists during the Ben Ali
and Bourguiba period are rather poorly documented (Gray, 2012, p. 286).
Women of Ennahda members often had to assume multiple roles while their
male relatives, as the head of the household, were in prison. Furthermore, they
faced harassment and micro-aggressions from police, neighbors and families,
expressing the interpersonal domain of power structured around "secularism".
Doris Gray finds that women of Ennahda in particular "have developed a practical stance on women's rights that is reminiscent of women in World War II
who pushed emancipation forward" (Gray, 2012, p. 292). This collective experience of being persecuted for ideas has surely made Islamist women in Tunisia
more sensitive to the importance of individual rights.

Feminist spaces challenging state feminist knowledge production also targeted the representational dimension of the public sphere. The bilingual feminist
magazine *Al Nisaa* was first published in April 1985 and was "in direct line of
descent" of the first feminist magazine *Leila* published from 1936-1941 (Labidi
L., 2007, p. 12). Whilst the first, which I described earlier, was born in the context of a colonial struggle, the second, which also had its roots in Tunis' Tahar
Haddad club, aimed to defend women's rights within a more Universalist approach and establish an autonomous female voice. Fighting patriarchal structures
and their manifestation in the dissimulation of sexist stereotypes at the representational dimension of the public sphere constituted a pivotal aim in the counterpublic. In a flyer accompanying the first issue of *Nissa*, the editors expressed
their wish to "construct another image of the women, opposing the one spread
by 'other' news outlets, perpetuated by a sexist discourse and profoundly anchored in the individual and collective consciousness" (quoted in: Weber A. F.,

2001, p. 65). The quote also shows the cautious formulations that the women took on when talking about "the other" news outlets that were, in fact, state-controlled.

However, according to *Nissa*'s founding members, an initial trigger to produce a feminist magazine was the Israeli invasion of Lebanon in June 1982. Disappointed by the weak reaction of the government and opposition groups, the women from the Tahar Haddad club joined forces with the newly established women's section of the strong labor union UGTT to create an outlet to raise their concerns (Dwyer, 1997, p. 486). The creation of the magazine and the emergence of the association ATFD, which would later be influential, were two processes that ran in parallel (Dwyer, 1997, p. 493). I claim that these parallel structures emerging from the cultural center demonstrate interest in tackling all three dimensions of the public sphere. Here, the concept of counterpublics traces how the space of the cultural center and exchange between women was then institutionalized and translated into associations and media projects alike.

Finally, academic knowledge production as a form of counterpublic participation targets the hegemonic domain of power. I have previously pointed to the aim of feminist intellectuals to re-introduce the ideas formulated in the Tahar Haddad club to challenge state feminism, even before the *tahawwul* was introduced by Ben Ali. This can also be deduced from several academic publications of the time that managed to bypass censorship and other mechanisms of control. They give an entry point to discover feminist academic counterpublics at the time. Ben Said Cherni writes in 1986, that Tahar Haddad's "suppressed thoughts have to regain surface" (ben Said Cherni, 1986, p. 11) and identifies four fields of thoughts that must be revitalized: worker's socialism, democracy, total gender equality and the adaption of sharia to modernity. A second concern in feminist academic counterpublics was shedding light on the women's role in historic struggles for independence (El-Masri, 2015). In the field of gender studies, Dalenda Larguèche, Professor for Gender Studies and president of CREDIF after the uprisings, states a relative freedom during the times of Ben Ali in the academic public. For example, sociological inquiries around the social construction of female bodies, such as the change in the perception of virginity or the "sociability of prostitutes"[67], were undertaken in 2010 and published to a greater audience after the uprisings (Matri, 2012; Guedri, 2012). However, religious approaches to gender studies were excluded:

> "I've always been teaching, and it is me who is in charge of the schedule and content of my teaching schedule, the way I want it. But some questions were censored… Religion. Religion is a difficult issue. I remember

---

67 Sex work was legal, organized and regulated by the Ministry of Interior. For further inquiry of these policies and any changes therein after the uprisings, see the study from Nicolas Silva (Silva, 2013).

> once we wanted to organize a colloquium on religion and it didn't get the
> authorization of the ministry of education" (Dalenda Larguèche, Tunis,
> October 2014).

The taboo of discussing religious aspects within the academic setting of gender
studies illustrates just another form of repressive state policies against any platform of knowledge creation that could challenge the hegemonic ideology of the
state. Sara Salem notes from a post-colonial theoretical perspective: "The silence
around feminism and religion is a profound one, and its roots lie in the metanar-
rative of secularizing that influences knowledge production in the field of feminism (and more broadly the social sciences)" (Salem, 2013).

Newer research in political literature points to Arabic novels and books that
have entangled gender and resistance in Ben Ali's regime (Labidi L., 2016):
Mas'udah Abu Bakr's *Tarshqanah*, published in 1999, Fadilah al-Shabbi's *al-
'Adl* ("Justice"), written in 2005 and banned for three years by Ben Ali's government, and Fathiyah al-Hashimi's 2009 *Maryam tasqutu min yad Allah* ("Maryam Falls from the Hand of God"). These books have been analyzed as "subversive strategies" exposing, among other things, "the intersection of gender with
class as a site of disenfranchisement" (Head, 2016, p. 1). It appears that Arabic
Tunisian literature constituted an important medium for feminist counterpublics
at the time and is worth a more detailed exploration.

In conclusion, the feminist counterpublics developed within a framework of
constant surveillance, threats and imprisonment of both secularist and Islamist
opposition. The configuration of the hegemonic domain of power had an impact
on the content of gender issues raised. Labidi critically concludes: "the feminist
discourse of the 1980s... [put] forth only stereotypical slogans and cliché demands and is consequently incapable of confronting the geopolitical issues of
the day" (Labidi L., 2007, p. 23). Here we see how state-feminism can be read
as one important pillar of the authoritarian system, by excluding important emancipatory debates: This lack of a *débat de fond*, a fundamental debate taking into
account religious issues, economic, post-colonial dependencies and geopolitical
issues of war and peace (Marzouki, 1993, p. 270)[68] can also be discerned as a
repeated pattern in the transformation period from 2011-2014.

---

68 Ilhelm Marzouki, one of the most prominent feminist scholars in Tunisia of the 1990, remarked
in 1993: "The feminist approach is by far not constituting a clear position. The absence of a
collective research on this notion and its implications has originated a great number of contro-
versies. The fundamental issues of this debate touched on the real or supposed relation between
feminism and politics" (Marzouki, 1993, p. 270).

6.2   The 18th October Movement of 2005

The international World Summit on the Information Society (WSIS) that took place in Tunisia in 2005 constitutes an important event in challenging the hegemony of the public sphere. A new counterpublic aimed to utilize the presence of this international public on Tunisian soil to shed light on human rights abuses in the country. This alliance was secured institutionally in 2005 when oppositional forces from civil society and political parties, namely Ennahda, the Democratic Progressive Party (Parti Démocratique Progressiste, PDP) and the Communist Worker's Party (Party Ouvrier Communiste Tunisien, POCT), published an initial common declaration named "The Committee of the 18th October" ("Le collective du 18 Octobre pour les Droits et les Libertés," later also referred to as the 18th October movement). They initially organized around three themes: freedom of expression and the abolishment of censorship, freedom of organization of political parties and the liberation of all political prisoners. The committee organized a hunger strike of eight opposition activists belonging to the left and Islamist camps (Ayari M. B., 2012, p. 69). It gained the attention of most Western governments and produced a "diplomatic choc wave" expressed in numerous condemnations of the Ben Ali regime in the frame of the WSIS. Only France, Tunisia's former colonial power, ignored the protest at first for reasons of "Realpolitik" (Geisser & Gobe, 2005-2006, p. 16). The movement was also supported by international NGOs such as Amnesty International, Reporters Without Borders and the International League for Human Rights.

The founding document expresses the intent to institutionalize a public forum, wherein "academics and intellectuals" of all ideological and political backgrounds could participate to discuss "fundamental questions posed by the arrival of democracy to the country" (Collectif 18 Octobre pour les Droits & les Libertés en Tunisie, 2007).[69] The unfolding dynamics in the aftermath of the WSIS within this counterpublic entails special empirical interest with regards to the negotiations of women's rights that hasn't yet been fully explored, hence providing interesting parallels to negotiations in the transformation period after 2011. The brochure published in November 2007 resumes the negotiations in the counterpublic around two themes: Gender equality and freedom of consciousness. The choice of debate is not surprising, given the very diverse composition of the members of the counterpublic, which aimed to further deepen the discussion

---

69 The Publication of the collective entitled "Notre Voie vers la Démocratie" can be found online incorporating translations in French, Arabic and English. The source of Nachaz provides a declaration of the secular counterpublic, including many signatures of the ATFD, criticizing the work of the collective entitled "A propos d'une dérive" (Concerning a diversion) http://nachaz.org/blog/doc-1-brocure-du-collectif-du-18-octobre-pour-lesdroits-et-les-libertes/#_Toc439340003

around topics other than the initial three themes mentioned above. While the members agreed on the need to preserve the CSP and foster the participation of women in the public sphere, two issues remained unresolved: The gender-segregating inheritance laws and the ratification of "international convention codifying women's rights." While not stated explicitly, it can be deduced that the text refers to the CEDAW, whose position for national legislation has not been resolved. The very same debate appeared during the transformation period and will be analyzed in the following chapters. It shows the centrality of gender politics to negotiate political camps, not only in the politics of transformation, but also in the creation of cross-party counterpublics.

Finally, in a third declaration, they detailed several positions introducing the principle of equality as "complete and effective for every citizen without any discrimination or disadvantage based on social origin, sex, intellectual and existential orientation". The clear commitment to the CSP and gender equality expressed in the three joint *communiqués* of the cross-ideological counterpublic thus challenges the view that the "process of discursive redefinition of women's rights in terms of Islam" had only been initiated after a "shift to the center of the political field" of Ennahda after the uprisings (Khalil, 2014, p. 191). That is to say that it had already been initiated within the counterpublics in 2005-2007. For example, Jaziri Hussein from the Ennahda movement was part of the "coordination committee" of the collective. Furthermore, Rached Ghannouchi, the political and spiritual leader of the Ennahda movement, took part in the National-Islamic dialogues that had been taking place since 1994 at the Center for Arab Unity Studies in Beirut in the beginning of the 1990s (Browers, 2006, p.9). Browers states that the "women's question" constituted the most contested issue in these forums (Browers, 2006, p.10). Ghannouchi had experience in debating these question in a transregional couterpublic that aimed to bring together the marginalized political forces from the respective authoritarian regimes of the region in Beirut and in the 18th October counterpublic.

The efforts were countered by a public *replique* by a secularist counterpublic, including many signatures of the ATFD, criticizing the work of the collective entitled "A propos d'une dérive" (Concerning a diversion, 2006). They explicitly referenced their position towards women's rights and referred to a secular state as the only option, fearing cooperation with the Islamic Ennahda which would entail a state project endangering women's rights. The defenders of the cooperation included members of Ettakatol and the CPR, the parties that would form the Troika government in 2011 after the elections for the constitutional parliament.

The constitution of the 18th of October showcases the dilemma of feminist counterpublics in merging with other political counterpublics as soon as the Islamic opposition was included. The counterpublic brings to light the agreements and limits of women's rights discussions between different political opposition parties at the time. Furthermore, the negotiations within and around the 18th October Committee exemplify the pivotal role that women's rights play both in coalition buildings and in the separation of counterpublics.

6.3 Counterpublics Against Internet Censorship

The Tunisian "exceptionalism" that I have problematized in chapter II can be also be applied to the field of the digital infrastructure, in which Tunisia also pioneered. In the following, I demonstrate how possibilities for the opposition to create and participate in counterpublics and produce alternative knowledge have increased through a widening of the communicative infrastructures. However, these new opportunities need to be analyzed in their dialectic relationship with mechanisms of control and surveillance of the opposition set in place by the authoritarian regime.

Tunisia was the first African (and the first Arabic-speaking) country to go online. The Internet was introduced in 1991 and became public in 1996, but remained under strict government supervision. Nevertheless, an online community emerged by the end of the 1990s, which was also backed by the Tunisian diaspora (Lecomte, 2009). The Tunisian government presented itself as an active promoter of the ICT infrastructure, incorporating it into the modernization paradigm of the country.[70] However, at the same time, the government was employing online and offline practices, such as its elaborated Internet censorship system, to block content related to human rights, news or religion nationally. The important role of new media was expounded during the World Summit on the Information Society (WSIS) that took place in Tunis in 2005. In the same year, Tunisia was ranked as one of the biggest "internet enemies" according to Reporters Without Borders (Reporters Withouth Borders, 2005). The summit was in fact under high surveillance by national state authorities, to the point that even the transmission of the opening speech of the Swiss co-president of the summit was censored (Khechana, 2009, p. 101).

For the regime, the WSIS constituted another opportunity to polish its *"vitrine démocratique"* in relation to women's rights: The digital divide and its gendered dimension[71] was addressed and guidelines put forward to specifically

---

70 According to official sources of the time, internet connectivity in the education sector (universities, schools, research laboratories) was officially reported by 100% (Open Net Initiative, 2009). While this percentage is hard to verify, and also unlikely, it does show the will of the regime to appear a connected and modern nation.

71 This digital divide is not only gender specific but also divide along spatial lines: "Compared to female Internet usage in the rest of the world, it would seem that women in the Arab world are in the deepest recesses of the digital divide." (Wheeler, 2004, p. 138)

improve women's access to the Internet. While it remains crucial to address the unequal redistribution of resources and access to the Internet according to gender, Ben Ali's principal aim was to hide the authoritarian practices of his regime in an international public sphere by instrumentalizing women's rights. The modernist agenda in the frame of the WISI intersected technological innovations and women's rights.

Internet censorship was imposed by the Ben Ali regime in various ways: From a restricted press code, affecting journalists and bloggers, to the use of sophisticated spy and filtering software[72], and the blocking of websites and taking down of internet servers (Open Net Initiative, 2009). The Tunisian Internet Agency (ATI) established by the Tunisian Ministry of Communications to regulate the country's internet and domain name system (DNS) services was controlled all Internet servers in the country. The ATI managed a "cyberspace police" that has been in effect since 2002, blocking political and critical content (Khechana, 2009, p. 104). Website distributing proxies (such as the very popular "hotspot shield" or those developed by Tor) that enable the user to de-block content online were also targeted. At the same time, cybercafés (referred to as *publinet* in Tunisia) and their owners were observed and infiltrated by the regime's (civil) authorities. In some parts of the country, internet users had to show their IDs in order to go online, while owners of cybercafés could be penalized for the actions of their clients, thus establishing observation and snitch system between citizens (Deibert, Palfrey, Rohozinski, & Zittrain, 2010, p. 584). In their typology of internet censorship, Deibert et al. (2010) classify Tunisia at the time as using second and third generation techniques:

"Second and third-generation techniques [are] more subtle, flexible, and even offensive in character. These next generation techniques employ the use of legal regulations (…) extralegal or covert practices, including offensive methods, and the outsourcing or privatization of controls to 'third parties' to restrict what type of information can be posted, hosted, accessed, or communicated online" (Deibert, Palfrey, Rohozinski, & Zittrain, 2010, p. 6).

In my 2011 study, I found how the censorship system has qualitatively developed during the four weeks period of the uprisings (Antonakis, 2012, p.40 f.). YouTube was continuously blocked from 2008, while Facebook was unblocked after a couple of months of censorship. The decision as to why the ban was lifted remains unclear. Media scholar Khechana points to "firm internal and external

---

72 The ATI could rely on the most sophisticated and expensive monitoring and filtering software on the global market, employing, for example, the equipment of *Trovicor*, a German company developing interception technologies for intelligence surveillance (Jalalzai, 2014, p.172). The German NGO *Digitalcourage* publicly called out *Trovicor* (formally Nokia Siemens networks) for supporting authoritarian regimes, for instance in Iran, when awarding the company the "Big Brother Award" in 2009 (Süddeutsche Zeitung, 2010).

pressure" preceding this decision coming from the presidential palace (Khechana, 2009, p. 105).

It can be stated that state-run internet censorship was a complex system, interlocking juridical aspects in order to filter and block content online, prosecuting activists and *publinet* owners, and last but not least, creating a climate of fear leading to self-censorship in political communication among activists and journalists. The state's control permeated all three dimensions of the public sphere. At the same time, media ownership sustained the censorship system and the regime's control over the Public Sphere. Ben Ali assured that the telecommunication market would remain under the control of his family, illustrating again the monopolization within the structural dimension of the public sphere. Marouane Mabrouk, husband of Ben Ali's daughter Cyrine, entered the cell phone provider market in 2010, when the French company Orange launched a Tunisian branch – he held 51% of the shares and Orange was the first to obtain the license to launch 3G in Tunisia (Haugbolle, 2013, p. 168). Consequently, internet accessibility increased drastically.

Nevertheless, the internet censorship system imposed by the ATI was challenged by a small counterpublic of a "digital elite" even before the uprisings of 2010/2011. They used ICTs to bring attention to human rights abuses committed by the regime such as restrictions on freedom of speech and freedom of the press, the persecution and torture of activists (note that Tunisia signed the UN convention against torture in 1988). Due to a lack of statistics it is hard to investigate the scope of those infrastructures that were used to create counterpublics and challenge hegemony at the representational dimension of the public sphere. Starting with email lists of "takriz", spaces of communication were widened, and e-mags and blogs were created. It is assumed that websites like TUNeZINE (created by Zouhair Yahyaoui, who died after he had been imprisoned for his activism), Tunisnews, Kalima, Nawaat or Alternatives Citoyennes became important sources of information, even though the local Tunisian access to these sites was regularly blocked (Khechana, 2009, p. 102), and cyber dissidents were imprisoned (Richter, 2005). The sites were read and supported by the Tunisian diaspora as well as those who used proxies to circumvent censorship from within the country (Lecomte, 2009).

Slim Amamou, blogger and state secretary for youth and sports of the interim government in 2011, points to the first organized demonstration against "Ammar 404" in May 2010 in the capital: "Ammar 404" was the default page that appeared when trying to open a blocked website. According to Deibert et al Tunisia thereby employed a common second-generation censorship technique:

"Unlike other states (…) Tunisia's endeavors to conceal instances of filtering by supplying a fake error page when blocked website is requested. This technique makes filtering more opaque and clouds users' understanding of the boundaries of permissible content" (Deibert, Palfrey, Rohozinski, & Zittrain, 2010, p. 585).

Nevertheless, this technique could not really "cloud" the censorship: Yet, instead of targeting the Ben Ali regime, the activists had another enemy. "Ammar" was criticized ironically in a more open space (Ben Gharbia, 2015). By personifying the censorship, it was easier to covertly protest without explicitly referring to Ben Ali's regime (Antonakis, 2012). This first mobilization of a young digital elite forming shows the potential of internet censorship as a mobilizing factor, as expressed in the Tunisian campaign against Ammar404. For Amamou, this was the first appearance of an "apolitical" youth in the public sphere that was defending freedom of information and expression online:

> "Actually, even May 22th [2010] was pretty important, not only as it took a bit of fear from the people but also because, we, as a small group organizing this demonstration, insisted that it was apolitical" (Slim Amamou, Berlin, 2012).

Still, Slim Amamou was arrested and the demonstration forbidden. Activists appeared wearing white shirts as a sign of protest in the public space (Ben Mhenni, 2011, p.10). In a novel way, this specific bodily comportment brought questions of internet censorship and freedom of speech online into the interactional dimension of the public sphere. At the same time, the staged protest was visible to the counterpublic, yet escaped the disciplinary domain of power of the regime in the planning phase. The campaign, organized by a middle-class urban elite, partly deconstructs the "Tunisian paradox" that has been debated in scholarship concerning the lack of political freedoms of the opposition in a modern and neoliberal economy with relatively high living and educational standards (Chomiak, 2014, p. 37). This is in line with the argument of the overall theoretical framework of this study, looking at the restrictions in the hegemonic public sphere for which technological innovations certainly entailed structural changes. The role that ICTs will yet play in breaking the regime's monopoly over the public sphere in the uprisings starting just a couple of months later will be analyzed in more detail in the next chapter.

7 Challenging the Matrix of Domination

The two consecutive uprisings of 2008/2009 that started in Gafsa and 2010/2011, which has been framed as triggering the "Arab Spring", can be regarded as attempts to challenge the Matrix of Domination. Although women's rights were not the driving force behind the uprisings under examination, this is not to say that women weren't participating equally in the uprisings as advocates, online-activists, unionists, journalists or politicians. Numerous scholars studying the crucial days of the uprisings in the Tahrir Square in Egypt notice a "gender-bias free zone" (Sholkamy, 2012, p. 94). Similar statements have been made in my interviews with regards to the Kasbah protests, following Ben Ali's ousting. Departing from the epistemological reflections on "talking about a revolution", I will exhibit the narrative of the uprisings in Gafsa and Redeyef as a starting point of the uprisings in 2010/2011, framed as the beginning of the "Arab Spring". The second subchapter briefly summarizes the shifting public sphere constellations during the days of the uprisings leading to the transformation period under investigation. The last subchapter is concerned with the revolutionary protests at the Kasbah in Tunis, incorporating Tunisia's often forgotten "square moment" that lasted until March 2011.

7.1 The Uprisings in Gafsa 2008/2009

Sociologist Amine Allal calls for the "choice of a heuristic temporality" to understand the "ongoing revolutionary process" in Tunisia (Allal A. , 2012, p. 821 f.).[73] By marking the beginning of the Tunisian uprising with the events that took place in Gafsa in 2008, I am following the discourse of many inhabitants of the center of the country, where the uprisings in the phosphate region are considered

---

73 Amine Allal's analysis of the uprisings in 2008, serves as an important reference in the literature on Tunisian revolutionary history before the uprisings of 2011 (Allal A., 2010). Besides these rare studies from "on the ground", I also had the chance to interview Laila Khaled Labidi in November 2014. Her testimony introduces the role of women during the uprisings in Redeyef. A documentary was produced in 2009 centering on her accounts of the events entitled: "Laila Khaled, La Tunisienne" and is accessible on YouTube: (Chaîne de JaniJamel, 2009).

© Springer Fachmedien Wiesbaden GmbH, part of Springer Nature 2019
A. Antonakis, *Renegotiating Gender and the State in Tunisia between 2011 and 2014*, Politik und Gesellschaft des Nahen Ostens,
https://doi.org/10.1007/978-3-658-25639-5_7

the foreshock of the uprisings of 2010/2011. There are several reasons that justify subscription to this narrative:

Analysts consider the protests of 2008/2009 as the most important social uprisings since Ben Ali took power in 1987 (Remili, 2011) and they have been framed as an outcome of the neoliberal "structural adjustment policies" introduced in the 1980s. Tunisian author Boujemaa Remili has pointed to the structural communalities between the Gouvernorats Gafsa and Sidi Bouzid in terms of socio-economic inequalities since the post-colonial period (Remili, 2011, p. 13). They can both be considered "marginalized localities", produced by national state policies, as I have argued in chapter IV. Activists from Redeyef claim to have been the first to chant the slogans that were later reproduced all over the country and in the capital ("Work, freedom and national dignity") in 2010/2011. The leaders of the uprisings, some of them members of the local syndicate UGTT, were at the time calling on the people for *peaceful contestation*, a tactic that was also common during the uprisings 2010/2011.

The Gafsa governorate had the highest unemployment rates in Tunisia for people between the ages of 15 and 29 with levels reaching 52.8% and 46.5% for those with a graduate degree in 2010[74] (Institut National Statistiques). While the export of phosphate is one of the main pillars of the Tunisian economy, the region that is home to this resource has one of the lowest infrastructure and living standards in Tunisia. Redeyef is a town situated within the Gafsa governorate and mining area. It is the terminus of the railway line Redeyef-Métlaoui, which is used for transportation of phosphate and is situated next to the Algerian border. Métlaoui is then connected to the SNCFT infrastructure through which phosphate reaches the cities of Sfax and Gabes for further processing.

The initial trigger of the uprisings in 2008 was the publication of the selection of employees by the „Companie des phosphates de Gafsa" (CPG), which is anchored as "the only alternative to poverty" (Allal, 2012, p. 825). State-ownership and the exploitation of phosphate mines play a crucial role for the region as its main employer. Over the last 20 years, the state-owned company that runs the phosphate industry has been required to reduce its workforce in accordance with the reform program "mise à nouveau" set by the International Monetary Fund that started in 1986. Almost two thirds of the work force, equaling 10,000 people, lost their jobs (Allal, 2012, p. 824). The nature of the protesters' demands developed from initial calls for employment to an improvement in working conditions, to more general political demands that targeted the country's center of power, criticizing the widespread practices of nepotism and corruption to a neo-colonial capitalist system. Initially, only workers and political activist took to the streets to voice their concerns, but eventually gained support from students,

---

74 For an analysis of employments statistics in relation to education and region, shedding light on the regional disparities, see (Touhami, 2012).

professors and other sympathetic actors in the region. A driving force behind the mobilizations was the Union of Unemployed Academics (Union des travailleurs chômeurs, UDC), which grew into an institutional presence in the aftermath of the uprisings through the creation of a regional division in 2009 (Antonakis, 2015a). The UDC's presence had, however, been in preparation since 2006 (Al-lal, 2012, p. 824). While the UGTT organized mass strikes in the days before Ben Ali was ousted, the position of the UGTT in 2008 was very different. The agency of the UGTT was very limited in 2008, as national leaders were actually involved in the corrupt contracting procedure. Labidi confirmed this in our interview, recounting that the regional members of the UGTT-Gafsa gave their support at a later date. As a result, the relation between the syndicate and local activists in Redeyef remains shattered until today. Amine Allal finds a mutual finger pointing between local UGTT members and RCD-cadres in his analysis (Allal A. , 2010, p. 180).

Contrary to the uprisings in 2010/2011, the communication infrastructure was also very different in 2008 in that the internet penetration rate was much lower at the time: According to Internetworldstats, it was 17% for Tunisia, corresponding to some 1,765,430 users in 2008. The famous blogger Lina Ben Mhenni points to this in her 2013 book by asking the question: "What if we already had Facebook during the uprisings in Redeyef?" (Ben Mheni, 2013). At the same time, it is from 2008 onwards that rapid changes to internet infrastructure can be observed. The national report on Tunisia by the (Open Net Initiative, 2009) asserts that: "Government-brokered 'free internet' programs that provide web access for the price of a local telephone call and increased competition among ISPs have significantly reduced the economic barriers to internet access."

In the classical media landscape, only the TV channel Al-Hiwar El-Tounsi ("The Tunisian dialogue"), run by the leftist intellectual Tahar Ben Hassine, covered the events. At the time, the TV channel had a limited volume of broadcasting hours and, due to constant interventions by the regime, Al-Hiwar El-Tounsi was forced to broadcast from Great Britain via a South-American satellite signal and later via an Italian company (Khechana, 2009, p. 102). Instead of sending their own staff to report from the ground, the channel delivered some basic equipment to local activists.[75] This allowed for a well-informed and often more leftist elite in the country to access information about what was going on in the mining region. Al-Jazeera also provided news on the uprisings in the Gafsa (Khechana, 2009, p. 103). However, it can be deduced that the protests of 2008 were absent in the wider public sphere and the creation of a counterpublic was unsteady. The information monopoly by the state, delivering hegemonic ideologies, could not be broken. Although the protests in 2008 were rather isolated,

---

75 This is according to informal talks I conducted with local activists in Redeyef.

some rare video footage of the uprising in Gafsa do exist on the video platform *Dailymotion* (YouTube being blocked at the time). [76]

The crackdown on the growing protests was soon to follow and resulted in mass arrests by the police. The military took part in repressing the rebellion by besieging the cities of Gafsa and blocking access to them (Allal A. , 2010). It hereby assured that the protest remained in a local public and could not challenge the hegemony of the public sphere. By contrast, in 2011 it became clear during the first weeks of the uprising that the military would not shoot at protesters, as decided by Rachid Amar, general and chief of staff of the Tunisian Armed Forces, allowing a revolutionary counterpublic to grow.

Labidi recounts the days of resistance, of police brutality, and of long days of traveling from prison to prison to see her family members, because her husband, Bechir, and her son, Moudhafer, were both imprisoned. She highlights the fact that after the first arrests of demonstrators, women, sisters, mothers and wives, took to the streets demanding the release of the political prisoners:

> "And then, on April 8th or 9th, it was the women (taking to the street), it was their role: From the morning until the afternoon, we were in front of the administration (*markaz*) and we demonstrated. There was lots lots lots of police. It was almost all the women of Redeyef. The ones who had her father, her husband or even just her neighbor [in prison]. So all the women demonstrated for their release because they were using torture. (…) on the 10th they liberated the political prisoners, so it was a more quiet period and they started negotiations with the government" (Laila Khaled Labidi, Redeyef, November 2014).

What Leila Khaled Labidi describes here is the takeover of the public space by female protesters as a reaction to the mass arrests of their husbands and sons in the town of 27,000 inhabitants. Her narrative of the role of women who were occupying the space in front of the local authorities (*markaz*) sheds light on a highly symbolic strategy: Knowing that the police could not crack down on a women's counterpublic for fear of producing a fierce image of themselves that would endanger the women's rights propaganda (for a similar conclusion, see Chomiak, 2014). This is not to say that women would not have to fear prison and torture in the authoritarian regime: Much less is known, for example, of the fate of Zakia Difawi, who was arrested in July 2008 and sentenced to five months of prison after participating in a demonstration for the release of prisoners. Besides

---

76 One video shows the date of 24th April in the title and is "dedicated to the men and women of Gafsa and more particularly to the people of Redeyef, for their courage and the lessons they have taught us."(*Translation by the author*) http://www.dailymotion. com/video/x56k4e_lotfi-dk-redeyef-2008-tunisie_music;   http://www.dailymotion.com/video/x59e98_redeyef-wledecha3eb-24-04-2008_news.

the interviews conducted during my research, only the Arab Human Rights Institute for civil rights documented her imprisonment.[77]

Leila Khaled Labidi can be regarded as the keeper of a localized collective memory. In the interview, she claimed that "she didn't do anything" during the uprisings of 2010/2011, but watched the developments online and on TV and relates to the more general local discourse:

> "For us in Redeyef, there were almost no protests, nothing big going on in 2011 (…). It was like, we started the revolution and it's on you to finish it; that was the discourse" (Laila Khaled Labidi, Redeyef, November 2014).

Shortly after the Ben Ali's ousting, Labidi was introduced to broader publics: national and international media, activists and scholars visited her house because "they wanted to know what had been going on in 2008." The example of Laila Khaled shows how the unfolding events of 2011 and new publics opening also made the discussion and visibility of events in recent history accessible. She was honored by the ATFD and could establish herself as a new feminist actor with a much broader public to address and as an advocate for transitional justice. Talking to journalists, syndicalists, and researchers, Labidi also gained access to the structural dimension of the public sphere: She participated in the building of new political institutions in Tunisia, by taking part in the commission on elections on the local level (IRIE Gafsa) and giving testimony during a public hearing organized by the Dignity and Truth Commission (Mosaique FM, 2016, 54:10). Besides this institutional involvement, Laila Khaled Labidi represents a revolutionary discourse that is very critical to the further developments of the "transformation" after 2011. For example, the debates in the constituent parliament took place around the issue of whether the people killed during the uprisings of 2008 would be counted as martyrs. In Labidi's eyes, the transitional justice process should also include investigations into the killings and injuries that occurred during the events of 2008 in Gafsa.[78] Another issue requiring attention would be the continued ownership of the land by the state-run phosphate company that the city of Redeyef is built on. As the inhabitants cannot have property of their own, clearly the revolutionary demands were not satisfied. That is to say, the relation of the local public sphere to the state and its institutions as well as the CPG and the sub-contracted transport companies remains the same (Chennaoui, 2015).

---

77 Documented on the monthly bulletin for Civil Rights Watch– civitus http://www.civicus.org/csw_files/CSWMB_Sept-Oct_No39.htm (Civil Society Watch, 2008).

78 Today, the Truth and Dignity Commission, the institution created on constitutional grounds for transitional justice was established on December 10th, 2014 and is charged with processing and investigating state crimes dating back until 1955. Within one month, it received 3,000 complaints and 12,000 complaints in May 2015 (El Gantri, 2015).

7.2   The Uprisings in 2010/2011

On December 17th, Mohamed Bouazizi, a young fruit vendor immolated himself in front of the *markaz,* the local authority in Sidi Bouzid, after a presumed dispute with a female policewoman harassing him. The role of the "national heroes" triggering uprisings in different countries is debated in literature. The mystification of "martyrs" like Khaled Said in Egypt and Mohamed Bouazizi in Tunisia and an overinterpretation of their role in the uprisings have been critically discussed in this context. Ali traces back the history of the fruit vendor who was in the counterpublic being stylized as an unemployed academic. This can be read and has been described by activists as a strategy to create a higher potential for identification. Also, the Union des Diplomés Chômeurs (UDC), who created another office in Sidi Bouzid just before the uprisings, quickly allied themselves with the cause.[79] His public act expressed the despair of a whole generation of young people living in the structurally neglected local public of the interior of the country that has been subjected to corrupt despotism and a lack of infrastructure in culture, transport, jobs and health services.

The mobilizations that were triggered by this individual act can be read as a process of shifting from a counterpublic to the wider public sphere challenging the hegemonic ideals of stability and prospect established by the regime. In the first stage, information on the protests and killings were circulating within social media and satellite TV channels (Al-Jazeera, mainly) in December 2010. The local protests soon reached the national and international public sphere. *YouTube* had been blocked[80] in Tunisia since 2008 so videos were mainly spread via the platforms *Vimeo* and *Dailymotion.* Social media, especially Facebook, were of crucial importance to the spread of information, to communication and to "make sense" of the content and also organize protests. One of the findings of my study conducted in 2011 was that most of my interviewees were informed of the self-immolation of Mohamed Bouazizi on Facebook and followed developments online. The Arab Social Media Report details a similar dynamic. (Dubai School of Government, 2011). However, family and friends and face-to-face contacts remained crucial to gather and distribute "trusted information" (Antonakis, 2012).

---

79 Ali provides many details on Khaled Said's life, a "de-mythologization" of the young man (Ali, 2012). The ambivalence of heroic figures in the uprisings is described by (Armbrust, 2013) who reiterates the story of Sally Zahran, a young woman killed during the uprisings and mystified as an icon.

80 It was made accessible on January 13[th,] 2011, shortly after the final speech of Ben Ali, where he guaranteed more freedoms to the Tunisians. This promise could immediately be verified. As a reaction to this sign of change, activists created a Facebook group called "I won't give up my freedoms for YouTube" to encourage further mobilizations.

Tunisian activists and bloggers such as Azyz Amami, Lina Ben Mheni and So-fiane Chourabi[81] circulated information about the uprisings in the counterpublic sphere. They were shared on (anonymous) profiles, sites on Facebook (for example, "Ma Tunisie" or "Tunis today") or the hashtag #sidibouzid on Twitter (Antonakis, 2012, p.23 ff.). Videos and photos from the events, showing protesters and police violence, were very efficient for mobilization. Also, satellite TV stations played their role in representing and following up on the protests early on, such as the satellite TV station Al-Jazeera, based in Qatar.[82]

The protest, initially a sign of social unrest in the center of the country, became increasingly politicized through a rise of political communication from Sidi Bouzid, over Kasserine, to Sfax and Tunis. The first demonstrations in the capital were led by lawyers and oppositional youth and were only amplified when the youth of the marginalized suburbs of Tunis joined in and confronted the police forces. The opposition knew that it was crucial for them to bring their demands to the capital and thereby to a broader public in order to succeed and bring about a cessation in police violence. Protest in "marginalized localities" alone would not be able to reach wider and international publics.

Another factor of these dynamics was the organization of mass demonstrations by the UGTT, which were held in the cities of Sfax and Sousse on 12th January, 2011, and announced a general strike in Tunis for January 14th. This mobilized tens of thousands of people. Their role as important political actors has been analyzed in literature pertaining to the uprisings and the transformation period that followed (Chayes, 2014). However, the efficiency of the instruments they used, for example the mass strike, has barely been analyzed. This could be particularly interesting with regards to the unity between the political and economic struggle that characterizes mass strikes according to Laclau and Mouffe, building on Rosa Luxemburg's 1906 work "The Mass Strike, the Political Party and the Trade Unions" (Laclau & Mouffe, 1985, p. 8). This under-thematization of the mass strike can be regarded as symptomatic for the decoupling process of socio-economic rights and political rights during the transformation process.

The dynamics between the web and the streets finally broke the information monopoly of the state in the public sphere. Against the background of the information that was given by state TV and official press channels, I have reframed the information and communication spaces created online as *anti-state counterpublics*. Those who were using social media and actively circumventing internet

---

81 See for example their testimonies on YouTube in the frame of the online project "memories of a journalist" https://www.youtube.com/watch?v=l8h5yv9BTf0. With regards to recent developments in the state and the region, those attempts to keep counterpublic memories and knowledge recorded appear to be an important tool to reconstruct history.

82 In the next chapter on the transformation period, I will briefly address the shift in the perception of the Qatari satellite TV station in Tunisia.

censorship to acquire information can be regarded as internet activists. They accessed and shared information challenging the hegemonic domain of power. Emphasizing the dynamics within the online counterpublics should not at the same time downplay the role of young men and women who were literally fighting in the streets, nor neglect the interaction and overlapping of different forms of activism. According to the official report investigating the crimes of the security forces, 338 people were killed and more than 2000 injured during the uprisings between 17 December 2010 and March 2011 (Bouderbala, 2012).

During the uprisings, Ben Ali addressed the nation in three televised speeches. The last one, on January 13th, is particularly important because Ben Ali addressed Tunisians in the Tunisian dialect for the first time, thus demonstrating that he had understood the demands of the people (*"Ana fahamtkoum"*). He announced that he would not be candidate for the elections in 2014 and promised to implement measures to fight regional disparities in Tunisia and create jobs. The lift of the internet censorship system was announced and put in place immediately after the speech as a final attempt by the regime to calm the situation. However, the protesters did not consider the liberation of the online sphere to be enough. This is documented by the Facebook group called "I won't give up my freedoms for YouTube" that was founded after Ben Ali's speech on the 13th January 2011. According to my empirical studies, I started by the beginning of January 2011, their members rose to 17,000 within 18 hours (Antonakis, 2012).

I argue that the processes described below were vital in triggering the shift in the public sphere: At first, videos and photos were the materials mostly shared by internet activists to convince people to join them by giving them proof about what was actually going on in the country, penetrating the representational dimension of the public sphere and challenging the hegemonic ideology of safety and stability that the authoritarian state claimed to provide. The classical media were silent about the uprisings and the regime's authoritarian reaction to the demonstrations. However, an information flow of videos showing the protests, as well as injured and dead Tunisians, was developing in the counterpublics situated at the interface of online and offline spaces: From previous studies, I learned that many activists actively communicated information they acquired online in their local communities by visiting other neighborhoods. They reached out to those who might not be informed or didn't have internet access and showed them materials on their phones (Antonakis, 2012, 52 f.). Activists aimed to address the information gap within the state-owned public sphere using all tools available to them. Secondly, in the first days after the uprisings, internet activists were aware that the flux of information needed to be approved and guided somehow: Recognizing the downside of social media as having the potential for high levels of *intox* (i.e. wrong information or often purposely falsified news, nowadays it would simply be translated as "fake news") as well as problems in the verification of information due to the speed of its dissemination in the 'many-to-many' framework. Thirdly, projects like the swarm *Anonymous* and *Wikileaks* certainly helped to bring the demands of the activists to an international public sphere. While *Wikileaks* cables published in September-December 2010 proved the corruption of the Ben Ali regime and his family, Anonymous recruited hacktivists from all over the world to take part in Operation Payback starting on the 2nd of January. Gabriella Coleman, indubitably the most distinguished researcher of Anonymous, states that the operation in the Tunisian uprising was the first time that Anonymous engaged as a political actor:

"Although Anonymous initially intervened to stamp out censorship, the same team continued to lend a helping hand as country after country in the region underwent revolution. Individuals organized in a dedicated AnonOps chat room, and the operations became collectively known as the 'Freedom Ops'" (Coleman 2013, p. 7).

While the role of Anonymous during the uprising is still under debate, they constitute an important element in the analysis of shifting publics as they are a solely online phenomenon that helped to draw the international mass media's attention to Tunisia.

With Ben Ali fleeing the country in 2011, the priorities of the information and communication flows within the counterpublics changed drastically. The hegemonic public sphere was liberated from authoritarian rule, the internet censorship system was dismantled, people now took to the streets for various demonstrations, and the regime's editorial lines did not dictate the content of audio-visual and print media anymore. I find that in this specific period, a mosaic of publics was set in vibration, the hegemonic domain of power was yet to be defined and the "field of democratic struggles" was widened (Laclau & Mouffe, 2014 p.xvii).

During the four weeks of the uprisings, categories and conflict lines within society, such as gender, religiosity, party affiliations and geographical location, were almost invisible. The head of the nation state, his family and the RCD party were perceived as the main constructors of the Matrix of Domination, incorporating various structures of oppression that affected everybody in the country. The system was challenged on the basis of a national category that over time united different segments of the society (Zayani, 2015, p. 74) and can be considered the driving force behind the uprisings. However, eventually, issues related to security, religion and gender re-appeared in the public sphere initiating a struggle over state–power. Also, "political identities were "constituted and re-constituted" (Laclau & Mouffe, 2014 p.xvii). through debate, protest and other (also violent) interventions in the public sphere. The question of gender was now addressed in terms of the maintenance of rights for women in the new Tunisian state. The fear of an Islamist movement that could fill the power vacuum underpinned these claims and can be regarded as the main reason for the re-appearance of gender politics and feminist mobilizations in different dimensions of the public sphere. As we have seen, after the independence struggles of colonial times and the *coup* against Habib Bourguiba, the same function of gender politics was also present in discussions regarding the (re-)distribution of power within the state.

In the following chapter, I will scrutinize these renegotiations within the developed theoretical framework. I contend that it is in the synopsis of the different dimensions of the public sphere, and their reciprocal relationship with the four domains of power, that the exploitation of gender relations becomes clear.

7.3   Menzel Bouzayane and the Kasbah Square Moment

I have previously argued that a re-modelization of the Tunisian case was established in reference to the "procedural democracy" in the so-called transformation period. Against this background, it is important to highlight that the Tunisian roadmap was not decided by the first provisional government, but put in place by the revolutionary sit-in of the Kasbah. These protests brought down the two first post-revolution interim governments (Boubakeur, 2015), demanded the dissolution of the RCD party and the elaboration of a new constitution. Therefore, it was not a result of negotiations taking place in institutions at the structural dimension of the public sphere, but rather pushed through by the protesters occupying the urban public space in the crucial weeks after Ben Ali's ousting.

Accordingly, I start the analysis of the changes at the structural dimension of the public sphere by presenting a counterpublic operating at the interactional dimension of the public sphere. The protests targeted the structural domain of power and actually succeeded in pushing through demands that would lead to a political transformation. However, the institutional outcomes of the Kasbah protests did not prevent them from being re-marginalized in the transformation process that followed. Also, their place in the historical narrative on the "Tunisian Revolution" and transformation appears narrow. This can partly be explained by the international focus at the time on the uprisings in Egypt and the UN intervention in Libya.

The marches organized by activists from the cities of Sidi Bouzid, Gabes and the Gafsa governorate to the capital, starting from Menzel Bouzayane[83] were

---

83 Menzel Bouzayane is a town of 6,000 inhabitants situated in the governorate of Sidi Bouzid. Shortly after Bouazizi's immolation, uprisings broke out which is why it is considered the town where the first "martyr" had died in the clashes with the police. Journalist and political scientist Thomas Léger, who has worked extensively on the UDC, argues that it remains until this day a space of resistance (Léger, 2014).

dubbed as the "liberation caravan" or "dignity caravan"[84] or simply "the protest march towards the capital" (*Kalfala Ettahir, Kalfala Karama, Masirat aihtijajiat fi aittijah aleasima*) and initiated the Kasbah I (from 22/23rd/until the 28th January) and Kasbah II movements (20th February 2011 until 6th March).

Protesters held sit-ins and occupied the Kasbah square, situated in front of the Prime Ministry in the city center of Tunis, to demand the first interim government that was headed by Prime Minister Mohamed Ghannouchi to step down and hold elections for a constitutional parliament. A young protester from Menzel Bouzayane, interviewed by journalists of *Nawaat,* remembers what pushed them to actively transgress local boundaries, march to the capital and occupy the *Kasbah* Square:

"We felt the danger of a counterrevolution. That's why we were thinking of a novel idea, consisting in occupying the square of the Kasbah, symbolizing the political power. The other day, we started the march [to the capital]. After a while, a number of towns joined in and we finally took buses and cars to get to our destination on the same day" (interview with Safouen Bouzid in: Chennaoui H., 2015).

The space was highly contested: protesters were dispersed from the *Kasbah* by tear gas and other forms of violence. One week after Ghannouchi had announced the elimination of all RCD ministers from the first transitional government, the first sit-in had been violently repressed. During the sit-in, the walls of the Prime Ministry were tagged with slogans in Arabic and French, as well as stencils and works of graffiti, which expressed the protesters' political contestations on the one hand and a re-appropriation of the urban space on the other. However, after the dispersion of the sit-in, the walls were whitewashed and there is no longer a reminder of these times in public space in Tunis.

The protesters returned to the *Kasbah* about one month later to try again to expel Ghannouchi from the interim government. The police again employed force to disperse the crowd. However, during the second sit-in the protesters were well organized. Adding to that, the legitimacy of their protest had resulted

---

84 In Anglophone representation, the protest march from the center west of the country to the capital are often referred to as the "caravan of freedom," changing slightly the sense of the protest from liberation to freedom. This can be explained by the similarities in French of "liberté" and "libération," but makes a difference, as the former concept encapsulates firstly an oppressor from which one wants to be "liberated" and secondly points to a process, while the concept of "freedom" lacks these two crucial elements. In videos from the scene, however, protesters speak of either "ettahir," or "karama". See the YouTube videos from the 22nd January 2011: the first from Menzel Bouzayane (Mr. Abassi 2007, 2011 during the day, the second when the caravan passes by in Kairouan, on their way to Tunis (according to the caption) in the evening: (afrit 1975, 2011).

in increasing support from the inhabitants of Tunis. [85]

The relation between the liberation caravan coming from the center of the country and the *Kasbah* protests remain highly undocumented in literature engaging with urban spaces as spaces of protest and their symbolic significance in Tunis[86]. However, their conceptualization is highly relevant for the *Kasbah* protest, where the local and the imaginary nation are linked. One important exception in literature represents Choukri Hmed's analysis, where he conceptualizes the *Kasbah* protests of 2011 as a synchronization of space and time (Hmed, 2011, p. 74).

I hold that these marches and the occupation of the formerly highly monitored public space illustrate the battle against the hegemonic and disciplinary domain of power. Actors from "beyond the center" occupied the centers of power with their bodies, their tents and their demands. Furthermore, the regional components of the occupation are, to my knowledge, unique in the protests and occupations of squares in the capitals of Yemen, Egypt and elsewhere at the time. Of course, the small size of the country made moving to the capital a relatively easy endeavor. Judith Butler concludes with regards to the numerous forms of public protest that have been seen in urban spaces since 2011, "for politics to take place, the body must appear" (Butler, 2011).

The *protesting bodies* were mostly men who, by virtue of their locality, had previously been excluded from the public sphere, and, in light of the analysis of the Tunisian revolutions, continue to remain on the periphery of the national public sphere. Locality can also be considered a factor in the process of racialization when it is noted that in the Tunisian dialect, the word *tamaiouz* is used for both "racism" and "discrimination based on locality" interchangeably.

Abdesselem Mahmoud, Head of the Town Planning Department at the University of Carthage, cites Manuel Castells in his analysis of the urban protests at the time and integrates the dimension of new technologies as creating a "space of autonomy" and a "third space":

> "They reach togetherness, a space of autonomy and occupied places (Bourguiba Avenue, Kasbah 1, 2 and some called for Kasbah 3 and 4, Bardo place across the ANC headquarter...). As Manuel

---

85 I remember an incident that I observed while participating in one of the (numerous) debates in Tunis in a theater during the first days of March 2011. It was organized by a newly founded initiative to debate what the future constitution should look like. The public consisted mainly of a cultivated urban middle class. Shortly after the beginning, the doors opened and two self-identified *Kasbah* protesters entered, denouncing the event vocally and wondering why nobody had thought of inviting the people, or at least a "delegation" from the *Kasbah* protesters. After his announcement, some twenty to thirty protesters from the *Kasbah* rushed in. A feeling of shame was to be perceived in the public, including myself, sitting in the red theater chairs for not having invited those who had been squatting in the Kasbah and fighting the police for weeks to demand a constitutional process, while we were debating what this constitution should look like in safety. Symbolically, most of us got up to offer our chairs to the new arrivals, however, it felt like a gesture of embarrassment, because for a real act of solidarity, it certainly came too late.

86 For a non-recognition see for example (AlSayyad & Guvenc, 2013, p.4f.), (Tripp, 2015).

Castells argued: This hybrid of cyberspace and urban space constitutes a third space that I call the space of autonomy. This is because autonomy can only be insured by the capacity to organize in the free space of communication networks, but at the same time can only be exercised as a transformative force by challenging the disciplinary institutional order by reclaiming the space of the city for its citizen (Castells, 2012:222)" (Mahmoud, 2014, p. 54).

In a similar vein, an oppositional journalist described the innovative protest elements as illustrating the connection of the on- an offline space and the interplay of "cyberspace and urban space" as a "third space" in the frame of the *Kasbah* protests in an interview I conducted in 2011:

> "As soon as an information was confirmed by three people, we considered it as right and we informed the people at the Kasbah. At the Kasbah, there was a journalist who somehow functioned as an 'office of the Kasbah' and was connected with a 3G and she was always there to secure the information" (M.D., Tunis, March 2011).

The Kasbah protesters did not only demand a structural shift in the public sphere but actively produced this shift by taking over the public space and creating a third space. Controls of the police had previously monitored closely and prohibited these bodies from entering the capital. On that account, during the sit in, their locality of origin was emphasized by indications on each tent, stating the hometown of the protesters. Amel Amrawy, who took part in the Kasbah occupation, remembers:

> "At Kasbah 2, we demanded the establishment of a constituent assembly (…) We had a tent of the preparatory school and the engineering school, we were together in that tent and there were no problems at all. What was impressive though was that I got the impression to be in a global village. There was a tent from Gabes, from Gafsa and so on..." (Amel Amrawy, Tunis, May 2014).

What Amrawy describes as a "global village," illustrates the structural change in the public sphere when the Matrix of Domination was deconstructed for a certain period of time and the oppressive structure of locality as constituting the public sphere drained[87]. As an activist from the capital, Amrawy enjoyed the structural shift engendering relations in the square, not only based on locality but also the gender mixed occupation, which created "no problems at all".

As well as creating a moment of "togetherness" which, I claim, marked not only a Tunisian generation, the protests could also exert political pressure: Ghannouchi, who had served as prime minister for over twelve years in the regime of Ben Ali resigned on 27th of February 2011, and was proceeded by Beji Caïd Essebsi. Essebsi, the elected president since 2014, shall become one of the most important architects of post-revolutionary Tunisia. He continued his political career, despite his public announcement stating his refrainment from running for highest political office (Preysing, 2015, p.80). An experienced politician in the Bourguiba cabinet, he occupied the posts of the Ministry of the Interior, of Defense and of Foreign Affairs and was a close confidant and admirer of the first president. After having integrated the RCD, and being elected deputy, he later became President of Parliament, a position he had already occupied from 1990 until 1991. He remained deputy until 1994 and hence cannot be regarded as "independent", despite his claims to the contrary (Boubakeur, 2015, p. 5). The appearance of Béji Caïd Essebsi on the political scene has been analyzed as the starting point of the end of a revolutionary process that would overthrow the old system, and instead mark the establishment of a "bargained competition":

> "The endorsement of Essebsi as a Destourian technocrat set the stage for the political comeback of old regime members and their networks. Essebsi's interim government may have agreed to disband the RCD and the secret police, but only second-rank RCD members and businessmen were in fact tried for corruption; the majority of Ben Ali's close associates were allowed to exit the country" (Boubakeur, 2015, p. 6).

After the replacement of Ghannouchi by Essebsi, the sit-ins continued to demand that Interim President Mebazza step down, increasingly feeling that the fruits of their struggle thus far would only benefit the urban elites (Ayari M. G., 2011). Protests in May and July of 2011, demanding that Essebsi step down, were dubbed Kasbah 3 protests, however, they were violently repressed. From now

---

87 In response to the liberation caravans that initiated the *Kasbah* protests between February and March 2011[87], the citizens of Tunis (*'Tunisois'*) organized the solidarity caravans ("caravans de solidarité") that travelled to the South and center of the country in January 2011. These two marches can be seen as symbolic renegotiations of locality, while shifting the narrative from one of liberation (from the periphery to the center) to "solidarity" (from the center to the periphery), illustrating the urban-rural divide of the country. In the first caravans, the people from the capital were welcomed by their hosts, however, the expression of solidarity was highly criticized by an activist interviewed in March 2011: "There were two or three caravanes de solidarité (solidarity marches) towards Sidi Bouzid. What? Girls with makeup with the Tunisian flag taking pictures. That's not what it is about!"[87] (Slim*, Tunis, March 2011). While at the beginning, the counterpublic from the interior of the country was acting towards "liberation," it was turned into a discourse of "solidarity" that was based on victimization. The Matrix of Domination, organizing locality as a structure of oppression has reinstalled the dependency between the capital and the center of the country.

on, these protests were delegitimized and regarded as threatening the political and economic stability of the country (Boubakeur, 2015, p. 6), marking a slow re-establishment of the hegemonic power in the public sphere.

Part II
Analyzing Negotiations of Gender in different Dimensions of the Public Sphere in Tunisia (2011-2014)

This study investigates how gender relations are renegotiated in this multifaceted web of (counter-)publics, taking a variety of possible modes of communication into account, which challenge, build, interpret, and alter the different structures that define the hegemonic domain of power. Drawing on intersectional methodology, I put specific emphasis on different narratives that were voiced by the participants of this study. This responds to the need to further differentiate counterpublics in the regional context in order to do justice to the complexities of power structures creating subordinated positions. To introduce this relation empirically, I will give the example of locality and class hereafter. Departing from the framework of the public sphere within Matrices of Domination, I quote Amany Ltifi, a 24-year-old activist from Sidi Bouzid, who sees the capitalist system as the main cause of her oppression:

> "I see for example that men and women are suffering on the same level with regards to the state. Here I speak from the perspective of class struggle. The day that the men will be liberated, the women will be liberated as well. Nevertheless, women suffer from a double colonization: first within the family in the region, and second from the nation as a whole" (Amany Ltifi, Sidi Bouzid, April 2014).

Ltifi points to a "double" oppression: she mentions the family situated within the region on one hand, and the state on the other. Weaving together the family and their locality points to the importance of regional disparities in internal family structures. The state appears here as a producer of marginalized localities. Ltifi thus sees how women and men [of her region] suffer from the state's economic oppression and believes that ending this oppression will alter norms conveyed within the family as well. The specific feeling of oppression related to locality mirrors a systematic marginalization.

Amany Ltifi has clarified in the interview that she understands her activism within the broader framework of an anti-capitalist class struggle. Adding to that, she elaborates on the patriarchal structures affecting her activism, explaining that she is not happy with the situation and that her region offers almost no spaces for women, claiming that she would be the only woman in the meetings with her comrades from the workers party and the UDC. At the same time, she discusses how she empowers her female friends to take up a more active role in politics, demonstrations or their lives in general, and communicates this through social networks (see Interview Ameni Ltifi, Sidi Bouzid, April 2014, p.9 f.).

Her activism can be situated within the differentiation of counterpublics as laid out by Fraser, whereby "for some less privileged women, access to public life came through participation in supporting roles in male-dominated, working class protest activities. Still other women found public outlets in street protests and parades" (Fraser, 1992, p. 61). This understanding is problematic on the following grounds: Ltifi is not only engaging in a "supportive role" but leads marches herself and explains that she would often also act as a mediator, based on her experiences acquired during various demonstrations. Furthermore, she claims to be asked her opinion on different issues within the counterpublic owing to her actions therein. The workers movement constitutes a space of participation for her, and she participates actively within this counterpublic.

In light of this introductory illustration of the intersection between empirical findings and methodological and theoretical considerations, I will now turn to the part of the analysis presenting different women's counterpublics encountering patriarchal power structures that I situate in the three dimensions of the public sphere: the structural, the representational and the interactional. In the following, I will provide an analysis according to several dimensions of the public sphere, their interaction with power and a closer examination of the relation between the hegemonic domain of power and counterpublic spheres for the period under investigation from 2011 until 2014.

8 The Structural Dimension of the Public Sphere

This chapter engages with the changes in the structural dimension of the public sphere, focusing on the negotiations of institutions that would limit and open up access to the public sphere in a gendered analysis. I employ the term of political transformation with reference to the new state institutions that were created following the Tunisian uprisings, namely, the interim governmental institutions, the Independent High Authority for Elections (Instance Superieure Indépendante pour les Elections, ISIE), which prepared the elections of 2011 and 2014, the National Constituent Assembly (Assemblée Nationale Constituante, ANC) and, most prominently, the new Tunisian constitution of 2014. This specification with regards to political transformation aims also to clarify the theorization of state institutions and their implication in structuring hegemonic publics as well as counterpublics.[88] Nevertheless, many of the interviewees outright refused the term 'transformation', pointing to a non-identification with the institutional process.

It can be stated that even before the constitutional parliament could start its work in November 2011, the discourse in the Tunisian public sphere already revolved around gender constituting the "political frontline in the new Tunisian identity politics" (Gray, 2012, p. 285f.) and "[w]omen's rights stood out as one of the most fiercely contested issues in the campaigning that preceded Tunisia's October 23, 2011 elections" (Marks, 2013, p. 224). I argue that the renegotiation of gender at the structural dimension of the public sphere was deeply influenced by the hegemonic domain of power. This claim empirically grounds Yuval-Davis' theorization of women as not only the biological, but also the "cultural reproducers of the nation" (Yuval-Davis, 1997, p. 116). Norms and values, constituting the hegemonic domain of power, were being redefined within the nation and its institutions. Andrea Khalil concludes for the post-revolutionary period how "the women's status (...) was embedded within an ideological debate between 'Islamist' and 'secularist' discourse" (Khalil, 2014, p. 197). The following will go into more detail and trace the roots of this dynamic, which mainly took place in the structural dimension of the public sphere.

---

88 Yuval-Davis points to the need to theorize state, nation and civil society separately in order to allow an in depth analysis of gender relations and nationalist projects (Yuval-Davis,1997, p. 12).

© Springer Fachmedien Wiesbaden GmbH, part of Springer Nature 2019
A. Antonakis, *Renegotiating Gender and the State in Tunisia between 2011 and 2014*, Politik und Gesellschaft des Nahen Ostens,
https://doi.org/10.1007/978-3-658-25639-5_8

I have analyzed this political transformation according to three different phases elsewhere (Antonakis, 2015a). The first is constituted by the time between the Kasbah protest and includes the elections of October 2011. The second phase encompasses the time of the TROIKA government. The third phase of the transformation, triggered by the Bardo Protests of August 2013, leading to the installation of a technocratic government (Joyce, 2015), is characterized by the conservative, consensus-oriented politics that were reproduced within a staged polarization, paving the way for elections between October and December 2014.

I hold that this chronological approach proves helpful in tackling the contestations over political institutions: The analysis focuses on gender and family commodification, in particular, those that could lead to the return of cadres of the previous regime(s). However, tracing changes on the institutional dimension constitutes only one part, and certainly the most researched one, to understand the complex dynamics of gender renegotiations and is completed with the findings of chapters IX and X of this study.

8.1   Redefining Legislations for Gendered Inclusivity

With the ousting of President Zine el-Abidine Ben Ali, who left Tunisian soil on January 14th, 2011 to seek exile in Saudi Arabia, the country's hegemonic ideologies were renegotiated in public sphere. The subsequent decision to elect a constituent assembly was an important step towards restructuring the Tunisian public sphere under new premises: respecting human rights, promoting socioeconomic justice as well as individual and press freedoms. Under PM Mohamed Ghannouchi, who stayed in office until the end of February 2011, the Ministry of Communication was completely abolished, political prisoners were freed and organizations like the Tunisian League for Human Rights were allowed to operate publicly.

During this first phase, the "Higher Commission for the Fulfillment of Revolutionary Goals, Political Reform, and Democratic Transition" (Haute Instance pour la Réalisation des Objectifs de la Revolution, des Réformes Politiques et de la Transition Démocratique, HIROR) took a leading role. It was an interim government body created via an emergency decree on 17th February 2011 and was issued by interim president Fouad Mebaza, coming into effect on 6th March 2011. The commission was the product of various institutionalization processes that followed Ben Ali's ousting and consisted of the "National Council for the Protection of the Revolution" (Conseil National de Protection de la Révolution, CNPR) and the "Political Reform Commission" (Commission Supérieure de la Réforme Politique). In this phase, even the "The Front of January 14th" (Front du 14 Janvier), consisting of leftist opposition forces, who had initially rejected the idea of joining any political institutions, eventually joined the CNPR. The latter was established on February 11th and included human rights organizations, Ennahda, the UGTT and the lawyers' bar organization.

Furthermore, Prime Minister Ghannouchi appointed a number of secularist and young intellectuals to the new government. For example, the scholar Lilia Labidi was appointed Minister of Family and Women's Affairs, while Slim Amamou, who was arrested on January 6th along with his fellow activist Azyz Amami, took the position of the State Secretary for Youth and Sports in the interim government. In the following, I will look at the "first round" of the debate on the women's quota taking place within the HIROR to illustrate the specific negotiation on the codification of women's access to the parliament as a "strong public." Second, I will identify the changes in civil society law and finally, the first democratic elections as instruments to manage and define inclusions and exclusions to the Tunisian public sphere.

8.1.1 Negotiations within HIROR: The Women's Electoral Quota

By 8th March 2011 provisional President Fouad Mebazza bowed to pressure of the Kasbah protests and announced direct constitutional elections. The assembly would firstly be charged with drafting a new constitution for Tunisia within one year and secondly, with serving as a legislative body during the transitional phase. The High Commission for the Fulfillment of Revolutionary Goals, Political Reform and Democratic Transition (HIROR) was created and mandated to elaborate the new electoral code. After public contestation, Ennahda left the HIROR in June 2011, accusing it of not respecting rules of consensus and lacking democratic legitimacy (Naudé, 2011). The Commission presided over by law professor Yadh Ben Achour laid an important foundation for the next steps in the political process: Its composition (that had continuously expanded its number of members since March 2011 until its final board) mirrored the struggles over inclusiveness and charted the dynamics for the following process. The process followed a participatory approach, "fostering legitimacy, national ownership, and the inclusion of diverse groups" (Tamaru, Holt-Ivry, O'Reilly, 2018, p. 1). The composition of this institution mirrors the inclusiveness of the structural dimension of the public sphere, where basic rules and norms of the future nation-state would be negotiated.

The Commission was one of four, besides the National Commission for the Establishment of Facts about Corruption, The Commission to establish the Abuses and Violations against the Population since December 17th and fourth, the High Commission for the Elections (Khalil, 2014, p. 195). HIROR was composed of two committees: The "Expert Committee" and the "Committee of Representatives". These, in turn, were composed of political parties, representatives of neglected regions, journalists, feminists, martyrs, as well as various NGOs. While the composition charts the attempt to present inclusive bodies, male membership dominated both committees: the former having six female members out of a total of 18 and the latter 36 out of a total of 155 (Khalil, 2014, p. 194). A negotiation of the structural limitations of the public sphere that would challenge the patriarchal hegemonic public sphere must be read against the background of these quantitative inequalities as they can be regarded, I argue, as an important element of the disciplinary domain of power still influential at the institutional level.

However, the women participating in these commissions, despite their low numbers and owing to the strength of their resources, were able to participate (significantly) at the structural domain of power. It was feminist figures such as Ahlem Belhaj from the ATFD and Noura Borsali (both listed as independent "national personalities" and interviewed for this study); Saida Ben Garrach, (officially representing the ATFD); and Radia Bel Haj Zekri (representing AFTURD in the High Commission), that vitalized debates on women's rights within the institutions they were party to[89]. According to their testimonies, debates focused on how to increase women's participation in politics in the years to come. The represented feminists were especially vocal in pushing for women's quotas in democratic institutions. Borsali remembers the days of these struggles and recalls the resistance they encountered from within the HIROR when they called for electoral quotas:

> "At this time, when we were at the High Commission, we could do many things, you know. The parity law [for the electoral lists], we had to impose it! Because under the former prime minister, who is Béji Caïd Essebsi, who is nowadays coming back. He is 86 years old and he is the head of the country. It was him who refused to go along with the parity law. We made a sit-in and so on. We imposed the parity! And then imagine if you have to impose [already] the quota for men and women, how can you impose that the women are on the head of the list in 50%? It is his [Caïd Essebsi's] ambiguous vision of gender equality that prevented us from progressing" (Noura Borsali, Tunis, May 2013).

Note that Borsali refers to Beji Caïd Essebsi as the "head of the country" long before he was elected president in 2014. His opposition to parity, mentioned in the quote, may come as a surprise considering women's rights and gender equality were important pillars of Nidaa Tounes' party identity that he would go on to form in 2012 and place in direct opposition to the Islamic Ennahda party. In

---

89 The document listing the different members of the institution by category and affiliations at the official site of the Tunisian Government: http://www.tunisie.gov.tn/index.php?option=com_content&task=view&id=1488&Itemid=518&lang=french

Noura Borsali's account, it becomes clear that the renegotiation of gender in the structural dimension demanded specific efforts by women, who had to use extraordinary means ('sit-ins') to impose their wish for the fulfillment of quotas for the first elections.

Against this background, the promulgation of the parity law of the electoral code, which codified their aim in legislative text, can be read as a success by the established feminists, who had already learned to navigate the pressures exerted upon them by the disciplinary domain of power under the former regime. Voted on April 11th of 2011, the law requires 50% of candidates on the election lists to be female. Furthermore, the law even established the principle of *alternance* of male and female candidates, preventing political parties from privileging men in their internal hierarchy. Civil-society organizations and national and international media outlets alike have largely celebrated the adoption of the parity law in Tunisia.

Tunisia could claim an exceptional position in the MENA region, as this law was the first of its kind in the Arab-speaking world.[90] AFTURD qualifies it as an "historical turning point," as the law recognizes women's rights to political participation and access to public space.[91] However, this discursive and legislative commitment to gender mainstreaming lacked the notion of "horizontality." This principle would not only make parties and independent lists to alternate between male and female candidates, but also between the heads of lists. According to Noura Borsali, quoted above, resistance from the secular camp had prevented the establishment of complete parity in the electoral lists. The majority of parties were reluctant to nominate women for their electoral campaign as heads of the lists. In the end, only 6% of the heads of the lists were women. And it was only the leftist party Pôle Démocratique Moderne that showed a voluntary commitment to apply alternating parity up to the head of the lists (Antonakis, 2012; Haddaoui, 2014).

This general pattern exemplifies the limits of an exclusive analysis of the structural dimension in that it neglects the domains of power that interfere with it. A concrete case being that patriarchal norms preventing parties from nominating women to the top of their lists because of a perceived lack of votes during

---

90 See, for example, the article of the AWID organization, which is stresses the aspect of Tunisia being the first country to introduce the parity extensively: http://www.awid.org/fre/Actualites-et-Analyses/Dossier-du-Vendredi/Tunisie-Une-nouvelle-loi-institue-la-parite-totale-lors-des-prochaines-elections-de-l-Assemblee-constituante
91 See an interview with Radhia Bel Haj Zekri, Presidente of AFTURD (Association des Femmes Tunisiennes pour la Recherche et le Développement) with the international organization AWID: https://www.awid.org/fr/nouvelles-et-analyse/tunisia-new-electoral-law-prescribes-gender-parity-upcoming-constituent

elections. The party's reluctance is comprehensible, because of a of a proven gap of representation of female candidates in the media and a smaller chance to be elected.[92]

8.1.2 Institutionalizing a Pluralist Public Sphere?

Besides the quotas that would prepare the ground for a greater representation of female politicians, I regard the reform of the civil society law as another institution shifting access to the structural dimension of the public sphere. The interim government passed the reform on civil society law (n° 2011-88) on 24th September 2011, which allowed the creation of new associations, leading the way, on the structural dimension, to establish a more vibrant landscape at the interactional dimension. Associations, initiatives and networks could engage in institutionalization and professionalization, work openly and acquire money from local or international donors[93]. With the reform, the responsible institution for approval for the creation of an association was no longer the Interior Minister, but the General State Secretary (Association Tunisienne de Gouvernance, 2014). Before this, the arbitrary practices of the Ministry of the Interior had prevented the official registration of many counterhegemonic organizations. Consequently, the number of organizations and associations has almost doubled from 9,969 associations registered in 2010 to more than 17,000 in 2014.

Hayet Amami founded the "Association for the Victory of the Rural Woman" together with trusted friends in Sidi Bouzid in July 2012. In the interview, she specifically references this law and contrasts it with the former situation where only money and contacts would prove to be effective when trying to obtain an official registration for an association:

> "I asked 1000 questions, I took papers and formulas, I went to the administration and they told me 'no, this is not the moment, you can't do this now. Do you have anybody who supports you?' At Ben Ali's time, when you didn't have a person with you, who is really a chief executive or a director or manager, something like that, you couldn't do anything! I said: 'No, I'm just a simple citizen and I'm unemployed'. So he told me: 'Go back home, you have no rights here' and he also revealed the real reasons for his refusal saying: 'You don't have money, you don't have people who support you, you don't have a space' and all of this.' [...] After that, with Article 88, that was created by Yachia Ben Achour for the reform of

---

92 For a presentation and interpretation of the media monitoring reports as conducted by the ATFD and others, see chapter 9.1.

93 I analyze the issue of foreign funding in more detail 10.1.1. because it impacts the possibilities of creating counterpublics at the interactional dimension of the public sphere.

the association, [this has changed]. I was very happy and so we got started" (Hayet Amami, Sidi Bouzid, April 2014).

The example of Amami's association shows the impact of changes at the structural dimension on the creation of counterpublics situated within the interactional dimension of the public sphere. In their work, the members specifically go against the established hegemonic idea of feminist organizations by integrating an intersectional perspective of women ("Femme rural"). The rural woman is proudly taken as a label that would effectively challenge the established notions of feminist action. Amami's episode shows a state controlled public sphere and the establishment of a plurality of publics opening up, precisely because the Interior Ministry was discharged of this important gatekeeping function. The association law furthermore exemplifies the interaction between the structural and the interactional dimensions of the public sphere and its relations to the creation of sustainable counterpublics, where citizens could meet regularly around a common purpose.

8.1.3 Elections for the Constitutional Assembly

Another milestone illustrating the change in the structural dimension of the public sphere in this first phase was the first post-uprising elections held on October 23rd, 2011. Ennahda emerged as the winner, though it had to share power with two smaller parties, emerging from the former opposition, in order to form a government[94]: the Democratic Forum for Work and Freedoms (Forum Démocratique pour le Travail et les Libertés FDTL, usually referred to as Ettakatol) and the Congress for the Republic party (Congrès pour la République, CPR)[95]. Together the three parties followed the call for a "government of unity" and formed the interim "Troika" government. Power was shared in the government between the Head of Parliament Mustapha Ben Jaafar (Ettakatol), the President Moncef Marzouki (CPR) and Prime Minister Hamad Jebali (Ennahda). With regards to the agreements that had been negotiated between the parties during their participation in the counterpublic of the 18th October from 2005-2007[96], this coalition could draw from a common history of activism and opposition under the Ben Ali regime.

---

94 Ennahda built on 89 of the overall 217 ANC seats. Its coalition partners won 29 (CPR) 20 (Ettatol, FDTL) seats respectively.

95 Their political orientation can be disputed but includes secular and socio-democratic stances.

96 For an analysis of the 18th October movement that I have framed as a counterpublic that was constituted under authoritarian rule, see 6.2.

Despite the introduction of electoral parity on the party's lists, the outcome of the elections didn't reach 50% representation of women in the National Constituent Assembly, but regrouped 27% of women in the elected Parliament 'only'.[97] This gap can be explained by the fragmented electoral landscape of Tunisia, counting more than 200 electoral districts and the reluctance to implement a horizontal zipper (see the so-called parity law) as outlined with regards to the first quota debate. Their number did increase to 31% (67 members) in the assembly mainly because male parliamentarians who died or withdrew from the ANC were replaced by the next (female) candidate on the list (Cherif, 2014, p. 2). Now, female parliamentarians constituted nearly one third of the constitutional assembly: Valentine Moghadam recalls, by relaying on UN action plans to increase women's share in parliaments, that around a 30% representation of women in parliament constitutes "the threshold at which women can make a difference in policy and political decisions" (Moghadam, 2014, p. 138).

Women from Ennahda represented a majority of female parliamentarians, first because Ennahda won most seats in the elections of 2011 and second because of the vertical quota being mandatory. I find it worth recalling that women's representatives from different localities were elected deputies and, taking into consideration Ennahda's history of oppression, for the most part they didn't stem from the national political establishment but were new to professional politics.[98] Scholar Andrea Khalil recalls that the leftist parties usually associated with feminist issues failed to include "poor, local networks and rural women to the extent that Ennahda did" (Khalil, 2014, p. 187).

The parliament represents, according to Nancy Fraser, a "strong public" where women had, in our conceptualization, the chance to actively participate in the renegotiation of the structural dimension of public sphere by discussing solutions in committees, crafting legislations and voting on the constitution. The (quantitative) representation of women in these institutions constitutes only one aspect for our analysis, because women who could access the institutions were nevertheless confronted with the disciplinary and interpersonal domain of

---

97 For an overview by countries employing (voluntary or legislative) quotas, see for example the "quotaproject" online for 2013: http://www.quotaproject.org/country.cfm. Tunisia appears to fall within the global average with regards to the percentage of women in parliament. (Quotaproject, 2013).

98 In the frame of this study, a systematic biographical analysis of Ennahda female deputies cannot be undertaken. Marsad presents all biographies of the parliamentarians on their website. To underpin the argument, I will just point to deputy Jawahra Driss, born in 1985 from Tataouine (south of the country) who pursued her education in her home town Ghomrassen joined Ennahda shortly before the elections http://majles.marsad.tn/fr/deputes/4f4fbcf3bd8cb56157000033. Samia Ferchichi from Siliana on the other hand, joined the MIT from a young age and is the wife of a former political prisoner http://majles.marsad.tn/fr/deputes/4f4fbcf3bd8cb5615700004c.

power. Laila Khaled Labidi, who participated in the Regional Independent Authority for the Elections (IRIE)[99] of the Gafsa governorate, recounts that she was one of the few women in the IRIE of her region (Gafsa, Tozeur, Kebili). She stood for candidacy to find out firsthand whether the elections were really free and fair. In the interview, she recalls how she was ridiculed based on her gender and social position in order to delegitimize her participation in politics:

> "How can you put a woman in here who is unemployed, a housewife who is member of IRIE?" (Laila Khaled Labidi, Redeyef, October 2014).

While I hold that the parliament and the regional institutions of the ISIE present an exceptional make-up of differently positioned people in the structural dimension of public sphere, Labidi and others were then perceived as political intruders. The hegemonic domain of power that pervaded the public sphere before the uprisings was mainly interspersed with women (and men), who could marshal strong political and economic networks and were able to draw upon educational and financial resources. Women from different backgrounds, or clear religious stances, such as co-president of parliament Meherzia Labidi Maiza, would challenge the dissembled secularism. After the uprisings these women suffered stigmatization and ridicule at the interpersonal dimension of power even within the institutions, independent from political ideologies.

Besides the challenges for women within the institutions, the democratic institutions themselves were observed with great skepticism by many of the interviewees, as they were not perceived to be effecting any changes within the Matrix of Domination. Tellingly, most interview participants participated in the elections of 2011 but not those of 2014. An activist from Tunis expresses a general discontent with the democratic election process:

> "For me, these aren't free elections. No matter what parties will win, I don't consider their outcomes as the expression of the popular will. There were manipulations, there were even Human Rights violations in this electoral process, so I decided to boycott and I even tried to support boycott campaigns" (B.L., Tunis, May 2014).

While the two elections in 2011 and 2014 are regarded as the major achievement of the "transformation process" in literature for the simple fact that they met

---

99 There were 33 IRIEs subjected to the ISIE. They usually consisted of 14 nominated members. These nominations occurred shortly before the electoral inscriptions were opened, charging them with getting constituted and controlling the inscriptions in a short time period. The report on the elections of 2011 by the US-based Carter Center states the absence of women in the IRIEs (The Carter Center, 2011). In the frame of this research, I couldn't find official numbers of a gendered repartition in the IRIE.

most democratic standards with only few "irregularities"[100], much more skepticism was expressed in the interviews conducted during this study. Some pointed to the lack of education and socio-economic inequalities, which would render this elementary instrument of structuring the public sphere obsolete:

> "How do you want to organize elections? How do you want to assure equality between men and women if the women have other problems? How will she think of making political decisions when she needs food for her and she doesn't even have money to go to school, how will she be interested in these things? She is not. And in the *Dakhel* region, there are many illiterates" (Laila Khaled Labidi, Redeyef, November 2014).

Labidi points again to the category of locality and the *Dakhel* region, as a marginalized locality, influencing education and predefined gender-based discrimination. In her opinion, many women are not able to make responsible political decisions. She hereby introduces a debate on the relation between social inequalities and the exercise of democratic practices, such as voting, that I will pick up on in the conclusion of this work. Hayet Amami, who was running for parliamentary elections on one of the numerous independent lists[101] in Sidi Bouzid in 2011, testifies how she encountered lack of education and poverty during the election campaigns:

> "A woman asked me [during campaigning at the countryside]: 'When we vote your list, what do you give us?' And one woman told me: 'Give me your scarf at least'. And I replied to her: 'If I give you this scarf it will be torn after three months, but the constitution that is about to be created, will stay for millions of years'. So I dropped [campaigning for] my list aside and started to explain to them about what a constitutional assembly is, how you elaborate a constitution, what a parliament is. And then the women replied: 'This is not what our husband told us!' Believe me, there was an old woman of more than 70 years, who told me: 'Look, we made a revolution against the colonizers so that you young girls can go to school and you didn't make any effort to make us understand how to vote and all of this!" (Hayet Amami, Sidi Bouzid, April 2014).

---

100 See, for example, the press statement by the civil society group ATIDE (Association Tunisienne pour l'Integrité et la Démocratie des Elections) observing the elections: http://www.atide.org/communique-24-octobre-2014/

101 According to the report of the European Delegation for the observation of the elections, 1517 lists have been registered in total, there from 645 independent in the 27 circumscriptions in Tunisia. Adding to that, 145 lists were registered from foreign countries. The report expresses careful criticism with regards to the definition, lack of sanctions and inequality of public and private funding in the electoral campaign. It stipules a tardy distribution of public funds to electoral lists for political campaigning (Albertini, 2011, p.4). Lilia Labidi states that for the elections in 2014, a majority of the independent lists are run in the interior governments (Kasserine, Gafsa, Jendouba and Sidi Bouzid) (Labidi, 2014, p.2). This underpins the argument that traditional party politics and representations are mostly mistrusted in the underdeveloped regions of the country.

In the situation of a public encounter, Amami choose to function as an educator and renounced her political campaigning. She shared knowledge on the political institutions. Amami, who had decided to become a candidate for Sidi Bouzid as a young educated woman, hereby (re-)presents an exceptional type of politician focused more on the democratic education of voters than actually gaining their votes. The observation of a lack of political education to prepare for the elections is backed by the general findings of the European Delegation for the observation of the Elections (Albertini, 2011, p. 5).

The democratic elections reveal the entanglements of the structural and the interactional dimensions of public spheres in representative democratic systems, whose main function is to organize the elections of representatives: It is at this intersection that material benefits, as well as hegemonic power and the manipulation of ideologies and symbols can influence the decision-making processes of the individual citizen.

8.2 Renegotiating the Constitution

The second phase consists of the period following the elections for the National Constituent Assembly (Assemblée nationale constituante, ANC) that were held on October 23rd, 2011. From then, the Assembly was the legitimate institutional body influencing the process of transition by drafting a new constitution. The constitutional process takes a central place in the examination of gender renegotiations in the structural dimension of the public sphere.

The political landscape of Tunisia transformed in 2012 during the TROIKA government with the emergence of new political parties. Béji Caïd Essebsi and secular forces founded the Nidaa Tounes party in June 2012. Tunisian journalist and publicist Seif Soudani called the Nidaa Tounes party, "less a party but rather an assemblage of components driven by the re-activation of pre-existing structures of the former single party" (Soudani, 2014). Nidaa Tounes was able to fill a vacuum that would stand in direct opposition to Ennahda by taking advantage of the fragmentation of leftist parties that didn't unite until nearly half a year later. Numerous leftist parties merged into the coalition Popular Front a few months later in October of the same year. During the time of my interviews, the drafting of the constitution was an ongoing process, which charted the dynamics between old and new political camps and parties.

8.2.1 Whose Feminist Frameworks?

The question of whether Tunisia's Personal Status Law (CSP) from 1956 would remain untouched by the political change was raised early on in the public sphere. I would distinguish two different stages of different political quality. At first, concerned feminist activists that staged demonstrations against a potential backlash against women's rights took to the streets by the end of January 2011. Later on, the issue reflected the political struggles over state power, as I will detail with the example of the National Women's Day on August 13th 2012. Conservative political forces would exploit feminist concerns to build a political front against the Ennahda-led government.

The first women's march after the uprisings in January 2011, in which a feminist counterpublic claimed the urban space, was led by a secular-feminist coalition at the Avenue Habib Bourguiba, the main street of Tunis, which can be considered the most mediatized urban public space[102] where people's demands are expressed. Noura Borsali, who had taken part in the gathering herself, sees this first public appearance and renegotiation, critically, in retrospect as not "organized" enough and "*maladroit*":

> "I think it was an inapt (maladroit) demonstration, because it was too early, but it is a question of slogans as well. I remember well, in the streets, it was the Avenue Bourguiba. We were chanting 'Laicism! Laicism!' And the people were watching, I remember well, because I took part and sometimes broke off the march, taking pictures, so I could see peoples' reaction. They were like: 'Laicism? Laicism? Does that mean...?' In my opinion the demonstration was not well organized, the slogans not clear enough and accessible. I didn't like that. I think it was made in a hurry and we paid a hard price for it afterwards" (Noura Borsali, Tunis, May 2013).

She especially points to the demand of "Laiquia!" ("laicity") that wasn't understood by the people who passed by in the streets. Because the slogans were not "accessible" enough to a wider public, they were easily misinterpreted and linked to the old regime's attempts to resurface in public. This, especially, must be read against the background of the conception of feminism as exclusively Western in the first place, evoking not only post-colonial power structures of economic dependencies but also modernist state-feminist practices that the people wanted to liberate themselves from. The actress and activist Amira Chebli remembers:

---

102 I have previously laid out the occupation of the Kasbah, which gained little to no attention at the representational dimension of the public sphere. The images of the uprisings, constituting the hegemonic narrative on the revolution, are set at the Avenue Habib Bourguiba.

> "I didn't participate in all of these marches [women's march and march for laicism taking place in January and February 2011 at the avenue Habib Bourguiba in Tunis, note of author], but I was disappointed, as I felt that even the march for the women was quickly politically reincorporated and the people who really made the revolution have been marginalized, because again, the political scene created space for the intellectual scene but not for the people" (Amira Chebli, Berlin, May 2013).

The account shows how the hegemonic domain of power continued to affect the interactional dimension of the public sphere and consequently the struggle that counterpublics face to take over and remain in control over dynamics at the interactional dimension. It becomes evident how feminist appearances had to find a way to demark themselves from the hegemonic domain of power that had incorporated feminist demands within their dissembled secularism. In the new pluralist public sphere, autonomous feminists had to reframe their demands that were associated with legitimizing the crackdown on Islamists and largely excluded the underprivileged classes.

Blogger Afef Abrouigi explores the problematic religious versus authoritarian state binary that emerged with the first women's march after the revolution:

> "They [referring to Ennahda] have been and they are exploiting religion and Islam. They see themselves as those who protect religion and this works. You know why this works? This works because there is ignorance about religion and there is ignorance about secularism. People actually think that secularism equals the Ben Ali regime and the Bourguiba regime. And it [the respective regime] is oppressing and I know that many people were actually harassed, many women. I have been talking to former classmates and asked: 'Why did you vote Ennahda' and, she was like: 'I don't wanna have a regime that prevents me from putting on the headscarf.' It kind of works, cause it's still in the memory of many Tunisians, so there is so much to do when it comes to raising awareness" (Afef Abrouigi, Tunis, May 2014).

The women of the march were perceived as bringing back the ideas of the old regime, associated with the oppression of religious beliefs in the public sphere. A wrong perception that, according to Borsali, could have been countered with more preparation and discussion beforehand. The slogans were not thought through enough, as the public appearance came "too early." The positions and reflections of other women were evidently not taken into account and no time was afforded to build new inclusive feminist counterpublic regroupings before taking to the street. There should have been more thought on how to approach gender politics after Ben Ali had left the country. Borsali points to the "high price," and certainly refers to the problematic establishment of a polarized system in which she didn't want to side with any political camp and certainly not the one regrouping the old secular forces.

While the CSP was an issue after Ben Ali came to power in 1987, the concerns of feminists were even more heightened by the formation of the Ennahda-led government and its majority in the Constituent Assembly. Despite its statement to actively preserve the progressive women's rights legislation in contrast for instance to the Muslim Brotherhood in Egypt (Al-Ali, 2012, p. 31), Ennahda was suspected to have a "hidden agenda" and stood accused of "double speech" (Hamza, 2016, p. 225).

According to scholar Andrea Khalil

"the massive social shift brought about by the revolution ushered in renewed interrogation of the reformist principles upon which the CSP was built. The politics of secular reformism, now discredited by the revolution, which were behind the crafting of the CSP, were replaced by a political hegemony dominated by Islamist-leaning political actors!" (Khalil, 2014, p. 191).

However, I argue that the fear that an Islamic party would be responsible for crafting the legislative framework of Tunisia was deeply anchored in the hegemonic domain of power. This provided fertile ground for the opposition's claim that Ennahda's state project equated the full implementation of *sharia* law. Against this background, it comes as no surprise that Ennahda renounced taking up the women's ministry. It appears that at the beginning, all three parties of the Troika were reluctant to take up the Ministry of Women's Affairs, and in particular Ennahda renounced the move as part of a political calculation. Marouan Habita, consultant to the CPR women's minister, explains the hesitance of the parties to take up the portfolio of the Women's Ministry because of its strong association with the *ancien régime*:

> "It was the ministry of the Tunisian woman, and that equaled the woman of Ben Ali. (…) But we finally decided to take it to make a real difference, because the tasks attributed to the ministry allow to work very closely with the people" (Marouen Habita, Tunis, May 2013).

His account underpins the argument of the particular importance of gender politics and the ministry of women affairs as carrier of state feminism and the hegemonic domain of power in particular: For CPR and Ettakatol, it would be challenging to demark themselves from the former state–feminist hegemony, while in the case of Ennahda, competence in the field would be denied *a priori*. It was finally accorded to the CPR and Sihem Badi succeeded Lilia Labidi, women's minister of the interim government of 2011, in office. The ministry of women's affairs thus took not more than a consultancy role in the process of negotiating the new constitution.

Old Cleavages Regaining Surface:
Complementarity and National Women's Day 2012

Previously, I stated that the institutional, representational and interactional dimensions of the public sphere cannot always be strictly separated. Their interconnection becomes apparent when looking at the debates revolving around the four different drafts of the constitution, engaging different publics at the institutional, representational and interactional level. Four constitutional drafts were published between October 2011 and January 2014 (in August 2012, December 2012, April 2013 and June 2013) before the final text was adopted in January 2014.[103] In the debates following each new draft, identity issues, incorporated in women's rights, took over "the bulk of discussions" in the public sphere (Mersch, 2014). The discussions in parliament were streamed on national TV, thus producing media output that was scrutinized by associations, and triggered discussions at the interactional dimension of the public sphere.

To demonstrate these relations, I will present the reactions to the first draft of the constitution on National Women's Day (13 August) 2012 in more detail as it entails an important shift in power arrangements in Tunisia. The mobilizations on National Women's Day 2012 constitute indeed a turning point for the discourse on gender equality in the transformation period and have engaged leading scholars working on Tunisia's transition with respect to questions of gender (Charrad & Zarrugh, 2014; Moghadam V. M., 2014; Khalil, 2014; Khélifa, 2012, p. 25).

The first draft of the constitution that was published in the first days of August 2012 provoked a huge outcry. Article 28, which was leaked to the press and circulated on social media, stated that women were complementary to men. It also stated that the *acquis* of women's rights have to be protected and men and women are equal partners in building the nation. Salma Mabrouk Sadaa, a deputy from the Ettakatol party and a member of the Rights and Liberties Committee, circulated the paragraph on social media before the first draft was officially published. Omezzine Khélifa stresses the role of her visibility on social networks that enabled her to mobilize against the potential dangers of this law and attract international public attention to the work of the rights and liberties committee (Khelifa, 2012, p. 25). In response to the formulation of "complementarity", a coalition including leading feminist organizations such as ATFD and AFTURD called for a mobilization on the streets on National Women's Day on 13th

---

103 You can find all drafts in Arabic and English on the international forum constitution.net: http://www.constitutionnet.org/country/constitutional-history-tunisia; the national NGO Bawsala provides three drafts in French on their website http://majles.marsad.tn/fr/constitution (the draft from August 2012 is missing in this list, but can be accessed here: http://www.marsad.tn/uploads/documents/traduction_FR_verifie.pdf.) Note that I have mainly worked with the French version of the four drafts.

August 2012, linking the movement to the proposed Article of "complementarity" that would jeopardize the progressive family laws providing a loophole for misogynist and Islamist legislation. One week ahead of the march, on August 4th, a number of other Civil Society organizations and the strong labor union UGTT published a joint communiqué that gained widespread public attention.[104] The coalition was able to rely on a network that guaranteed extensive circulation on social media. Three days before the march, the ATFD held a press conference with AFTURD and the LTDH. This assured additional coverage by traditional media ahead of the march (Ghorbani, 2012, p.54). The organizers managed to mobilize thousands of people with estimates varying drastically, ranging from 10,000 to 200,000 participants (Ghorbani, 2012, p. 55).

Apart from civil society organizations and activist groups, the above coalition also included political parties, most prominently among them the newly formed opposition party Nidaa Tounes. The public defense of women's rights was thus not an exclusively feminist cause that would be situated within a counterpublic. In the mainstream media, it was framed as a successful mobilization against "obscurantism." It became an occasion to unite those fearing the project of an Islamic state and an "Islamization of Tunisia." Ennahda's opposition was able to take advantage of the rallies, as chants for gender equality alternated with slogans against the Islamist party. While Ennahda professed to recognize the CSP, it stood accused of reintroducing inequalities at the constitutional level through the introduction of its complementarity clause (Antonakis, 2015a, p. 8).

Different Positions towards the Mobilizations against Complementarity

The events of the 13th August 2012 featured as a topic in my interviews as they offered the possibility to formulate diverse stances towards the march. In the following, I will point out four different critiques of the march from different positionalities deduced from the interviews: First, the celebration of the march as showing the power of women's rights in the public sphere. Second, the politicization and exploitation of the march by *secular* forces, namely the recent party Nidaa Tounes that was linked to criticism of the media as an event. Third, a critique from an intersectional perspective focusing on the exclusion of women of marginalized positions in society. Finally, I shed light on a more radical

---

104 You can find the communiqué signed by representatives of ATURD, the Human Rights League, the labor union, Amnesty International and the national council for freedoms (CNTL) on Face-book: https://fr-fr.facebook.com/notes/association-tunisie-tol%C3%A9rance/commu-niqu%C3%A9-commun-atfd-afturd-amnesty-international-ltdh-cnlt-ugtt/358043447598389 (accessed 5 March 2016).

feminist critique, denouncing that the CSP was presented by feminists as the ultimate codification to defend women's rights, glossing over the pitfalls and non-secular basis of the current family code.

M.T., a feminist from Kairouan in her 40s and member of the local women's committee of the Popular Front, recalls that feminist politics have "always been used for political reasons." Reviewing her own history in feminist activism, she summarizes that the image of women serves to merely construct a "façade." Nevertheless, as for the march on the 13th August she finds:

> "There, I participated in a big women's movement to secure women's rights at least, so this is where you really see her influence" (M.T., Kairouan, April 2014).

According to the respondent, the demonstration on National Women's Day 2012 created space for women's participation and resistance. She perceives the mobilizations in the streets as a demonstration of power that may be anchored in a state feminist ideology but is nevertheless necessary and a source of pride. At the same time, she claims that sustainable participation of women within parties is also needed. Otherwise, women's political influence would remain restrained to marches and "events" instead of changing structural gender relations within party politics.

Others, especially feminist activists from the younger generation, express disappointment as they regarded the march as an expression of a political recuperation of the fight of women's rights by the newly formed oppositional party Nidaa Tounes. Y.T. points to the powerful resources they could mobilize to re-appear on the public scene as the defender of women's rights. She felt that their voices were homogenized when participating in the demonstration:

> "I was there because I had to be there. The ATFD was behind the organizations, but besides, the main organizers were of the kind Nidaa Tounes, you know?(…)The place of the Popular Front was not really apparent in this march (…)There was a huge political recuperation [of the march]: You participate in the demonstration and you get the impression that you are a member of Nidaa Tounes (...) You go to these demonstrations, but they have so many resources. They have money, you have their slogans, their flag, everywhere. And still, you are present with them, because you have to do it. You don't really have a choice" (Y.T., Tunis, March 2014).

Her account expresses a dilemma that women's activists face when their rights become a token for political campaigning and sound familiar with regards to the history of state-feminism in Tunisia previously laid out. Yasmine* expresses despair as she identifies with the promotion of women's rights against possible backlashes in the new constitution. At the same time, she doesn't want to ally herself with political forces of the *ancien regime.* In that, the prevailing *secular* forces could re-establish the maintenance over women's rights in opposition to the Troika Government. Borsali backs the observation of the previous interview participant and expresses how the march has been exploited for party political reasons as well:

> "I left the march, because I was sad. At the time [before the uprisings], we were maybe only hundreds of women, but we were real feminists. Sometimes we faced violence, but it was a march for women's rights. While this time, a certain political party has invaded it and their slogans of which several had nothing to do with women's rights" (Noura Borsali, Tunis, May 2013).

While some faced the dilemma unfolding at the interactional dimension of the public sphere or left the march out of disappointment, other respondents consciously skipped the march and reacted in a more detached way: Eya Turki, a young activist, with affiliations to the Tunisian Pirate Party, claims in the interview that the mobilizations around the complementarity clause were just a showcase that fitted into media's sensationalist logics and reflected negotiations over political power behind the scenes. In her opinion, the fact that the word "complementarity" didn't appear in the second draft was not because of the mobilizations on the streets, but because of new political agreements and negotiations:

> "I thought by myself, well, we wait two or three weeks and it will be over. And that's exactly what happened. It's not because of the demonstration that the notion of 'complementarity' disappeared. So, I thought with this thing on complementarity it's a start. Something is going on. As soon as something is going on behind the scenes of the assembly, they start to leak us what's going on. For example, they say:' Ah today there is X who got into an argument with Y because of an article', or I don't know what. And then everybody gets angry and we create a sort of a tempest in a teapot. We debate this the whole day and then that's it" (Eya Turki, Tunis, May 2013).

From the very beginning, Turki trusts that the *acquis* of women was never really in danger, but she understands the polemic around the complementarity clause as a proxy for political bargaining. Instead, she points here to the attention economy of social media and the Tunisian counterpublic on Twitter that she participates in and exposes the dynamics of political parties creating publicness via social media.[105] Her claims are supported by Mounira Charrad, who has researched the history of feminism and nationalism in Tunisia. In her analysis of the changes in the Tunisian CSP between 1930 and the 1990s, she concludes "shifts in legislations always expressed a struggle over state-power instead of

---

105 Her descriptions can be related the discussions in social media scholarship on the shifts in attention economies and the emergence of "online firestorms." They reshape government–citizen relations by "Word of Mouth" propagation of new ideas (Pfeffer, Zorbach, & Carley, 2014, p. 117).

true commitments to women's emancipation" (Charrad M. , 2008, p. 111). For Turki, it appeared clear that in the current political situation, the hegemonic domain of power encapsulated in the CSP would remain untouched.

A third position is put forward by Ameny Ltifi from Sidi Bouzid, who is active in the local UDC. She criticizes the march from an intersectional perspective, pointing to the class background of the women who demonstrated that day in Tunis. While expressing support for the claimed purposes of the march, she raises the issue of the representation of women:

> "For me that was a thing from bourgeois women. Really, we neither, we do not want to be complementary to men, but those women who went out, they are not complementary in a first place. They defend the marginalized women but it's the marginalized women who have to create and participate in these actions themselves[106]" (Ameny Ltifi, Sidi Bouzid, April 2014).

She argues that the demonstrators taking the streets and claiming to represent marginalized women come from a privileged position in society. These women take center stage in renegotiating the structural domain of power and with it the writing of the constitution, while those who, in her opinion, are more concerned and affected by restricted gender roles in the public sphere and the family remain excluded from the struggle. It is pertinent to examine this misrepresentation due to the connections it draws between the event in question and the representational dimension of the public sphere.

A fourth critique centers on the content of the CSP, the document constituting the shared basis and least common denominator of the mobilization on August 13th. The blogger "La pomme empoisonnée" (the poisoned apple), published a blog post two days before the march entitled "How can we preserve what we never had?" Therein, she calls out "feminists of the 25th hour" and points to the hypocrisy in the debate around the complementary law and the CSP as a legal text that may have been progressive 50 years ago but should not serve as the ultimate framework in 2012. She hereby expresses a feminist position from a younger generation that feels alienated by the feminist struggles and debates that build their defense on the grounds of outdated legislation, instead of attacking this very structural domain of power.

"Let's say that if this text (CSP) was revolutionary at the time - a text containing various gaps that can be criticized- it is not revolutionary anymore, after 50 years of existence. Because if we can still be astonished today by its avant-gardism, despite its incomplete character that we voluntarily omit to address, that means that in 56 years, we have not only made no progress at all, but even regressed" (La pomme empoisonné, 2012, *translated by the author)*.

---

106 In the course of the complementarity debate, there were indeed many actions, roundtables and demonstrations staged all over the country.

Her position reflects the broader camp of feminists whose interest is to "kill" or "decolonize" Tunisian hegemonic feminism. A critique of the CSP was also brought up in the interviews:

> "You feel, when you read the CSP, that it entails some revolutionary laws at the time, but *grosso modo*, it remains Sharia law" (Henda Chennaoui, Tunis, May 2013).

Her critique concerns the very basis of the CSP of *idjdihad*, which negotiates the Tunisian family law on the basis of Islamic law. Her position can be related to the refusal of blogger "la pomme empoisonnée" to engage in a discussion that would defend a legislative framework, the CSP "this famous talisman that the Tunisians take out of the box as soon as they are confronted with their own contradictions" (La pomme empoisonné, 2012) that the young feminists do not agree upon in a first place. Her position probably represents the most radical one that confronts the hegemonic domain of power incorporating *dissembled secularism*. Instead of defending the *acquis*, this position addresses the "gaps" within the CSP and calls for a reform. She reveals the irritation of defending institutions that do not stand on the "right grounds". Reforming the CSP thus implies a renegotiation of gender relations challenging the hegemonic domain of power and the national consensus.

I argue that the mobilizations around the complementarity clause illustrate the re-institutionalization of old cleavages between the Islamic and the secular camp. The *ancien regime* could revitalize hegemonic narratives impacting the structural and representational dimension of the public sphere. I argue that the march represents not only a huge coalition that was publicly opposing any regression in political rights for women, but adding to that, it represents a powerful reappearance of *secular* feminism, as it has been constructed in the *ancien state feminist doctrine*. The hegemonic ideology re-appeared as the only protector of women and their rights against an Islamist regime in the making.

I will demonstrate herein the transgression of boundaries of the CSP set in place by Habib Bourguiba and that demanding more rights entails a renegotiation of the hegemonic domain of power. This bears the risk of violent backlashes and defamation. These entanglements will be analyzed in the next section, which engages with the international codification of women's rights, the "Convention on the Elimination against All Discrimination against Women" (CEDAW).

8.2.2 CEDAW-Trouble and the Limits of State Feminism

In the following section, I claim that analysis of the debate around CEDAW embodies the practice of stigmatizing women who are trying to negotiate the institutional dimension of public sphere. The concept of "stigmatization" to silence gender-based movements was coined by professor of sociology Myra Marx-Ferree (Marx Ferree, 2012). Political scientist Susanne Zwingel, who works on international women's rights and their translation, frames the CEDAW as the "first international public space for debates on the advancement of women" (Zwingel, 2005, p. 403). "Bringing CEDAW home," is understood as the process of "active appropriation and interpretation" at the national and sub-national level shaped by feminist organizations (Zwingel, 2005, p. 411 f.). I strongly agree with Zwingel's assumption and I would elaborate specifically on the dimension of the political struggles encapsulated by the process of translating international legislation to national legislation. The national level has a specific political relevance in the period under study, because a presumed "failure" in 2011 of the interim government(s) turned the CEDAW into an instrument serving as a campaigning tool for national politics and creating further polarizations.

Tunisia signed the CEDAW in 1985, and in doing so it preserved important reservations (UN Women, 2009): These mainly concerned article 1 of the Tunisian Constitution of 1959, which places Islam as the state religion and respectively as the religion of the state, pointing to the majority of Tunisians. The reservations harmonize the international legislation with the CSP and uphold discriminatory practices such as non-equality in inheritance. In fact, the designation of article 1 remains disputed as the Arabic formulation can be translated in different manners allowing a couple of interpretations on the place of religion within the state: It can be read as either a cultural reference of the identity of the state, Islam as a state religion or Tunisia as a state with the majority of Muslim citizens (Hached, 2011). The CEDAW legislation was an important reference point in the work of the ATFD, the AFTURD and other independent feminists before the uprisings (see Arfaoui, 2016, p. 226). As an international women's rights framework, it helped to connect feminist counterpublics globally. They initially demanded lifting reservations to conform the CSP, with the international treaty (ATFD, 2010).[107] After the uprisings, and by virtue of their presence in the legislative bodies of the first phase of the transition, they formed a counterpublic at the structural level of the public sphere and pushed for a full recognition of the CEDAW under the new auspices.

---

107 A declaration by the ATFD in October 2010 at the CEDAW committee can be found online at the website of the Office of the High Commissioner for Human Rights: http://www2.ohchr.org/english/bodies/cedaw/docs/ngos/ATFD_Declaration_fr.pdf

Under Béji Caïd Essebsi's interim government in 2011, the decision to withdraw the reservations of the CEDAW was made. However, this decision was proclaimed on a national level, without notifying the UN, and its general-secretary, as the depository of the convention. Consequently, the decision had no legal effect. After the elections of 2011 and under the Troika government, the Tunisian withdrawal has been pushed aside and the process of legalization was not pursued during this period. Noura Borsali, who took part in the negotiations, summarizes the struggles they faced as follows:

> "We had to pay a hard price, so they don't pass the article one (…). You see, the CEDAW has a whole feminist dimension. And for the feminist side, they pay great attention. There is the religion which shall not be touched. And then lifting of the CEDAW reservations was achieved indeed, it was in front of the ministerial council! You know what they did? They didn't send it. That was under Essebsi, who will become the next president. Okay, we have buried it. And when the Islamist came to power…The Islamists consider certain articles of the CEDAW to be against the Islamic principles [they campaigned against it by linking it to the rights for homosexuals, note by author]. And we couldn't do anything. We are still blocked" (Noura Borsali, Tunis, May 2013).

In this account, neither the secular forces, nor the Troika government wanted to assume the structural changes in gender politics that the CEDAW represents. The feminist counterpublic was effectively "blocked" in between the two governments and unable to achieve their aims. While the Troika coalition declared that lifting the reservations of the CEDAW was not part of their political interest, the interim government under Essebsi pretended to have committed a procedural "mistake." They hereby couldn't be held accountable for a political decision. Dalenda Larguèche rates the CEDAW trouble differently, seeing the Troika government alone responsible for not having forwarded the decision on the lifting of the reservations to the UN:

> "Tunisia had withdrawn from the reservations with Béji Caïd Essebsi, and the Troika didn't want to send the text at the UN, so what to do?" (Dalenda Larguèche, Tunis, October 2014).

One of the main issues of the CEDAW trouble is situated at the constitutional and legislative level of the family code, which is organized by Sharia law and remains the last bastion of religious rights. In the interview, ATFD member and active participant in the negotiations Ahlem Belhaj makes an allusion to the defamation campaigns stigmatizing feminists lobbying for an application of the CEDAW lifting in legal practice under the Troika government:

> "When the ATFD prepared their alternative report for the CEDAW, they spoke about the de-penalization of homosexuality as well and we are one of the rare associations, if not the only one, who dared bringing up the

> issue that you are not supposed to bring up: homosexuality and inheritance (…) so they started a defamation campaign that we want to integrate the international treaties, because we want homosexuality and the equal inheritance, because we are atheists and so on… but these were the two major issues they brought up publicly" (Ahlem Belhaj, Tunis, April 2014).

Belhaj hereby exhibits the limits of the hegemonic domain of power, characterized by a dissembled secularism. It incorporates two major issues: First, the freedom of sexuality and consequently the acceptance and de-penalization of homosexuality, and second the more economically-based dimension of equal inheritance. The later exemplifies the privileging of men over women, concerning the right to property, that is to remain uncontested from a religious argument.[108]

On the other hand, homosexuality (male and female) is punishable under the penal code §230, which was created under colonial rule in 1913 and thus represents a colonial hegemonic legacy. The homosexual subject was explicitly outlawed under colonial rule and since then excluded from the construction of the Tunisian nation.[109] Abolishing article §230 constituted the common ground around which an LGBT counterpublic was created and reached wider publics in 2015.[110] The challenge to "bring CEDAW home" (Zwingel, 2005) is thus stopped by national state feminism that remains anchored in patriarchy.

The blogger Lina Ben Mheni adds some perspective to the discussion of the CEDAW, placing it within elitist publics that the majority of people are ignorant of. She hereby summarizes a critique of the framework stating that it was indeed elaborated by middle-class women that were mostly experiencing gender discrimination only (Zwingel, 2005, p. 404).

> "Now we are all scandalized by the reservations of the CEDAW. But in Tunis there are those who have no consciousness at all about what the CEDAW is, so what to say about the other regions of Tunisia? You have

---

108 The equal inheritance laws will be presented later as one of the "hot topics" at the representational dimension of the public sphere.

109 In this regard, concepts of "homonationalism" and "gay assimilations" come into focus in Western knowledge production, where the "war on terror" has opened new windows of opportunity for homosexual subjects to be strategically integrated into the national discourse. See (Puar, 2009). I will come back to the negotiation processes of gender via homosexualities in 2015 in the outlook of this dissertation, as it doesn't fit into the period under study and opens new dimensions of investigation and theoretical conceptualizations.

110 These developments, where demands to accept and decriminalize homosexuality were openly articulated in the hegemonic public, were taking place after the interview conductions. The accounts of 2014 mirror the struggle for the acceptance of homosexuality within the international framework of the CEDAW, while later on, they have been discussed more widely on the national level and culminated in the official creation of the organization *Shams*, which defends LGBT rights, in May 2015.

> to approach these women and discuss with them. Understand their prob-
> lems and try to help" (Lina Ben Mheni, Tunis, 2014).

While Ben Mheni argues that the CEDAW legislations are no priority in the lives of the majority of Tunisian women, the issue remains an important indicator to the political power games linked to gender renegotiations within the structural dimension of the public sphere.

In April 2014, after three years, the situation changed under the technocratic or "independent" government that was installed after the national dialogue in January 2014: On 17 April 2014, the reservations were officially withdrawn, but the government included a general declaration, stating that "The Tunisian government shall not take any organizational or legislative decision in conformity with the requirements of this Convention where such a decision would conflict with the provisions of Chapter I of the Tunisian Constitution" (UN, 23rd April 2014)

The lifting of the reservations underlined Tunisia's exceptionalism, being the first country in the region to have withdrawn from any reservations (albeit its declaration). The decision certainly reflects lobbying by feminist organizations over the last two decades. However, it appears that this general declaration only replaces the former reservations and the CEDAW trouble remains *de jure* and *de facto* unresolved. In an official declaration, the ATFD express their "pride," while at the same time proclaims to "continue the struggle against the general declaration that could be used to hamper women's rights as declared by the constitution" (ATFD, published by Nawaat, 29th April 2014, translated by author). The "CEDAW trouble" illustrates a sometimes paradoxical consensus paradigm, which respects religious rule in the last instance but supports universal women's rights codifications as well. It exposes the limits of dissembled secular hegemony upholding the matrix of domination in Tunisia.

8.3   Elections and a New "Patriarchal Bargain"

The final phase under investigation now is marked by the end of the elected interim government and the installation of a technocratic government (under which the constitution was proclaimed) and finally the "pacted transition" (Boubakeur, 2015, p. 5) leading to a coalition between the Ennahda party and the Nidaa Tounes party. In July and August 2013, opposition forces, including the Nidaa Tounes Party, took over the square in front of the Tunisian parliament, disavowing the legitimacy of the constituent process, as the ANC's one-year mandate had long since expired. This protest against the Troika government was realized in the aftermath of the killings of two opposition figures of the Popular Front, Chokri Belaid and Mohamed Brahmi. Since the 25th of July 2013, 60 members of parliament had suspended their activity in the ANC and joined the protest, also known as the Erahil ("departure") sit-in. This time, the public protest did not focus on the Kasbah as representing the structural domain of power but the Bardo, situated in front of the Constituent Assembly. A weakened and shocked left secularist camp joined forces with the Nidaa Tounes party in the "National Salvation Front" (Front de Salut National, FSN). The protests took place during Ramadan in a festive ambiance, including celebrations and fireworks and were mainly supported by inhabitants of the capital.

In this phase of negotiations of the structural dimension of the public sphere taking place within and outside of the parliament, the National Women's Day played a decisive and dividing role. Gender politics illustrated the political polarization further and played into the "bargained competition." Two marches were announced for this day: One initiated by Hrayer Tounes (Free Women of Tunisia), a collective regrouping previously mentioned feminist groups, including the women's section of the UGTT and – most importantly – the former state feminist institution of the UNFT[111] (Schmidt, 2014, p. 23). On the other hand, Ennahda called their supporters to celebrate National Women's Day at the avenue of Habib Bourguiba under the theme "Tunisian women, pillars of the democratic transition and national unity," *(translated by the author)*.

The former announced their gathering for the "Victory of the Tunisian Woman" at the *Bab Saadoun*, to later join the *Erahil* protest in front of the Bardo. On the Facebook event page of *Hrayer Tounes*[112], the "special taste" of National Women's Day in 2012 and 2013 (both under the Troika government) is emphasized: "These two last years, our celebration has a special taste, our struggle has a special character as well, which gives the charm to our mobilization, our marches and our demonstrations" (translated by author).

The threat of seeing women's rights curtailed by religious extremism and political Islam can be regarded as providing a common ground for the Bardo protest coalition and the willingness of autonomous feminists and other organizations to ally with a former state-feminist institution, the UNFT. In our interview, former women's minister Lilia Labidi points to the lack of discussion on the interdependencies of the feminist organization and the state that haven't been explored after the uprisings:

> "I'm really surprised that we don't really have a debate on the role of the UNFT. I think it is a duty and responsibility to talk about the role of the national [feminist] organizations" (Lilia Labidi, September 2016).

To recall, the UNFT continued to be a parallel structure to the ministry of women

---

111 For a presentation of the UNFT in the historical context, see 5.2.1.
112 The event page of "Hrayer Tounes - Réseau de femmes Rahil" can be found on Facebook: https://fr-fr.facebook.com/events/1400506783499621/ (accessed 19th August 2016).

affairs, that was run by the CPR at the time. Their participation in the Erahil protests demanding the departure of the Troika government reveals the important competition between the two institutions. The Bardo protests could draw from a feminist legitimacy with *Hrayer Tounes*, despite or even because of the inclusion of the former state feminist institution UNFT.

The protests were followed by the formation of the "Quartet", composed by UGTT, the Tunisian League for Human Rights (Ligue Tunisienne des Droits de l'Homme, LTDH), the Tunisian employers' organization (Union Tunisienne de l'Industrie, du Commerce et de l'Artisanat, UTICA) and the Tunisian Bar organization, offering a roadmap, initiated through national dialogue, to overcome the political deadlock. Ennahda finally took part in the dialogues after having boycotted former initiatives, pointing to Nidaa's associations with the old regime. On 18th August 2013, an unofficial meeting between the head of Ennahda, Rached Ghannouchi, and the head of the Nidaa Tounes party, Béji Caïd Essebsi, took place in the presence of Slim Riahi,[113] revealing the "bargained character of the Ennahda–Nidaa Tounes competition" (Boubakeur, 2015, p. 12). The Troika handed over power to a technocratic government in January 2014.

It can be argued that during the process, Ennahda's defensive position as not embracing modern gender politics on the one hand, and poor organization and fragmentation of various leftist and youth groups paved the way for a return of old party members and presidential candidate Essebsi. Lilia Labidi summarizes the important compromises Ennahda made in this time of the Bardo protests thus: "agreeing not to vote for the law excluding former members of the Ben Ali regime and his political party from political activity; agreeing not to adopt an age limit on presidential candidates, thus allowing Béji Caïd Essebsi to run for president; and agreeing to leave the government in January 2014 to give way to a government of technocrats" (Labidi L. , 2015, p. 2). The following institutional outcomes structuring the public sphere must be analyzed against the background of this political climate and mobilizations that I have sketched out here.

8.3.1 The Constitution of 2014: Manifesting a Paradox

Besides the elections of 2011, the finalization of the constitution in 2014 constitutes a second important benchmark as defined by democratization theory. After extensive work in consensus committees, the initiation of national dialogues (for further details see (Antonakis, 2013)), the final document of the constitution was

---

113 The Tunisian media outlet Assabah and Mosaique FM claim that the meeting was intermediated by Nabil Karoui, director of the Nessma TV who is also politically close to the Nidaa Tounes party.

adopted on January 26th 2014, only two days before Prime Minister Ali Laarayedh handed over power to the technocratic government of Medi Jomaa.

Article 46 of the Tunisian constitution of 2014 is considered the key-article for the national gender codification: It states that "The state commits to protect women's accrued rights and work to strengthen and develop those rights" and hereby commits not only to the status quo of women's rights, but also entails the perspective of further improvements. Furthermore, the same article states that "the state works to realize parity between women and men in elected councils." This commitment was taken up by feminists when entering the second round of the quota debate before the elections of 2014 analyzed hereafter. Finally, violence against women is recognized in the constitution: "The state shall take all necessary measures in order to eradicate violence against women." This very recognition of structural violence against women can be read as a success of the feminist groups. However, the ATFD and others had pushed for the criminalization of moral and physical violence against women in public spaces before (Antonakis, 2015a, p. 8). On 27th July 2017, new legislation criminalizing gender-based violence was passed after months of negotiations. It included the criminalization of harassment in the streets and easier prosecution of domestic violence.

These positive developments on the legislative level are an outcome of new negotiations taking place at the legislative level, which could certainly draw from the basis laid by the constitution. This illustrates the argument made by Voorhoeve and others, who stated that the actual outcome of the Tunisian transition will take place on a different level, namely in the field of proper legislation and legal practice (Voorhoeve, 2014)." In this context, the creation of a constitutional court,[114] with exceptional competences inscribed in Chapter V of the constitution (Pickard, 2015), constitutes an important step to translate international and constitutional codifications on the legislative level of women's rights. Furthermore, the court will be crucial in harmonizing international laws with current national legislation that has been ratified, but not put into practice (Mersch, 2015). Lilia Weslaty, a journalist and human rights activist recognizes the importance of feminist themes pushed through by counterpublics to be integrated in the constitution, but she also highlights the constitutional court as an institution of justice whose installation should be a priority:

> "I know that there is people specialized on these issues [women's rights].
> I have another methodology: for me justice passes before feminism. To

---

114 For an analysis of the legislative frame for the constitutional court from the perspective of comparative and international law, see (Grote, 2014). The author positively evaluates the extension of the right to submit legislation for prior control to 30 members of parliament and the court itself, even of existing rights. Under the previous regime, constitutionality of laws could be checked solely on the instigation of the president and only prior to its promulgation.

> guarantee women's rights, we need a constitutional court. This will be the
> next debate in June. We should focus on this, because it's the constitu-
> tional court that will harmonize the constitution with the existing legisla-
> tions. I confront the root of the problem, which are the institutions. We
> have a problem with institutions in Tunisia" (Lilia Weslaty, Tunis May
> 2013).

Weslaty's position reveals the idea of tackling the structural domain of power
that will then, in a second step, be translated into gender justice. However, at the
time of writing, the Court has still not been established. The stagnation in the
process, which has seen no agreement being reached, may be explained by the
selection of judges, which first requires the establishment of a Supreme Judicial
Council, a body that would select four out of the twelve constitutional court
judges. Furthermore, four other members must be proposed and voted in by the
parliament. Importantly, leading Tunisian law professors have cautioned against
the 'politicizing' of these votes (Bellamine, 2015).

From the model of the Matrix of Domination, we can discern that changes in
the structural dimension of power can only be applied if the disciplinary domain
of power that sets in place rules and organizes the translations of structural
changes does so up to the interactional level. In this context, an institution would
need to set the constitution in harmony with the laws and, last but not least, those
who effectually defend the hegemonic domain of power legitimizing the social
contract. Consequently, the executive state institutions such as the police and the
military would need to be trained to implement these changes on the interpersonal dimension of power. I will later discuss this issue with regards to police
violence against women.

In the reception of the constitution by activist of different positionalities, it
becomes clear that the elaboration of the constitutional framework stood in contrast to the diverse hopes Tunisian citizens carried after the uprisings. The following claim by Y.T. shows that the constitution gave hope to a new generation,
while also mirroring the increasing delegitimization of the parliament and the
government for their general tardiness during the transition:

> "It's true that it is important that we have a constitution that it is well
> edited and discussed. But in terms of representativeness, it was Ennahda
> that decided on everything. They had the majority in Parliament. So,
> whatever the other alliances did, there was always the majority of the
> Ennahda party. And it has taken so much time…They were constantly
> hanging behind, so I lost interest. But I have to admit that the day they
> passed the constitution, I was happy. Finally!" (Y.T., Tunis, March
> 2014).

Y.T. doubts the representativeness of the document that was in her view elaborated by Ennahda in particular. Moreover, she points to the very long process of
the drafting procedure, which took up three years instead of the announced one

year. She cites a diffused feeling of "nationalism" that emerged with her happiness later in the interview. The celebrations for the adoption of the constitution aired nationally and internationally did indeed create a moment of pride, even for those who had been skeptical about the process itself.

When asked about their view on the "last three years," the respondents facing unemployment immediately referred to the socio-economic situation and their feelings of huge stagnation, rather than any changes during the period. From their positionality, there have been no changes despite the final agreement on the constitution and found no proper representation of their interests:

> "Always, the priority is work. Until this day, we are unemployed" (N.M.
> and S.M., Sidi Bouzid, April 2014)

Access to labor markets and job opportunities is an outcome of and manifested in the structural domain of power (Collins, 2000, p. 277). While the constitution incorporates articles defining the right to work and engaging with regional developments, these commitments did not translate into citizens' realities. Najoua Karim, who is also from Sidi Bouzid, clarifies the priorities of the 2011 protest, remaining, in her opinion, underrepresented on the structural. These structural grievances cannot be encountered by political cosmetics:

> "Because we didn't make a revolution to change the constitution. I'm sure. Everybody took the streets to protest against unemployment, against poverty, against marginalization. After three years we have nothing. Even the employment laws, they have changed nothing. For instance, now we will pass the CAPES... we have protested against the CAPES on 18th December [2011]. So what have we changed? We have changed nothing, so we have to continue to work on these issues here in Sidi Bouzid, Kasserine and Gafsa. This is our real problem: If there is no work and unemployment rates remain that high and they continue to rise, there will be another revolution for sure" (Najoua Karim, Sidi Bouzid, April 2014).

The importance of locality and class as analytical categories for the changes at the institutional level surfaces. While in the hegemonic public sphere, the constitution was celebrated as the "endpoint" of the transitional phase, Karim points to the common situation in the governorates in the center of the country still struggling with high unemployment rates, announcing a second revolution. The Matrix of Domination defining her reality is still in place and the allusion to the "revolution" entails the wish to change the structural domain of power. Indeed, in 2018, a new wave of women's movements from the governorate of Sidi Bouzid, intersecting gender, class and locality pushed the institutional boundaries (Antonakis & Chennaoui, 2018).

In this context, various respondents have stated the relation of socio-economic development as a necessary pre-condition for libertarian development and democratic practices.

> "In my opinion, freedom will [have to] be supported by a certain degree of economic well-being, a certain comfort that permits to canalize the freedom of expression, because if I'm free and I have a job at the same time, I can canalize this freedom in a development, a progress however it looks like. However, if I'm free and frustrated because I don't have a job, I have nothing, I could canalize this freedom of expression in a destructive way, in any form of destructive power and that's why no freedom of expression and real democracy [can function] without economic development" (B.L., Tunis, April 2014).

B.L.'s critique can be linked to Fabio Merone's observations on the radicalization of the disfranchised youth as part of "the struggle of marginalized social classes to be included in the Nation" (Merone, 2015, p. 76). Pluralism has provoked a further fragmentation in the spectrum of religious parties and movements that could capitalize on the frustrations that B.L. describes. I will come back to these dynamics impacting on issues of security and gendered outcomes later in chapter 9. Similar as with regards to education as a necessary but precondition for voting during elections, economic stability is seen as a necessary pre-condition for libertarian democracy.

8.3.2 The Negotiations Around the Electoral Quota in 2014

I have previously outlined the negotiations of the quota for women candidates in the 2011 elections. Its successful implementation can be regarded as the outcome of the lobbying of feminists targeting the structural dimension of the public sphere. The debate on parity inscribed in the electoral code gained new ground during the pre-election period in the first half of 2014. Women's rights activists were pushing for a reform of the electoral code of 2011 to finally adopt the horizontal quota, or vertical zipper, that were refused before: Then, parties would have to assign 50% of the head of their electoral lists to women. In the following, I argue that its re-assessed rejection illustrates the persistence of the hegemonic domain of power that does not only discriminate against women in politics, but specifically against women in politics of marginalized localities. As female politicians are very rare in the Dakhel region, the quota would have empowered them in particular.

The new electoral code was debated in the Constituent Assembly during the first half of 2014. This time, the legislation was elaborated in constitutional grounds, because Article 45 of the Tunisian constitution codifies the commitment of the state to foster parity in all elected bodies. A regress in gender equality in the electoral code would have been anti-constitutional.

However, while there was no regression, there was no progress either. On 1st May 2014 the parliament, still operating under a technocratic government, finally rejected the amendment of "horizontality" pertaining to the quota for the heads of the lists because the proposal did not secure the number of votes required in the Assembly.[115] The vote resulted in 69 votes in favor, 67 against and 44 abstentions. The Ennahda bloc, represented by 74 deputies opposed it with 33 votes against and 29 abstentions, indicating a polarization within the party.[116]

The vote on the quota in parliament illustrates again the political exploitation of gender politics: On the one hand the oppositional camp, Afek and Nidaa Tounes,[117] had brought in the amendment and supported the reform. On the other hand, Nidaa Tounes and Ennahda showed common grounds when they published their respective electoral lists: The polarized adversaries both had only three women nominated as heads of their lists in the following elections of 2014, contrary to Afek Tounes (ten women) and the CPR (seven women) (Labidi L. , 2014, p. 5 f.). This gap was reported by the Huffington Post Maghreb, indicating the hypocrisy of political parties when it comes to the application of a law that they had voted for just months before. Most strikingly, the fewest head of the lists are found in the districts in the center of the country, again reproducing gendered marginalizations in their intersection with locality.

As a reaction to the rejection of the horizontal zipper, a group of women's rights activist appealed to the provisory instance in charge with controlling the constitutionality of the laws. Basing their argument on Article 45 of the constitution, guaranteeing parity in all elected institutions, they sought to introduce the vertical zipper in the quota. However, the initiative was rejected without giving further explanations (Chekir, 2014). This raises the issue of the actual benefit of the constitution, if contradictory laws persist. Certainly, the initiative did not get enough political or media support to wrench a public explanation from the provisory instance.

This debate exemplifies another limitation of Tunisian state feminism, besides the de-criminalization of homosexuality and the discriminatory inheritance law. The vertical zipper was in line with the hegemonic domain of power that acquires a formal inclusion of women to defend Tunisian exceptionalism. However, the horizontal zipper would have given the right to access the structural

---

115 The rejected amendement to Article 23 states: « Les candidatures sont présentées sur la base du principe de parité entre femmes et hommes et à la règle d'alternance entre eux sur la liste et entre les têtes de listes partisanes et de coalition. Toute liste ne respectant pas ce principe est rejetée, sauf dans le cas d'un nombre impair de sièges réservés à quelques circonscriptions. »

116 The voting results can be found on the website of the watchdog and advocacy NGO Marsad (Marsad, 2014).

117 Despite the fact that Nidaa Tounes didn't participate in the elections in 2011, they had deputies in parliament, because many parliamentarians defected from other smaller parties to Nidaa. For details, see (Antonakis, 2013).

dimension of the public sphere *independently from her locality*. It would have enabled many more women from different localities to access the structural dimension of the public sphere as heads of the lists.

With regards to the policy debate, it fed the purpose of party politics and camp building between progressives and conservatives, but in the end, most of the parties didn't substantially engage in respecting the vertical zipper in practice. Tunisian journalist Tarek Mandhouj writes for Nawaat with regards to the quota debate and its outcome in the electoral lists in 2014:

> "Observing the heads of the electoral lists, I do not recognize the Tunisia that I belong to and that I thought being more evolved. The image of the heads of the lists in their 'overall masculinity' scare me, make me feel ashamed" (Mandhouj, 2014, *translated by the author*).

His claim represents progressive counterpublics, in which men and women alike would have supported employing the instrument of the vertical and horizontal quota in order to push for further equality in politics in the whole country. The quote above furthermore reveals "fear" and "shame" of a young male journalist with regards to hegemonic masculinities. These masculinities mirror the overall conservative consensus that was about to be re-established in the election of 2014. The debates on the legislative level proved to fall short in challenging the hegemonic domain of power.

8.3.3 Elections of 2014: The "Vote Utile"- Campaign Revitalizing Bourguibism

In the following, I argue that contrary to the elections in 2011, the electoral campaign of 2014 very much revitalized old cleavages of secular versus Islamic ideologies in a newly formed political landscape. For their adversaries, "Islamist backward" camp was represented not only by Ennahda, but after their involvement in the Troika, Ettakatol and CPR as well[118]. All parties were held responsible for the political terror that occurred under their rule and the killings of leftist politicians Choukri Belaid and Mohamed Brahmi. Nidaa Tounes, on the other hand, represented the old secular, modern camp. For their opposition, they incorporated the *ancien regime* and counter-revolutionary forces with links to the security apparatus and the media (Merone & Cavatorta, 2013). In the run up to the elections, journalist Sana Sbouaï affirms in our conversation:

> "I'm afraid that the elections will go by this logic as well. To talk about identity as if the people would have an identity problem, and to only focus on that. A majority of the issues of women's rights are negotiated by this.

---

118 As of 2018, both parties, the CPR and Ettakatol, are politically marginal. The CPR had integrated into the party "The Tunisian Will" founded by Moncef Marzouki. In the elected parliament of 2014, both parties were not represented.

When you assure economic and social rights to women, you grant her full
citizenship" (Sana Sbouaï, Tunis, May 2014).

However, in light of empirical developments, the campaigns focused on identity,
rather than citizenship and operated within simplistic metaphors. The Nidaa
Tounes party and Beji Caïd Essebsi mobilized voters to cast a "*vote utile*," the
necessary, or "useful" vote. Slogans implied that Nidaa Tounes would compose
a strong counter-weight to the Ennahda party evoking the danger of fragmented
voting results. In the campaign, the party positioned itself as the only credible
alternative to Ennahda, playing on the fears of the Tunisians regarding economic
chaos, the growth of political violence and terrorism and Islamophobia. They
stated that liberty and individual rights would only be upheld within the *secular*
program they proposed (Alexander, 2016, p. 100). Hereby, secular was being re-
translated as "utile", useful and therefore the only alternative.

Essebsi's presidential campaign was marked by a revitalization of Bourguibism to gather support among Tunisians. I have previously laid out how the
former president personified not only the "father" of the Tunisian nation after
independence, but also the liberator of women and architect of post-colonial
state–feminism. Regarding the campaign of Nidaa Tounes, and its leader Béji
Caïd Essebsi, it becomes clear how politics for gender equality continue to be
inscribed in a post-colonial understanding of "modernity" that serves *secular*
party politics.

Salim Ben Hamidaan, co-founder of the CPR party and minister under the
Troika, assesses how Essebsi exploited Bourguibism as a "wrong copy instrument capable to transfer the identification between the past and the future" (Ben
Hamidane, 2014, translated by author). Capitalizing on his participation in politics on the side of Habib Bourguiba, Essebsi managed to carefully omit his involvement with the former regime of Ben Ali. This revitalization of Bourguibism
was actually staged at the annual meeting of the Nidaa Tounes party in Sousse:
In a video installation, Bourguiba's larger than life head was projected on a wall
and after a couple of minutes of silence, Béji Caïd Essebsi's voice is heard speaking through Bourguiba's projection, while moving his lips and addressing his
followers. The technology enabled an illustration of the continuity of past and
present in a strong symbolic way, not only to the interactional public at the meeting but also to a wider public, as the video was put on YouTube by the media
outlet Business News entitled: "Bourguiba reprend à Sousse" ("Bourguiba takes
back over in Sousse") (Business News, 2014, 01:38).

In the parliamentary elections of October 2014, Nidaa cast 37% of the votes
compared to the 27% of Ennahda. Beji Caïd Essebsi won the presidential elections after defeating interim President Moncef Marzouki in December 2014. The
candidate Hamma Hamami who was sent in the race by the popular front got
7.8%. For a first time, a female candidate, the judge Kalthoum Kannou took the

symbolic initiative to compete with the other 27 male candidates for the highest office in state; she received 0.56% of the votes (ISIE, 2014).

Former president of the ATFD, deputy and member of the executive bureau for the Nidaa Tounes party, Bochra Bel Haj Hamida states in an interview before the presidential elections of 2014 that it is precisely Bourguibism that unites the Nidaa Tounes party: "If there's something that unifies the party it's Bourguiba's modernist social project" (Strickland & Verghese, 2014). It becomes clear how the modernist project of Habib Bourguiba, which was analyzed in the contextual chapter, re-appears and is supported by a leading feminist of the country.[119] The hegemonic ideology of modernism, created in the aftermath of decolonization and its specific relation to gender is again established in the post-revolutionary period.

Ironically, after having focused on the delegitimizing campaigns before the election period, the Nidaa Tounes party and the Ennahda formed a coalition government together with UPL and AFEK. This could be framed as a 'historical bloc' representing by definition "an alliance of ruling class fractions would continuously sustain hegemony by building consensus" (Clarke, Hall, Jefferson, & Roberts, 1975, p. 102). The only party alliance excluded from this so-called historic bloc is the Popular Front as well as some other independent parliamentarians, who would remain the only opposition with parliamentary party status. This coalition between the two fierce adversaries reveals the "staging" of the confrontation on ideological issues, while both representing the interests of a conservative middle class that would not touch on established neo-liberal policies in the country. Their compromise illustrates the consensus orientation of the hegemonic framework that dominated the third phase of the transformation process.

Ben Ali himself famously put the particular culture of consensus forward in his speech on the 7th of November 1990 (Ayari M. B., 2012, p. 64). The consensual government is not only promising stability, it has been perceived as a victory for women and women's rights as well, preserving Tunisia's exceptionalism. As representative of Nidaa Tounes' "feminist wing," Bochra Bel Haj Hmida has defended the coalition with the Islamic Ennahda party, declaring that Ennahda had been transformed. She states: "We are against the project of Ennahda, but when you hear their discourse today, they speak like us, we have brought them to our project, they are unrecognizable" (Soudani, 2014). The Ennahda party, which would later separate itself from a "movement," was integrated and defending the hegemonic domain of power. The coalition shows the development of dissembled secularism, in which a religious party identity can be integrated into the nation-state when committing to the basic principles of state feminism.

---

119 It has to be stated that Hmida run for the Ettakatol party in 2011 but could not succeed in entering the ANC, partly because of a lack of support of her own party. Nidaa Tounes offered her a reliable opportunity to enter the strong public of the parliament.

Fabio Merone, studying Salafi and Islamist movements in Tunisia also assumes a "middle class compromise upon which the new Tunisia is being constructed," (Merone, 2015, p. 79) established through the democratic institutions. He argues that the compromise came at the expense of further radicalization of a disfranchised youth representing the lower classes that remains "materially and ideologically" excluded. It can be deduced that "Bourguibism" became the consensual frame for "the middle-class consensus" that was, I argue, furthermore underpinned by and up-to-date feminist legitimacy. I will later argue that radicalization and extremism of local youth posed a challenge for women, especially in marginalized localities.

In light of the increasing marginalization of left parties besides their effort to unite in the Popular Front, one could ask whether the elections can be considered the right tool to institutionalize the revolutionary demands of 2011. The skepticism towards democratic institutions has been expressed in my interviews with regards to a lack of education and socio-economic pressures that wouldn't allow for informed decision-makings at the ballot boxes.[120] Indeed, the turnout for the parliamentary and presidential polls in October and December 2014 casts doubt on the assumption that the demands of the Tunisian uprisings were channeled effectively through participation in elections. Rather, an abstention rate of 40% of registered voters in the parliamentary elections demonstrated a lack of trust in the established institutions. Significantly, the lowest turnout occurred in Sidi Bouzid, where the abstention rate was 52%, according to the INS. These figures mirror the continuation, and in some instances, deepening disparities between the center of the country and its coastal areas (Antonakis, 2015, p.18f.).

8.4   Conclusion: Renegotiating Gendered Institutions

The purpose of this Chapter was to detail the shifts in the structural dimension of the public sphere by analyzing changes in the electoral legislation, the association law, the national constitution and the international women's rights codification of CEDAW, while exposing the limits of a powerful state feminist legacy. The analysis of access and representation of women in the political institutions after 2011, with regards to the interim institutions, the parliament and the democratic elections, showed that it was predominantly a small, but very well-organized group of feminists within the interim institutions that imposed a quota system for the electoral lists prior to the democratic elections in 2011. Furthermore, I have argued that institutional changes such as the reform of the associa-

---

120 The arguments were outlined with regards to the first elections in 2011 Tunisia under 6.1.3

tion law have enabled feminist counterpublics from different localities to become organized.

In contrast, respondents advanced that a lack of education, poverty and biased reporting in the mass media impeaches the overall efficiency of a representative democratic system. They point to systematic oppressions inherent in the neo-liberal system that structure inclusion and exclusion to the public sphere and the democratic system.

Finally, I have argued that Nidaa Tounes party's success in the elections was due to a revitalization of *Bourguibism*: They could reactivate the state feminist legacy incorporated in the hegemonic domain of power, linked to secularism and modernity, in opposition to the Islamic camp and the Troika government. Finally, the unity government is not only an expression of a "middle class compromise" that includes an elite that has been sidelined under Habib Bourguiba but can be regarded as a new "patriarchal bargain" legitimizing the pursuit of the same neo-liberal politics that initially triggered the uprisings in 2008 and 2010/2011.

The next chapter offers a gender analysis of the representational domain of the public sphere and examines more closely the mechanisms that lead to an identity-focused discourse, which greatly impacted the ballot boxes and point to the themes that fed into the staged polarization between the secular and Islamic camp.

9 The Representational Dimension of the Public Sphere

Freedom of the press and freedom of expression, anchored in new press codes and legislations, have been regarded as one of the major outcomes of the revolutionary process in Tunisia so far (Zayani, 2015, p. 195) and are furthermore manifested in a multitude of local media outlets. These created local spaces of debate and the institutionalization of various civil society organizations and parties have led to a vibrant and more fragmented societal landscape. However, new democratic institutions were elaborated to regulate the media sector and ban hate speech and propaganda from the public sphere.

The Independent High Authority for Audio-Visual Communication (HAICA) was created in 2013 on the basis of a decree consented on in 2011 and also contains sanction mechanisms to monitor and regulate sexist and racist content. Its contested role was to "ensure the independence, pluralism and diversity of the media" in the critical post-revolutionary phase, but it was under constant attack by the political system (Article 19, 2014).

I argue that the mass media continue to be inscribed in a hegemonic domain of power drawing more on polarization than dialogue. Within Patricia Hill Collins' framework of the Matrix of Domination, the mass media plays a crucial role in propagating and maintaining the hegemonic domain of power: "…an increasingly important dimension of why hegemonic ideologies concerning race, class, gender, sexuality, and nation remain so deeply entrenched lies, in part, in the growing sophistication of mass media in regulating intersecting oppressions" (Collins, 2000, p. 284). A central question, then, is whether the representational dimension of the public sphere has substantially changed with regards to more pluralist depictions of gender since the uprisings (Silva & Mahdhaoui, 2016). The structural, or "hard repression" of the state has certainly changed but, as Marx-Ferree points out, this is not the only element that should be under investigation:

"States can exercise hard repression on the media in the form of censorship (...) my focus on soft repression by civil society, including institutionalized media practice excludes voices and produces silence, even when there is no direct censorship. The issue is therefore not if the media is free or not, but what a free media does" (Marx-Ferree, 2005, p. 147).

Fenton states that media "routinely access and privilege elite definitions of reality and are claimed to serve ruling hegemonic interests, legitimize social

© Springer Fachmedien Wiesbaden GmbH, part of Springer Nature 2019
A. Antonakis, *Renegotiating Gender and the State in Tunisia between 2011 and 2014*, Politik und Gesellschaft des Nahen Ostens,
https://doi.org/10.1007/978-3-658-25639-5_9

inequality and thwart participatory democracy" (Fenton, 2016, p. 2). In this respect, Habermas distinguishes four core characteristics of the *modus operandi* of the sensationalism of entertainment to create de-politicized subjects within the neo-liberal media system: "personalization, the dramatization of events, the simplification of complex matters, and the vivid polarization of conflicts" (Habermas, 2006, 27; quoted in: Fenton, 2016, p. 54). From this discussion, I deduce that the marketization of the media has influenced political communication and deeply informs the representational dimension of the public sphere.

There are various ways to explore where gender negotiations are manifested in the representational dimension of the public sphere. Scholars working on the relation of women in the media sector have pointed out that an analysis should not be limited by pure quantitative data on women in the media, but an examination on the oppressive structures that are reproduced in the hegemonic media needing a qualitative stance.[121] While a gendered perspective on the structures within media outlets would be incorporated in the structural dimension of the public sphere, this chapter is more concerned with two other perspectives that serve as entry points to analyze gender negotiations at the representational dimension of the public sphere: first, women as subjects of media productions, and the topics related to them. The aim to integrate "diversity" into theories of communication studies is discussed with regards to "essentialisation" and "othering" on the one hand, and the need to integrate wide ranges of representation of people on the other hand (Richter, Dupuis & Averbeck-Lietz, 2016, p. 5). The second perspective looks at counterpublics in their "factual dimension," which understands counterpublics as alternative media (in particular feminist media spaces created online) and counterthematization (Wimmer, 2007, p. 158) by investigating content appearing at the representational dimension of the public sphere. This second perspective has remained understudied for a long time compared to research on media representation of women and female audiences (Byerly & Ross, 2006; Minic, 2014, p. 134).

Firstly, I will engage with who is represented in the mass media, drawing upon interview material and two quantitative studies monitoring male-female representation in Tunisian mass media in 2011 and 2013. Then I will investigate feminist counterpublics online. Secondly, three particular contested themes –polygamy, inheritance laws and Femen – will be discussed: I deduced these from

---

121 Mohamed Ayish shows the under-representation of women in leading positions in the media sector, as producers, directors and decision makers (Ayish, 2010). Most strikingly, women played a role in the media sector in the transition period: To just give one example, Imen Bahroun has been appointed as the head of Tunisia's public television network in August 2012, which was deemed illegal by Decree-Law 2011-116 of 2 November 2011, stipulating that such appointments must be made in full consultation with the High Authority for Audiovisual Communications (HAICA) (Weslaty, 2012).

my interviews, but they have also been identified as "hot topics" in secondary literature (Marks, 2013). The themes can be set at the heart of negotiating the hegemonic domain of power, namely at the representational dimension of the public sphere: they were not concerned with concrete legislations. To put it frankly, lots of ink, bits and bytes were accorded to them but never revolved around concrete policy proposals or outcomes related to the structural dimension of the public sphere.

Next, I show how this media discourse has been engrained within the reappearance of pre-revolutionary ideologies and was integrated into party politics. Consequentially the feminist subject was re-constructed and the inscription of feminism in universalist presumptions of representing the (read: *all*) "women" of Tunisia. Finally, I will explore ways of resistance against the one-dimensional hegemonic depictions of women and gender relations in the public sphere by means of counterpublic productions in the representational dimension of the public sphere.

9.1   Who Is In? Media Representation of and by Women

A rise in quantity of media outlets and a liberalization of the press code does not necessarily translate into ground breaking changes at the representational dimension of public sphere. Media activists Mahdhaoui and Silva state with regards to possible renegotiations of gender relations and identities:

"Despite the apparent abundance of media spaces, Tunisian media continues to reproduce the same heteronormative and patriarchal patterns of domination. It is from this perspective that we decided to use journalistic and audio-visual knowledge and tools to create this new safer media space of expression and artistic and political development" (Silva & Mahdhaoui, 2016, p. 98).

Drawing upon feminist media theory, the approach of Silva, Mahdhaoui and others can be positioned as 'women's media enterprises', referring to the independent, often small, media outlets created by feminists themselves to produce their own knowledge and distribute it in their own media with maximum control (Minic, 2014). Collins distinguishes two levels of knowledge creation for a politics of empowerment. While creating new knowledge about one's own experiences of oppression can be empowering, she pleads that: "activating epistemologies that criticize prevailing knowledge and that enable us to define our own realities *on our own terms* has far greater implications" (Collins, 2000, p. 274).

9.1.1 The "Classical Media": Persisting Underrepresentations

The quantitative reports I analyzed for this study were produced by the "Coalition of NGOs for a democratic transition" in 2011 and by the "Arab Working Group for Media Monitoring" in 2013. In the same field, researchers at the "Center of Arab Women for Training and Research" (CAWTAR),[122] through monitoring of the media, have made efforts to introduce new theories offering practical guidelines to media outlets in the interests of implementing gender equality (interview with Atidel Mejribi and Soukaina Bouraoui, May 2013).[123]

The first study was conducted by the ATFD and other NGOs monitoring the period of August 2011 to November 2011 before the Tunisian elections. The study is entitled "Media monitoring in the transition period" (Coalition des ONG Tunisiennes pour la Transition démocratiques, 2011) and was supported by "International Media Support." Most importantly for this work, the study includes gender as an analytical category: It highlights mass media coverage of the activities of female politicians, while also providing data on the media coverage of topics related to gender. The study investigated seven print media publications, four TV channels and four radio stations within three rather short different time periods: First, when registrations for the elections were set (1st to 25th August); second, during the crucial time of the election campaign (1st to 22nd October); and finally the period after the elections and the preparation of the constitutional parliament (23rd October until November 30th).

When interpreting the results, strikingly, the representation of female politicians is higher during the second period in all media, reaching a maximum of 10% on TV. In comparison, the report mentions 6,000 female candidates for all electoral lists, constituting approximately 50% of the overall candidates (11,313). However, this included other categories of politicians as well (members of government, leaders and parties' spokespeople). The change in representation is highlighted in TV, where the representation of female politicians doubles before the elections and drops back down right afterwards.

---

122 I visited the center in May 2013 to speak to the director and a research assistant specialized in social media. It was created in 1993 and headed by Talal ibn Abd al-Aziz Al Saud. It is situated in Tunis next to the Saudi Embassy, which gives it a rather surprising location. Besides the oppressive policies against women in Saudi Arabia, the center's self-proclaimed aims are to "enhance the status of women and collect data, indicators and statistics." Their work is based on principles of human rights and gender equality" (see their mission statement, http://jamaity.org/bailleur/center-of-arab-women-for-training-and-research/, translated by author). I find it important to note that their reports are not publicly accessible.

123 In the first step, they have looked at research conducted in different countries to find common patterns and harmonized established methodologies. Second, they have developed a software for media houses to discern the gender gap within their own institution along different categories, such as salaries and gender distribution in decision making positions (Interview Mejribi, Atidel, Tunis, CAWTAR, May 2013)

Overall, the representation of female politicians remains very low in all three phases.

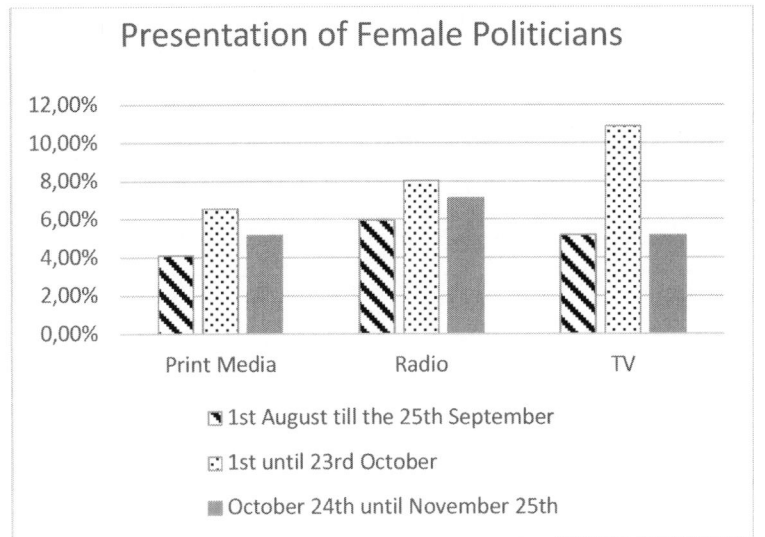

Chart 1: Presentation of Female Politicians in selected national Mass Media before, during and after the elections 2011 as found by (Coalition des ONG Tunisiennes pour la Transition démocratiques, 2011, pp. 45-49).

The quota system as an element of the structural dimension of the public sphere certainly reflects on the results because more female political figures running for elections and were thus more represented in the second phase under investigation. This finding illustrates the interconnection between the structural and representational dimension of the public sphere. From an intersectional perspective however, it would have been interesting to further diversify the category of "female politicians" by locality or educational background. Furthermore, the study finds that discussion of gender issues was almost absent in the media under investigation. 2.32% of the media content was related to gender related topics:

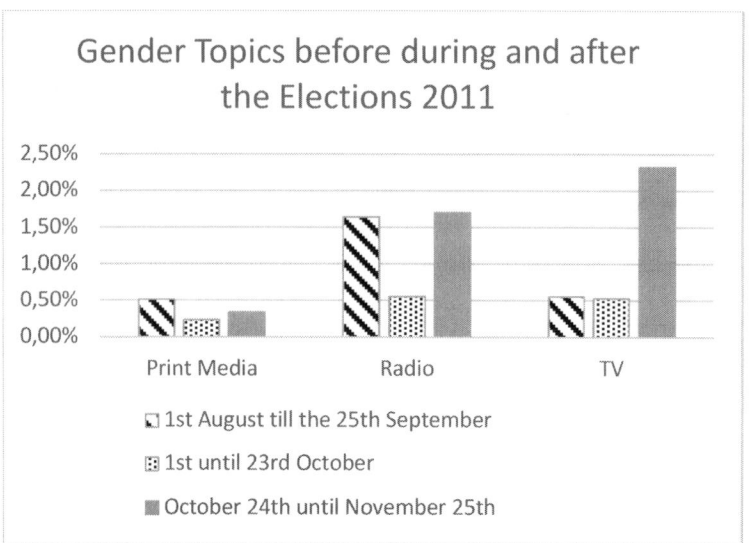

Chart 2: Coverage accorded to gender issues in percent as found by (Coalition des ONG Tunisiennes pour la Transition démocratiques, 2011, pp. 50-85)

The numbers expose opposing trends with regards to the coverage of female politicians: While their presence rose in the pre-election period, the percentage of gender related topics declined during periods of political campaigning, only to rise after the elections. Again, this dynamic is the most accentuated in TV coverage, where gender topics were increasingly discussed after the victory of the Ennahda party and the formation of the Troika government. However, the quantitative design of the study doesn't allow for a more differentiated examination of which gender topics have been handled and by whom. In light of the analysis of the structural dimension of the public sphere, the figures on media coverage reflect the centrality of gender issues during coalition building and the proceeding constitutional drafting process. These results back the argument that gender was increasingly politicized only after the first elections in 2011 and represented from now on as an important element for criticizing the government.

The second study, published by the Arab Working Group for Media Monitoring, using a more differentiated methodology, covers a timeframe of eleven weeks in 2013. The monitoring of the presence of women in relation to their profession allows for vital insights into the representation of gender and class in the classical media landscape. From the quantity of women appearing on TV, radio and in newspapers, politicians are the most represented (810 representations in total), but in relation to male politicians, they constitute only 7.2% of total presence.[124] However, it shows that the profession of politician allows women to access the public sphere the most.

With regards to the overall male-female partition by profession; female representation as housewives (60.4%) and as students/pupils (50.9%) are most prominent: the figures here revealing the more traditional repartition of labor and the reality of male-female percentages in the society respectively. Furthermore, women have a significant presence as celebrities (36%) and artists (25.9% and also compose an important share of the representation of health professionals (28.4%) in the mass media.

The lowest representation of women, however, can be found in the fields of security, namely soldiers and policewomen (1.3%) and religion (2.7%) (Arab Working Group for Media Monitoring, 2013). Security and religion can be discerned as important fields within the disciplinary domain of power, which regulates gender relations in society at the very interactional dimension of the public sphere. These representations can be related to the findings of the challenges women face on an everyday basis. I identified extremism and radicalizations on the one hand, and police violence on the other, as major challenges impacting female participation in the interactional dimension of the public sphere. Against this background, one could assume a causal relation between under-representations of female role models speaking on religion and security and its repercussions on everyday lived experiences. However, this relation constitutes an interesting starting point for further investigation. For example, during the elections in 2014, female soldiers securing polling stations in Tunis were a popular illustration of the elections, especially in Western media outlets. Furthermore, in 2015, the Tunisian National League of Police Women was created, which constitutes the first step for more representation of women in the security sector.

Unfortunately, due to the lack of data covering the whole period under study here, this analysis cannot make exhaustive claims. However, it is striking that there seems to be a contradiction, or paradox, between the room of negotiations in the structural dimension of the public sphere (note that a consensus commission had to be employed in order to deal with issues of women's rights causing a slowing down of the overall constitutional process), and the actual airtime and text accorded to the various issues. This interpretation can be attributed to the wider "gender-paradox" in the political process, as stated by Andrea Khalil. (Khalil, 2014, p. 196).

Andrea Khalil has studied the accounts of media studies professor Fathia Saidi and Ennahda deputy Farida Labidi who both agree that women were particularly absent from the media and went on to implore a lack of diversity in

---

124 This finding corresponds roughly to the percentage of female politicians as found in the previous report, note that the report of 2013 summarizes the findings for radio, TV and print, presenting the average that has been detailed out by media in the previous report.

women's representation, especially pointing to the absence of veiled women. According to Farida Labidi, "dominant classes that controlled the media had inherited, and were continuing the tradition of Ben Ali's anti-Islamist ideology" (Khalil, 2014, p. 196). Analyzing these claims from the perspective of the Matrix of Domination, the representational dimension of the public sphere was persistently inscribed in a hegemonic domain of power: stoking fears of an Islamist state project to be enacted by Ennahda would reproducing feelings of Islamophobia and increase the legitimacy of modernist hegemony.[125]

According to my respondents, there was not only a lack of diversity in the representation of women in the media, but in the overall representation of Tunisia's citizens. Only a few actors monopolized the discussions in the wider publics, impacting in our understanding the representational dimension of the public sphere. This monopolization is described by Borsali as a personalization of trained opinion makers that would take over the majority of airtime on TV and prevent an informed in-depth discussion. She specifically mentions political parties as the main opinion makers:

> "It's always the same people who participate in the debates on television. Sometimes you have the same people going from one TV panel to another the same evening. They control very well their discourse and express their opinion. Political parties are always there. When it's about the project of society we want, civil society is there, but they don't reflect enough either. (…) But there were no debates, neither on television, nor in the print media. What I want to say is that nothing is been done on a profound level" (Noura Borsali, Tunis, May 2013).

Revisiting the authoritarian legacies employed by the Bourguiba and Ben Ali-regimes would have implied a critical assessment of state feminist practices supporting a patriarchal order. The absence of debate, especially with regards to women's rights and the subject of feminism was therefore expected.

In this context, it could be argued that TV talk shows are not the most appropriate place to have in-depth and informed discussions on political issues in any case. I will now turn to the parliament, as a public where alternative gender identities could be displayed. Some interviewees have pointed to the quota system, which allowed for increased visibility of female parliamentarians. This produced the perception that it would be possible for female politician to succeed in Tunisia, which in turn would have a long-term positive effect on gender equality in the country. Framing and codifying gender equality at the structural dimension

---

125 Throughout the period under study, the media system stood accused by members of Ennahda of still operating within the logics of the former regime, while on the other hand, it has been affirmed that Ennahda wanted to "put its hand on the media," by appointing Ennahda friendly strategic positions.

of the public sphere has indeed impacted the representational dimension positively. As a strong public, the Tunisian parliament certainly brought to the fore
a plurality of women that played an important role in upholding diversity in the
representational dimension. The fact that they came from different backgrounds
and regions, each with their own circumscriptions, certainly fostered further
identification within the female audience. Debates were aired live on national
TV, videoclips were shared on social media. One politician who unsettled the
established hegemonic domain of power by her very presence was Mehrezia Labidi of the Ennahda party, who was elected vice-president of the ANC. Her political position assured her visibility in the hegemonic public. Journalist Sana
Sbouaï summarizes Labidi's role within the context of the media:

> "This is the reality! It's a woman from Ennahda, even though this is op-
> posing the ideas we had received. It's a woman from Ennahda who has
> somehow managed the ANC for two years. Who is veiled! So the first
> ideas we had and you could hear was: It's a woman who is not in her
> place, a woman from Ennahda has to be conservative, looked at as a
> woman who will stay aside, not able to manage anything. This woman
> has shown to everybody that she is capable" (Sana Sbouaï, Tunis, May
> 2014).

Sbouaï recognizes how Labidi was capable of breaking with powerful stereotypes, not only of women in politics but also religious women in particular.
Against this background she surely has integrated a new lawyer of a gendered
challenging the hegemonic image of "the modern Tunisian woman" by representing a strong veiled woman managing political debates. She can, however, be
considered an exception in the Tunisian public sphere not only by her gender
and religious identity, but due to the stances she took as a politician, sometimes
even against the majority of her party[126]. In the interviews, secularist feminists
have even referred her as a "surprise". Her performance in parliament contributed to the de-colonization of the hegemonic feminist conceptions linked to the
secular project of modernity.

On the other hand, placing women as a 'window dressing' after the revolution was common practice in the public sphere. Y.T. references her experience
in a small secularist political party:

> "I gave many interviews after the revolution when I was still part of the
> party [political left party]. Every time there came journalists who want to
> talk to young people, they called me up. (…) It's the party who puts you
> in front of the camera or the micro and that's it. (…)It's practical of
> course, but of course it's just for the media" (Y.T., Tunis, March 2014).

---

126 For example, Labidi received sex workers to discuss their working conditions after the uprisings
   (See 9.3.1.).

As a young woman with political aspirations, she felt exploited by the party to serve their representational agenda only. Despite having participated in the interim institutions renegotiated in the codification of women's rights, she never participated in any fundamental decision-making within the party. Y.T. eventually decided to withdraw entirely from party politics, which, under the Ben Ali regime, had offered a counterpublic that was better organized and equipped with (limited) resources of protection. She then decided to inscribe her participation in the field of civil society and finally to create her own media space, while others with a similar story dedicated themselves to professional media work.

Journalist Henda Chennaoui, points to a quantitative misrepresentation of women, but also points to the restricted range of topics that women are invited to speak about:

> "If you are not in this gender approach, the equality of men and women in the talk shows [and television programs] you will find yourself with 10 talk shows without any women. This is the case today in Tunisia. Even female journalists find it hard to impose women for political or societal subjects. We insist on the stereotype that when you are a woman, it has to be on family and sexuality, only this " (Henda Cheannaoui, Tunis, May 2013).

I suggest that this qualitative restriction of topics accorded to feminine subjectivities has further nourished a disconnection of feminist counterpublics from female representation in the mass media. The (few) women representatives in the hegemonic public sphere were depoliticized and lacked a space for subversive discursive politics that could show oppression in its various dimensions. This finding supports the importance of qualitative media studies that allow for an in-depth analysis of topics that bring to surface intertwined domains of power, rather than just in and exclusions to the public sphere.

When, Najoua Karim, a feminist activist from Sidi Bouzid discusses the representation of women with regards to pre-defined topics accorded to them:

> "All the time! All the time in the media, women who are activists and women in political parties, they are focusing on polygamy and that the women will wear the hijab! But the real issues: no. I don't see that there are discussions of these problems" (Najoua Karim, Sidi Bouzid, April 2014).

Polygamy and the veil, for example, are inscribed in a line of the "sensationalism of mass media" that proves to attract a high level of attention, thus feeding into the mobilizing discourse of a secular opposition that would challenge the legitimacy of the Islamic party in power. Women function as carriers of the messages that remain restricted to their symbolic bodies. It has also been displayed earlier, that they were practically excluded from discussing security and religion. In order to understand the repeated critique of the centralization of topics in the hegemonic public sphere and the marginalization of the "real issues," the next chapter will investigate them in more detail. After having focused on the "classical" mass media TV, radio and print, I will first look at the representational dimension of the public sphere created by many-to-many media in the next section

9.1.2 Counterpublics Online: Multifaceted Visibilities

Internet communication and social media represent therefore an alternative to the hegemonic public sphere. The new potential for women's emancipation processes online, that could challenge the Matrix of Domination by interfering and informing hegemonic productions of knowledge must therefore always be seen within, what I call a the "Matrix of Domination 2.0." Building up on critical scholarship on digital media, I employ intersectional theory as a tool to "push against peculiarly narrow presumptions about the universality of digital experience" (Coleman, 2010, p. 489). This unequal access "can translate into new hidden hierarchies of power" (Murphy, 2011, p. 110) manifested in digital divides. However, they can constitute a domain, where women renegotiate topics that remain marginalized or overlooked at the hegemonic public sphere. Lubna Skalli states for the MENA region the high costs of publishing alternative knowledge as they are "targeted by both religious and political circles" (Skalli, 2006, p. 41).

Eya Turki summarizes the importance of social networks as a counterpublic, functioning according to different rules that are entirely detached from the hegemonic domain of power:

> "The world that has been created on social media with projects, analyses and all the debates that come with it, I think this is completely different from what they say on TV panels with the old people who smell the naphthalene. It's not at all the same thing. It shows how disconnected we are from them and they are from us. This is ugly because we are not represented by anybody. Somebody that communicates our ideas, a person who has the guts to speak up at the right moment. And this is what makes us even more detached from the political class and affiliates us even more with the community we created on social media. There, we are free to say what we want at least, even though it doesn't have any impact. At least we communicate our standpoint, that's it already. That people listen to you when you talk about this and that and that. It's pretty important" (Eya Turki, Tunis, May 2013).

Her statement reveals the resignation of a younger generation. The disconnection from the political class is substituted by communication between peers on Twitter, hence Turki doesn't claim to be influential. The counterpublic online represents a different "world" that young people have created by themselves, with its own rules and debates thus eluding the structures and representations imposed by the state media and private mass media. The interaction between peers, where new knowledge is communicated, becomes a source of individual empowerment. The relief of being heard and the possibility to speak freely is considered a pivotal advantage. However, Turki mainly refers here to the Twitter community as "a small circle" with an "elitist" character in Tunisia, pointing to a small and exclusive number of people participating in that counterpublic. However, one member of the Twitter community, Slim Amamou, alias @slim404 (an account with over 300 000 followers), did integrate to the structural and representational dimension of the public sphere under the interim government when he took the post of a State Secretary of the Youth and Sports on January 18th 2011. His appointment became a symbol of the will to integrate the youth and digital elite from online counterpublics into the interim government. After using his increased political visibility to advocate for freedom of speech, he resigned from government.

In the interview, Henda Chennaoui mentions the characteristic of "Young" as an identity generating characteristic of the counterpublic. Young is not to be understood in terms of age, but rather in terms of ideology. She is part of the transregional feminist network "The uprising of women in the Arab World" that was created with a Facebook group in 2012. For fear of instrumentalization and co-optation the group refuses any funding and points out its autonomy.[127] It expresses an overcoming of feminist thoughts of the 1970 and the attempts to negotiate being a feminist differently, taking into account specific contextualities such as geographical locations, class or sexual orientation. Chennaoui brings up the issue of changes and reform from within feminist circles when describing the online counterpublic she engages with:

> "This is the term that we should use: the label 'Young'. Not the movements that started in the 1960s, who continued the independence struggles of the Arabic countries, these are the same movements which endured in Tunisia and that have the monopoly on feminism in Tunisia or the Arab World and it's a single experience that is obsolete and outdated a bit by our societies, outworn by its own clichés, by its convergence to power, by its fatigue as well" (Henda Chennaoui, Tunis, May 2013).

Her criticism shows the importance of the category of age: Her goal is to overcome the debates of the 1960s and challenge their monopoly. Feminist theories that were inscribed in anti-colonial struggles, as we have seen, were very much

---

127 I organized an exhibition in December 2013 in Berlin and had the chance to get to know one of their founders Sally Zohney and gain an insight into their integer funding policies. In the course of our cooperation, it has been discussed repeatedly that the network never wanted to depend on any political actors or (Western) donors and we actively sought alternative funding for the event.

inspired by nationalist thoughts. The revolution of 2011 stands as a specific reference point and its struggle is put as a continuity of the revolutionary process of demanding dignity. "Chaml" can be regarded a feminist counterpublic, tackling the representational dimension of the public sphere by creating a blog online. It is described as a "safe space" and in their self-definition they state: "the blog is the outcome of the encounter between young Tunisian women who wish to change the regard of the society on women and 'deconstruct *the myth of the modern Tunisian woman*"[128] (Homepage Chaml: About us, translated by author, emphasis added).

In this context, "Young" can be conceptualized on the most part with regards to three facets: First, the channels of communication used by the feminist actors, namely, many-to-many forms of communication and blogs bearing the potential to create trans-regional networks and alternative spaces of knowledge production at low costs[129]. Second, in opposition to feminist concepts of state feminism implemented within a nationalist and modernist framework of state building during colonial struggles and a refusal to be categorized within the ideologically constructed dichotomy of "Islamist" vs. "secular." Third, "Young" refers to a self-definition and the actual group of age of a generation that has mainly grown up under Ben Ali's regime that was established in 1987 and, in contrast to the generation before, are not the "children of the CSP"[130] that were adopted by the "father of the nation" Habib Bourguiba in 1957.

In the digitalized environment, they face particular challenges: Social media can function as an accelerator when it comes to attacks against feminists. This was a major point addressed in the interviews. For example, the ATFD, stood accused of atheism when lobbying for the full introduction of the CEDAW at the structural dimension of the public sphere:

> "We were particularly attacked on Facebook: Defamation, moral attacks against each of our members, threats, deformation of the history of the ATFD, everything has been used. (…) It's true that concerning communication, we are a bit late, but I think we did pretty well in facing the counter-attacks and we got over it. We could at least re-establish a bit the militant image of the ATFD, but concerning communication strategies, we are now elaborating them. It is not over yet and a difficult domain" (Ahlem BelHaj, Tunis, May 2014*).*

---

128 Find the website of the blog here https://collectifchaml.wordpress.com/: A piece by BBC contextualizing the initiative within the wider struggle of violence against women can be found here: „Has Life got worse for Tunisia's women?" http://www.bbc.com/news/world-africa-35743663

129 I hereby refer mainly to the Independent Tunisian Feminist Movement of the 1980s, emerging from the circles of the club Tahar Haddad in Tunis (Daoud, 1993) (Labidi L. , 2007).

130 The Family Status law (Code du Statut Personnel, CSP), introduced in 1957 is considered to be the most progressive women's rights codification in the Arab World (Charrad, 2008).

While, on the one hand, the feminist organization could rely on social media to create visibility and mobilize people to take the streets, the emergence of peer-to-peer networks has also led to an increase in often personalized attacks and accentuated misogynist oppression. This blessing and curse of social media in feminist activism can be regarded as *multi-faceted visibilities* (for an elaboration of this concept, see Antonakis, 2018*)*. Shaming and discrediting women and, for instance, female politicians or women' rights advocates became a common strategy in web 2.0 contexts. Online harassment reaches from personal attacks and *doxing*[131] to, for example, posting private photos or hacking and compromising websites of women's rights NGOs, such as Sisters in Islam in Malaysia (Jensen, sm Kee, Venkiteswaran, & Randhawa, 2012, p. 73). Feminist counterpublics that attempt to leave behind the "space of withdrawal" and target the hegemonic public sphere face different obstacles. Ridiculing and stigmatizing marginalized groups delegitimizes knowledge claims. Instead of creating new knowledge, they find themselves in a reactive position defending themselves constantly against accusations most often voiced by those of privileged positionalities. This illustrates the argument exposed earlier that in a digitalized environment, the state is not the only actor to implement censorship and regulations of the hegemonic domain of power defining gender and sexuality.

Certainly, opening up the public sphere, enabled by lifting internet censorship, allowed for increased interactions that hold the potential to challenge national power arrangements. ICTs are employed to put in place networking processes allowing nascent transregional feminist counterpublics to emerge. At the same time, strategies by anti-feminist movements are internationalized. Describing these phenomena always bears the pitfall of technology optimism and reproduction of an elitist paradigm that I problematized earlier. I will come back to this in my discussion of the Matrix of Domination 2.0. in the conclusion. However, I believe it is necessary to shed light on these initiatives because they create important pockets of resistance that may grow with the resources the participants hold.

Henda Chennaoui expresses the need for physical space. She insists that in order to implement and discuss long-term strategies, the women need to meet face-to-face, which creates various logistical problems, e.g. arranging and paying for flights

> "The virtual cannot replace a physical presence. Now we are at the third action of the movement, but you cannot meditate on [long term] strategies at long distance. We can organize collective actions, ok, this is not so hard. But you cannot think of a common strategy that needs to be discussed, argued, and negotiated. We have to meet each other concretely to

---

131 Doxing refers to publicly exposing the address and other personal information of a person on the internet without consent.

> spend one or two weeks together face-to face and discuss all the details. To come up with a strategy after all, to say: What will the movement do, in one year, in two years. This is who we are, this is what we want to achieve and this is what we want to do. (…) In order to come together, we need money, and this is the challenge we face" (Henda Chennaoui, Tunis, May 2013).

While it is possible to coordinate common actions virtually, Chennaoui exhibits that in order to create a sustainable feminist counterpublic, identities ("this is who we are"), common goals ("this is what we want"), and modes of action ("this is what we want to do") need to be negotiated among the core group of the movement. These three components are defined by Chennaoui as the "strategy" that the movement needs. In order to negotiate strategies, physical encounters and the need for a common space become crucial. This displays the limits of virtual forms of communication in establishing sustainable counterpublics and its vulnerability in challenging the hegemonic domain of power perpetuating all dimensions of the public sphere.

9.2   What Is On? Discussing the "False Problems"

This section engages with content and output of the media with regards to representation of gender relations and gender identities in the frame of political transformation. With the rise of Ennahda as the possible winner of the elections of 2011, the fears of falling behind the 'progressive' status of Tunisia was nourished in national and international media outlets alike (Marks, 2013, p. 225). Tunisian exceptionalism appeared endangered by an Islamic party taking power. Questions of national identity were negotiated not only in law texts and the compositions of political institutions as analyzed in the previous chapter, but also at the representational dimension of the public sphere. On the national level, I argue that the representation of women's issues was mis-focused and merely served to play on ideological cleavages, rather than address structural reforms that would benefit all citizens of Tunisia. "Derailing," "real issues" and "wrong debates" were formulations, employed repeatedly in the interviews in this context. Najoua Karim points to the exploitation of gender issues for pure power politics:

> "They [the parties with support of the mass media] will create many false problems. They will create problems for the women, they tell you: 'You will have a backlash, you will lose all your acquis. We have done this and that'. On the other hand, there is the problem of the new ones, who took power [Ennahda, in occurrence A.N.] who don't want the revolution to be accomplished either. They want to create false problems around

> women and youth as well and with everybody. Because it's a power ne-
> gotiation. Not more. All the rest is not really important to them" (Najoua
> Karim, Sidi Bouzid, April 2014).

Karim's account reveals a deep mistrust towards both the "new" and "old" parties and the mass media. She claims that questions of gender and youth cannot be regarded as independent from power politics. She feels that they serve to create "false problems" that would derail public attention from revolutionary aims. She clarifies that both political camps, the old and the new parties in power, can profit from the same strategy. Habiba Trifi employs the same argument:

> "False problems have been created. Amina [Sboui, who protested topless
> as part of the Femen counterpublic, see 9.2.3] and others, that's not the
> issue. The revolt has started based on the right to work, poverty and all
> these issues, later on it got derailed to questions of the Niqab and nudity.
> Was the revolt sparked by the Niqab or Amina? No. The revolution has
> started by the people and for the people. All the rest are false problems"
> (Habiba Trifi, Kairouan, April 2014).

The topics that have been addressed in the interviews, illustrating the focus on ideological and identity questions, were central in the discussion of gender after the uprisings and are contrasted with the issues that the interviewees highlighted.[132] They constitute "wedge issue[s] or flashpoint conflicts between Islamist and secular trends" (Marks, 2013, p. 224).

In contrast to the hypervisible "flashpoint conflicts," the media monitoring report by CAWTAR, concludes that the topics related to issues of gender were marginalized during their observations in 2012 and "women were almost systematically excluded" (Ben Salem & Mejbri, 2015).

---

132 I had previously included the issue of single mothers in this section, due to its importance for the maintenance of the Matrix of Domination and their entire deprivation of political rights. The structural domain of power simply excludes mothers and their children from state services or makes it extremely difficult to access government services (Marks, 2013, p. 240f.). With the constitutional process, the position of "single mothers" in Tunisian society was debated despite the fact that no concrete policies on the issue were discussed by political parties. It thus became a normative formulation of polity. In one interview I conducted with two young women form Sidi Bouzid, they addressed it to give an example of what "is not important in Sidi Bouzid" and attached it to a debate happening in the capital only, where "things like that" would matter. At the same time, I hold that it constitutes a struggle for many other respondents and should thus not be considered as a "hot topic" only. For instance, the counterpublic "Women and Citizenship" in ElKef has started to work on assisting single mothers and have described the difficulties to actu-ally get to the women and create an informal network to assist them (See interview Amel Cherni, ElKef, April 2014, p. 1 and p. 5). It was Ennahda deputy Souad Abderrahim who sparked the debate by declaring single mothers as "sinners" in a radio interview and renouncing their "right to exist" (Marks, 2013, p. 240). Souad Abderrahim herself became a symbol for Tunisia's excep-tionalism in 2018, when she was elected mayor of Tunis.

9.2.1 Polygamie

Polygamy had been abolished in Tunisia since 1957 by the introduction of the Personal Status Code (CSP). It bans polygamy and criminalized also the "person who knowingly marries someone liable under the forgoing clauses" (Mahmood, 1987, p. 157). Ennahda, for their part, had proclaimed its stance to preserve the CSP in 1988. As the Movement de Tendance Islamique, they formally accept the CSP (Labidi L. , 2016b, p. 141) and renewed this commitment within the anti-regime coalition of the Comité of 18th October in 2005.[133] Finally, during their first press conference after the uprisings in February 2011, they defined the strengthening of women's rights on the basis of the CSP as part of their political program (Trabelsi, Houda quoted in: Ayari & Geisser, 2011, p. 147). There was a political consensus that poligamy would not be re-introduced. Open calls for a reform would have challenged the hegemonic domain of power.

During the political transformation, no proposal for reform has ever been introduced to the legislative body, still, the scenario of the re-introduction of polygamy has taken a central place in the national and international public discourse. Tim Lister's piece for CNN for instance has the tendentious title "After the Arab Spring: Islam, democracy, bikinis and polygamy" published in October 2011 (Lister, 2011) after the elections. This underpins the argument about the entanglement of international and national public spheres that have been perpetuated by similar themes. The debate around polygamy became a yardstick that seemed detached from actual policy debates and concerns in counterpublics alike.

Many of the interviewees, especially those participating and acting outside of the capital, expressed serious doubt and disbelief that the introduction of polygamy would fall on fertile ground, because it would just not 'correspond' to Tunisian ideas regarding the organization of family. Hayet Amami shares in the interview that "even women from uneducated backgrounds" would refuse the idea of reintroducing polygamy, while men have advanced the argument of simply not earning enough money to be able to take care of more than one wife:

> "Even the 'simple' women, those who don't have a great cultural education they say: 'no, it's Ennahda who brought this up.' And that she can never change her lifestyle. Even in the debate on polygamy and the right to marry four women, these women said no! And even the men said: We wouldn't have enough money to live comfortably" (Hayet Amami, Sidi Bouzid, April 2014).

Amami, as well as other interviewees, stresses that no women, independent of her education, would agree to polygamy. Furthermore, it is considered an issue

---

133 For the historical context of the coalition, see Chapter 6.2.

for the middle- and higher-class, because poor men would not be able to pay maintenance. In her analysis, Ennahda is considered to have brought this topic up in political circles.

It has been repeatedly argued that the focus on identity issues prohibited a debate on structural reforms of the country. Najoua Karim, who is an active member of a diverse local civil society project in Sidi Bouzid has repeatedly pointed to the derailment of "real issues" in relation to mis-representations of the applications of the revolutionary demands and identifies polygamy as a case in point, affirming:

> "I see that we have to work on women's incomes, on their health, social insurances to work in the fields... There are many issues for these women. They don't only need their husband not to marry another wife, Ok, that's fine, but they need many, many different things as well" (Najoua Karim, Sidi Bouzid, April 2014).

Karim highlights the socio-economic situation of women and access to public services, needing political debate and reform. Income and the gender pay gap, especially in the agricultural sector, equal access to health care and a development of the social insurance system do not serve as easy identity markers. They do not represent topics that fit into binary logics of sensationalism but require more technical discussion. However, they constitute the most important themes discussed in the counterpublic she engages in. Many other interviewees raised these issues and they will be discussed separately hereafter. This goes in line with the methodology that this study engages in, attempting to shed light on counter-narratives beyond hegemonic negotiations of gender.

9.2.2 The Inheritance Legislation

It has been stated before that the inheritance law embodies one of the last "barriers" representing access to property and power inspired by Islamic law. It entitles women to inherit half of the amount of their brothers. The question of introducing equal inheritance was important during the transformation phase at various encounters. The legislation is based on the sharia law, where it is stated that "to the male the equivalent of the portion of two females, (Surat An-Nissa, 4:11): Defending equal inheritance was therefore easily placed under the stigma of atheism. Besides its religious character it also has a pure economic dimension which privileges men over women. The religious legislation[134] can greatly mask the maintenance of men's economic power.

---

134 The legislation was progressive at the time, because it stipulates that women do have the right to inherit at all.

A reform has been discussed within the international framework of the CEDAW, outlined in the previous chapter. The commitment to an equal inheritance law was directly linked to the defense of homosexuality. Feminist Ahlem Bel Haj from the ATFD provides insights into the negotiations on the inheritance laws and claims that it remains a symbolic gatekeeper to sustain gendered division of labor. The argument advanced is of a paternalistic nature, "protecting women" from a double burden:

> "We were at the commission and we have said it before. They came to us saying that women's political participation is no problem, but that it is the equality in private space that will burden women. Cause if we would ask women to participate economically to the investments of the family – as if the Tunisian women wouldn't do it already- that this would constitute another burden. All resistance in public is concerned with the head of the family, the right of child custody, but most importantly the inheritance. They are completely against it. And the battle is on that level as well" (Ahlem BelHaj, Tunis, May 2014).

Her explanations reveal the anachronism of the argument, as women are indeed already an integral part of the Tunisian labor force and breadwinners for the family. The husband is considered the "head of the family" according to the family code CSP. The question of inheritance is then crucial in the systematic organization of labor, especially in privileged families.

According to the PEW report of 2013, Tunisians are on top when it comes to defending the right of women to divorce (81% agree with the current codification) or the freedom to choose their dress (89%). However, this study finds that regarding equal inheritance Tunisia (and Morocco) comes last of all in the MENA region with only 15% of the respondents believing that sons and daughters should have equal inheritance rights (PEW-Report, 2013, p. 95). In light of the results of these polls, the political parties in Tunisia treated the subject carefully. Parties on the left, with their connections to various feminist pressure groups, were the only ones to defend equality. However, Najma Labidi recalls that while defending it on paper, they didn't actually mobilize for it in any wider publics, such as the media or the Tunisian parliament:

> "I quote for example the communist party: It defends total equality and goes with the horizontal and vertical equality [in the electoral lists]. It's the only party that states in its program that they are for the equal inheritance. But did they, later on, fight for it in the assembly or lobbied for it in the media? No!" (Najma Kousri Labidi, Tunis, May 2014).

This reveals how political parties exploited the inheritance laws to secure votes, albeit only within their own restricted publics of support that would sympathize with this policy. Nevertheless, they wouldn't take up a reformist position in the public sphere, at least in the period under investigation. Labidi also reveals the importance to tackle both dimensions of the public sphere, the structural and the representational, to foster feminist politics.

A proposition to reform the law was brought to parliament in May 2016 following the publication of a new study from the national survey institute Sigma, whereby the majority of Tunisians (73%) indicated their preference to give the choice to the concerned parties of which quotation should be adopted in the inheritance laws (Huffington Post Maghreb, 2016). A connection between public opinion polls and policy suggestions seems likely here.[135] Consequently, the debate on equal inheritance changed and became more substantial, as an actual policy proposition was then discussed.

In her study on gender relations and property in Palestine, anthropologist and expert on Muslim family law, Annelies Moors offers a more distinctive view on the inheritance issue. She highlights the importance of shifting the focus from property as "material resource to a social relation" because "inheriting property could have widely divergent meanings, calling into question both the centrality of the nature of the property involved and the assumed direct relation between property and power" (Moors, 1996, p. 69 f.).

Implicitly, the exclusive focus on the materialistic dimension of equal inheritance in an intersectional setting would mean very different things to women from different positionalities. The reform of the inheritance laws was considered a bourgeois feminist policy. "We don't have anything to inherent" was a response that reflected the social realities of women over the need to reform the discriminatory legal practice. S.C. criticizes the universalist grounds of dominant feminist politics, and exemplifies her claim with regards to the inheritance laws:

> "They [the feminist organizations at the capital. N.A.] always work on a very superficial level and make statements on 'the women' in general. For example, the pledging for the economic equality and the equal inheritance. They have no consciousness that even with a new code for the inheritance, these women don't have anything (S.C., Tunis, April 2014).

S.C. calls out the 'superficial' analysis and claims of universality in activism for gender equality. Indeed, a more intersectional approach would help to identify and define different needs according to different localities and levels of resources. She questions the hegemonic subject of feminism that is defended by the more influential NGOs. They, on the other hand, were stigmatized by religious conservative sides, but also revolutionary feminist positions, for pursuing a Western modernist model.[136]

---

135 The proposition does not fall under my period of investigation. However, it would have been interesting to look at the methodologies and concrete questions asked in the two different surveys from 2013 and 2016.
136 On this issue, see chapter 8.2.2. and 10.2.1.

The debate to reform the inheritance laws exemplifies different prioritization in challenging the matrix of oppression according to different positionalities. It entails a materialistic and ideological dimension that is structuring oppression. It appears that the feminist counterpublic lobbying directly within the institutions via international frameworks for a reform of the law could not communicate on the symbolic importance for a negotiation of gender relations beyond the materialistic dimension across different classes. Just like the debate on polygamy, an actual consensus between the secular and Islamic parties to maintain the status quo and the discriminatory law can be observed for the period under study.

9.2.3 Femen and Amina Sboui

In the period under study one of the most disputed and controversial non-legislative issues was the protest of former Femen member Amina Sboui. Freedom of sexuality and bodily comportment in the public sphere has been negotiated here as one aspect of feminism. Amina Sbouri, an 18-year-old high school student, circulated topless images of herself on social media in March 2013.[137] Her protest was directed against religious moralization of the female body conveying the slogan: "My body belongs to me and is anyone's honor." The strategy of protesting naked is not new and has a long tradition in African history, where the women's body is used as political action. Nigerian feminist scholar Ogundipe-Leslie accounts: "If she threatens to strip and go naked, even governments will go down" (Ogundipe-Leslie, 1994, p. 212).

Amina Sboui's participatory bodily act was thus situated within the translocal counterpublic of Femen, who had, for their part, used their protest tactic previously in a European setting. Femen's understanding is very much an embodiment of binary thinking, which does not take into consideration the complexities and intersections of power relations that produce women's everyday life experiences obstructs the view on modern patriarchal hegemony. This is not surprising, when looking at their initial ideas, in which their activism is positioned in a logic of war, as expressed by Inna Shevchenko, self-identified "leader of the feminist movement Femen":

"Make no mistake about it: we are at war. This is an ideological war, a war of traditionalism against modernity, oppression against freedom, dictatorship against the right to free expression. We are targeting the three principle manifestations of patriarchy: religion, the sex industry, and dictatorship" (Shevchenko, 2013).

---

137 For an interpretation of the arrival of Femen in Tunisia from a cultural studies perspective, see (Labidi L., 2014, p. 89)

International women's rights defender and scholar Chitra Nagarajan qualifies their action as "racist colonial feminism" and reminds that "the role of feminists from outside should be to support the work of the women in the communities concerned, not to add to the problem. (…) A true ally does not use racism to attempt to defeat patriarchy" (Nagarajan, 2013). Slogans such as "Nakedness is freedom" or "Arab women should be liberated" demonstrate a lack of awareness from a post-colonial perspective. Their methodology does not include a discussion of differences among women, and exposes a White Savior complex that relies on biased and racist stereotyping.[138]

In the content analysis of the interview material, three different positions towards Amina's protest can broadly be distinguished, which will be layed out here after:

1) Approval, but Contextualization in Media Sensationalism

First, Amina's protest was welcomed as both an act that confronted the liberal democratic camp with the limits of their own hypocrisy in their definition of freedom and a courageous act against radial Islamism (see interview, Eya Turki, Tunis, May 2013, p. 6 or Lina Ben Mheni p. 7). In our interview, Lina Ben Mheni explains how it took her some time to formulate a position towards her before she fully supported Amina. It inspired her to write a blogpost entitled: "I quit being hypocrite –I support Amina" (ben Mheni, 2013). At the same time, feminists who defended and supported Amina were cautious about the sensationalist media coverage that would derail any truly in-depth discussion on feminism as an ideology and confine it to the realm of mere entertainment. Indeed, Amina Sboui's "buzz" in the representational dimension fits into the logics of entertainment relying on polarization and personalization.

It can be regarded as an act of self-chosen hypervisibility, to turn the gaze on the hegemonic domain of power producing gendered subjects with regards to respectability (Amar, 2011, p. 304). The concept of "hypervisibility" was developed by critical race scholars and entrenches referring to

"processes whereby racialized, sexualized subjects, or the marked bodies of subordinate classes, become intensely visible as objects of state, police and media gazes and as targets of fear and desire (...) Paradoxically, when subjects are hypervisibilized, they remain invisible as social beings: they are not recognizable as complex, legitimate, participatory subjects or citizens" (Amar, 2011, p. 305). While Amina's topless uprising as a Femen activist attracted attention within the

---

138 For a reply to the critique see for example Pyzik's piece: "White doesn't always mean privileged: why Femen's Ukrainian context matters" (Pyziks, 2013). She argues that Femen has to be seen in the context of post-communist masochism and its oppressive sex-industry. The Femen disputes are very diverse and can be regarded from different contexts and angles. Unfortunately, I can't go into more details here.

logic of the mass media and social media, her body protest became an important identifier and revealed conservative thinking even within the self-declared "progressive" and secular camp.

International public spheres again accelerated this dynamic of sensationalism that would marginalize the actual message conveyed by the teenager. Ahlem BelHaj points to international media's sensationalism fueling the debate around freedom of expression, women's rights and Islam:

> "In the case of Amina, there was no problem of communication at the level of the freedom of expression, on the contrary, there was an over-mediatization, I think. Especially from foreign media. This over-mediatization has helped neither the victim [allusion to Amina's political imprisonment, that will be laid out later] neither the cause. When it's over-mediatized, you are not in a fundamental discussion, but in the entertainment section".

In more general terms, she adds:

> "The media is an event, they don't work in the logic of continuity. There is the possibility to fraction an established order, but there is no elaborated strategy in place yet" (Ahlem BelHaj, Tunis, May 2014).

Her argument can be related to the Habermasian idea of de-politicizing power of the entertainment industries outlined above. Even if the hypervisibility was her choice, she was not able to direct the discussion away from her body to the actual message at hand:[139] the right of women to possess their own body and the liberalization from the patriarchal norms inscribed to it.[140] While her protest may have originated in a counterpublic, its main dispersion was "decreed by corporately-controlled mass communications" (Fenton & Downey, 2003, p. 200).

Amina Sboui was attacked from various sides: She received death threats from religious radicals. The preacher Adel Almi who had called for stoning her to death before on social media was invited onto a TV show along with Sboui: "When he appeared on Tunisian television, while refusing to occupy the same chair that Amina Sboui had sat in earlier, he recanted his earlier call for punishment, emphasizing his view that the young woman needed psychological treatment" (Labidi L. , 2014, p. 164). So, while death threats were not pronounced in the hegemonic public sphere, her protest was thus stigmatized and delegitimized as the act of a "mentally ill" person. The personalization and pathologization,

---

139 To extend the argument, it would be interesting to analyze the Femen protest within McLuhann's paradigm in media theory on "the medium is the message," situating the message conveyed by the naked body within the wider structure of the internet and TV as a medium within the medium.
140 This struggle is thus incorporated into other initiatives that were created in 2016, such as the video: "60 years after independence, our bodies are still colonized" launched by the initiatives Chaml and Chouf minorities that I will explore in more detail later (Amal Bint Nadia, 2016).

both outcomes of the sensationalist logic of the mass media, hindered a negotiation of the sexist oppressive structure that she initially wanted to address.

2)   "She added to the problem"

Second, most of the respondents argued that Amina in fact "added to the problem," despite her intentions, advancing a broad range of arguments. Women criticizing feminism as practiced by NGO representatives in the capital felt somehow assured in their opinion and qualified her protest as "disgusting" and "not the right way to do it." O.L., a lawyer from Tunis, affiliated with the pirate party whom I met in Berlin, analyzes the reinforcement of stereotypes and refusal of feminist concepts within the protest of Amina that received intense media attention in April 2013:

> "For example, to talk about politics still makes people uncomfortable in Tunisia. Not to speak about feminism, which makes people even more uncomfortable and adding the emergence of the Femen movement. The people who already mistrust feminism in itself, they perceive 'feminism' in a really wrong manner (now)" (O.L., Berlin, May 2013).

I have outlined before, how Femen's founder Shevchenko uses an overtly warlike rhetoric that ignores the actual struggles feminists face on the ground. Young feminist Najoua Karim expressed deep concerns on the backlash against women from religious extremists after the uprisings. In Shevchenko's logic, she would be on the front line of this everyday war, but Karim points out how the Femen movement has added fuel to the fire during a crucial and sensitive period. At the same time, she acknowledges the topless expression of Amina Sboui as a form of political protest, while posing the question of adequate methods:

> "They are free in the way they manifest themselves, it's a form they have chosen, okay. (…) But, in the current context especially, with the problems of Salafists, the terrorism and all of this and people instigating against the Tunisian women, this Femen movement has derailed the real issues, it didn't really help to ask the right questions. On the contrary: It created a buzz which had negative repercussion on the situation of the Tunisian women" (Najoua Karim, Sidi Bouzid, April 2014).

One of these negative repercussions is related to the actual local communication context where Salafist and *Wahabist* ideologies could infiltrate the local mosques after the uprisings in 2011. This issue has been raised various times in the interviews and I will go into more detail about this later.[141] Hayet Amami's

---

141 For an analysis of the rise of radicalization and extremism as perceived by women, mainly from outside the capital, see Chapter 10.1.2.

reasoning takes a similar direction: She situates the protest within an actual sensitive political situation that women felt, especially in Sidi Bouzid. She claims that she would have supported Amina's protest if she had conveyed her message during the regime of Ben Ali (see Interview Hayet Amami, p. 11). However, with regards to the tensions that female activists in Sidi Bouzid encountered, the topless protest did not serve their interests, but imposed a hegemonic image of feminism they had to distance themselves from.

The polemical actions of Sboui obliged women activists all over the country to position themselves towards Femen's activism. This lead to the necessity to re-legitimize their participation at the interactional dimension of the public sphere:

> "Those who are in direct contact with the people need to control their method and their image. An image of self-respect and respect of her community. Me, who is living in this tension, I cannot wear shorts and provoking clothes. I have to take care of my image, so when people see me [in photos] in demonstrations the next day or weeks later, they can't say that I'm like Amina-Femen. I need to show that I'm respectful, at the same time active; who mobilizes to help this city to progress and develop and [someone who] demands the rights of men and women alike" (Ameny Ltifi, Sidi Bouzid, April 2014).

Ltifi first introduces an implicit distinction based on class and locality: There are those who are in direct contact with the people, like herself as a woman in a counterpublic engaging in street protests in Sidi Bouzid. On the other hand, she regards those organizing among women only around personal libertarian and women's rights in the capital as detached from revolutionary feminist counterpublics. She voices her concern that all those active (and respectful) feminists, who actually live in a situation characterized by economic oppression and constant conflict, would all to easily be associated with Amina and need to renegotiate their position. In this way, Femen has further marginalized her and her female comrades in the local patriarchal order. The image of their body becomes crucial here, especially in a digitized world, where pictures of protests in public can re-appear at any moment to de-legitimize especially women's action for inappropriate bodily comportment and clothing.

The topless protest also created discussions within the feminist counterpublics and an urge to reposition themselves internally, as Amel Cherni from the "Association Femme et Citoyenneté" remembers:

> "One of our members, she shared the photo of Amina on our group page on Facebook... We told her: Erase it! Erase it! (…) On the streets they said: Ah you're feminist so you are Amina. They take this decision for you systematically. We had to talk to person by person to explain our standpoint" (Amel Cherni, ElKef, April 2014).

Collective decisions and standpoints had to be agreed upon internally before communicating them on social media. In the interviews, especially feminist activists from localities outside the capital, argued that they felt the real consequences on the ground of the media buzz triggered by the Femen protest. In contexts where women were already struggling for appropriate feminist expressions in the public sphere, Amina's protest merely compounded the problem and backfired on women's emancipatory counterpublics. The accounts of pressures to have to take a position towards Amina Sboui in order to not lose legitimacy in the local feminist organizations highlight the relation of the representational and interactional dimension of the public sphere. The processes of making sense of the media outputs directly impacts feminist counterpublics in their everyday work.

3) A victim of political violence

A third position framed Amina as a victim of political violence. This focus was taken up especially by the ATFD. After reluctance to take her defense considering that their struggle would be even more delegitimized, ATFD took up the case of Amina Sboui as a "political prisoner" after she was arrested in Kairouan. She was accused of carrying tear gas for self-defense, being a member of a criminal organization and insulting moral values (Labidi L. , 2014). In my interviews and in the media alike, ATFD members refused the method of topless protest, but instead insisted on the importance of defending women as victims of political violence.

In reaction to Amina's arrest, three European members of Femen staged a topless protest in front of the Tunisian Ministry of Justice to demand her liberation. The activists were arrested, but eventually released, even before Sboui, sparking a debate on their privileged positionality, thus raising the issue of postcolonial heritage. In the course of the events, activists of Femen also staged a "topless jihad day" in European capitals, carrying the controversy into international public spheres. This also provoked the reaction of Muslim feminists online (For example in the Facebook group: Muslim Women against Femen), condemning Femen's universalist feminism that is "silencing Islamic feminism".

Sboui distanced herself from the Femen network that she qualifies as "Islamophobic organization" (Hamadi, 2013). She then started to focus on issues of female prisoners and state violence. For instance, Amina Sboui supported the demonstrations in front of the court treating the case of "Meryem" who was raped by police agents. In 2016, she was the first woman to come out as loving women on national TV and has since been a prominent defender of LGBT rights. Needless to say, her reflections upon her activism did not generate anything close to the same quantity of media output with regards to her topless protest.

9.3   Counterthematizations: "Let's Talk About the Real Issues"

I have previously argued, that the "hot topics" of polygamy, the inheritance laws and Femen have played into a secular-religious divide, structuring and re-producing the hegemonic domain of power at the representational dimension of the public sphere. By contrast, addressing "real issues" has been used both as rhetoric employed by conservative and patriarchal actors to delegitimize feminist positions in the public sphere in Tunisia (as in other societies as well), as well as by feminists in my interviews. Talking about marginalized issues touching upon gender relations can be read as a participatory empowering act in creating new knowledge about particular experiences. I hold that it is important to contextualize the critique of gender renegotiations covering up other forms of structural oppression. In an intersectional setting, it becomes clear that the "real issues" do concern women's rights but have to be tackled in their intersections with labor, health and education, in order to bear emancipatory potential.

9.3.1 Gender and Labor

Besides these observable statistical gaps, issues concerning the labor market in relation to higher education and the marginalization of working-class women remain under-thematized in the hegemonic public sphere. They were, however, repeatedly addressed in my interviews. Women outnumber men in universities, but their unemployment rate remains twice as high: According to the National Statistics Institute in 2016, unemployment by gender reveals a gender gap with female unemployment at 23.5% (a slight decrease compared to the percentage of 25.6% in 2012) compared to 12.4% unemployment among men (compared to 14.6% in 2012). This gap is even more accentuated in relation to higher education: 40.4% of unemployed women have a university degree compared to 19.4% of men (Institut Nationale des Statistiques, 2016). The statistics also reveal a division in the type of labor undertaken by men and women with the latter being mostly employed in the "service sector," followed by manufacturing industries and agriculture (Tunisian Ministry of Employment and Qualifications & National Observatory on Employment and Qualification, 2013, p. 10).

This non-thematization can be regarded as an expression of the continuity of an exclusive state feminist legacy. The marginalization of working-class women and a lack of representation of their needs is also stated by Andrea Khalil, for the Tunisian context, and by Errazzouki in a Moroccan context, showing the exclusivity of the state feminist paradigm (Errazzouki, 2014, p. 262; Khalil, 2014, p. 198 and chapter 4.2.2.).

M.T., a member of a leftist party and also of the party's"women's committee" finds the needs of working-class women underrepresented:

> "This majority feminism doesn't represent the working class or the pop-
> ular classes, because they work within and remain in their cultivated up-
> per class" (M.T., Kairouan, April 2014).

In order to encounter the "majority feminism" or hegemonic understanding of feminism, it is up to women from working class positionalities themselves push for more recognition and an eventual change of their specific situation. I will engage with examples of counterpublics that make these intersections apparent during the political transformation. Different strategies to bring their interests into the representational dimension of the public sphere can be revealed: firstly, by strikes, secondly by public demonstrations and petitions issued to politicians and thirdly by gathering data and issuing reports.

In Tunisia, female unemployment is lower in areas with a textile industry: namely the coastal governorates of Tunis, Monastir, Nabeul and Sousse. Hence, women effectuate a good share of the workforce in this sector with many factories employing only female staff. The successful strike by the female workforce in the factory of *Mamotex* in the city of Chebba that started in 2013 can be seen as an example of a women's counterpublic organized around labor. The female workers organized together against their male superiors because of belated payment and unfair working conditions, but also because of abuse: They were screamed at by their (male) superiors and treated disrespectfully at the workplace.[142] In order to resist the abuse, the factory workers agreed that every time a woman was humiliated and screamed at the others would immediately strike collectively, hereby defending the dignity of them all. Initially, the women formed syndical structures within the factory against the pressure of the factory owner. The creation of the syndicate resulted in an improvement in working conditions and halted verbal and physical abuse from the supervisors.

In 2016, the female workforce even acquired provisory self-management through strike action, protests and negotiations with the local syndicate of the UGTT, constituting a first in Tunisia (Bertoluzzi & Spocci, 2016). While the coverage of their breakthrough does not fall into the period under study here, it is nevertheless noteworthy that women took the opportunity to speak up against psychological mistreatment by their male superiors, thus actively challenging the Matrix of Domination as manifested in the workplace. According to a testimony given to *Inkyfada*, Houda Charfeddine claims: "Now we have established a dialogue between us, we speak about our salaries and the working conditions.

---

142 Concerning the material at hand, it was especially the newly funded online-media "Inkyfada" specialized in investigative reporting, that followed up on the case in two reports. See (Mzalouat & Sehiri, 2016) and (Ben Hamdi, 2016).

We make our voices heard to claim what we deserve. Personally, I have learned a lot, I have learned that I have to fight for my rights" (Ben Hamadi, 2016, *translated by the author*).

Despite this success in the workers' counterpublic, I argue that the struggle for women's empowerment within the workspace remains bound to the artificial separation of the economic and the political struggle (Laclau & Mouffe, 2014, p. 3), which is upheld in the representational dimension of the public sphere. The case of *Mamotex* was surely inspiring for other working-class women in Tunisia and the (restricted) readership of the investigative outlet *Inkyfada*. The case was followed up in global socialist counterpublic media as well.[143] However, it didn't transgress the boundaries of the factory in question and generate what Laclau and Mouffe consider to be a general pattern in bourgeois society where "economic struggle is split into a multitude of individual struggles in every undertaking and dissolved in every branch of production" (Laclau & Mouffe, 2014, p. 3).

A second counterpublic representing the intersection of gender and labor is the demonstration of sex workers that raised attention to their conditions after the revolution. Prostitution is legal in Tunisia in specific brothels under the supervision of the Ministry of the Interior. Their passports classify them as workers of the Ministry of the Interior, which is supposed to provide a healthy and secured workspace including regular health checks. In the course of the uprisings however, "state brothels" were destroyed and in the following period, many of them were not renovated or rebuilt, depriving the women of their workspace. By a court ruling, the brothel in Sousse was closed in November 2012 in order to "establish order in the neighborhood", after attacks from Salafists. See for an in-depth study on the relation of sex work and the security apparatus in the aftermath of the uprisings (Silva, 2013). In 2013, formerly employed sex workers organized a demonstration at the Bardo Square to point to their increasingly precarious working conditions since the closing of many state brothels. They formulated a petition and gathered 120 signatures, demanding a re-opening of the brothel in Sousse that they handed over to the Vice-President of Parliament Meherzia Labidi (Ennahda party). The latter used her position as representative of the people to draw attention to the subject by welcoming the group of delegates and bringing their demands into a wider public. The meeting between the Vice-President of Parliament and the sex-workers was recorded by Tunisian radio broadcaster *Mosaique FM* and shared with *CNN Arabic*. Labidi is considered the only politician to take up the issue. She told *Mosaique FM*, "These women are Tunisian and they have rights, and our duty is to serve them. I am ready to listen

---

143 See for example the coverage for the outlet „Red Latina sin Fronteras": https://redlatinasin-fronteras.wordpress.com/2016/07/23/21908/; or the „Dawn News," a counterpublic media concerned with international popular struggles: http://www.thedawn-news.org/2016/07/28/made-in-tunisia-women-textile-workers-resist-poor-working-conditions/

to everyone on the condition that I have the time and if their demands are possible and can be addressed in such circumstances; they have the right to be heard by everyone" (Benazis, Smith-Spark, & Abedine, 2014). She regards them as equal citizens, however, at the same hinting at that their demands are not related to "normal labor", but that the brothels are, in fact, part of the problem. Their struggle is hereby perpetuated by a hegemonic ideology, impacting their representation. This strategy of the female counterpublic by relying on the vice-president of parliament guarantees access to a hegemonic public sphere on the one hand, but on the other hand, it loosens their control on framing their intervention.

Besides these concrete cases of counterthematizations around gender and labor that found representation in the wider public sphere, a major problem consists in the lack of statistics dealing with the intersecting relation of gender, work and education in specific localities. It is therefore paramount to gather and report on data regarding these intersections. Hayet Amami has investigated the situation of rural women in the region of El-Hanya, in the governorate of Sidi Bouzid, where she conducted in-depth interviews with women from rural areas within a sociological frame (Amami, 2014). The study aims to "understand the problems and shed light on the suffering and needs of the inhabitants".

The (unpublished) report, reveals interesting patterns with regards to gender and labor introducing the issue of gender and class-segregated work migration from the rural contexts.[144]She found that many women stay alone and work the fields while their husbands leave the family to migrate to other places in search of work, such as the capital Tunis and the wealthier coastal regions but also Europe. Another form of work migration is housemaids moving from the center of Tunisia to work for wealthier families in the northern part of the country. Tunisia's housemaids are deprived of any working rights and are part of Tunisia's informal labor market. The discussion around housemaids proved fruitful in Jendouba, where registrations by the official employment office were set up, guaranteeing at least some security for the women (see interview Hayet Amami, p.4). Hayet Amami highlights that, in order to address these issues, she is obliged to gather data on these relations by herself to shed light on the actual realities that many women face.

In a similar objective, Ghofrane Heraghi, who works for the association "Women and Citizenship" in ElKef, explains the importance of data on the socio-economic conditions in different localities, that are publically not accessible:

> "The solution we found with this project was to launch a socio-economic study on the situation of women. To gather data and concrete numbers that can be of support for the association and even for the parties that are going to work there. It helped us a lot because we know the situation on

---

144 According to the study that she has conducted in the region of El Hania, while 90% of the husbands had emigrated, women still claim they have a good relation with them (Amami, 2014).

> the ground better, and have insights into this and that locality, so that we can interfere to launch a sensibilization in terms of anti-poverty or hygiene or cancer and so on" (Ghofrane Heraghi, Tunis, May 2013).

Gathering data on women's lives in rural contexts in an explorative setting can help to formulate counterthematizations. The local NGOs need these information to design programs that correspond to the needs on the ground. However, Heraghi also underlines the importance of their work for the political parties to obtain a clear picture on the specific situation of women. While the Tunisian National Statistical Institute does provide data on the labor market, households and other data, even in rural areas, categories of health and labor or income, for instance, are often not gendered.

However, these reports on the most part do not contribute or trigger debates in the hegemonic public sphere and often remain in restricted counterpublics of scholars and local NGOs, rather than mass media and "strong publics", such as the parliament.

9.3.2 Gender and Locality

With the popular uprisings in 2011, the interior regions of the country came into focus of international and national media publics. "The rural woman" soon became the symbol of the politics of systematic marginalization and appeared as the "other" in relation to the modern secular, urban Tunisian woman that has been more prominently promoted. While blogs and Facebook pages have certainly helped to diversify the media output in the representational dimension of the public sphere with regards to locality, the classical media continues to operate from the capital and produce rather stereotypical images of women from outside Tunisia's urban centers. B.L., who works as a journalist and producer, clarifies the misrepresentation of the intersection of gender and locality leading to disengagement with liberal feminism:

> "Why not go to film a talk show in Gafsa or ElKef? It's very interesting to go and meet the women there. As long as you are based in Tunis and you try to centralize everything, nobody will feel represented by the media. I assure you that women are mostly not conscious because when they see women of the elite talking about women's rights on talk shows, they feel less and less concerned. They feel that women's rights and feminism is something like a story. It's an issue linked to the bourgeois class and to educated women [only]. (...) In a talkshow based in Tunis, you invite women who are already influential and who spend their evenings regularly in TV or radio debates. It strikes me that these women [from different class and locality] are not included. And you always have this notion of victimization, when you go and film women in the region, you have to film the very poor women or at the image of the victim while no, there

are success stories there as well, strong women!" (B.L., Tunis, April
2014).

She sheds light on the relation between locality (and related categories such as
labor and education) and the central structure of the media system, which would
need to change for more inclusive representations. Being involved in the media
sector herself, she claims to have actively pushed for the integration of more
women of different positionalities. Her approach to renegotiate the representational dimension of the public sphere can therefore be regarded as the "media
professions to politics" path, identified by feminist media scholars (Byerly &
Ross, 2006, p. 124).

B.L. speaks about a victimization of the rural women who will not, as a result, be perceived as agents of their own destiny. Hayet Amami observes a similar trend of victimization with regards to representations of rural women in development projects, which on the most part she finds to be inadequate. Consequently, in order to counter this passive image, Amami has named her association the Victory of the Rural Women to increase strong images of women working in the agricultural sector.

While discussions on the need of decentralizations with regards to political
structures were present in post-revolutionary Tunisia, the monopolization of the
mass media system in the capital that fails to represent local challenges and dynamics remains understudied. Drawing on empirical evidence from Sweden, media scholar André Jansson states: "the mediatized reproduction of an urban/rural
divide holds a hegemonic function in contemporary society"(Jansson, 2013,
p.88). I argue that stereotypical and classist representations of marginalized localities feed into the hegemonic domain of power. This urban-rural divide is even
upheld in the representation of party delegates:

> "With regards to information, it [the classical media] is not really repre-
> sentative, because it is the members of the national parties' board [who
> are speaking], it is not regional. The media do not represent me anymore
> of course because they don't speak about the parties' political program,
> the problems of women. What is mediatized is: 'so, the women have
> taken now a part of their rights!' and that's it" (M.T., Kairouan, April
> 2014).

From her positionality, M.T. argues that the classical media do not represent her
for two intersecting reasons: The first is concerned with locality, because national media do not include regional issues and centers on representatives of national parties. Secondly and with regards to gender representation, coverage of
"women's issues" is centered on the rights-based approach to enhance women's
emancipation. She is thus active in a counterpublic concerned with women in
the working class from the perspective of a marginalized locality. The intersectional debates she addresses are thus not represented at all in the mass media.

Consequently, she does not trust the mass media, ven though state control has officially been lifted since 2011.

Media skepticism in general and criticism with regards to coverage of different localities in particular, is expressed by Marouen Habita, who worked as a consultant for the Ministry of Women under the Troika government. He claims that the promotion and enhancement of the situation of women in rural areas was a work priority. The Ministry of Women worked along two major axes and budgeted accordingly: Assistance for demands and of initiatives of the rural women and female drop-outs from schools. The Ministry hereby addresses more technical and local issues that cannot be exploited within parallel debates. However, he felt that the work of the Ministry wasn't well mediatized, claiming:

> "The media is a very different story. If we start to talk about the media now, I would turn it upside-down. (…) At a certain time, we boycotted specific media and avoided going to talk shows where we would get humiliated anyways" (Marouen Habita, Tunis, May 2013).

The possibility to get messages across does not only concern feminist counter-publics, but also workers within government ministries. Gender politics as a politicized issue affected their ability and legitimacy to speak. Humiliation on TV shows, by the hosts can be discerned here as another mechanism of "silencing," in this case the CPR-lead Ministry.

Finally, the image of rural women conveyed in the mass media has proved to be a mobilizing force for women of rural background. In order not to reproduce a binary between "the rural woman" that is stereotyped as a victim in contrast to the "modern Tunisian woman", some have claimed the production of this image for themselves. A.L. is a young farmer, defining herself as *"a sort of a rural woman,"* coming from a village in the governorate of ElKef. She is determined to shoot a movie herself and "put it on YouTube to show the realities." When we met, she was taking part in camera training offered by a local NGO and had started to identify characters for her movie:

> "I love everything related to the promotion of the rural women, because I'm so to say, a rural woman myself. (…) This is why I would like to make a documentary of the ten women and I really want to convey the realities with it. We feel, that they are not represented" (A.L., ElKef, April 2014).

One year after the interview, the short movie "Amel" is indeed online. Her participation is defined by the need for representation. Conceptualizing, and shooting the movie constitutes then a process of emancipation. While the movie gives insights into the lives of two women (contrary to her initial idea to portray ten women), they cover a wide range of topics such as having to drop out of school because they cannot pay for the bus fare, divorce, the situation of a single mother in a rural context, and everyday life struggles defined by sickness and poverty. Besides treating hard realities, the film does not convey an image of victimization per se but presents the women's agency and everyday resistance. One of the protagonists, a divorced field worker, who gets paid five dinar per day (around 2.50€ in 2016) states: "I feel like a strong woman, because I do the work of both, the men and the women." Unfortunately, the film is no longer accessible on YouTube in Tunisia[145] because of copyright violations, most probably in relation to the musical soundtrack used in the film. As of March 2017, it has generated only a couple of clicks. This not only highlights the small scope of the project, but also exemplifies the dependence of counterpublics as feminist media projects in the communication infrastructure of a hegemonic (globalized) public sphere and media enterprises such as youtube.

9.3.3 Gender and Health

Over the last six decades, Tunisia has developed a basic health care system with a large health care network all over the country. This was in line with the modernization of the country and can be related to the needs of the state's family planning policy. In their study, the Tunisian public health scholars Mohamed Kouni Chahed and Chokri Arfa evaluated the Universal Health Care coverage in Tunisia and point to a remaining gap in access to health care between the poorer and wealthy population of the country. They also address an unbalanced development of the health care system, with a stronger private sector and a less efficient public sector.[146] This inequality characterizes "marginalized localities": the coastal areas have a more developed private system that is almost absent in the center and south of the country. Despite these structural inequalities, the authors find only one issue that would prevent Tunisia to meet their Global Development Goals, the high mortality of women giving birth: "Tunisia would seem on track to timely meeting the MDGs targets without further policy efforts, only for maternal mortality" (Chahed & Arfa, 2014, p. 1).

Studies in public health reveal the relation between locality, access to health care and gender. At the same time, the high mortality rate was addressed in the interviews I conducted in Sidi Bouzid. Sidi Bouzid has the lowest percentage of birth assistance in Tunisia (still 88%, compared to an average of 98% in Tunisia (Gribaa & Depaoli, 2014, p. 3). There are no actual numbers available classifying mortality rate by region, however, numbers from 2008 suggest that it is three

---

145 The movie "Amel" is accessible on *YouTube* in other countries: (Cinemovel, 2015).
146 According to the numbers given in the report, the private sector deals with 20% of the population and benefits of 60% of total health expenditures. The public sector deals with 80% of the population and recieves only 20% of total health expenditures.

times higher in the rural region (Mestiri M., 2016). Maternal mortality and badly equipped hospitals constitutes an important reality for women and men in Sidi Bouzid. Within this context, speaking about the lack in health infrastructure in Sidi Bouzid in public has caused problems to the respondent S.M., who was invited for a radio debate as a representative of her association:

> "For example, I gave an interview at the radio. I was in a debate with the general secretary of the governorate and I was live on air. He was talking about the situation in Sidi Bouzid, and me at a certain moment, I forgot that I'm at this broadcast to represent me and my association and so I started to talk honestly. I made the general secretary angry (...) and I had a real problem with my boss: 'Why did you do that? Did you forget about the association?' Honestly, I'm very happy. At this moment I forgot that I'm XY, working for XX and the sister of XX who was injured during the revolution. The debate was on the situation of the hospital in Sidi Bouzid. And the secretary was like: 'We have done...' and I interrupted him that he shouldn't talk like that. The day of my brother's injury, he was transferred to Sfax with an ambulance that had an accident on the way. I could have lost my mother and my brother at the same time. What situation? We are transporting invalids in ambulances (to other cities) that break down on the way!" (S.M., Sidi Bouzid, April 2014).

This episode reveals the pressure on young woman to speak 'respectfully' and not to address the "real issues." It marks the lack in health infrastructure as a public taboo. Furthermore, it shows her personal relief, when she finally spoke her mind. This is not to say, that her act of courage would lead to a change, as she clarifies later. In her opinion, she "gained courage to speak up," but this would be useless if "nobody listened." Her experience and the interpretation of it raise questions on the lack of channels that respond to the pluralization of voices in Tunisia's post-revolutionary public sphere. While in the liberal idea of the public sphere, the focus is on strengthening the plurality of opinions and "voices," the issue of channeling and responding to these voices remains under-theorized.

Another example is the explorative study, the President of the NGO "Victory of the Rural Women" Hayet Amami, conducted on the situation of rural women. She found a strikingly high number of handicapped children in the area, whose needs are not addressed. At the same time, health coverage is assured by a medical center consisting of a doctor and a gynecologist, opening one day per week with consultations for three to four hours. While by law, the women have access to healthcare via the *carnet de soin*[147] by the National Health Insurance Fund

---

147 Since 1960, Tunisia has had a basic social protection system funded through employee distribution and subsidized by the government for the poorer sections of the population (Chahed & Arfa, 2014). The carnet de soin is subdivided by color: The basic, which women working in the field could claim is the white one.

(Caisse Nationale d'Assurance Maladie), according to the study, 75% of the re-spondents refuse any relation with the local authorities, and only 23% have ad-dressed the *Omda*[148] to obtain a *carnet de soin*. The report points to an "almost absent" relation between women and the local state authorities, resulting in a high ignorance of their rights in general and with regards to healthcare in partic-ular.

A political dimension between gender and health becomes clear when con-sidering suicide by immolation of women. Psychologist Laila Labidi states that self-immolation, such as the one committed by Mohamed Bouazizi that triggered the uprisings, are not a new phenomenon and constitute a serious public health problem. Between January and June 2011, 111 self-immolations were reported by the hospitals with 31 of them committed by women. The press reported seven of these cases. Labidi resumes: "Despite the shocking nature of these cases, there was no collective outcry, no call to understand what was happening in the heads of these women. The absence of a public and collective response to such events reflects the lack of a broad expression of solidarity with women who were suf-fering" (Labidi L. , 2016b, p. 122). Additionally, all of the women came from the center, east and west of the country. Public suicide in this context can be regarded as the most radical and desperate act to raise attention to lived oppres-sions. On the one hand, it can be argued, along journalistic deontological stand-ards, that suicides should not be covered in order to avoid the "Werther effect" - an increase of suicides in imitations of these acts. On the other hand, these were all public acts, with the women in question choosing to immolate themselves in front of public buildings expressing their despair at the official social policy.

9.4   Conclusion: Gender on the Mediatized Battlefield

This chapter dealt with the changing representational dimension of the public sphere between 2011 and 2014. By drawing upon quantitative data sets and the qualitative interviews I conducted, I have pointed to a general marginalization of women in the mass media. In a second step, I laid out the hegemonic repre-sentations of women and I have shown how the topics and depictions under study have fed into a general polarizing discourse that would sideline the complexities of women's lives. By contrast, I have outlined the topics related to gender as they were addressed in my interviews and in feminist media projects and pointed to the intersections of structures of oppression. I gave three examples of coun-terpublic interventions tackling the representational dimension of the public

---

148 The *Omda* is a kind of mayor of the villages, forming the directorate of the smallest administra-
     tive unity in Tunisia, the *Imada*.

sphere. It became clear that these attempts to "spill over into wider publics" (Antonakis, 2015 b), carry the risk to feed into the discourse of political polarization. Relaying on multiplicators such as the parliamentarians or mass media beard the pitfall to means losing control of the message that can then be stripped off its subversive potential and be disintegrated by the hegemonic domain of power and channeled into sensationalism and polarizations.

Reports gathering data and information challenging the hegemonic domain of power that do not enter the dominant public at all are another example. My results confirm what Fenton and Downey have defined as a structural problem of counterpublics as "one of translation, of communicating across a wider arena of discursive contestation" (Downey & Fenton, 2003, p.195). Although, the representational and interactional dimensions cannot be strictly separated, I have mainly engaged with the counterpublics in their "factual dimension" (Wimmer, 2007, p. 157 ff.) entailing counter-narratives and alternative media spacesI found that the digitalized environment holds double sided visibilities for feminist counterpublics: While the space for regroupment is enlarged and encompasses the possibility to create transregional networks, attacks on social media constitute new multifaceted threats (Antonakis, 2018).

In the next Chapter, I will turn to the interactional dimension of the public sphere and focus on counterpublics in their "social dimension" as specific types of publics and specific cultural practices to investigate challenges, practices and diverging interests.

10 The Interactional Dimension of the Public Sphere

In this last chapter, I argue that the uprisings of December 2010 have certainly cleared the way to renegotiate gender and discuss new feminist approaches on a more local level in Tunisia. While these developments may hardly be visible within the institutional or representational dimension of the public sphere, I claim that they induce long-term change in gender relations. The women's counterpublics and women in counterpublics analyzed here, target "patriarchy" in its various everyday expressions and manifestations and refuse to be absorbed in formal political processes. Instead of focusing on the structural domain of power and trying to change the mechanism of in- and exclusion into and from political institutions, the interpersonal domain of power is the field tackled first or, depending on the positioning, is the only public the activists can engage with. The frame of activism is very much defined on a community level and includes everyday physical and verbal abuse, social and spatial immobilities, family education, confrontations with security forces and "bodily comportments"[149] policed by individuals, the community or the police. In my analysis, I follow Collins, who shows that the complexities of the different domains of power "produce particular patterns of domination" and consequently, women's action to counter these are widely ranged and diverse. In the US context, Collins suggests that it is "more useful to assess black women's activism less by the ideological content of individual black women's belief systems — whether they hold conservative, reformist, progressive, or radical ideologies based on some predetermined criteria — and more by black women's collective actions within everyday life that challenge domination in these multifaceted domains" (Collins, 2000, p. 203). In the highly politicized environment of a political transformation, where issues of gender are easily exploited for ideological purpose, my approach focuses on the actual common actions and issues within women's counterpublics.

The organizations "Victoire de la Femme Rural" from Sidi Bouzid and "Femme et Citoyenneté" from ElKef, or M'nemty, founded by Black Tunisians, exemplify different approaches to de-center the promoted image of the "modern Tunisian woman" as part of the hegemonic discourse of state feminism from the

---

149 For a discussion of the concept of bodily comportment reframed as participatory practice in the public sphere, see the typology of counterpublics within the matrix of domination, 3.2.3.

© Springer Fachmedien Wiesbaden GmbH, part of Springer Nature 2019
A. Antonakis, *Renegotiating Gender and the State in Tunisia between 2011 and 2014*, Politik und Gesellschaft des Nahen Ostens,
https://doi.org/10.1007/978-3-658-25639-5_10

perspectives of locality and race. The following analysis illustrates paths to break with nationalist gender politics, decolonize the hegemonic domain of power and find local, intersectional solutions for women's emancipation instead.

First, I present issues imposed on women participating in counterpublics that I situate in the interactional dimension of the public sphere and are defined by interpersonal domain of power. Three main challenges will be differentiated that were highlighted by the interviewees of different positionalities: political co-optations, extremism and radicalizations, and finally police violence against women. In the second part of the analysis, I investigate forms of participation aimed at influencing hegemonic publics: The notion that a "space for regrouping needs to be claimed first is a principal argument in this context. I then look at "space" with regards to fighting violence against women and as a necessary requirement to engage in long-term strategies and to "decolonize" feminism. Finally, and building up on the last point, different approaches to challenge state feminism as a form of authoritarian legacy will be laid out. I identify three branches of strategies to "decolonize" the hegemonic concept of feminism at the interactional dimension of the public sphere.

10.1   Shaping Negotiations of Gender on the Ground

By the following, I attempt to illustrate the problematic assumptions of modelizations laid out in chapter II[150] by pointing to three challenges that stand in opposition to the model. Firstly, political co-optation that is driven mainly by two interrelated factors: On the one hand by foreign funding and on the other by the political process of polarization and the "bargained competition" between Islamists and old regime elites (Boubakeur, 2015, p.1). Secondly, I look at extremism and radicalizations as a local challenge that is encountered on a daily basis. I received specific insights here from the male respondents from ElKef who claimed that they would interact with young radicalized men differently than women would. The third challenge that will be pointed out is that of police violence incorporated in the disciplinary domain of power, in particular the role of the executive forces, the police, in implementing gender orders by policing women's and men's bodies.

---

150 I deduced three problematic claims. The first bears a relational argument, whereas a country is stylized as a "model" with regards to a specific region in a geo-political context. Second, the modelization entails the coupling of rights and values that attach the model within a pre-defined value-system. Thirdly, modelization easily glosses over actual existing discontent within the population with regards to the application of democratic institutions, the persistence of socio-economic injustice and the lack of reform in parts of the Tunisian state, notably the Ministry of the Interior.

10.1.1 Political Instrumentalizations and Foreign Funding

I identified the nexus between political instrumentalization, women's rights and Western funding as a first challenge. Political instrumentalization and co-optations of gender issues by national political parties and other groups and movements re-surfaced quite early after the uprisings. This re-politization again hampered the struggles for autonomy of women's rights groups and feminist activists. Feminist activism has been perceived by some to feed into and even create political debates, while the actual struggle itself should be confined to the social domain:

> "Unfortunately, a big feminist current in Tunisia uses social action to exercise political pressure. It's true that participation in an association is a political action as well, but... It shouldn't be too much exploited [by politics], it shouldn't become a symbol" (O.L., Berlin, May 2013).

The respondent O.L. summarizes a dilemma, in which feminist issues can enter the political arena but are then perceived as a tool for political pressure and serve only as symbolic politics. In her opinion, when women's right become no more than an "empty signifier", it prohibits finding actual solutions. This representation of feminist issues, in which the symbol rather than the solution(s) appear as most important, can be linked back to the idea of women as the cultural reproducers of the nation, or according to Tahar Haddad's thoughts: "It's the women who make a nation" (quoted in Khalil, 2014, p.190).

The struggles at the very interactional dimension of the public sphere that feminist activists faced must be explained from a post-colonial perspective. I hold that international actors should be a central component of the analysis here, especially after the toppling of the authoritarian regime against the backdrop of the "decoupling" process, as described by Nicola Pratt in the Egyptian case of gender and other factors such as class, education and locality:

"Over the long term, the demise of radical, secular movements has led to a decoupling of secular women's rights agendas from local popular projects, paving the way for their cooption and instrumentalization by authoritarian regimes and international actors and rendering secular women's rights activists vulnerable to accusations of representing foreign agendas" (Pratt, 2016).

The emphasis on feminist counterpublics focuses on funding from the European Union and the US, where "gender," most importantly in the axis of gender mainstreaming, has been adapted in many programs for the promotion of democracy in the transition period in Tunisia.[151] Many of the interview partners have been involved, in one way or another, in projects that have received financial support

---

151 It would be interesting to investigate the funding of the Gulf states to build up civil society structures, often in the field of education.

from the EU or Ministries of EU member states.[152] Issues originating from this foreign funding in transformative contexts have previously been explored in studies on Palestine and Lebanon and have been evaluated as a "mixed blessing" (Carapico, 2002, p.379; see also: Brynen, 2000). Post-colonial theorists have pointed out the "neo-colonial paternalism" characterizing these relations (Spivak, 2007, p.177).

The struggle of feminist NGOs was considered as "westernized" or following a Western agenda and could be easily stigmatized as such by the Islamist political forces and conservative groups. This is a common pattern that has already been stated in different contexts with regards to feminist projects in the global South. Secondly, various authors have stated how the Western support for women's right in Arab countries have been attacked by conservatives as an "imperialist/Christian/Zionist plot to undermine Muslim countries and their culture" (Keddie, 2007, p. 104), for example in Malaysia (Spiegel, 2010, p. 132) and India (Mitra, 2013, p. 138).

There is no doubt that Western governments can exert political influence by funding civil society organizations and hereby uphold hegemonic norms. However, it is important to differentiate because, according to Yuval Davis "it would be westocentric stereotype to view women associated with NGOs in the South as puppets of Western feminists" alone. A distinct analysis of these NGOs and associations "according to their specific projects and practices" (Yuval-Davis, 1997, p. 121) should be highlighted. Similarly, Nikita Dhawan who has investigated the gender and development discourse from post-colonial perspective (Dhawan, 2009, p. 54) points to the "ambivalence" of processes. She stresses the lack of accountability and democratic legitimacy that international civil society operate in. "International organizations have become more powerful than states,

---

152 Funding has been provided in this context by governments around the world, often partnering with institutions of their respective countries that then implement the projects. It often follows a complex system of subtractors that cannot be laid out in detail here. For example, Germany created the Transformation partnership to "support the processes of democratization and stabilization that have been launched" and put a "spotlight on Tunisia" in the course of the transformation phase (see website of the German foreign Office: http://www.auswaertigesamt.de/sid_4CDC765737C1B5F057ABB0D0E6031EFB/EN/Aussenpolitik/RegionaleSchwerpunkte/NaherMittlererOsten/Umbrueche_TSP/150624_TransfPartnerschaften_node.html (accessed 13 October 2015; the content is unfortunately not available anymore). On the supranational level, as „reaction to the uprisings in the region," the European Union has launched its initiative PASC (Programme d'Appui à la Société Civil) in September 2012, in the frame of their program "SPRING" (Support to Partnership, Reform and Inclusive Growth) and implemented by an NGO based in Brussels. While the internal problems within the project, especially in relation to their director, who was a public supporter of Ben Ali, some former regional coordinators decided to address a letter pinpointing abuse and inefficient handling of the funding and the overall vision of the project to the coordinators in Brussels and a collective voluntary termination of their work contracts (see for a critical investigation (Robert, 2016).

but they are not accountable to people in the same way that democratic governments should be" (Dhawan, 2013, p. 148).

While a lot of the potential for political mobilization of the younger generation has been channeled through the new possibilities of employment in associations and NGOs, the outcomes of this process were very different: besides a diversification of associations working on women's issues, it led to a professionalization of the NGO work. At the same time, it advantaged NGOs and organizations that could rely on established structures and knew how to deal with international donors, apply for funding, or communicate expected outcomes and provide evaluation criteria for their projects. On an individual level, the professionalization of NGOs constituted a possibility for upward social mobility and new pockets of funding possibilities. For many activists I interviewed, to engage with an NGO constituted a conscious political decision, while for others their pressing financial situation was the priority. When engaging in the study of associations as counterpublics, funding must always be a key consideration.

On the other hand, international donors also financed important studies that were conducted by local organizations, providing data on the socio-economic situation of women, illiteracy rates and health in Tunisia. These reports constitute an important element to negotiate gender relations in their intersections by first providing an input that can enter the representational dimension of the public sphere, and second, by providing information for local women's associations to optimize their work. A solely critical perspective on foreign funding of feminist initiatives in Tunisia turns a blind eye to the work that local women's organizations can actually put into practice.

In the interviews, selective support of feminist counterpublics by Western donors that represented a hegemonic type of feminism has been dispraised. Sana Sbouaï speaks about the relation between international donor organizations and their selective support, reproducing the same exclusive structures of feminism:

> "These organizations had most of this space and the donors are partly responsible because they always address the same people, because indeed, you know that the same people will be accustomed to succeed with the projects. But if you want democracy, you integrate everybody, you have to broaden your view. Unless you say: I want my project [to be done] good, and it doesn't matter if it's always the same people who benefit from it. But I don't think that this is 'helping democracy' if you do this. You have to help the young women…Feminism means many things, you can't assume that it is an issue of secularist democratic, bourgeois, francophone women. That's not what it is. This division has to stop. Feminism, that's the female students who goes to the university in crowded buses and answers to guys harassing her" (Sana Sbouaï, Tunis, May 2014).

This quote opens up a variety of issues that this study engages with. It highlights the monolithic conception of feminism prevailing in post-colonial and post-rev-olutionary Tunisia in terms of class ("bourgeois"), educational background ("francophone") and political position ("secular") as understood by Western do-nors, thus impacting access and resources for renegotiating structural power. Sbouaï points out a value system that is manifested rather than changed by in-ternational monetary support. In this sense, feminism is an ideology that "ab-sorb[s] and thereby depoliticize[s] oppressed groups' dissent" (Collins, 2000, p. 299) and can be understood as part of the hegemonic domain of power. Further-more, Dhawan reminds us that "Elite actors in civil society obtain remarkable amounts of political power and access to transnational public spheres, without being directly elected by the people whom they claim to represent (Dhawan, 2013, p. 153 f.). Other activists have expressed that "needs assessments" by NGOs are often happening in very restricted spaces only. Also, presenting pro-jects in coffee breaks of conferences in a concise manner requires specific re-sources. While the real work happens outside of the conference rooms, activists need to participate and perform well in these events in order to secure funding.

Nadje Al-Ali and Nicola Pratt have coined the term "five-star democracy tourism" to designate the same pattern in the context of post-invasion Iraq, where support of civil society mainly happened within hotels, utterly removed from realities on the ground (Al-Ali N. , 2016). This nexus also points to the depend-encies of women on international organizations and donors, who take up roles that should basically be taken care of by the state. As we have seen earlier, how-ever, the Ministry of Women Affairs and the UNFT had limited resource and did not conduct qualified field work for the promotion of women in rural areas.

Adding to that, a complicated cooperation between the ministries, for in-stance of those of agriculture and artisanal and the Ministry of Women Affairs for the gender sensitive regional development hampers the establishment of do-mestic solutions.

K.E., who originally comes from a small village in Siliana, works with young Tunisians especially and warns of abuses taking place in the NGO sectors:

> "NGOs use the volunteers to realize their aims and I'm against it. I work
> with NGOs and associations who work for the youth and for Tunisia. I'm
> against political parties and I'm against those who abuse the youth to cre-
> ate street pressure as well "(K.E., Siliana, April 2014, p.4).

Her quote is illustrative of a general mistrust with the political elite in the country and international donors that, on the one hand, abuse voluntary work for political gains, and on the other, manipulate a youth that has so far not experienced any political education or media literacy. She also points to the manipulation of youth groups to create street pressure for political purposes.

However, the possibilities to engage in the civil society sector have impacted the lives of many of the activists I interviewed, including A.L., who summarizes what has changed in her personal life as follows:

> "I'm unemployed. Nothing has changed [since the revolution], except for
> a bit more freedom of expression. And I know the associative work now,
> I didn't know it in the past" (A.L., ElKef, April 2014).

Besides this, A.L. points to corruption in the civil society sector and reveals how the project manager would keep money for himself and not pay her adequately when she was working in an EU-led project on the promotion of rural women and water accessibility (see Interview A.L., ElKef, April 2014, p. 2). Abuse and corruption within the NGO sector constitutes a sensitive issue rarely discussed in public (For a critical investigation of one case in Tunisia see a report by the French journalist residing in Tunis, Diane Robert (Robert, 2016)).

Similar to issues of gender relations, the question of Islam and radicalization of a youth became an important political battlefield for ideological camp buildings and discrediting of the Ennahda party. Religious extremist groups, have also narrowed the space of participation on the local level.

10.1.2 Extremism and Radicalizations

I will now turn to a second challenge that was expressed in the interviews of this study: extremism and radicalization of young men. I situate this issue at the interactional dimension of the public sphere, permeated by the interpersonal domain of power that controls everyday life practices of women. While the "war against terror" in Tunisia and elsewhere has led to the restriction of freedoms for all citizens, the origins and consequences of this "war" for young women in particular have often been overlooked. Also, the trap that local feminist organizations fall into when fighting against Islamist fundamentalism is their association with the West, which has severe consequences for women's rights organizations. Law professor Karima Bennounehas pointed out this mis-conception: "Criticizing Muslim fundamentalists is mistakenly equated with support for Western governments. This is just wrong and entirely overlooks the fact that not everything is about the West" (Bennoune, 2013).

With the liberalization of the public sphere in Tunisia, religious expression by ordinary citizens became part of everyday interaction. Disputes around political and ideological beliefs had been under strict control under the authoritarian regimes of Tunisia. The newly found expression of such beliefs in public represents a novelty at the interactional dimension of the public sphere. The quick spread of associations based on religious moral identification have been analyzed as a new "social counter power" (Merone & Soli, 2013). Due to a lack of access, this study cannot inspect actual Salafist counterpublics and consequently does not represent the experiences of Salafist women. It can, however, shed light on the different perceptions of their new freedom of expression in public spaces by the women interviewed as part of this study. In the much-politicized climate polarized around Islamism, women's rights and the attempts of the counter revolutionary forces to re-install their regime for the sake of security, it is important to highlight the danger that was felt by women's organizations, especially in marginalized localities. I argue that long term solutions to radicalizations include investments into the educational, economic and cultural structures of the marginalized localities were only rarely articulated in the public sphere. Addressing these solutions drawing from concepts of "human security" can easily be derailed as "supporting terrorism".

Amel Cherni is treasurer of the association "Femme et Citoyenneté" in ElKef. ElKef, as part of the *dakhel*, is located along the same mountain range that runs along the Tunisian-Algerian border, constituting a stronghold for Islamist extremism where numerous attacks, mainly against security, forces were executed since 2011. She describes her concerns after 2011:

> "We regarded it as an *acquis*, but after the 14th of January with the Salafists on the rise, I really was afraid that women's rights are at stake. That even the women's rights which were already not satisfying for me could really be in danger" (Amel Cherni, ElKef, April 2014).

The respondents from Sidi Bouzid lament the polarization between "Salafists" and "Muslims" that didn't exist in their community before and hold local mosques responsible for "brainwashing" the youth. They claim that verbal harassment based on their clothing has increased after 2011. Their jeans and trousers were targeted as "non-Muslim" and as a result they had to defend their clothing. S.M. recounts an episode when she and her friends were harassed in public by Salafi youth. She defends her right to be present in public in this encounter:

> "I reply! I'm capable to reply. I have a bit of knowledge about the Koran, so it's not necessary to lecture me about my religion. I know well what I'm doing. It's my relation between God and myself. You are not an intermediary between us. I'm grown up, I know, and I'm convinced by what I'm doing. I'm wearing the hijab, because I'm convinced of it. I don't want to hear anybody telling me to unveil me or to put the veil, to wear or not to wear jeans!" (S.M., Sidi Bouzid, April 2014).

S.M. reveals how conservative and modernist discourses alike have exerted pressure on her bodily comportment and clothing. They have taken the form from national legislations banning the veil to street harassment. The attitude of responding to insults and threats at the interactional dimension of the public sphere is very different from the interaction with a Salafi taxi driver, as stated by Tunisian activist O.L.:

> "Even with my mother, when I get into a taxi with a Salafi driver and he starts to exclaim his path and more. I reply: 'yes, yes...sure, of course' but I don't really pay attention, I don't want to create conflicts. But my mother replies sort of: Me too I did my [Koranic] studies, do you think I'm illiterate? I know more than you, here and there and this and that'. My mother has never lost a debate until now. She is a great woman" (O.L., Tunis, May 2013).

While O.L. avoids discussions of religious nature, her mother on the other hand engages in disputes when she feels that expressed statements are not correct and offend her. The fact that the driver referred to above is at the service of both women, thus bringing in a dimension of unequal social status, cannot be neglected. At the same time, the category of age appears to be a regulative factor for the interaction and brings in a generational component. The younger woman "doesn't want to create conflicts" while the older woman challenges the driver with her knowledge. In the end, she expresses an admiration for her mother who does not avoid an argument, while it could be discerned that her mother's experience and positionality allow her to take this liberty.

The two viewpoints exemplified above also reveal the different stances women take in the interactional dimension to renegotiate their position towards Salafists and oppression in the name of religion. While on the one hand, O.L., a law student and feminist living in Tunis, can ignore it and does not need to care much because her encounters with these ideologies are very limited. On the other hand, the young woman in Sidi Bouzid is constantly confronted with new forms of oppressive ideologies that would restrict her freedoms and subject her to more aggressive behavior.

When the ATFD opened their new office and took over the physical space with demonstrations in Kairouan, violent confrontations at the interactional level had to be dealt with. Anissa Saidi president of the ATFD office in Kairouan and philosophy teacher recounts the first demonstration of the ATFD in Kairouan that was attacked by Salafists. She finds the behavior of a young feminist courageous, who stood up against them:

> "Yes, sometimes there is a lack of security. In April 2011, it was the first time that the ATFD accessed the public space here in Kairouan. We were the only organizers of an activity in a cultural center here in Kairouan. We were attacked by salafists, and it was hard for us. They were trying to pull out our activity" (Anissa Saidi, Kairouan, April 2014).

Saidi can look back on a career in teaching philosophy. She can draw from certain legitimacy, as she has taught subjects related to religion, freedom of expression and the state under the authoritarian regime of Tunisia. Nowadays, she confronts her Salafi students with "suppleness". She relates a tendency to radicalization in the youth in Kairouan to the "lack of culture" and deficiencies in an educational system that emphasizes the re-production of knowledge over intellectual reflection. She raises the issue of fostering a critical attitude towards taught knowledge.

Slim Magri is the regional coordinator for the support of civil society of the European Program PASC in ElKef argues along same lines. According to him, the priority lies in educating the youth:

> "So, that makes me want to work with children and teenagers even more, because really these Salafists are victims. For me they are sleepwalkers, they march while asleep. Hence, culture hasn't been on the daily agenda for the last decades of our dear Tunisia. Especially in the interior regions, there is a huge percentage of analphabetism, the rural exodus, social and economic problems and all of these factors. Therefore, culture has been absent and now it's just normal that these people will be manipulated" (Slim Magri, ElKef, April 2014).

Saidi and Magri have both experienced actual violence at the hands of Salafists at the interactional dimension of the public sphere: The first in the frame of a feminist demonstration, the latter for his engagement in the cultural field.[153] Still, they do not put their experience in a context of political polarizations. They highlight long-term strategies instead, tackling the interpersonal domain of power by investing in cultural and educational development. The radicalization of the youth, in ElKef and Kairouan respectively is explained, through the deficiencies of a failed centralized cultural and educational policy of the *ancien regime*. In an environment of a "war on terror" focusing on short-term solutions that have led to the restriction of newly gained freedoms in Tunisia,[154] their argument of intersecting radicalizations of a Salafist youth with education. Hereby, another important dimension of the concept of "marginalized localities" is laid out. I claim that the lack of cultural education and the patriarchal culture within the dissembled secularism that did not allow for different forms of masculinities to appear in the public sphere, provided fertile ground for the propaganda of *daesh*

---

153 Slim Magri has a background in education, He is a member of a local theater organization "Association of Arts for Cinema and Theather ElKef" (L'association des Arts pour le Cinéma et le Théâtre) in ElKef where his theater was attacked by salafists in 2013. His efforts to file complaints have so far not resulted in finding the perpetuators. It can be stated that the cultural counterpublics of resistance that could operate under Ben Ali, but where constantly under surveillance and threat, were after the uprisings a target for salafist groups as they represented the "nonbelievers" or "infidels." They nevertheless received only little support by the police and state security. 2012 was marked by confrontations between artists and Tunisians working in the field of culture and a "vocal minority" of salafist groups; as a result, cultural events and festivities were canceled.

154 See for example the article and call for action by Human Rights Watch on the new anti-terrorism from 2015 in Tunisia, considered to endanger rights such as freedom of expression (Human Righst Watch, 2015).

and other radical islamist groups in Tunisia to "manipulate" a youth of "sleep-walkers" and recruit their army in post-revolutionary Tunisia by activating sexist role models.

10.1.3 The Police and Gender Based Violence

In this section and their role in reproducing rigid gender roles. The idea of *"Karama watanya"* (national dignity), chanted through the streets during the uprisings, can be regarded as a demand to eradicate a system of corruption and illegitimate forces that were seizing the nation, which in the case of Tunisia were embodied by the police and the Interior Ministry. A lack of reform of the security sector stands out as an important characteristic of the procedural democratic pro-cess in Tunisia, while it was one of the major demands of the Tunisian uprisings.

Police forces can indeed be regarded as the employers of the hegemonic power in the interactional dimension of the public sphere, by policing the bodies of the citizens, showing an intimidating presence in the urban space and having the monopoly over the legitimate use of force. Harassment by the police based on gender has been mentioned in different contexts in the interviews. Below, different encounters with the police, mirroring a general patriarchal sexist atti-tude as well as strategies of resistance will be outlines. They will be recounted and analyzed according to the varying positionalities of the interview partners.

According to figures from the US State Department from 2007 concerning sexual violence committed by security forces (i.e. militaries and government-supported militia, police, and prison guards), Tunisia has been placed in category 3 (out of 4) entailing that, „There were 'numerous reports' of 'rape', 'sexual assault' or 'sexual abuse' by security forces, which were 'routine', 'common', 'widespread', 'systematic', 'reported repeatedly', or 'rape', 'sexual assault', and 'the threat of rape' against detainees and their family members was used as a tool of torture 'to extract information, to intimidate and to punish'" (Butler, Gluch, & Mitchell, 2007, p.683). While such statistics must be handled with care as they rely on "reports" only (for Libya for instance, there is no sexual violence by security forces reported), they do show a trend of a massive employment of sexual violence by security forces. Research linking sexualized violence and the production of masculinities and radicalization processes outlined above consti-tute an important field of research, that remains understudied.

The issue of police violence against women has been addressed in different counterpublics and remains a key challenge for (feminist) activists and citizens in general. I situate it here at the interactional domain because women can en-counter this type of violence on an everyday basis. At the same time, it reflects a wider system of state repression. The following accounts can be linked to the theorization of Paul Amar who analyzed the role of the security apparatus of Egypt as an "agent of sexual harassment and sexualized torture," which was able to remain invisible after the uprisings by shifting the attention to poor men as perpetrators (Amar, 2011, p. 314). In Tunisia, comparable to what Amar describes for the Egyptian context, the bodies of law enforcement could re-appear after the uprisings as agents that would re-establish order and portray themselves as the only alternative to create safe spaces for women in the interactional dimension of the public sphere by the means of physical presence and surveillance.

Who files reports? Privileged Positionalities and the Police

In the interviews, various women from different backgrounds addressed the feeling of being mistreated by the police. Najma Kousri Labidi points to a general increase in sexual harassment after the uprisings. Within this context, the police appear not only as an attacker, but also as a bystander, at times ridiculing situations of sexual harassment experienced in public spaces. I argue that, while new legislations for women's rights and the constitution had been discussed in parliament and the media, the actual implementation entering the disciplinary domain of power, was not put into practice:

> "I think sexual harassment has increased in the streets. The people feel impunity in the air. When I go to a police station to file charges there is never a follow up. The police always tell you to come back the next day. (…) There was a girl with me once, who got harassed. So we went to file charges, even though there were security agents, I mean street police, that would have had to hold the guy back. [But] he was laughing about the situation! He is laughing when a woman is getting harassed in front of his eyes. And he started to insult her. [The other guy] had threatened her to show her his genitals. It's terrible to be a woman in Tunisia" (Najma Kousri Labidi, Tunis, May 2014).

Kousri Labidi admits that nobody who she has filed reports against has been actually charged with any form of sexual harassment (verbal or physical), yet she continues to file charges when necessary nevertheless. Kousri Labidi makes these efforts from a position of privilege, being a law student herself and enough resources at her disposal to negotiate her positionality against police abuse. She stresses her position in the interview pointing to her education and the support she would get from her family for denouncing harassment and abuse by publically filing charges (Interview with Najma Kousri Labidi). Her proactive actions at this level are more the exception than the rule, given that very few women actually receive justice when charges are usually dropped.

Religion and Class

The previous example of interactions with the police exposes a more privileged positionality. I found in the interviews that experiences of women from smaller villages and less material resources and/or veiled women's experiences change drastically from there. Rather than seeking to file reports for themselves and remind the police of its duty to protect women's interests in the public sphere, they go for the safer option and try to remain invisible. S.C. brings up her background from a small village as an additional risk factor to being harassed by the police:

> "It's a bit class segregated: This class can participate in associations, clubs, travels, but the other… Generally, it's like that, in my opinion. Even the police at the university, anytime we entered, we had to take precautions, because I'm originally from a small village. I don't have any weapon to defend myself. So if I get randomly into trouble I won't find anybody who supports me, so I prefer to live by my norms, but always keep it smart" (S.C., Tunis, April 2014).

Furthermore, she points to the need of resources to encounter police harassment, which exposes more vulnerability of women in terms of class and locality in the interactional dimension of the public sphere. Her account also exposes the role of the police in restricting access to public spaces, such as the university to veiled women, before the revolution. The specific positionality of veiled women when exposed to police, however, continues to be a source of discrimination after the uprisings.

When her brother was injured during the December 2010 uprising in Sidi Bouzid, the activist S.M. took over the role of a representative of her brother's rights as she is the most educated in her family. She explains that her veil has always been an issue when dealing with the authorities. Even after the uprisings, she felt that it hindered her because authorities would try to 'put her in her place' based on religious rhetoric. She narrates an episode when she was at the local administrative office where she demanded to see the Governor (or an equal person in charge) of the indemnity procedures of those wounded during the uprisings.[155] When she demanded her right to be heard, she was confronted with harassment because of her being a Muslim woman:

> "He said: You are not polite! And I replied: 'I'm very proud not to be polite with you, but this is my opinion. And he replied: 'How come you talk to me like that? You have to respect the veil that you are wearing' and I replied: The headscarf, I respect it. If the headscarf will knot my tongue, I will take it off. That's not worth it. Our religion is not like this, and it's not gonna be you to tell me what I want to do and what I don't

---

155 One demand and struggle for the families of the injured was to receive social assistance based on the inability to work.

> want to do. So he asked me my identity card to find a problem… he didn't
> find anything" (S.M., Sidi Bouzid, April 2014).

S.M. finds herself in a situation of harassment where she has to defend her position as a Muslim woman. The harassment she encounters by the police is not only gender based but invokes religious morality as well. Her argument is similar to the episode when she had to defend herself as a Muslim woman against the Salafist youth: She finds herself in a positionality where she has to defend her gender and her religion against state authorities and extremists alike.

Leftist activism

Ameny Ltifi, who is part of the unemployed workers union (Union des diplomés chômeurs, UDC), has had confrontations with the police because of her anticapitalist activism. The UDC and other counterpublics mobilizing for the right to work often face harsh oppression by the police. The forms of participation that the UDC employ to demand socio-economic justice can all too easily be framed as "disruptive": The means of political participation they have at their disposal, such as demonstrations, occupations and strikes, expose them to direct repression, against which they do not receive any protection (Antonakis, 2015). Ltifi reveals her strategy to overcome police violence when demanding access to new job opportunities:

> "I met women at the ministry who were waiting to be heard. Even if you
> would organize a hunger strike inside the ministry, they will finally come
> and beat you and arrest you. So you have to look for quantity. Why? To
> attract the media, to attract the civil society, to attract political parties to
> claim your right. And the unemployment is something that touches upon
> the whole society"(Ameni Ltifi, Sidi Bouzid, April 2014).

Ltifi brings up the protective factor of being "many" people to encounter police violence. After the uprisings, exposing police violence by employing channels that would mediate abuse at the representational dimension of the public sphere is considered an important way to reform the relation between citizens and police. The liberated public sphere that didn't exist before, can function as a protector against oppressive practices.[156]

The analysis of gender-based violence by the police, as an expression of the disciplinary domain of power needs to address the political context. According to Lina Ben Mheni, the surveillance of women's bodies and behavior in public

---

156 This has been stated by Amel Amrawy as well who claims that during her arrest, she told the
police that she would film and document everything he will be doing to her as to intimidate him.

illustrate different phases.[157]Ben Mheni analyses the gender-based harassment by the police as an expression of the disciplinary domain of power linked to a specific time context, claiming that there were waves of targeted arrests. Police would structurally harass and attack women who go out at night, consume alcohol and gather with male and female friends, standing for a more "secularist" lifestyle. In the interview and blogpost, she describes that once she published her first blog about the supposed systematic attack more testimonies were sent to her and she discerns a "period" in which police violence against women had increased. By opening the discussion, the blogger would in turn receive more replies and break the taboo of addressing everyday harassment by the police. It is hard to say here, whether these demonstrations of power by the law enforcement were in fact part of a campaign controlled by the higher authorities, or an expression of internal power vacuum under the Troika government or whether they were happening within the interactional dimension only, without mirroring the political power games.

(Transitional) Justice and Gender Based Violence

The Dignity and Truth Commission tackled sexualized violence by the state in their report of 2016. Hundreds of testimonies have been presented to the commission, including accusations of sexual assault and rape by policemen. A women's committee presided over by Ibtheld Abdelatif is part of the Dignity and Truth Commission. It aims to uncover gender based sexualized violence and facilitate women to testify (Abdelatif, 2015). While the vast amount of material still needs to be validated, researchers like Hind Ahmed Zaki demand to include an overall gender component in the transitional justice process instead of separating it into a committee. Raising a feminist voice, within the frame of transitional justice, may prove to be the most significant challenger to break the disciplinary domain of power and the Matrix of Domination.

In November 2016, the first public hearings organized by the Dignity and Truth Commission (also broadcasted on national TV) took place in the context of transitional justice. Leila Khaled Labidi, was among the first women who publically spoke out about police abuse during the uprisings in Redeyef in November 2016 (Mosaique FM, 2016, 54:10). However, scholars working on the process of transitional justice in general, paint a more negative picture and also

---

157 After the uprisings, there was unanimity among the security corps. Tunisia witnessed the creation of two, often competing syndicates of the security forces: the National Union of the syndicates for Tunisian Security Forces (Union Nationale des Syndicats des forces de Sûreté Tunisienne UNSFS and the National Syndicate of Security Forces of the Interior (Syndicat Nationale des Forces Securitaire Intérieures SNFSI). Investigations into this split would be desirable, but cannot be undertaken in the frame of this work.

point to the political parties of Ennahda and Nidaa Tounes who would hinder a successful process. Zaki states with regards to the process that: "The country's two main political parties seem to be seeking reconciliation in the interest of national stability but seem less interested in justice" (Zaki, 2016).

One particular case that had broken the taboo of sexual violence committed by police forces was debated in a broader public: The case of "Meryiem Ben Mohammed"[158] exposes how the interconnections of the three dimensions of the public sphere can be used efficiently by feminist intervention to challenge the Matrix of Domination that legitimizes a culture of violence against women. The young woman was raped by three policemen in 2012, when she was stopped in a car while travelling with her boyfriend. After the attack, she filed charges against the aggressors but was afterwards accused of "indecency." This strategy of blaming the victim" sparked a public outcry, triggering a debate on the criminalization of rape in Tunisia. "Women's organizations joined in the debate, while feminist journalists followed the case closely. The case also received some attention from national and international NGOs, such as Amnesty International.[159]

The case was taken to trial in April 2014 and the policemen, who stood accused, were sentenced to seven years in prison. After an appeal by the victim, the judge extended the sentences to 15 years in November 2014. The trial in April was accompanied by demonstrations outside the courthouse of Tunis. There were around thirty supporters, among them young, publicly known feminists Lina Ben Mheni, Amina Sboui and members of the ATFD. Far from a mass protest, the sensitive issue and the well-developed networks of the pressure groups demonstrating gained the attention and even the presence of national and international reporters.[160] When asked, why she had decided to participate in the demonstration, the former Femen activist Sboui replies:

> "It's important to be here to support Meryem and with her all women who have been victims of rape in Tunisia. It gives me a hard time to know that only because they are policemen, they are still free, this is not normal. (…) Even if it's only one or two women in front of the trial, it's important for us to designate to her that we are here" (Amina Sboui, Tunis, April 2014).

Feeling ashamed and being held responsible for abuse is one of the main reasons why women do not speak up against their aggressors, as a study by Amnesty

---

158 The real identity of the woman has not been revealed until today, which speaks for an ethical treatment of the case by journalists and a careful course of action from the rape survivor and her supporters.

159 For example the trans-regional NGO „Women Under Muslim Law" was following up on the case http://www.wluml.org/news/tunisia-police-rape-meriem-attackers-sentences-doubled

160 This account is based on my own participatory observations during the demonstration.

International in Tunisia shows (Mughrabi, 2015). In the case of Meryem, it was the attempt to codify the practice of victim blaming that brought about a well-orchestrated response by women's rights defenders, journalists and NGOs who highlighted the structural (police) violence against women. Finally, the process contributed to challenge Tunisia's archaic laws on sexual violence. According to Article 227 of the penal code, perpetuators who marry their victim can be exempt from punishment. Furthermore, the Arabic translation of "rape" doesn't appear in the penal code (Ben Achour, 2013, p. 32). In August 2017, the article was abolished and the legal practice dissolved in Jordan, Lebanon and Morocco, around the same time. This speaks for a strengthened transregional feminist counterpublic that could lobby their governments at the same time (Antonakis, 2017, p.10). At the same times, public "local triggers", such as the case of "Meryem" generate national attention.

10.2   Decolonizing and Localizing Feminist Terminologies and Practices

In the previous Chapter I have suggested a conceptualization of a "Young feminist approach". This can be linked to the wider issue of contested concepts of feminism incorporating a hegemonic domain of power. I have exhibited how state feminism has degraded terminologies and controlled the definition of an emancipatory concept. Re-negotiating this concept that served to legitimize the old regimes' structural power is certainly one of the challenges of young or newly institutionalized feminist actors.

10.2.1   Unveiling Authoritarian Terminologies

Drawing on conclusions of the previous Chapters and building up on the issue of foreign funding laid out previously, the next section elaborates on the persistent manifestation of a feminist ideology, which is embedded in the hegemonic domain of power and sheds light on different attempts to (re-) negotiate hegemonic feminism. Access to the structural dimension of the public sphere, media outlets, academia and strong publics can certainly facilitate this renegotiation, but I argue that slow changes can as well be set in motion in counterpublics.

Firstly, the women I interviewed that come from outside Tunis, would argue that feminism is not the label they would take on themselves as it is somewhat "occupied" by Western, bourgeois women in the capital. Feminist scholar Ogundipe-Leslie speaks to the dilemma of drawing from feminist knowledge creation in Western societies, often implying racist stances: "African Women must read white feminists but with discrimination and with a critical sensitivity to their relevance or non-relevance to the complexity and differences in our history, sociology and experience as different peoples. In the final analysis though, African women, I think must theorize their own feminisms" (Ogundipe-Leslie, 1994, p. 208). Abu-Lughod also highlights the relation between "local feminisms" and the West, trying to find a "measured course between the glossing over and underemphasizing the West" (Abu-Lughod, 1998, p. viii).

Addressing oppression and injustices to women in their respective societies consists in an empowerment approach to increase women's participation that would depart from the local level. First developed in the 1990s, the empowerment approach was considered a new paradigm in development studies and one that was supposed to confront the "women in development" approach. The respondents to this study have argued in favor of inducing change by working at the interactional dimension of the public sphere and most importantly integrate men to renegotiate the "subject of feminism". Consequently, the label of "feminism" is either abandoned or replaced by other concepts to frame local activism. The journalist B.L., who moved from a Western town in Tunisia to the capital reveals the self-censorship with regards to feminist terminology linking it to Western and colonial feminism:

> "The term feminism recalls foreign countries, it recalls the Western woman, it relates to the Western notion. It doesn't fit with oriental and Muslim values and norms and so on. That's why we try to avoid calling it 'feminism', but 'justice' instead, or 'against violence'. There you go, different nominations. But this is just to not to fall into the exploitation of the causes" (B.L., Tunis, April 2014).

Secondly, and closely related to the problematic assumption of feminism as a Western colonial concept, is Feminism as an authoritarian modernist concept as it was employed under Bourguiba and Ben Ali. Anissa Saidi, who is the head of the ATFD office in Kairouan that the association opened as part of a decentralizing strategy in 2013, recalls the connection of feminism to the *ancien regime*:

> "I think that Tunisians have a prejudice against feminism, because before under the regimes of Ben Ali and Bourguiba, it was always the image of the woman who is part of a political party, that is the single political party that is ruling [Neo-Destour respectively the RCD, note from the author]. So this is not feminism, it may be a female struggle but not a feminist one" (Anissa Saidi, Kairouan, April 2014).

Saidi relates the problematic conception of feminism to the practices of the *ancien regime*, stigmatizing counterpublics organizing around the dominant lexicon. According to her, the practices of the former regime were not an expression of feminism, but a female struggle. B.L. presents one way to detach it from the hegemonic representation of feminism:

> "If you show the people that feminism means that the rural woman is more and more autonomous economically, when the rural woman has the same rights as men, that the women working in the agricultural sector have the same salary and the same work, that women have rights that protect them against every aggression, when women have access to information and education, this is the real struggle for me. Feminism cannot only be claimed by holding a poster in demonstrations or by pretending it on TV shows"(B.L., Tunis, April 2014).

B.L.'s account illustrates that "feminism" should be read as "empty signifier"[161] that could incorporate a number of critical positions to advance women's rights and establish gender equality in education and labor, but it has been attributed to the middle class, secular woman in demonstrations and talk shows supporting a hegemonic ideology.

The decolonization of the terminology goes in line with finding different methodologies and methods for their struggle that includes a shift-away from a pure rights-based approach and focus on issues of justice, and against violence. The feminist counterpublic "Chaml," providing an online platform for young women to speak about experiences of violence encountered on a daily basis as well as debate new trends in Tunisian feminism, aims to revolutionize classical feminist participations on the basis of deconstructing the "myth of the modern Tunisian woman." To this end, co-creator, Amel Amrawy calls for a shift in priorities of feminist work. Focusing only on the structural domain of power, i.e. by changing the codification of women's rights, upsets her:

> "It makes me even more sick that because of Article 45 that is codifying women's rights to see all the women being very happy to have this Article. However, the problem is not the Article but the realization and implementation of the Article. Our issue doesn't lie in a piece of paper, but in the mentalities outside" (Amel Amrawy, Tunis, May 2014).

"Mentality" can be regarded as a problematic concept as it presumes fixed identities and is therefore not helpful when analyzing the construction of gendered discourses among different structures of oppression. I have previously presented the pattern found in my data that can be summarized as the "revolution in the mentalities" that would lead the way to "real" gender equality. I have so far used this as an *in vivo* code. The respondents use it as an expression in opposition to the "paper," the rights based-approach, a practice that points to the importance of structural changes at the interactional dimension of the public sphere when it comes to the daily implementation of the laws by policemen, judges or other people in positions of authority. The critique expressed here can be related to

---

161 On the importance of having empty signifiers by the idea of political theorist Ernesto Laclau (1996) in feminist movements, as „as a 'surface of inscription' for a number of disparate – and sometimes contradictory – political ideas and feminist demands," see (Gunnarsson Payne, 2012, p.188).

Mervat Hatem's analysis of Islamist and modernist feminist understandings in the MENA region in 1993, where she states a "depersonalization" of women's problems by "emphasizing the importance of introducing macro-changes in these societies, which they claim will improve the public conditions under which women operate. They avoid a discussion of the personal, familial norms of women, which in fact significantly influence public attitudes" (Hatem, 1993, p. 45).

The assumption that changes at the structural dimension of the public sphere would trickle down to the interactional domain of power and then influence lived experiences positively is refused. The demand for a "cultural revolution" that would challenge patriarchy "bottom up," at the interpersonal domain of power cannot only be situated within any specific dimension of the public sphere but is supposed to target the structure of Tunisian society as a whole, including the family and spaces situated within the "private realm." When looking into initiatives created by feminist activists and women in various counterpublics, the cultural "transformation" tackling the hegemonic domain of power at the interactional dimension of the public sphere can be discerned as one path to help this revolution on its way. Cultural change can be regarded here as complementary to the institutional changes that have been described earlier and includes a variety of forms for negotiating gender outside of legal texts, reaching from artistic and media productions diversifying stereotypes and gender relations to sexual education within the family and in public institutions such as schools, music, film and theatre. Hereby the "hegemonic domain of power" and cultural practices as sites of resistance is being activated.[162]

10.2.2 Reviewing the "Subject of Feminism"

While feminist scholars in the 1980s and 1990s were constantly imploring a lack of fundamental debate to find a "clear" position on what feminism means (see quote of (Marzouki, 1993), it appears that a younger generation of feminists participating in the public sphere by redefining ideologies have agreed to disagree. "Tunisian philosopher Soumaya Mestiri understands here the recognition of difference as an important practice to "decolonize feminism": "This necessary revision of the history of occidental feminism appears even more legitimate since the second half of the last century, when feminism has developed, sometimes in a radical way, a paradigmatic slogan that resonates all too well with our ears: "Recognizing difference" (Mestiri, S., 2016, p. 9; *translated by the author*).

---

162 Yuval Davis has pinpointed the "two co-existing elements in the operation of cultures" understood as "dynamic social processes": the tendency for stabilization and continuity on the one hand, and that for perpetual resistance and change on the other (Yuva-Davis, 1997, p.41).

The respect of individual freedoms and acceptance of differences among women is considered the driving force of women's emancipation, also by the activists I interviewed:

> "The right to believe what you want is an individual freedom. If I will defend an atheist woman, I will defend a Muslim or a Christian woman as well" (Y.T., Tunis, March 2014).

This generation, raised by mothers who could profit all of their lives from the personal status law is more eager to integrate other subjects, bodies and issues into their participation as well and possess resources to create novel possibilities of coalitions. Their aim is to deconstruct and revitalize feminist approaches, with their analysis extended by the categories of class and labor. This illustrates the intersectional paradigm replacing a mono-dimensional approach to gender analysis and feminist activism. Fenton and Downey have coupled the need to recognize differences to the effectiveness of counterpublics through "the language of community" relating it to "the extent to which it admits difference and differentiation within its own borders, is capable of accepting multiply-determined identities and identification" (Downey & Fenton, 2003, p.192).Many interviewees referred to the period after the uprisings as a time when Tunisians could simply meet and have the chance to get to know each other. This is particularly true for the periods of increased mobility within the country. It was also a period when veiled women could enter public institutions again as the ban of the veil in public institutions that Habib Bourguiba had introduced by a public decree in 1981 (Ben Salem M. , 2010) was lifted. The new legislations that changed the structural dimension of the public sphere also had direct repercussions on the interactional dimension.

S.C. and other interviewees who wear the veiled, made this point several times. S.C. stresses the feeling of being "a whole citizen now" who "had taken precautions to access the public space as a veiled woman" before. It allowed her to become more engaged and increasingly active in civil society. With other friends she founded a local cultural initiative in Kairouan. As a student and activist, S.C. has encountered many stereotypes. Her approach is to change these slowly by seeking interaction with people. While before, the legislative frames took away her freedom to express herself in public, she is now using new spaces to get in touch with other people. She travels to conferences, organizes local initiatives and as part of the international green network she also travels abroad with her activism. In her account:

> "This [stereotypes against veiled feminists, note by the author] is bad, so we tried…It will change of course but it will take time. It can change, when you are in contact (with other people), you get used to see friends, that are not veiled; there is no difference between us. There are also jokes,

> there was a trend of posting photos from veiled women within the communist party (…) Okay, they are veiled, and they are part of the communist party, how can that happen? They always link the veil to Islamism. It is slowly changing, I think that as soon as you are a bit included in the society, its changing" (S.C., Tunis, April 2014).

The trend to "expose" veiled women in apparently inappropriate contexts, such as at the meetings of a communist party, or sitting at tables where alcohol is consumed, can on the one hand be problematized as a strategy of ridiculing women and excluding them from the public sphere. S.C., on the other hand, deduces that it could help to disentangle the image of the veiled women from an Islamist ideology in the long run[163] and even connect them to an Islamic feminism. In this regard, S.C., a woman in her mid-twenties, who is originally from a tiny village in the Kairouan Governorate, can be seen as an example of a new social mobility that allows young, well-educated women to overcome hegemonic power in terms of class, religious and local hierarchies. For her, seizing the opportunity to get involved with foreign NGOs and networks was the right choice to push for her aim to fight regional injustices in Tunisia and at the same time become "included in the society."

Colonial rule and the established state feminism have deeply marked Tunisian society until today and impacted the rural urban divide specifically that is until today felt in the language barriers that exist between Tunisian citizens. Najma Kousri, a law student who is part of the youth section of the ATFD in Tunis, speaks about her own difficulties in overcoming these language barriers when the association was expanding its activities to other regions and reached out to local publics in the aftermath of the uprisings:

> "I handle standard Arabic well. But, for example, when I go to the regions like ElKef or Sidi Bouzid where we went with the caravan, they speak Tunisian only. They don't speak French. I had some difficulties there, but it has been three years already [since the uprisings] and I speak more or less not in standard Arabic anymore but in clear Tunisian without employing French words" (Najma Kousri Labidi, Tunis, May 2014).

The experience of finding a common language in the Tunisian society can be linked to the epistemological reflections I outline in Chapter II. Actively overcoming language barriers entails the subversive potential of translational feminist politics that seek to include "unsettled and deauthorized modes of

---

163 The dialectical relationship of double sided visibilities play into this question as well.

knowledge" to challenge the Matrix of Domination (Butler, 2013, p. 213). Common language, in terms of de Saussures conceptualization of *"langue"*, [164]appears to be a crucial pre-condition when constructing counterpublics aimed at sharing knowledge and establish a powerful "language of community" (Fenton & Downey, 2003, p.192).

However, language barriers are pushed into the background, when a *language* of solidarity is found that entails to actively engage with stereotypziation that the hegemonic domain of power has constructed. S.C. describes the inherent stereotypes among women that hamper coalition buildings based on the category of "women":

> "From my personal experience, I took part in a UN program for capacity building for women in Tunis. Women from Ennahda and from the left were present. At first, it was really chaotic, even the tone of the discussion. The women were nervous and did not feel comfortable even during the coffee break; they spoke about each other. But later there was a lot of communication. (…) On the third day, we were trying to find common grounds and forget about our differences and focus on the most important points, because after all there will always be stereotypes from both sides." (S.C., Tunis, April 2014).

Contrary to the challenges of stereotypes discussed before, these do not result from mis-representations of feminism at the representational dimensions, but rather concern internalized stereotypes from within feminist counterpublics as well:

> "Now we talk about the difference between veiled and non-veiled women. In my association, however, there are friends with degrees in arts, in design and theater, and we are veiled and non-veiled women and we like each other a lot and we work a lot together" (Hayet Amami, Sidi Bouzid, April 2014).

Amami contrasts the "hot topic" of the veil debated in national and international publics with her own experience in work and feminist resistance in the counterpublic that she has created. She emphasizes the constituencies that bring them together, pointing to "high culture" (Yuval-Davis, 1997, p. 40), their university education and common interests despite differing religious practices and expres-

---

164 The term « langue » derives from the linguistic separation by Ferdinand de Saussure into „Langue, Langage and parole" and designates the „principle of classification" (de Saussure, 1916, p. 25) and the „linguistic organism" of the language needs to be studied. An analysis of the relation between the trias of language, langage and parole, seems particularly interesting to investigate with regards to the establishment of counterpublics and its supposedly required common language of community.

sions. In this counterpublic, the practice of an inclusive understanding of emancipatory politics is emphasized and set in opposition with a middle class, modern feminism that continues to reinforce ideological markers of difference.

The acceptance of difference among women as a decolonizing strategy is not only emphasized with regards to local or class boundaries but is pushed also within urban and middle-class feminist counterpublics with regards to sexualities and gender identities. One activist expresses discontent at having to hide her femininity (or *femme* identity) when entering feminist circles because otherwise she wouldn't be taken seriously. She critically reflects the internal structures that systematically exclude women based on appearance and lifestyle:

> "I don't want to be assimilated to the feminist movement here in Tunisia: To be feminist, you need to be single, and you're not allowed to be feminine. There is a lot going on like this. And this is stigmatizing and excluding other people." (Y.T., Tunis March 2014)

The respondent opens a debate on the interpersonal domain of power and how activists "treat each other," while hinting to internal hierarchizations and exclusionary processes. She goes on that even in her circle of friends she notices sexist reflexes, proving there is still a lot of work to do. As a self-identified bisexual woman, she furthermore expresses the need to overcome heteronormative hegemony within feminist circles as well. The authoritarian state feminist paradigm excluded "queer" identities and theories from the public sphere. However, queer and intersectional ideas guide, explicitly or implicitly, the participation and visions of a younger feminist generation socialized in a digitalized environment.

A last strong dimension of decolonizing and localizing feminist concepts is to strip feminist politics off the hegemonic assumption that it addresses "women's issues" alone. The association "Women and Citizenship" (Femme et Citoyenneté), based in ElKef, decided to employ the notion of citizenship in its name to involve men in their work. Their work revolves around gender and labor equality, but they also stress the inclusion of young boys and girls, offering them a space to spend time together, experience associative work and have a space to debate freely. When I was visiting the organization, the women praised the common work with young men. Amel Cherni from the association describes the problems they faced when first establishing their association in ElKef. With the ATFD being the most present feminist counterpublic actor within the structural and representational dimension of the Tunisian public sphere, the local NGO had to defend their own local identity first:

> "For example, our association, it was new for them. Here, in ElKef, the majority calls us democratic women, they say: 'Ah you are the femmes democrats [ATFD]'. But we reply: 'No! We are the association 'Women and Citizenship'. From ElKef!'" (Amel Cherni, ElKef, April 2014).

The episode shows how a redefinition of the hegemonic domain of power can start at the interactional dimension of the public sphere. The demarcation from the hegemonic understanding of feminism as a metropolitan ideology is emphasized when clarifying who they are in the interaction with others from the ElKef. Besides this local aspect, the association advances a different methodology as well that breaks with the hegemonic understanding of feminism. They actively want to integrate men as they identify them as the representatives of patriarchal mentality that they want to change:

> „It's more about the mentality, it's about the patriarchal society that we are living in. That's what we are trying to change, but I think you have to work with men. It's true that you have to work with women, but you have to work with men as well. Change will happen by [changing] the men's mentality"(Ghoffrane Heraghi, ElKef, May 2013).

At their office in ElKef, they introduced me to Ayoub Trabelsi, a 28 year old physical education graduate, wanted to talk to me as well.[165] Besides his early sensitivity, he knew the locally grown organization "Femme et Citoyenneté" as well. From the interview, two major points can be deduced:

First, Ayoub Trabelsi, himself and, according to his testimony, many other young men from ElKef, have decided to work on feminist issues after the uprisings and the coming to power of the Ennahda party. They felt that locally, Salafism was on the rise and nationally, the Ennahda-led Troika government would endanger women's rights. He says that the situation for women was "a bit complicated" and "there were some menaces." Second, his experience as an openly declared feminist illustrates the importance for the members of feminist organizations to work with men as well, when he explained how he directly talks to Salafi young men in his neighborhood. Asked whether he will not be discriminated by them and feel lonely in his position, Trabelsi admits that the discussions on gender equality and feminism are possible because they are neighbors and he is drawing on that resource to share his knowledge and convictions with them. He also employs religious arguments, using their own language, to debate gender issues. He is able to access their circles, which could also be described as a counterpublic, from his position of a man much more easily. Interestingly enough, he employs the self-description feminist without hesitation and explains that many other young men in ElKef describe themselves as feminists, which in his approach means to defend women's rights:

---

165 For the members of the associations, it was essential to present the young men as part of their counterpublic and that his account should be heard as well. They hereby actively pushed a new epistemology by challenging the way I had intended to create knowledge to define their realities on their own terms. This can be related to Patricia Hill Collins' appeal of activating critical epistemologies as an emancipatory practice.

> "No, I don't feel alone. In our association already, there are many men who all defend feminism and even the youth in the region of ElKef, who are feminists. It's true that they may not participate in associations, but they are feminists and they defend women's rights. Especially in the demonstrations, you see a lot of youth and young men" (Ayoub Trabelsi, ElKef, April 2014).

Trabelsi's account raises the issue of new masculinities in post-Ben Ali Tunisia. He represents a male generation that openly embraces feminist issues and was educated on women's rights within the local association "Women and Citizenship" that represent for him a space of withdrawal and learning. His example furthermore demonstrates how young men can function as women's rights advocates at the interactional dimension of the public sphere by engaging with peers of their neighborhood network. Employing a "language of the community" that is in this case defined by religious and local elements, he functions as a mediator between counterpublics.

K.E. brings up a similar issue in the interview, calling for an integrative and exhaustive gender approach and work with men and on masculinities as well. She goes so far as to say that self-declared feminists would even harm women in the long run. Her account reveals the close association of "feminist politics" and an authoritarian, destructive legacy:

> "If you really want to follow a strategy, find real solutions and correct things, you have to talk about the human being. But if you speak as a feminist and you address women only and you don't work on men it's the contrary. If you want to help women, you have to work on men. But there are many feminists who work on women only, so the same problems are still in place. If you work on men and the family, you can correct things. You have to follow a clear strategy, the women are here but you have to work on men" (K.E., Siliana, April 2014).

The female-only approach reproduces power structures and the "same problems" persist. A "strategic" approach to women's rights would integrate those who hold the privileges in patriarchy. Her account examines the urge to depoliticize women's rights issues linked to an exclusive feminist doctrine and focus on dignity and justice for everybody. Meaning that gender equality would best be achieved by working with men within the communities and families.

10.2.3 The Family and Community as "Site of Transformation": Deconstructing 'Naturalized Hierarchies'

Decolonizing feminism at the interactional dimension of the public sphere finally concerns the naturalized hierarchies within the family, which structure family life and usually give the father and male members of the family more privileges. Feminist scholar Ogundipe-Leslie stated: "All theoreticians of African liberation have failed to confront the issue of gender within the family or to confront the family as site of social transformation" (Ogundipe-Leslie, 1994, p. 210).

Discussing naturalized hierarchies within the family illustrates the limits of the frameworks of the public spheres and counterpublics that has been offered here. The assigned space of the "family" from which others are excluded is in literature usually associated with the "private space", most commonly a house or an apartment, in opposition to the public sphere. Centering the family in analysis of political transformation also bears explanatory potential as it reproduces the hegemonic domain of power from within. My argument draws from on Collins' illuminating essay "It's All in the Family" where she finds that "naturalized hierarchies" are embedded in the traditional family idea, that is "articulated not only with hierarchies of race and nation but also with hierarchies of economic or social class" (Collins, 1998, p. 73).

I have argued before, that the state feminist paradigm could externalize patriarchy on an Islamic "other", hereby omitting an exhaustive societal debate on patriarchal state feminism. Relating to this, despite the rights offering women more choices for a self-defined life, state feminism did not address patriarchy in its formulations within the family and secondly, excluded women and families by marginalizing localities.

In her 1988 article, Deniz Kandyoti argues for a systematic comparative analysis of the different strategies women employ to counter patriarchy according to their specific contexts (Kandiyoti, 1988) and sheds light on the under-theorized concept of patriarchy and the roles (older) women play in supporting it:

"The cyclical nature of women's power in the household and their anticipation of inheriting the authority of senior women encourages a thorough internalization of this form of patriarchy by the women themselves. In classic patriarchy, subordination to men is offset by the control older women attain over younger women" (Kandiyoti, 1988, p. 279).

Within the social contract of the "Patriarchal bargain," older women and mothers gain security and protection in the framework of family roles as mothers, daughters and mothers-in-law. In turn, they impose the rules of a patriarchal order on younger and dependent women. While Deniz Kandyoti mainly talks about the mother-in-law who will exercise authority on the daughter-in-law, Hayet Amami, gives the example of the relation between mother and daughter. She sheds light on the education of girls focusing on a *lookism* that serves the role of finding a future husband. She describes how girls are expected to dress modestly and unobtrusively when they are younger, but as soon as they reach an age to get married, mothers will suddenly encourage them to go to the hairdresser and 'dress up' without giving them any explanation. For Amami, this behavior triggers deep incertitude in a girl's comprehension of her body and self-expression:

> "So, that's my work now. I revise the attitudes passed on from mothers
> to their daughters. In my opinion, it's a bit foolish, but I think that our
> mothers have bequeathed us with a wrong culture. (…) The girls go crazy;
> they don't know how to behave. For me, the hardest thing to see is that
> even the women who are in their 40s today reproduce the same culture to
> their daughters, so the problems are being reproduced. (…) The biggest
> problem is, that they are afraid of their bodies" (Hayet Amami, Sidi
> Bouzid, April 2014).

For now, Amami says, her ideas are confined to a restricted counterpublic, where she mainly exchanges with other activists. Her approach to a feminist emancipatory work engages with the category of age: She finds that hierarchies and practices between mothers and daughters constitute the major interpersonal domain of power she aims to tackle to initiate change in gender relations. As another related problem, Amami identifies, that women are actually afraid of their own bodies. Her approach to tackle the naturalized hierarchies within the family consists of two different elements. On the one hand, she has created citizen cafés in Sidi Bouzid, where she mainly addresses young mothers directly. These gatherings usually take place in private houses, due to the lack of public spaces where women can meet.[166]On the other hand, she also wants to reach broader publics that may not be situated on the direct interactional level of publics. One way to reach them is to produce videos exposing the "wrong culture":

> "We want to make an ad or a documentary film, we try to call out this
> wrong culture and to make a revision, even to shock young mothers, and
> even the mothers in their 40s. And they can then complete with them the
> same approach" (Hayet Amami, Sidi Bouzid, April 2014).

In her opinion, only shocking and disrupting acts can help to make older and younger mothers understand their participation in maintaining the hegemonic domain of power from within the family. Amami's work can be related to what Nigerian gender studies scholar Molara Ogundipe defines as "Stiwanism," a term she coined to describe an African centered theory of feminism focusing on "Social Transformation in Africa Including Women" including the particular categories of age and kinship roles. A woman's status in society is mediated and improved by age, economics, kinship roles and by the class she comes from as well as birth and the achievements in her lived experience (Ogundipe-Leslie, 1994, p. 219).

Mothers in my interviews also expressed tackling gender negotiations from within the family and reveal its importance to organize resistance. Leila Khaled Labidi, a mother of three children clarifies the reasons she decided to take the

---

166 An exception here is the space of the mosque where women can gather together, exchange information and so on.

streets, mobilize women and directly confront the authorities during the uprisings in Gafsa in 2008:

> "The education still states that men are better than women. But for me, the first time I went out (for demonstration and the sit-in) that wasn't for feminism. I was fighting for my family, to defend my family" (Laila Khaled Labidi, Redeyef, November 2014).

Her account reveals the perceived disconnection and opposition of feminism and the family and can be related to the discussion of state feminism earlier. When state authorities crossed the boundaries to the family, because her husband and her son were arrested, Laila Khaled decides to take to the streets. Concerning gender equality, she identifies education within the family, as essential to fight discrimination. Talking about family, rather than rights and ideologies, detaches the feminist concept from problematic ideologizations.

10.3   Conclusion: Encountering (Violent) Excertion of Influence

This chapter's purpose was to, in a first step, empirically ground the connection of feminism to both the colonial history and the old regime and its manifestations at the interactional dimension of the public sphere. Foreign funding was framed as an important entry point to analyze the creation and development of emerging counterpublics and the ambiguous constitution of foreign funding in promoting gender politics has been highlighted. I have looked at specific forms of violence against women by the police and found that the security forces are enforcing the disciplinary domain of power as bystanders and perpetuators. They cannot be considered an ally to reduce sexualized violence. Furthermore, I distinguished different forms of discrimination and abuse by the police through the lens of positionality and found how religion, class and activism challenging the neo-liberal consensus affects treatment by the police.

At the interactional dimension, negotiating gender in an emancipatory way consists in localizing feminist concepts that overcome former ideas of secular middle class and women-only approaches often imposed by Western influence and funding. Two important processes that happen in counterpublics is then the review of terminologies and feminist practices. Newly established organizations must often struggle against stereotypes and hegemonic images that derive from the representational dimension of the public sphere in order to gain legitimacy and credibility in their community. Re-inventing a "common language" incorporates then recognizing differences, integrating men to re-define the "subject of feminism". Soumaya Mestiri speaks of a "muslim cultural feminism" or "muslim differentialist feminism" born with the uprisings of 2010 (Mestiri S. ,

2016, p. 81). Finally, the family and naturalized hierarchies have been identified as a major site of transformation. I have pointed to the concept of *Stiwanism* proposed by feminist Ogundipe-Leslie as a counter-draft to the legacies of feminism that appears more adaptable to the empirical realities and more appealing to improve gender justice for everybody.

11 Conclusion

This study set out to explore multifaceted dynamics of gender relations in the post-revolutionary Tunisian public sphere. Departing from the complexities of the empirical world necessitating a multi-layered analysis, a theoretical framework was developed in chapters 3 and 4 based on the epistemological and methodological premises outlined in chapter II. This allowed very different negotiation processes to be grasped in relation to women's positionalities and their resources. The study displayed how state feminism has deeply marked discourses on feminism and consequently the field of NGOs and women's networks. The field of women's rights remains profoundly politicized and vulnerable to instrumentalizations by parties and actors playing on polarization. In her piece from 2011, young feminist Ons Bouali called for the death of state feminism (Bouali, 2011). In the following, I summarize the argument with regards to political rearrangements and bargains first and show the political exploitation of gender politics in the political transformation. I then conclude with the analysis of the different dimensions of the public sphere. Finally, I emphasize four main issues I see emerging within the Matrix of Domination 2.0 showcased in this study.

11.1 About the Exploitation of Gender Politics

In the historical analysis within the public sphere and the Matrix of Domination, I have shown the development of a state feminist doctrine linked to the construction of modernity in the post-colonial period in Tunisia that characterized its "exceptionalism". At the same time, most organizations and spaces, including media and academia, were controlled and co-opted by state feminist politics. This came at the expense of a deeper debate about the relationship between women's rights and religion. One of the traces of an authoritarian legacy was the unique representation of "the Modern Tunisian Woman" promoted by the state-led institutions and the wife of the President, Layla Trabelsi, privileging the urban, secular, middle- and upper-class woman. The state and its institutions thus remained deeply patriarchal.

© Springer Fachmedien Wiesbaden GmbH, part of Springer Nature 2019
A. Antonakis, *Renegotiating Gender and the State in Tunisia between 2011 and 2014*, Politik und Gesellschaft des Nahen Ostens,
https://doi.org/10.1007/978-3-658-25639-5_11

This research showed in detail how the patterns of an installed dichotomy of colonial rule, of 'modern and secular' versus 'Islamic, traditional and backwards' that constituted an important pillar of the Ben Ali and Bourguiba regimes, could be mobilized again in formal politics over the period under study. Gender politics have been re-ideologized in a publicly staged confrontation between the two major political camps, the Nidaa Tounes party as the "secular and nationalist" party and the Ennahda as the "Islamic" party. Negotiating gender relations was carried out in a frame of sensationalism and ideologization, reproduced in powerful channels of political communication constituting the national, hegemonic public sphere. However, it has been demonstrated that both camps reproduce conservative oppressive and sexist politics. Drawing from the historically implemented hegemonic domain of power, "Bourguibism" could be presented as the only possible alternative to defend women's rights. The centers of power thus remain in the hands of a defined elite that has certainly enlarged its core circle, namely by sharing power with the Islamic party Ennahda, but continues to maintain a consensus-oriented system that delegitimizes autonomous voices. In this context, gender politics were defined by the middle- and upper-class, excluding socio-economic justice as an integral dimension. Furthermore, far from defending a secularist agenda, Nidaa Tounes upheld religious argumentation in the family code, thereby discriminating against women. Feminists who challenged the legislation and pushed for revolutionary legislation on the basis of *de facto* secularism were – ironically – sidelined. The recent years prove "dissembled secularism" to remain a pivotal hegemonic element legitimizing the conservative politics of a middle and upper class. The consensus-oriented norm of negotiations in the public sphere has re-marginalized revolutionary actors. The aim of consensus-building endangered political freedom and silenced those who challenged political power bargaining. I conclude that in order to foster sustainable change, an agonistic pluralism should be defended within the mosaic of public spheres.

11.2 Changes and Persistency in the Public Sphere

In light of the review of state feminist scholarship on Tunisia and Egypt that I embedded into the conceptual approach in chapter III and my empirical findings, I conceptualized state feminism, besides its benefits, as an oppressive structure within the hegemonic domain of power, legitimizing the Matrix of Domination. This continued to define the gendered discourse in the structural and representational dimension of the public sphere, while at the same time, I concluded that this authoritarian legacy continues to be challenged by counterpublics through new intersectional associations, transregional networks, media projects and work alliances alike.

11.2.1   Interdependencies: Political Institutions and Media

There is no doubt that important changes at an institutional level have introduced a liberalization of the former state-owned public sphere that lead to a more vibrant and pluralistic landscape of associations and new media projects at the representational and interactional dimension of the public sphere. The following section summarizes the most important findings of this study with regards to persistent power structures and changing dynamics within the three dimensions of the public sphere.

First, chapter VIII demonstrated how the structural dimension of power, as defined by Patricia Hill Collins, was renegotiated in the constitutional process in Tunisia: It set the judicial framework for women to access "strong publics" (Fraser, 1992, p. 75). Quotas represent a mechanism of inclusion and exclusion that impacts the representational dimension of the public sphere. I showed that it was mainly a small but very well-organized group of feminists within the interim institutions that imposed a quota system for the electoral lists prior to the democratic elections in 2011 and again in 2014. On this structural level, the introduction of the quota in Tunisia served at least two purposes: firstly through strengthening women in decision-making positions, shaping new women's rights codifications and secondly in opening access to the parliament and to representation in the public sphere to women of different backgrounds.

Integrating more participatory elements into local politics is certainly urgent and indispensable for an inclusive political process. Against the background of Article 46 of the Tunisian constitution and the parity in electoral law, local elections would change gender relations at the local level drastically, as women's lack of visibility in local politics has repercussions on their overall acceptance in public space. Mechanisms excluding women from entering local political institutions are much more fortified than on the national level. The rejection of the vertical zipper of the electoral quota that would have obliged parties to put women at the heads of their lists in 50% of the country's circumscriptions has divulged the government's reluctance to proactively alleviate the persisting marginalization of women in politics outside of the capital and cities in the coastal area.

While in Tunis, I outlined how women and feminist organizations with real bargaining power at their disposal can enter national political and media institutions and claim individual rights, but the situation is very different for women outside the capital. Regional (on the level of governments) and local (on the level of municipalities) politics in ElKef or Sidi Bouzid are very male-dominated. However, after years of postponing, local elections finally took place in Tunisia in May 2018. The electoral list from Sidi Bouzid also included female revolutionaries (Antonakis/Chennaoui, 2018).

Besides these successful negotiations at the institutional level, my study gave insights into deceptions expressed by women from their local perspective: It has been argued repeatedly how more freedom of expression or the finalized constitution alone would not help to overcome the oppressions that the women were suffering from. More so, the constitutional process that quickly came to revolve around identity and gender issues has been regarded as derailing "public opinion" from the need to structurally reform the country and respond to the initial demands of the 2010/2011 uprisings: these centered around work and dignity, regional development and political freedoms.

Second, the analysis of the representational dimension of the public sphere engaged with the absence of women from the classical mass media and explored feminist media projects. It brought to light a consistent marginalization of women in general and, more specifically, in their intersection with class and locality in the mass media. The (few) women representatives in the hegemonic public sphere lacked a space for subversive discursive politics that could expose oppression in its various dimensions. I suggest that this qualitative restriction of topics accorded to feminine subjectivities, such as women's issues, family or health, have nourished the further disconnection of feminist counterpublics and hampered feminist solidarity across local and class boundaries.

Additionally, gender negotiations were subjected mostly to the characteristics of entertainment, expressed in political polarizations, stereotypes and reductionism. An example here was the representation of "the rural woman" as a "victim," forming an antithesis to the "modern Tunisian woman." I have argued that the conceptual terms "modern" and "secular" that remain inscribed in the representation of "the Tunisian woman" are a part of post-colonial terminology that reflects the hegemonic domain of power. The study showcases that more pluralism does not necessarily lead to a plurality of gender roles and a decentralization of feminist discourses and views: I have shown that that the feelings of marginalization and a lack of representation of women in general and working class women or women from rural background especially, persist beyond victimization. Still, expressions of counterpublic resistance that localize feminist concepts should not be overlooked. The analysis of counterpublics as counterthematizations at the representational dimension of the public sphere revealed the aim to address gender in their intersections. I have identified three major themes that were considered "real issues" in contrast to the identity loaded women's rights debate, fueled by polygamy, Femen and inheritance laws: gender and labor, gender and locality and gender and health. I have presented successful counterthematizations and the deconstruction of stereotypical representations of gender by feminist activists, scholars and media producers. However, the communication infrastructure presented in the study (strikes, reports, petitions) remains highly vulnerable to political repression and ridiculing and therefore often remains in restricted counterpublics. This is also true for social media infrastructure, dependent on foreign global companies. I will get back to the latter point when concluding on the Matrix of Domination 2.0.

Third, when it comes to long-term changes and the application of institutional changes in the representational and interactional dimension of the public sphere, my research has shown that patriarchal hegemony remains the power structurally limiting the media output and the experiences of women. However, patriarchy can be challenged in more various independent ways now: It was voiced repeatedly in the interviews that the more traditional feminist instruments such as lobbying institutions and the media are not sufficient to address the patriarchal power structures that construct intersecting oppressions. Instead, the roots of hegemonic ideologies responsible for the structures of oppression that women suffer from in diverse ways need to be addressed.

11.2.2 Challenging Patriarchy, Decolonizing Feminism

The analysis of the second part of the study has shown that the areas of debate on the feminist principles and practices have indeed diversified. Liberating conceptualizations of feminism from their authoritarian and post-colonial notions is an important issue at stake and was outlined in chapter X. In contrast to the highly-controlled public sphere, where only a small circle of women at the capital could form counterpublics in the forms of associations or magazines, more subjects, both men and women, have taken over various communicative means to negotiate differences and positions in the interactional dimension of the public sphere. This has been illustrated by the formation of associations such as "Women and Citizenship" in ElKef, or "Victory of the Rural Woman" in Sidi Bouzid, the association "Chouf" with a clear intersectional outlook and various initiatives with an Islamic identity like *Nissa Tounissiat* ("Tunisian Women"). Soumaya Mestiri has coined the expression of "Muslim, cultural feminism" born with the revolution of 2010 that encounters a French feminism of the 1960s which was previously dominant in Tunisia (Mestiri, S. 2016, p. 80).

In their work, many activists have expressed the attempt to diversify and appropriate feminist ideas and practices in the interactional dimension of the public sphere. In this particular context, three mechanisms to challenge patriarchy from a decolonized approach emerge, which I relate to the recognition, exploration and demarcation of feminism as an exclusively secular modernist concept: firstly, by breaking with stereotypes and recognizing differences among women, within and outside of feminist spaces. This involves reflections on position and privileges in society. Secondly, it involves the emphasis and discussion of family structures and "naturalized hierarchies" and attempts to deconstruct these. The need to regard the role of mothers, and gender education at home in general, in upholding the patriarchal bargain was formulated especially in the *dakhel* region. Last but not least, this study has brought to light the attempts to localize feminist concepts.

These local emancipatory dynamics are characterized by integrating men into counterpublics and ensuring a local and open agenda, taking into consideration issues of access to healthcare, the regional job market or environmental issues. In this context, "young" counterpublics have been conceptualized mainly with regards to four elements: referring to (1) an actual age group and a generation; (2) their non-ideological stance; (3) their methodology and finally (4) their methods.

Firstly, "young" refers to a self-definition and the actual age group of a generation that has mainly grown up under Ben Ali's regime installed in 1987 and that witnessed the momentum of the uprisings in 2010/2011. In contrast to the previous generation, they are not the daughters but rather the granddaughters of the CSP, the personal status law that was adopted by the "father of the nation" Habib Bourguiba in 1957. While their mothers found themselves in a contradictory relationship with Bourguiba, this generation has taken for granted the rights accorded to them, for example, the right to divorce. Representatives of this generation confidently proclaimed the wish to "kill" state feminism and liberate themselves from the heritage of Bourguiba. Consequently, they were reluctant to support the revitalization of Bourguibism as performed by Nidaa Tounes and personified by Béji Caïd Essebsi. Their position is not to defend the CSP and reform it, but rather to erase it (also from its historical premises) and build up a new secularist code that guarantees equality between men and women.

Secondly, in opposition to feminist concepts of the state feminism implemented within a nationalist and modernist framework of state-building during colonial struggles, it could be defined as "post-ideological." The revolutionary feminist counterpublics refuse to be categorized within the ideologically constructed dichotomy of "Islamist" and "secular." The struggle to disentangle gender equality from identity politics is expressed, for example, by employing intersectional approaches to feminism, relying on the concept of equal citizenship or renouncing ideologically loaded terms such as "feminist" or "democratic." Consequently, young feminist counterpublics attempt to overcome state feminism as an ideology and the debates of the 1960s. Instead of identity, feminist counterpublics integrate class and locality and other forms of structural marginalization. The urban and rural divide in the context of a state legacy that has produced marginalized localities is incorporated within these feminist negotiations.

Thirdly, and closely related to the second point, the urgent need for a different methodology to tackle the challenges of the post-revolutionary period has been voiced. The need has been stressed for a shift from feminist struggles from the structural to the interactional dimension – from a rights-based approach to more comprehensive strategies that reach from transregional networking processes to discussions of internal family structures, and cultural change in the form of feminist media productions. This methodology emphasises the interpersonnal domain of power and leads the way to renegotiate gender with regards to sexuality, religion and violence beyond political exploitations. Promoting more cultural activities and working on masculinities has been emphasized especially in marginalized localities, where extremism and radicalization of young men were on the rise, particularly during the period when the interviews were conducted, in 2014.

Counterpublics that disavow from women's only approaches not only break with a hegemonic idea of feminism as a "women's issue" but also integrate questions of social justice and a renegeotiation of security approaches in their work, attempting to encounter radicalization processes especially in "marginalized localities" by improving the situation of women in highly patriarchal contexts and decolonizing feminist practices. In order to rethink sustainable concepts of human security of the 21st century, the distinct feminist methodologies arising from challenges faced at the interactional dimension of the public sphere deserve the utmost attention in feminist, policy and security scholarship.

Last but not least, I demonstrated how young feminist counterpublics rely on increasingly digitalized methods. The channels of communication, namely many-to-many forms of communication and blogs, bear the potential to create trans-regional networks and alternative spaces of knowledge production at low costs. The new methods at their disposal allowed them to orientate themselves further away from Western feminist concepts and networks with only European feminist groups and to initiate regional exchange South of the Mediterranean. My research has shown that a "new Matrix of Domination 2.0" must be taken into account, applied to a generation of "digital natives".

11.3   Hidden Hegemonies: The Matrix of Domination 2.0

In this study, I used intersectional theory to point to the power structures that include and exclude people according to their positionality from participation in public spheres and in counterpublics. These mechanisms should be central when analyzing the "structural shifts" of public spheres. The same is true for the shift imposed by technological innovations and especially in the field of ICTs.

While it is undeniable that the internet has had positive impacts on democratic practices, increased civic engagement, and "a clear factor in promoting participation" (Dahlgren, p. 170), we are currently engaging in more critical debates showing the other side of ICTs as an instrument of control, restricting freedoms, which have particularly gendered outcomes. The usage of the internet depends on factors such as class, education or locality. The category of age, educational attainment and socio-economic class are important when describing mobilization processes that use social media within specific settings and especially in relation to government protests. Then it is not only the coverage of internet infrastructure but also the demographic characteristics of the state which are important.

I want to briefly sketch out four illustrations of the Matrix of Domination in a digitalized environment that I deduced from the interviews: Firstly, with regards to the disciplinary domain of power, state practices and internet censorship –framed by political scientist Ron Deibert as the "architecture of control" – come into focus. This architecture has been elaborated with the growing political potential of the internet(s) and "shapes a new geopolitical information landscape" (Deibert, Palfrey, Rohozinski, & Zittrain, 2010, p. 3). The shift of surveillance from governments to companies is a question with both global as well as national repercussions.

Secondly, we are now assisting a "re-monopolization process" (DiGiacomo, 2016) of the communicative infrastructure: A platform needs to achieve a critical mass of users in order to be economically beneficial. On the one hand, this greater reach has enabled the providers of this communication infrastructure to exercise more political and economic influence and, on the other hand, has led to more possibilities to create and reach wider (counter-) publics. Following the distinction introduced by Dahlgren, these developments heavily impact the "structural dimension" of the public sphere. Currently, Facebook is by far the most used social media platform worldwide, the number of active users having reached 1.8 billion people as of autumn 2016 (Statista.com, 2016). Its monopoly on the internet is also expressed by the finding that in my interviews, Facebook is often used interchangeably with "the internet."

Another angle of investigating the Matrix of Domination 2.0 are the algorithms' lack of transparency and the deletion of content. With regards to my interviews and the feminist media projects under examination, the vulnerability of the communication infrastructure for feminist counterpublics became evident. They are situated within a global Matrix of Domination and subjected to the patriarchal norms of a hegemonic domain of power whose origins remain undefined. This became evident with the blocking of the short movie "Amel" on YouTube for copyright violations.

In this context, the policing of female bodies on social media needs closer investigation (Myers West, 2015). The censoring of photos of female bodies, i.e.

naked nipples, has become a subject of discussion in feminist media communities (Wong, 2016). In the case of the Facebook page "The uprising of Women in the Arab World," the photo of a young Syrian woman 'Dana' with short hair, showing her ID with her being veiled, was censored in 2012 and sparked a debate on censorship and transparency of decisions to erase content on Facebook (Salam, 2012). Most of the time, as in the case of "Dana", it is not clear whether banning content from the public platform is caused by "reporting" by a critical mass of other users or because of the internal moral standards and rules of the US-based social media companies themselves. This exemplifies the issue of hidden hegemonies that cannot be traced by classical methods of inquiry.

Last but not least, the digital environment can lead to "multifaceted visibilities" of feminist counterpublics (Antonakis 2018, 153 ff.). Against this background, women's rights organizations and feminist networks have to develop specific media and communication strategies to respond to online harassment and state surveillance. One issue is then how to react to these threats. The question whether to ignore or to react, take security measures or even try to file lawsuits, must be taken within the particular time and locality of the attacks. Responses, including digital security practices, acquire different resources, such as money, time and energy, which well-established NGOs may have, but often leave non-institutionalized actors and networks without protection.

New scholarship combining technology and social science open much needed perspectives to understand current dynamics in complex attention economies online, created by human and algorithmic interventions alike. Zeynep Tufekci mainly distinguishes two new forms of gatekeeping: networked gatekeeping function and algorithmic gatekeeping. Both lack transparency, while censorship can be re-conceptualized as simple denial of attention (Tufekci, 2017). Nevertheless, I would argue that with the #metoo hashtag the boundaries of a hegemonic public sphere were broken. The powerful cultural industry of Hollywood constituted the epicenter of the counterthematizations uncovering everyday patriarchy and could shift fixed attention economies.

12 Outlook: Negotiating Homosexualities in Tunisia: Inclusions and Exploitations in the Hegemonic Public Sphere after 2014

The discussion of homosexualities in the public sphere as part of a negotiation of gender in Tunisia constitutes a complex relation that weaves together issues of security and visa regulations, sexuality, morals, and citizenship and would require a specific in-depth study. In this regard, concepts of "homonationalism" and "gay assimilations" come into focus in Western knowledge production, where the "war on terror" has opened new windows of opportunity for homosexual subjects to be strategically integrated into the national discourse (Puar, 2009).

The question of LGBT activism can be framed as a part of renegotiating gender within the transformation period in Tunisia. Homosexuality was and remains criminalized and LGBT visibility is mostly excluded from all dimensions of the public sphere. Hence, from the interpretation of my interviews, the struggle to integrate the structure of oppression based on sexual orientation to the public sphere could be distinguished along all three dimensions of the public sphere. However, by the time of my data collection, it mainly consisted in processes of regrouping at the interactional dimension.

Thus, communication was set within counterpublic channels of communication online, such as "hidden" Facebook groups. In my interviews in 2013, it has been expressed that deputies were taken into confidence to defend LGBT rights. However, it was not considered the time to lobby more openly yet. I have previously outlined how defending homosexuality was used to stigmatize efforts to push for a lift of the reserves against CEDAW and equated with a loss of morals and atheism. Hence, this stigmatization campaign against the ATFD can be regarded as a demonstration of the hegemonic domain of power.

In 2015 however, the counterpublic gained more visibility in the hegemonic public sphere in terms of counterthematization and manifested in demonstrations and associations. The law criminalizing homosexuality, §230 was discussed by leading politicians, debates on homosexuality and queer identity and its place within Tunisian society were addressed in the representational dimension and

© Springer Fachmedien Wiesbaden GmbH, part of Springer Nature 2019
A. Antonakis, *Renegotiating Gender and the State in Tunisia between 2011 and 2014*, Politik und Gesellschaft des Nahen Ostens,
https://doi.org/10.1007/978-3-658-25639-5_12

the struggle for equal rights was institutionalized at the interactional dimension of the public sphere (Mzalouat, 2016).

An initial appearance of LGBT activism in the public space occurred at the World Social Forum in March 2015, when a small group of activists along with a huge demonstration composed of civil society actors from all over the world marched in the city center of Tunis under the rainbow flag (Voorhoeve M., 2015). At the Tunis Fashion week in April 2015, the young fashion designer Ayoub Moumene had a model wave the rainbow flag at the end of the runway show. The picture and video of the model dressed in a white robe and a white birdlike mask was mainly shared on social media (Tuniscope.com, 2015, 02:17).

Similar to the case of Meryrem that attracted public attention to police sexual abuse and was outlined in chapter 10.1.3, the case of Marwen, a young gay man that was subjected to the anal test, broke the taboo of homosexuality and exposed the anal test as a violation of human rights in October 2015. A structural reform of the law §230 was deemed to be an urgent matter and its abrogation demanded by a counterpublic of different minority rights defenders, for example the association *Mawjoudin* ("we exist"), the feminist association *Chouf* and *Shams*. The latter was the first association officially registered with the state secretary general in May 2015 defending openly the rights of homosexuals. The counterpublic was supported by the Tunisian Society of Clinical Sexology that issued a statement condemning the practice based on deontological medical standards that they are committed to de-pathologizing homosexuality (Société Tunisienne de Sexologie Clinique, 2015). This intervention illustrates the coupling of gender and health by the hegemonic domain of power.

One argument to abolish the criminalization of homosexuality is a legislative one: It can be regarded as anti-constitutional as the right to privacy is violated (Sbouai, 2015). Drawing from this argument, independent Mohamed Salah Ben Aïssa, then justice minister, spoke in favor of a depenalization of homosexuality on the radio Shams FM on September 28. One week later, president Béji Caïd Essebsi declared in an interview for the Egyptian TV that during his presidency the law §230 will continue to be enforced. He hereby publicly contradicted his minister of justice. Ben Aïssa left office only a couple of days after his initiative, on 20th October 2015, officially because of differences with the Prime Minister Habib Essid on the composition of the presidential council (Dahmani, 2015).

Rached Ghannouchi, leader of Ennahda party, argued in favor of an abrogation of the law departing from the right to privacy, while condemning homosexuality from a moral standpoint. His declaration that he gave in an interview to Olivier Ravanello has been received as a unique approach in a religious frame.

His argument re-arranges sexualities in the private and public dichotomy, exposing a more libertarian understanding of the state. On the one hand, he argues for decriminalization, on the other hand, he denies queer sexualities access to the public sphere.

The codification's history deconstructs the myth of homosexuality as an imported phenomenon by the West, as the criminalization goes back to colonial rule (Olomi, 2016) and was based on Western religious morals of the time rather than Islamic legislation. Renegotiating sexualities implies a renegotiation of masculinities, opening up the field of hegemonic and subordinated masculinities (Connell, 2013, p.111), but also persisting colonial legacies. The renegotiation of homosexualities sheds light on a gendered system of oppression that affects all genders and reproduces global inequalities in a post-colonial world.
d reproduces global inequalities in a post-colonial world.

References

Abu-Lughod, L. (1998). Preface and Introduction: Feminist Longings and
Postcolonial Conditions. In L. Abu-Lughod (Ed.), *Remaking Women:
Feminism and Modernity in the Middle East*. Princeton, New Jersey:
Princeton University Press.
- (2002). Do Muslim Women Really Need Saving? Anthropological
Reflections on Cultural Relativism and Its Others. *American
Anthropologist, 104*(3), pp. 783-790.
Abu-Zahra, N. (1992/1993). The Tunisian Personal Status Code, National
Policy, and the Homogenization of the Population. *Cambridge
Anthropology, 16*(2).
afrit 1975 (22 January 2011): القيروان إلى تصل الكرامة قافلة. [Video file]. Retrieved
16   March   2017,   from
https://www.youtube.com/watch?v=MeSNhmtg5J0
Ahmed-Ghosh, H. (2008). Dilemmas of Islamic and Secular Feminists and
Feminisms. *Journal of International Women's Studies, 9*(3), pp. 99-116.
Al-Ali. N. (2012). Gendering the Arab Spring. *Middle East Journal of Culture
and Communication 5*, 26–31.
- (2016, January). Interview with Nadje al-Ali. (E.-I. Relations, Editor)
Al-Amin, E. (2012). Tunisia: The Fall of the West's little Dictator. In F. Manji,
& S. Ekine (Eds.), *African Awakening: The Emerging Revolutions* (pp.
42-51). Oxford: Pambazuka Press.
Albertini, G. (2011). Final Report on the Tunisian national Constituent Assembly
Elections.European Delegation for the Observations of the Elections in
Tunisia. National Democratic Institute. Retrieved January 12, 2016
from: https://www.ndi.org/files/tunisia-final-election-report-
021712_v2.pdf .
Alcoff, L. (1992). The Problem of Speaking for Others. Cultural Critique(20),
pp. 5-32.
Alexander, C. (2016). Tunisia: *From Stability to Revolution in the Maghreb*.
London and New York: Routledge.

© Springer Fachmedien Wiesbaden GmbH, part of Springer Nature 2019
A. Antonakis, *Renegotiating Gender and the State in Tunisia between
2011 and 2014*, Politik und Gesellschaft des Nahen Ostens,
https://doi.org/10.1007/978-3-658-25639-5

Ali, A. (2012, 06 05). Saeeds of Revolution: De-Mythologizing Khaled Saeed. *Jadaliyya*. Retrieved 17 November 2013, from http://www.jadaliyya.com/pages/index/5845/saeeds-of-revolution_de-mythologizing-khaled-saeed

Allal, A. (2010). Ici, si ça ne bouge pas ça n'avance pas!" Les mobilisations protestataires dans la région minière de Gafsa en 2008. In M. /. Catusse, *L'État face aux débordements du social au Maghreb*. Paris.

- (2012). Trajectoires "Revolutionnaires" en Tunisie. Processus de radicalisations politiques 2007-2011. *Presse de Science Po*, pp. 821-841.

- (2016, January). Retour vers le futur. Les origines économiques de la Révolution tunisienne. *Pouvoirs, revue française d'études constitutionnelles et politiques*,(156), pp. 17-29.

Al-Mahadin, S. (2011). Arab Feminist Media Studies - Towards a poetics of diversity. *Feminist Media Studies, 11*(1), pp. 7-12.

Alwazir, A. (14. February 2012). No Spring Withouth Women. Retrieved 7 March 2014, from http://english.al-akhbar.com/node/4195/. *AlAkhbar English*.

Amal Bint Nadia (20 March 2016): 60 years of independence and our bodies are still colonized TUNISIA. [Video file]. Retrieved 16 march 2017, from https://www.youtube.com/watch?v=A8otd_B4k18&feature=youtu.be

Amami, H. e.al. (2014). *Rapport d'Analyse sur la Situation Economique et Sociale des Femmes rurales de la région d'El Hania, et sur leur Rôle de Citoyennes*. Unpublished Report.

Amar, P. (2011). Turning the Gendered Politics of the State Security Inside Out? *International Feminist Journal of Politics, 13*(3), pp. 299-328.

Antonakis, A. (2012). *Der Quellcode der ""Tunesischen Revolution" 2011 - Partizipation an der Schnittstelle von Gegenöffentlichkeiten*. (Vol. Working paper No. 5). (F. U. Middle East Institute, Ed.) Berlin. Retrieved January 12, 2016, from http://www.polsoz.fu-berlin.de/polwiss/forschung/international/vorderer-orient/publikation/WP_serie/WP5_info.html

- (August 2013). Tunisia's Legitimacy and Constitutional Crisis The Troika Has Failed. *SWP Comments*. Berlin.

- (2015a, October). Contested Transformation: Mobilized Publics in Tunisia between Compliance and Protest. *Mediterranean Politics*(21).

- (2015b). Hashtagging the Invisible: Bringing Private Experience into Public Debate. In *Hashtag Publics* (pp. 101-113). New York: Peter Lang.

(2018). Feminist Networks in Times of Multi-layered Transformations. Perspectives from Tunisia. In: Cilja Harders, Carola Richter and Anna Antonakis (ed.). *Media and the Politics of Transformation*. Springer VS. Wiesbaden.

Antonakis, A., & Chennaoui, H. (August 2018). Gender, Work, Locality - Female Protests in Tunisia Re-framing Socio-Economic Rights as Women's Rights . *Zeitschrift für Menschenrechte (Journal for Human Rights)*.

Arab Working Group for Media Monitoring. (2013). Image des Femmes dans les Medias Tunisiennes.

Arendt, H. (2012). The Human Condition. Chicago: University of Chicago Press.

Arfaoui, K. (2016). Women and Leadership in the Post-Arab Spring: The Case of Tunisia. In F. Sadiqi (Ed.), Women's Movements in Post-"Arab Spring" North Africa. New York: Palgrave MacMillan. pp 223-234.

Armbrust, W. (2013, May 8). The Ambivalence of Martyrs and the Counter-revolution. Cultural Anthropology Online - Fieldsights - Hot Spots. Retrieved 3 May 2015, from http://culanth.org/fieldsights/213-the-ambivalence-of-martyrs-and-the-counter-revolution

Aronson, P. (2003, December). Feminists or 'Postfeminists'"? Young Women's Attitudes toward Feminism and Gender Relations. Gender & Society, 17(6), pp. 903-922.

Asseburg, M., & Wimmen, H. (2015). Dynamics of Transformation, Elite Change and New Social Mobilization in the Arab World. Special Issue of Mediterranean Politics.

Association Tunisienne de Gouvernance. (2014). Gouvernance des Associations en Tunisie. Annual Report.

Association Tunisienne des Femmes Démocratqes (29 April 2014): La Tunisie lève officiellement ses réserves sur la Cedaw, mais maintient la Déclaration générale. Official declaration by the ATFD published on Nawaat. Retrieved on 15 December 2016, from https://nawaat.org/portail/2014/04/29/la-tunisie-leve-officiellement-ses-reserves-sur-la-cedaw-mais-maintient-la-declaration-generale/.

Ayari, M. B. (2012). Le "dire" et le "faire" du mouvement islamiste tunisien: Chronique d'un Aggiornamento perpétuel par-delà les régimes. In S. Amghar (Ed.), Les islamistes au défi du pouvoir. Evolution d'une idéologie. Paris: Michalon.

Ayari, M. G. (25. January 2011). Tunisie : la Révolution des «Nouzouh»* n'a pas l'Odeur du Jasmin. Retrieved January 12, 2016, from http://temoignagechretien.fr/articles/international/tunisie-la-revolution-des-nouzouh-na-pas-lodeur-du-jasmin.   Témoignage Chrétien. Le site chrétien démocraticque et fraternel.

Ayish, M. (2008). The New Arab Public Sphere. Berlin: Frank&Timme.

- (2010). Understanding Arab women's role in media industries – An empowerment-based perspective. Journal of Arab & Muslim Media Research, 3(3), pp. 191-206.

Azouzi, A. (2013). La « Révolution du Jasmin » en Tunisie et son Slogan « Ben Ali dégage !» Un Evénement Discursif. (R. P.-T.-F. E. Ballardini, Ed.) mediAzioni(15).

Bang, H., & Esmark, A. (2007). *New Publics with/out Democracy.* Frederiksberg: Samfundslitteratur Press.

Belkaïd, A. (2012, December 19). Y'en a marre de la «Révolution du Jasmin»! (http://www.slateafrique.com/79803/revolution-du-jasmin-tunisie, Ed.) *Slate Afrique.*

Bellamine, Y. (26. October 2015). La politisation de la Cour Constitutionnelle, crainte principale de nombreux juristes. Retrieved January 12, 2016, from   http://www.huffpostmaghreb.com/2015/10/26/politisation-cour-constit_n_8373428.html. *AL Huffington Post Maghreb.*

Bellin, E. R. (2002). *Stalled Democracy: Capital, Labor, and the Paradox of State-sponsored Development.* Ithaca, NY: Cornell University Press.

Ben Achour, S. (2013). *Etat du Droit Tunisien sur les Violences faites aux Femmes et aux Filles.* UNFPA and Tunisian State Secretary of Women and   Family,   Tunis.   Retrieved   from   http://www.unfpa-tunisie.org/images/stories/2014/publication/Publication%20Etude%20 violence%202014_f.pdf

Ben Alaya, D. (2013). The Tunisian Revolution: An Object under Construction. *Papers on Social Representations, 22*, pp. 2.1.-2.19.

- (2014). La reappropriation d'elements de l'histoire sur facebook, dans un contexte tunisien « post-revolutionnaire ».In: *Educaçao e Cultura Contemporânea*, 11(24), pp. 21-33.

Ben Gharbia, S. (2010): "Anti- Censhorship Movement in Tunisia: Creativity, Courage, and Hope! In. Global Voices. Advox. Retrieved on 1 August 2018, from https://advox.globalvoices.org/2010/05/27/anti-censorship-movement-in-tunisia-creativity-courage-and-hope

Ben Hamadi, M. (11 March 2016). Resister et produire : La Lutte des Ouvrières de   Mamotex.   Retrieved   14   March   2017,   from https://inkyfada.com/2016/03/resister-produire-la-lutte-des-ouvrieres-mamotex-chebba-tunisie/ *Inkyfada.*

Ben Mheni, L. (2011). Vernetzt Euch !. Ullstein Verlag : Berlin

Ben Mheni, L. [A Tunisian Girl] (2 July 2012): "Tunisie: les robes courtes dérangent la police!" Retrieved on 17 March 2017, from http://www.atunisiangirl.blogspot.de/2012/07/tunisie-les-robes-courtes-derangent-la.html;
- (6 July 2012). "Tunisie: Vivre dérange la police !" Retrieved on 17 March 2017, from http://www.atunisiangirl.blogspot.de/2012/07/tunisie-vivre-derange-la-police.html;
- (31 May 2013): Je cesse d'être hypocrite, je soutiens Amina! Retrieved on 1 August 2018, from http://www.atunisiangirl.blogspot.de/2013/05/je-cesse-detre-hypocrite-je-soutiens.html
Ben Said Cherni, Z. (1986). *Les Dérapages de l'Histoire chez Tahar Haddad: Les Travailleurs, Dieu et la Femme*. Tunis: Edition Ben Abdallah.
Ben Salem, M. (2010, December). Le voile en Tunisie. De la réalisation de soi à la résistance passive. Retrieved January 12, 2016, from http://remmm.revues.org/6840#bodyftn2, Ed.) *Remmm-Revue des mondes musulmans et de la Méditerranée*.
- (2010). Media Coverage of Women in the Arab Political Sphere. *Journal of Arab & Muslim Media Research, 3*(3), pp. 177-189.
Ben Salem, M., & Mejbri, A. (5. February 2015). The image of women in the Post-Revolution Tunisian Media. Retrieved January 12, 2016, from http://www.resetdoc.org/story/00000022499. *Reset Doc - Dialogues on Civilisation*.
Ben Youssef Zayzafoon, L. (2005). *The Production of the Muslim Woman: Negotiating Text, History, and Ideology*. Maryland: Rowman & Littlefield - Lexington Books.
Benazis, A., Smith-Spark, L., & Abedine, S. (March 2014). Tunisia sex workers call for brothel to reopen in resort of Sousse. Retrieved January 12, 2016, from http://edition.cnn.com/2014/03/12/world/africa/tunisia-prostitutes-brothel/ *CNN*.
Bendana, K. (2007). Leïla, Tunis, 1936-1941 : Revue Féminine ou Féministe ? (La Manouba. Institut Supérieur d'Histoire du Mouvement National, ed.) *Rawafid*,(12), pp. 296-299.
Benhabib, S. (1992). Models of Public Space: Hannah Arendt, the Liberal Tradition and Jürgen Habermas. In C. Calhoun, *Habermas and the Public Sphere* (pp. 73-98). London: MIT Press.
- (2011). The Arab Spring: Religion, Revolution and the Public Sphere. *Eurozine*, pp. 1-4.

Bennoune, K. (2013). *Your Fatwa does not apply here: Untold Stories from the Fight against Muslim Fundamentalism*. New York: W.W. Norton & Company.

Bertoluzzi, G., & Spocci, C. (25. May 2016). Tunisie : échec des ouvrières. (https://incendo.noblogs.org/post/2016/05/25/tunisie-echec-des-ouvrieres/, Ed.) *INCENDO- Sur le rapport entre Genre et Classe*.

Bessis, S. (1999). Le féminisme institutionnel en Tunisie. *CLIO - Histoires. Femmes et Sociétés*(9).

- (2004). Bourguiba Féministe: Les Limites du Féminisme d'Etat Bourguibien. In M. Camau, & V. Geisser (Eds.), *Habib Bourguiba. La Trace et l'Héritage* (pp. 101-112). Paris: Karthala.

Beth Radcliff, P. (1996). *From Mobilization to Civil War: The Politics of Polarization in the Spanish City of Gijón, 1900-1937*. Cambridge: Cambridge University Press.

Bhandar, B., & Ferreira da Silva, D. (21. October 2013). White Feminist Fatigue Syndrome - A Reply to Nancy Fraser. *Critical Legal Thinking – Law & the Political*.

Bond, P. (2012). Neoliberal Threats to North Africa. In F. Manji, & S. Ekine (Eds.), *African Awakening: The Emerging Revolutions* (pp. 252-272). Oxford: Pambazuka.

Borsali, N. (2006, March 15). Femme et Histoire: Nos souvenirs sont nos seuls repères. *Réalités*(1054), p. 26.

- (2008). *Bourguiba à l'épreuve de la démocratie 1956-1963*. Sfax: Samed Editions.

- (2012). *Tunisie: Le défi égalitaire - Ecrits féministes*. Tunis: Arabesques.

Bouali, O. (2011, March 22). Tunisienne, tu n'as pas choisi ton sexe, change donc de destin. Retrieved on 15 September 2013 from http://nawaat.org/portail/2011/03/22/tunisienne-tu-nas-pas-choisi-ton-sexe-change-donc-de-destin/. *Nawaat.org*.

Boubakeur, A. (2015, October). Islamists, Secularists and old Regime Elites in Tunisia: Bargained Competition. *Mediterranean Politics*(21).

Bouderbala. (2012 April). Rapport de la Commission d'enquête sur les dépassements et les violations. From http://de.slideshare.net/marsedkadha/ss-12834630

Bourdieu, Pierre (1995 [1985]): Sozialer Raum und „Klassen." Leçon sur la leçon. 2 Vorlesungen. Frankfurt a. M.

Bouziane, M., Harders, C., & Hoffmann, A. (2013). Analyzing Politics Beyond the Center in an Age of Political Transformation. In M. Bouziane, C. Harders, & A. Hoffmann (Eds.), *Local Politics and Contemporary*

Transformations in the Arab World - Governance Beyond the Center (pp. 1-21). New York: Palgrave MacMillan.

Brand, L. (1998). Women, the state and political Liberalization. New York: Columbia University Press.

Brynen, R. (2000). A Very Political Economy: Peacebuilding and Foreign Aid in the West Bank and Gaza-On the international assistance effort to the Palestine Authority,. Washinton: United States Institute of Peace Press.

Business News (23 October 2014) Meeting Nidaa Tounes. Bourguiba reprend à Sousse. [Video file]. Retrieved on 17 March 2017, from https://www.youtube.com/watch?v=s9pXjIwIK-g

Butler, J. (1990). Gender Trouble and the Subversion of Identity (Vols. *Thinking Gender*. Nicholson, Linda J. (Ed.)). London: Routledge.

- (2011, September*). Bodies in Alliance and the Politics of the Street.* Retrieved on 12 November 2014 from http://eipcp.net/transversal/1011/butler/en, Transversal.

- (2013). Parting Ways: Jewishness and the Critique of Zionism. New York: Columbia University Press.

- (2015). Notes Toward a Performative Theory of Assembly. (J. Butler, Z. Gambetti, & L. Sabsay, Eds.) Cambridge: Harvard University Press.

Byerly, C., & Ross, K. (2006). Women and Media: A critical introduction. Oxford: Blackwell.

Calhoun, C. (1992). Habermas and the Public Sphere. London: MIT Press.

Camau, M., & Geisser, V. é. (2004). La Trace et l'Héritage. In M. Camau, & V. é. Geisser (Eds.), *Habib Bourguiba. La Trace et l'Héritage* (pp. 9-17). Paris: Karthala.

Car, V. (2011, June). Critical Book Review: DAHLGREN, P. Media and Political Engagement: Citizens, Communication, and Democracy. *Quaderns del CAC, XIV* (36), pp. 123-124.

Carapico, S. (2002). Foreign Aid for Promoting Democracy in the Arab World. *Middle East Journal, 56*(3).

Carstensen-Egwuom, I. (2014). Connecting Intersectionality and Reflexivity: Methodological Approaches to social Positionalities. *Erdkunde, 68* (4), pp. 265–276.

Chabbi, N. (9. April 2011). Laïcité hysterique! Retrieved 10 November 2016, from http://nawaat.org/portail/2011/04/09/laicite-hysterique/, *Nawaat*.

Chahed, M. K., & Arfa, C. (2014). *Full Case Study: Monitoring and Evaluating Progress towards Universal Health Coverage in Tunisia.* Universal Health Coverage Measurement Collection. PLOS Medecine. Chaine de JaniJamel (15 october 2009): redeyef: le combat de la dignité. [Video file]. Retrieved on 17 march, from https://www.youtube.com/watch?v=AiBSBPS3NDE

Charrad, M. (2001). *States and Women's rights - The Making of Post-colonial Tunisia, Algeria and Marocco*. Berkeley: University of California Press.

- (2008). From Nationalism to Feminism - Family Law in Tunisia. In K. R. Yount (Ed.), *Family in the Middle East - Ideational Change in Rgypt, Iran, and Tunisia*. Oxon: Routledge. pp. 111-135.

Charrad, M. M., & Zarrugh, A. (2014). Equal or complementary? Women in the new Tunisian Constitution after the Arab Spring. *The Journal of North African Studies, 19*(2), pp. 230-243.

Chayes, S. (2014, March). How a leftist Labor Union helped Tunisia's Political Settlement. *Carnegie Endowment for International Peace*. Retrieved from http://carnegieendowment.org/2014/03/27/how-leftist-labor-union-helped-force-tunisia-s-political-settlement

Chekir, H. (2014). *Les Droits des Femmes en Tunisie*. Mittelmeer Institut, HU Berlin, Arbeitsstelle Gender Studies, Gießen,. Retrieved March 01, 2016, from https://www.uni-giessen.de/faculties/gender-studies-research-group/events/Discours_Chekir

Chennaoui, H. (19. January 2015). Redeyef: A Town of Hopes Betrayed. Retrieved 12 November 2014, from https://nawaat.org/portail/2015/01/19/redeyef-a-town-of-hopes-betrayed/, Ed.) *Nawaat.org*.

Cherif, N. (2014, November). *Tunisian Women in Politics: from Constitution Makers to Electoral Contenders*. (F. A. Action, Ed.) Policy Brief, p. 5. Retrieved February 11, 2016, from http://fride.org/download/PB_189_Tunisian_women_in_politics.pdf

Chomiak, L. (2014). Architecture of Resistance in Tunisia. In L. Khatib, & E. Lust (Eds.), *Taking to the Streets: The Transformation of Arab Activism* (pp. 22-52). Baltimore: Kohn Hopkins University Press.

Chouf-tech (2016). http://chouf-tech.org/ Accessed 17 March 2017.

Cinemovel (2015): Med-Itinerate- AMAL. [video file]. Retrieved on 17 march 2017, from https://www.youtube.com/watch?v=sX0W7BhIU14

Civil Society Watch (September-October 2008). Monthly Bulletin. (39). Retrieved on 2 May 2017, from http://www.civicus.org/csw_files/CSWMB_Sept-Oct_No39.htm. *Civicus*

Clarke, J., Hall, S., Jefferson, T., & Roberts, B. (1975). Subcultures, Cultures and Class. In K. Gelder, & S. Thornton (Eds.), The Subcultures Reader. London and New York: Routledge.

Coalition des ONG Tunisiennes pour la Transition démocratiques. (2011,

August/December). Rapport Final: Monitoring des Médias en Periode Transitoire. Retrieved 12 November 2014, from http://menamediamonitoring.com/fr/2012/03/07/rapport-final-dobservation-des-medias-en-tunisie-2012/

Cohen, W. (1971): *Rulers of Empire : The French Colonial Service in Africa.* California: Hoover Institution Press.

Coleman, G. (2010). Ethnographic Approaches to Digital Media. *The Annual Review of Anthropology*(39), pp. 487–505.

Collectif 18 Octobre pour les Droits & les Libertés en Tunisie. (2007). Notre voie vers la démocratie. Synthèse des débats sur le projet démocratique et ses enjeux nationaux La gauche - L'Islam Politique - Les Unionistes Arabes - Les libéraux à la recherche d'une approche tunisienne commune sur les bases de l'Etat démocratique. *Summary of discussions on the democracy project and its national challenges in Tunisia.*

Collins, P. H. (1998). It's all in the Family: Intersections of Gender, Race, and Nation. *Hypatia, 13*(3), pp. 62-82.

- (2000). *Black Feminist Thought: Knowledge, Consciousness and the Politics of Empowerment* (2nd ed.). New York, London: Routledge.

Connel, R. (2013). *Gender.* Gechlecht und Gesellschaft. Lenz Ilse; Meuser, Michael (Ed.) Wiesbaden: Springer VS.

Correia, J. C., & Maia, R. C. (2011). *Public Spheres Reconsidered. Theories and Practices.* Covilhã : LabCom Books.

Crenshaw, K. (1989). Demarginalizing the Intersection of Race and Sex: A Black Feminist Critique of Antidiscrimination Doctrine, Feminist Theory and Antiracist Politics. *The University of Chicago Legal Forum, 140.*

- (1991). Women of Color at the Center. *Selections from the Third National Conference on Women of Color and Law: Mapping the Margins: Intersectionality, Identity Politics, and Violence against Women of Color.*

Dahlgren, P. (2005). The Internet, Public Spheres, and Political Communication: Dispersion and Deliberation. *Political Communication*(22), pp. 147–162.

- (2009). *Media and Political Engagement - Citizens, Communication and Democracies.* Cambridge, New York: Cambridge University Press.

Dahmani, F. (17. November 2015). Tunisie – Mohamed Salah Ben Aïssa : « Pourquoi j'ai été limogé ». *Jeune Afrique* . Retrieved on 1 August 2018 from http://www.jeuneafrique.com/mag/275867/politique/tunisie-mohamed-salah-ben-aissa-pourquoi-jai-ete-limoge/

Dahou, T. (2005). L'Espace Public face aux Apories des Etudes Africaines. *Cahiers d'Etudes Africaines*(178), pp. 327-349.

Daoud, Z. (1993). *Féminisme et Politique au Maghreb. Soixante ans de lutte (1930-1992)*. Paris: Maisonneuve et Larose.

Darghouth Medimegh, A. (1992). *Droits et vécu de la femme en Tunisie*. Paris: L'Hermès.

Davis, K. (2008). Intersectionality as buzzword. A sociology of science perspective on what makes a feminist theory successful. *Feminist Theory* (9 (1)), pp. 67- 85.

Deb, B. (2012). Transnational Politics and Feminist Inquiries in the Middle East: An Interview with Lila Abu-Lughod. *Postcolonial Text, 7*(1).

Deibert, R., Palfrey, J., Rohozinski, R., & Zittrain, J. (2010). *Access controlled. The Shaping of Power, Rights, and Rule in Cyberspace*. Massachusetts: Massachusetts Institute of Technology Press.

Dhawan, N. (2009). Zwischen Empire und Empower: Dekolonisierung und Demokratisierung . Femina Politica (2), pp. 52-63.

   - (2013): Coercive Cosmopolitism and impossible Solidarities. In: Qui parle. Critical Humanities and Social Science. Vol. 22 (1) pp. 139-167.

DiGiacomo, J. (25. February 2016). Internet of Things Series Part III: Monopolization. Retrieved on 17 January 2017, from https://revisionlegal.com/revision-legal/internet-of-things-series-part-iii-monopolization/. *Revision Legal*.

Downey, J., & Fenton, N. (2003). New media, Counter Publicity and the Public Sphere. *New Media & Society*.(Vol5(2)), pp. 185–202.

Doyle, J. L. (2016). Civil Society as Ideology in the Middle East: A Critical Perspective. *British Journal of Middle Eastern Studies, 43*(3), pp. 403-422.

Dubai School of Government. (2011). *Civil Movements: The Impact of Facebook and Twitter*. Arab Social Media Report:, Dubai. Retrieved May 2015, from http://www.arabsocialmediareport.com/UserManagement/PDF/ASMR%20Report%202.pdf

Dwyer, K. (1997). Organizing for the Rights of Women: Tunisian Voices. In N. S. Hopkins, & S. E. Ibrahim (Eds.), *Arab Society: Class, Gender, Power, and Development* (pp. 479-497). Cairo: American University Press.

Dyczok, M., & Gaman-Golutvina, O. (Eds.). (2009). *Media, Democracy and Freedom. The Post-Communist Experience*. Bern a.o.: Peter Lang.

Eickelman, D. F. (Ed.). (1999). *New Media in the Muslim World : The Emerging Public Sphere*. Bloomington: Indiana University Press.

El-Masri, S. (2015). Tunisian Women at a Crossroads: Cooptation or Autonomy? Retrieved 8 December 2016, from http://www.mepc.org/journal/middle-east-policy-archives/tunisian-women-crossroads-cooptation-or-autonomy? *Middle East Policy Council, 22*(2).

Engelmann, I., & Scheufele, B. (2009). *Empirische Kommunikationsforschung.* Konstanz: UVK Verlagsgesellschaft.

Entelis, J. (2004). L'Héritage Contradictoire de Bourguiba: Modernisation et Intolerance Politique. In V. Geisser, & M. Camau (Ed.), *Habib Bourguiba. La trace et l'héritage.* Paris: Karthala.

Errazzouki, S. (2014). Working-Class Women Revolt: Gendered Political Economy in Morocco. *The Journal of North African Studies, 19*(2), pp. 259-267.

Faris, D. M. (2013). *Dissent and Revolution in a Digital Age - Social Media, Blogging and Activism in Egypt.* New York: I.B. Tauris & Co.

Fenton, N. (2016). *Digital, Political, Radical.* Cambridge: Polity.

Ferguson, A. (1998). Resisting the Veil of Priviledge: Building Bridge Identities as an Ethico-Politics of Global Feminisms. *Hypatia, 13*(3), pp. 95-113.

Fishman, R. (1990). Rethinking State and Regime. Southern Europe's Transition to Democracy. *World Politics. 42(3).* pp. 422-440.

Flick, U. (2006). *An Introduction to Qualitative Research.* London: Sage.

Foster, A. (2012). Tunisia: A global leader in reproductive health and rights. In A. M. Foster, & L. Wynn (Ed.), *Emergency contraception: The story of a global reproductive health technology* (pp. 153-168). New York: Palgrave MacMillan.

Fraser, N. (1992). Rethinking the Public Sphere: A Contribution to the Critique of Actually Existing Democracy. In C. Calhoun (Ed.), *Habermas and the Public Sphere.* (pp. 109-142). London: MIT Press.

- (2013) Fraser, N. (14. October 2013). How Feminism became Capitalism's Handmaiden - and how to reclaim it. Retrieved 3 November 2014, from https://www.theguardian.com/commentisfree/2013/oct/14/feminism-capitalist-handmaiden-neoliberal. *The Guardian.*

- (2014). Transnationalizing the Public Sphere: On the Legitimacy and Efficacy of Public Opinion in a Post-Westphalian World. In K. Nash (Ed.), *Transnationalizing the Public Sphere.* Malden, USA: Polity Press. pp. 8-42.

Fuchs, C., & Sandoval, M. (2014). *Critique, Social Media and the Information Society.* New York: Routledge.

Gana, N. (2015). Dissident Tunisia. Culture and Revolt. In F. Al-Sumait, N. Lenze, & M. C. Hudson (Ed.), *The Arab Uprisings: Catalysts, Dynamics, and Trajectories*. London: Rowman&Littlefield.

Geisser, V., & Gobe, É. (2005-2006). Des fissures dans la « Maison Tunisie » ? Le régime de Ben Ali face aux Mobilisations Protestataires. *Année du Maghreb*(2), S. 353-414.

Ghorbani, M. (2012). Mobilisations pour les droits des femmes : capacités d'influence féministe dans la transition politique tunisienne. *DUMAS*. (H. A. Ouvert, Ed.) Retrieved 10 February 2014, from http://dumas.ccsd.cnrs.fr/file/index/docid/826818/filename/201211GH ORBANI_MOB.pdf

Grami, A. (2008). Gender Equality in Tunisia. *British Journal of Middle Eastern Studies,, 35*(3), pp. 349–361.

Gramsci, A. (1971). *Selections From The Prison Notebooks Of Antonio Gramsci*. New York: International Publishers.

Gray, D. H. (2012). Tunisia after the Uprising: Islamist and. *Mediterranean Politics*(17:3), pp. 285-302.

Gribaa, B., & Depaoli, G. (2014). *Profil Genre de la Tunisie*. Report, European External Action Service.

Grodsky, B. (2016). *The Democratization Disconnect: How Recent Democratic Revolutions Threaten the Future of Democracy*. Maryland: Rowman&Littlefield.

Gunnarsson Payne, J. (2012). Feminist Media as Alternative Media?: Theorising Feminist Media from the Perspective of Alternative Media Studies. In E. Zobl, & R. Drüeke (Eds.), *Feminist Media: Participatory Spaces, Networks and Cultural Citizenship*. pp. 55-72.

Habermas, J. (1974). The Public Sphere – An Encyclopedia Article. In: *New German Critique*. (3). pp. 49-55.

(1992). *Faktizität und Geltung. Beiträge zur Diskurstheorie des Rechts und des demokratischen Rechtsstaats*. (2. ed.). Frankfurt am Main.: Suhrkamp.

Hached, F. (2011). La Laïcité : Un Principe à l'Ordre du Jour de la IIeme République Tunisienne ? *Confluences Méditerranée , 2* (77), pp. 29-36.

Haddad, T. (1978). *Notre Femme, la Législation Islamique et la Société*. Tunis: Maison Tunisienne de l'édition.

Haddaoui, N. (31. May 2014). Haro sur la parité : les limites de la justice constitutionnelle en Tunisie. Retrieved 10 November 2014, from https://nawaat.org/portail/2014/05/31/haro-sur-la-parite-les-limites-de-la-justice-constitutionnelle-en-tunisie/. *Nawaat*.org

Hafez, S. (2014). The revolution shall not pass through women's bodies: Egypt, uprising and gender politics. *The Journal of North African Studies, 19*(2), pp. 172-185.

Halimi, S. (October 2011). Tunisie, l'ivresse des possibles. (http://www.monde-diplomatique.fr/2011/10/HALIMI/21070, Ed.) *Le Monde Diplomatique*.

Hamadi, S. B. (August 2013). Amina Sboui Quits FEMEN: 'I Do Not Want My Name To Be Associated With An Islamophobic Organization. . *The Huffington Post*. Retrieved 1 August 2018 from https://www.huffingtonpost.com/2013/08/20/amina-sboui-quits-femen_n_3785724.html?guccounter=1

Hamza, N. (2016). Engendering Tunisia's Democratic Transition: What Challenges Face Women? In: F. Sadiqi (Ed.), *Women's Movements in Post-"Arab Spring" North Africa*. New York: Palgrave MacMillan. pp. 211-221.

Harass Map (2015): http://harassmap.org/ar/. Accessed 17 March 2017.

Haraway, D. (1988). Situated Knowledges: The Science Question in Feminism and the Privilege of Partial Perspective. *Feminist Studies, 14*(3), pp. 575-599.

Harders, C. (2011). Gender Relations. Violence and Conflict Transformation. in: B. Austin, M. Fischer, H.J. Giessmann (eds.) 2011. Advancing Conflict Transformation.The Berghof Handbook II. pp. 131-145.

- (2013). Bringing the Local back in: Local Politics Between Informalization and Mobilization in the Age of Transformation in Egypt. In M. Bouziane, C. Harders, & A. Hoffmann (Ed.), *Local Politics and Contemporary Transformations in the Arab World. Governance Beyond the Center*. New York: Palgrave Macmillan.

- (2015). "State Analysis from Below" and Political Dynamics in Egypt after 2011. *International Journal for Middle East Studies , 47* (1), pp. 148 - 151.

Hatem, M. (1992). Economic and Political Liberalisation in Egypt and the Demise of State Feminism. *International Journal of Middle East Studies*(24), pp. 231-251.

- (1993). Toward the Developpment of Post-Islamist and Post-Nationalist Feminist Discourses in the Middle East. *Gender Discourses*, pp. 29-47.

Haugbolle, R. H. (2013). Rethinking the Role of the Media in the Tunisian Uprising:. In N. Gana (Ed.), *The Making of the Tunisian Revolution:*

Contexts, Architects, Prospects (pp. 159-180). Edinburgh: Ediburgh University Press.

Hays-Mitchell, M., & Irvine, J. A. (2012). Gender and Political Transformation in Societies at War. *Journal of International Women's Studies, 13*(4), pp. 1-9.

Head, G. (2016, July). Transgender Subjects, Fairytales, and Red Light Districts: Strategies of Subversion in Tunisian Women's Writing under Ben 'Ali. *The Journal of North African Studies.*

Hennessy, R. (1995). Queer Visibility in Commodity Culture. (U. o. Press, Ed.) *Cultural* Critique(29), pp. 31-76.

Hermassi, A. (1994). Société, Islam et Islamisme en Tunisie. Cahiers de la Méditerranée, 49(1), pp. 61-82.

High Commissioner of Human Rights. (2015, April). Tunisian transition a model for the region and beyond. Retrieved 10 January 2017, from http://www.ohchr.org/EN/NewsEvents/Pages/DisplayNews.aspx?New sID=15866&LangID=E#sthash.81BPnD5u.dpuf

Hmed, C. (2016). « Le Peuple veut la Chute du Regime ». Situations et issues révolutionnaires lors des occupations de la place de la Kasbah à Tunis, 2011. Actes de la recherche en Sciences Sociales. (211-212) pp. 72-91.

Hoffmann, A., Bouziane, M., & Harders, C. (2013). Analyzing Politics Beyond the Center in an Age of Transformation. In *Local Politics and Contemporary Transformations in the Arab World. Governance Beyond the Center* (pp. 1-25). New York: Palgrave.

Hornig Priest, S. (2010). *Doing Media Research. An Introduction.* London: Sage.

Hsieh, H.-F., & Shannon, S. E. (9. November 2005). Three Approaches to Qualitative Content Analysis. *Qualitative Health Research*(9).

Hull, G. T., Scott, P. B., & Smith, B. (1982). *All women are white, all blacks are male, but some of us are brave."* New York: The Feminist Press.

Human Rights Watch. (2015). *Tunisia: Counterterror Law Endangers Rights.* Human Rights Watch. Retrieved 14 May 2015, from https://www.hrw.org/news/2015/07/31/tunisia-counterterror-law-endangers-rights

Institut Nationale des Statistiques. (2016, June). Retrieved 14 May 2015, from http://dataportal.ins.tn/fr/DataAnalysis?PjjB82FdwUWNC70aBlXrVA Tunis.

ISIE (2014) . Election Présidentielle 2014. Retrieved 1 August 2018, from http://www.isie.tn/resultats/resultats-presidentielles/

Janier, A. (14. January 2016). En Tunisie, les espoirs frustrés de la « révolution du jasmin » LeMonde. Retrieved 10 November 2016, from http://www.lemonde.fr/international/article/2016/01/14/en-tunisie-les-espoirs-frustres-de-la-revolution-du-jasmin_4846860_3210.html. *Le Monde*.

Jansson, André (2013). The Hegemony of the Urban/Rural Divide: Cultural Transformations and Mediatized Moral Geographies in Sweden. *Space and Culture*. 16(1). pp.88 -103

Jensen, H., sm Kee, J., Venkiteswaran, G., & Randhawa, S. (2012). Censorship, Surveillance, and the Body Politic(s) of Malaysia. In R. Deibert, J. Palfrey, R. Rohozinski, & J. Zittrain, *Access Contested - Security, identity and Resistance in Asian Cyberspace* (pp. 65-83). Cambridge: MIT.

Journalist Tunisien 30/10 (13 January 2011). Thourat alYasmine. Retrieved 3 May 2017 from http://journaliste-tunisien-110.blogspot.de/2011/01/blog-post_13.html

Kandiyoti, D. (1988, September). Bargaining with Patriarchy. *Gender and Society, 2*(3), pp. 274-290.

Keddie, N. R. (2007). *Women in the Middle East. Past and Present*. Princeton and Oxford: Princeton University Press. Kelly, J., & Etling, B. (2008). Mapping Iran's online public: Politics and culture in the Persian blogosphere. *Berkman Center research publication: no. 2008-01*. Retrieved 8 January 2017, from https://cyber.law.harvard.edu/publications/2008/Mapping_Irans_Online_Public

Khalil, A. (2014). Tunisia's Women: Partners in Revolution. *The Journal of North African Studies,*(19:2), pp. 186-199.

Khechana, R. (2009). Les médias tunisiens face à la préponderance de l'Etat partisan. *Confluences Méditerrannée*(69), pp. 99-106.

Khélifa, O. (2012). Women after the Arab Awakening. (W. W. Scholars., Ed.) *Middle East Programm Occasional Paper Series*, pp. 24-27.

Khiari, S. (2004). *Tunisie: le délitement de la cité : coercition, consentement, résistance*. Paris: Khartala.

Kollmorgen, R., Merkel, W., Mouna, G., & Wagener, H.–J. (2015). *Handbuch Transformationsforschung*. Wiesbaden: Springer VS.

Koopmans, R. (2005). Repression and the Public Sphere : Discursive Opportunities for Repression against the Extreme Right in Germany in the 1990s. In C. Davenport, H. Johnston, & C. McClurg Mueller (Eds.), *Repression and Mobilization*. Minnesota: University of Monnesota Press.

Kumari, K. (2010). Political Participation of Women in Inidia. In A. Kumar Gupta, & A. Bhandari (Eds.), *Women's Political Participation -*

Researching the Past and Designing the Future (pp. 197-210). Delhi: Authors Press.

Labidi, L. (2007). The Nature of Transnational Alliances in Women's Associations in the Maghreb: The Case of AFTURD and AFTD in Tunisia. *Journal of Middle East Women's Studies, 3:1* (6).

- (16. October 2014). The Role of Women in Tunisian Politics. *Wilson Center*. Retrieved on 11. February 2016, from https://www.wilsoncenter.org/article/the-role-women-tunisian-politics

- (2014). Political, Aesthetic and Ethical Positions of Tunisian Women's Artists 2011-2013. (A. Khalil, Ed.) *The Journal of North African Studies, 19*(2), pp. 157-171.

- (2015). Forming the New Tunisian Government: "Relative Majority" and the Reality Principle. (W. Center, Ed.) *Middle East Program - Viewpoints, 71.*

- (2016). Tunisian Women's Literature and the Critique of Authority: Sources, Contexts, and the Tunisian "Arab Spring." In F. Sadiqi (Ed.), *Women's Rights in the Aftermath of the Arab Spring*. London: Macmillan.

- (2016 b). Historic Women Figures and Women's Daily Struggles in Tunisia: Neglect and Societal Responsibility. In M. Ennaji (Ed.), *Minorities, Women and the State in North Africa*. Trenton, New Jersey: The Read Sea Press.

Laclau, E., & Mouffe, C. (2014) [1985]. *Hegemony and Socialist Strategy - Towards a Radical Democratic Politics*. London/NY : Verso

Lamloum, O. (2002). L'indéfectible Soutien des Francais à l'Exclusion de l'Islamisme Tunisien. In O. Lamloum, & B. Ravenel (Eds.), *La Tunisie de Ben Ali: La société contre le régime* (Les cahiers de confluence). Paris: L'Harmattan.

Larguèche, D. (2011). *Monogamie en Islam. L'exception Kairouanaise*. Manouba: C.P.U.

Laudel, J., & Gläser, G. (2013, May). Life With and Without Coding: Two Methods for Early-Stage Data Analysis in Qualitative Research Aiming at Causal Explanations. *Forum Qualitative Social Research, 14*(2).

Lecomte, R. (2009). Internet et la reconfiguration de l'espace public tunisien : le rôle de la diaspora. *tic&société,, 3*(1-2).

Liauzu, C. (2004). Bourguiba, héritier de Tahar Haddad et des militants réformistes des annés 1920? In V. Geisser, & M. Camau (Eds.), *Habib Bourguiba. La trace et l'héritage* (pp. 21-29). Aix en Provence: Karthala.

Lilleker, D. G. (2006). *Key Concepts in Political Communication*. London: Sage.

Lim, M. (11. July 2011). Tahrir Square was a Foreseeable Surprise - Tracing the History of Egyptian Online Activism. Retrieved on 11 February 2016, from http://www.slate.com/articles/technology/future_tense/2011/07/tahrir_square_was_a_foreseeable_surprise.html, Ed.) *Slate.com*.

Lister, T. (2011, October 29). After the Arab Spring: Islam, Democracy, Bikinis and Polygamy. *CNN*.

Löblich, M., & Musiani, F. (2014). Net neutrality and Communication Research: The Implication of Internet Infrastructure for the Public Sphere. In E. L. Cohen, & I. C. Association (Ed.), *Communication Yearbook* (pp. 339-369). New York: Routledge.

Lunnay, B., Borlagdan, J., McNaughton, D., & Ward, P. p. (2011, September 11). Ethical Use of Social Media to Facilitate Qualitative Research. *Qualitative Health Research*. Retrieved October 27, 2015, from http://www.researchgate.net/publication/265607508_Ethical_Use_of_Social_Media_to_Facilitate_Qualitative_Research

Lynch, M. (2006). *Voices of the New Arab Public. Iraq, Al-Jazeera, and Middle East Politics Today*. New York: Columbia University Press.

Mahmood, T. (1987). *Personal Law in Islamic Countries - History, text, and comparative analysis*. New Delhi: Academy of Law and Religion.

Mahmoud, A. (2014). Public Sphere: Power and Counter-powers in Post-Revolutionary Tunisia. *Open Journal of Social Science Research, 2*(2), pp. 52-58.

Mamelouk, N. (2008). *Anxiety in the Border Zone: Transgressing Boundaries in Leila: Revue Illustree de la Femme (Tunis, 1936-1940) and in Leila: Hebdomadaire Tunisien Independant (Tunis, 1940-1941)*. (D. p. Philosophy) Virginia.

Mandhouj, T. (2014, August 25). Tunisie : élections législatives 2014, la femme est peu présente comme tête de liste. Retrieved 12 March 2016, from https://nawaat.org/portail/2014/08/25/tunisie-election-legislative-2014-la-femme-est-peu-presente-comme-tete-de-liste/. *Nawaat.org*.

Manji, F. (2012). African Awakenings: The Courage to Invent the Future. In F. Manji, & S. Ekine (Eds.), *African Awakenings: The Emerging Revolutions* (pp. 1-19). Oxford: Pambazuka.

Marks, M. (2013). Women's Rights before and after the Revolution. In N. Gana (Ed.), *The Making of the Tunisian Revolution: Contexts, Architects, Prospects* (pp. 224-251). Edinburgh: Edinburgh University Press.

Marsad (1 May 2014): Vote sur l'amendement relatif à la consécration de la parité horizontale absolue dans l'article 23. Retrieved 17 March 2017, from http://majles.marsad.tn/fr/vote/5362543112bdaa078ab82510#.

Marx Ferree, M. (2012). *Varieties of Feminism*. Stanford, California: Stanford University Press.

Marx Ferree, M., & Choo, H. Y. (2010, June). Practicing Intersectionality in Sociological Research: A Critical Analysis of Inclusions, Interactions, and Institutions in the Study of Inequalities. *Sociological Theory, 28*(2).

Marx-Ferree, M. (2005). Soft Repression: Ridicule, Stigma, and silencing Gender-Based Movements. In Davenport et al. (Ed.), *Repression and Mobilization* (pp. 138 – 155). Minneapolis/London: University of Minnesota Press.

Marzouki, I. (1993). *Le Mouvement des Femmes en Tunisie au XXeme Siècle. Féminisme et Politique*. Tunis: Cérès.

Mason, M. (2010, September). Sample Size and Saturation in PhD Studies Using Qualitative Interviews. *Forum Qualitative Social Research, 11*(3). Retrieved November 4, 2015, from http://www.qualitative-research.net/index.php/fqs/article/view/1428/3027

Mataziasim, L. (11 August 2012). *Droits des femmes en Tunisie : peut-on préserver ce qui n'a jamais été ?* Retrieved 12 March 2016, from http://pomme-empoisonnee.blogspot.ch/2012/08/droits-des-femmes-en-tunisie-peut-on.html. *La pomme empoisonnée*.

McCall, L. (2005). The complexity of intersectionality. *Signs: Journal of Women in Culture and Society,, 30*(3), pp. 1771-1800.

McCarthy, R. (2014). Re-thinking Secularism in Post-Independence Tunisia. *The Journal of North African Studies, 19*(5), pp. 33-750.

McLuhann, M. (1962). *The Gutenberg galaxie the making of typographic man*. London: Routledge.

Mehrez, S. (2007). Translating Gender. *Journal of Middle East Women's Studies, 3*(1), pp. 106-127.

Mernissi, F. (1975). *Beyond the Veil: Male-Female Dynamics in Muslim Society*. Cambridge, Massachusetts: Schenkman Publishing Company Inc.

Merone, F. (2015). Enduring Class Struggle in Tunisia: The Fight for Identity beyond Political Islam. *British Journal of Middle Eastern Studies, 42*(1), pp. 74-87.

Merone, F., & Cavatorta, F. (March 2013). Ennahda: A Party in Transition. Retrieved November 4, 2015, from http://www.jadaliyya.com/pages/index/10762/ennahda_a-party-in-transition *Jadalyya*.

Merone, F., & Soli, E. (22. October 2013). Tunisia: the Islamic associative system as a social counter-power. Retrieved November 8, 2015, from https://www.opendemocracy.net/arab-awakening/evie-soli-fabio-merone/tunisia-islamic-associative-system-as-social-counter-power#_ftnref. *OpenDemocracy*.

Mersch, S. (21. January 2014). Tunisia's Compromise Constitution. http://carnegieendowment.org/sada/?fa=54260. *Carnegie Endowment for International Peace*.

- (10. April 2015). Judicial Reforms in Tunisia. Retrieved February 16, 2016, from http://carnegieendowment.org/sada/?fa=59746. *Carnegie Endowment for International Peace*.

Mestiri, M. (9 February 2016,). Disparités Régionales, Etat des Lieux d'une Discrimination. Retrieved 13 November 2016, from https://nawaat.org/portail/2016/02/09/disparites-regionales-etat-des-lieux-dune-discrimination/. *Nawaat*.org

Mestiri, S. (2016). Décoloniser le féminisme. Paris: VRIN.

Migdal, J. (2001) *State in Society. Studying How States and Societies Constitute and Transform One Another*. Cambridge: Cambridge University Press.

Mikdashi, M. (2012, February 28). The uprisings will be gendered! Retrieved 13 November 2016, from http://www.jadaliyya.com/pages/index/4506/the-uprisings-will-be-gendered. *www.jadalyya.com*.

Minic, D. (2014). Feminist publicist strategies: Women's NGO's media activism and television journalism in Serbia and Croatia. *Media, Culture & Society, 36*(2), pp. 133-149.

Mitra, A. (2013). *Voices of Privilege and Sacrifice from Women Volunteers in India: I Can Change*. Plymouth: Lexington Books.

Moghadam, V. (2003). *Modernizing Women: Gender and Social Change*. Boulder: Lynne Rieger.

Moghadam, V. (2004). *Towards Gender Equality in the Arab/Middle East Region: Islam, Culture and Feminist Activism*. Background paper for HDR 2004, United Nations Development Program.

- (2014). Modernising Women and Democratization after the Arab Spring. *The Journal of North African Studies*(19:2), pp. 137-142.

Mohanty, C. T. (1984). Under Western Eyes: Feminist Scholarship and Colonial Discourses. *boundary 2, 12*(3), pp. 333-358.

Moors, A. (1996). Gender Relations and Inheritance: Person, Power and Property in Palestine. In D. Kandyoti, *Gendering the Middle East* (pp. 69-85). London: I.B.Tauris & Co Ltd.

Mosaique FM (19 November 2016): *2ème séance d'audition publique à l'IVD : témoignage de Bechir Abid*. [Video file]. Retrieved 16 March 2017, from https://www.youtube.com/watch?v=1yqbJLuv2Qw

العاصمة اتجاه في احتجاجية مسيرة :بوزيان منزل :(2011 January 22) 2007 Abassi .Mr ,
[Video file]. Retrieved 16 March 2017, from
https://www.youtube.com/watch?v=Udlhex0K-SM

Mughrabi, M. (2015). *Tunisia must not turn its back on survivors of rape and abuse*. Amnesty International, Tunis.

Murphy, E. (2003). Women in Tunisia: Between State Feminism and Economic Reform. In D. Abdella, & P. Pousney (Eds.), *Women and Globalization in the Arab Middle East*. Boulder: Lynne Rienner.

- (2011). Between Image and Reality: New ICTs and the Arab Public Sphere. In M. S. Murphy, *The New Arab Media. Technology, Image and Perception* (pp. 103-122). London: Ithaca Press.

Myers West, S. (18 November 2015). Facebook's Guide to being a Lady. Retrieved 13 November 2016, from https://www.onlinecensorship.org/news-and-analysis/facebook-s-guide-to-being-a-lady. *Onlinecensorship.org*.

Mzalouat, H. (17. June 2016). LGBT Rights in Tunisia: The Fight will be Televised. Retrieved 13 Novemeber 2016, from https://www.boell.de/en/2016/06/17/lgbt-rights-tunisia-fight-will-be-televised. *Heinrich Böll Foundation*.

Mzalouat, H. &Sehiri, E. (14 July 2016). L'Autogestion de l'Usine Mamotex: Une Désillusion pour les Ouvrières. Retrieved 17 March 2017, from https://inkyfada.com/2016/07/autogestion-usine-femmes-mamotex-desillusion-ouvrieres-droit-travail-tunisie/. *Inkifada*.

Nagarajan, C. (2013). Femen's obsession with nudity feeds a racist colonial feminism. Retrieved 12 February, 2016, from http://www.theguardian.com/commentisfree/2013/apr/11/femen-nudity-racist-colonial-feminism. The Guardian.

Nawaat (29 April 2014): Declaration by the ATFD on the CEDAW: La Tunisie lève officiellement ses réserves sur la Cedaw, mais maintient la Déclaration générale. Retrieved on 15 December 2016, from https://nawaat.org/portail/2014/04/29/la-tunisie-leve-officiellement-ses-reserves-sur-la-cedaw-mais-maintient-la-declaration-generale/. Nawaat.org

Naudé, J.-F. (27. June 2011). Tunisie : Ennahdha se retire de la Haute instance pour la réalisation des objectifs de la révolution. Retrieved 13 October 2016, from http://www.jeuneafrique.com/180598/politique/tunisie-ennahdha-se-retire-de-la-haute-instance-pour-la-r-alisation-des-objectifs-de-la-r-volution/. *Jeune Afrique*.

Ogundipe-Leslie, M. (1994). *Re-Creating Ourselves: African Women and Critical Transformations*. Trenton: Africa World Press.

Olomi, A. (2016, June 3). The Roots of Homophobia and Anti-Gay Sentiment in the Muslim World. (http://islamiccommentary.org/2016/06/the-roots-of-homophobia-and-anti-gay-sentiment-in-the-muslim-world-by-ali-olomi/, Ed.) *Islamic Commentary*.

Open Net Initiative. (2009). Country Profile Tunisia. Retrieved 13 October 2016, from https://opennet.net/research/profiles/tunisia. *Open Net Initiative*.

O'Pry, Kay (2012) "Social and Political Roles of Women in Athens and Sparta," *Saber and Scroll*: 1 (2). Retrieved 29 April 2017, from http://digitalcommons.apus.edu/saberandscroll/vol1/iss2/3

Oxfam (2017). *Just 8 men own same wealth as half the world*. Oxfam. Retrieved on 2 August 2018 from https://www.oxfam.org/en/pressroom/pressreleases/2017-01-16/just-8-men-own-same-wealth-half-world.

Petzen, J. (2012). Queer Trouble: The Evasion of Race in Queer and Feminsit Practice. In G. *I. ativkolleg* (Ed.), *Gewalt und Handlungsmacht. Queer_Feministsiche Perspektiven* (pp. 48-59). Frankfurt am Main: Campus Verlag.

PEW-Report. (2013). The World's Muslims: Religion, Politics and Society. (P. R. Center, Ed.) Retrieved 5 April 2016, from http://www.pewforum.org/Muslim/the-worlds-muslims-religion-politics-society-women-in-society.aspx.

Pfeffer, J., Zorbach, T., & Carley, K. M. (2014). Understanding Online Firestorms: Negative Word-of-mouth Dynamics in Social Media Networks. *Journal of Marketing Communication, 20*(1-2), pp. 117-128.

Pickard, D. (2015). *Tunisia's New Constitutioinal Court*. Issue in Focus, Atlantic Council - Rafik Hariri Center for Middle East Studies. Retrieved February 16, 2016, from http://www.atlanticcouncil.org/images/publications/Tunisias_New_Co nstitutional_Court.pdf

Pratt, N. (2016, January 25). How the West Undermined Women's Rights in the Arab World. Retrieved 13 October 2016, from http://www.jadaliyya.com/pages/index/23693/how-the-west-undermined-women%E2%80%99s-rights-in-the-arab. *Jadaliyya*.

Prensky, M. (2001). Digital Natives, Digital Immigrants.*On the Horizon*. (5)9. pp.1-6.

Raupp, J. (2011). Organizational Communication in a Networked Public Sphere. *Studies in Communication Media*, pp. 71-95. Retrieved June 5, 2015, from http://www.scm.nomos.de/fileadmin/scm/doc/SCM_11_01_geschuetzt .pdf

Remili, B. (2011). *Quand le peuple réussit là où toute la société a echoué - Eléments de compréhension politique pour une révolution sans les politiques*. Tunis: Nirvana.

Reporters Withouth Borders. (2005). *The 15 enemies of the Internet and other countries to watch*. Reporters Withouth Borders.

Richter, C. (18. April 2005). Libyen geht online - aber wohin? Retrieved on 7 March 2016, from https://de.qantara.de/inhalt/Internet-libyen-geht-online-aber-wohinQantara.

Richter, C., & Badr, H. (2016). Communication Studies in Transformation – Self-reflections on an Evolving Discipline in Times of Change. (A.-G. Y. Academy, Ed.) Berlin.

Richter, C., Dupuis, Indira, & Stefanie Averbeck-Lietz) (Eds): *Diversity in Transcultural and International Communication*. Münster: LIT. Introduction. pp. 1-15.

Risse (Ed.). (2014). *European Public Spheres: Politics is Back*. Cambridge: Cambridge University Press.

Roberge, J. (2011). What is Critical Hermeneutics? *Thesis Eleven, 106* (1), pp. 5–22.

Robert, D. (10. August 2016). Soutien européen à la société civile : enquête sur un programme controversé. Retrieved on 7 February 2017 from https://nawaat.org/portail/2016/08/10/soutien-europeen-a-la-societe-civile-enquete-sur-un-programme-controverse. *Nawaat.org*

Sadik, N. (2013, March 8). The Uprising of Women in the Arab World. *New Internationalist Blog - People, Ideas and Action for Global Justice*. Retrieved January 8, 2015, from http://newint.org/blog/2013/03/08/womens-rights-campaign-arab-world/

Sadiki, L. (2008). Engendering Citizenship in Tunisia: Prioritizing Unity over Democracy. In Y. Zoubir, & H. Amirah-Fernandez (Ed.), *North Africa – Politics, Region, and the Limits of Transformation*. (pp. 109-133). London&New York: Routledge.

Salam, Y. (13. November 2012). The Uprising of Women in the Arab World censored by Facebook. Retrieved January 8, 2015, from http://www.genderit.org/feminist-talk/uprising-women-arab-world-censored-facebook, *GenderIT.org*.

Saldana, J. (2008). *The Coding Manual for Qualitative Researchers*. London: Sage.

- (2011). *Fundamentals of Qualitative Research*. Oxford: Oxford University Press.

Salem, S. (2013, December). Angela Davis in Egypt: On Feminist Solidarity. *Neo-colonialism and its Discontents*. Retrieved February 23, 2016, from https://neocolonialthoughts.wordpress.com/2013/12/01/angela-davis-in-egypt-on-feminist-solidarity/

Saussure (de), F. (1916): *Cours de linguistique générale*. (Bailly, Charles; Séchehaye, Albert Ed.) Paris: Edition Payot &Rivages.

Sayigh, Y. (5 February 2016): Bringin Tunisia's Transition to the Security Sector. Retrieved 7 March 2016, from http://carnegie-mec.org/2016/02/05/bringing-tunisia-s-transition-to-its-security-sector-pub-62563. *Carnegie*

Sbouai, S. (26. May 2015). Article 230 du Code pénal: La criminalisation anticonstitutionnelle. Retrieved February 23, 2016, from https://inkyfada.com/2015/05/article-230-code-penal-criminalisation-anticonstitutionnelle-homosexualite-tunisie/. *Inkyfada*.

Schankweiler, K. (2016). *Selfie-Proteste. Affektzeugenschaft und Bild-Ökonomien in den Social Media*. SFB 1171. Working Paper 05/16. Retrieved 2 May, from http://edocs.fu-berlin.de/docs/receive/FUDOCS_series_000000000562

Scheuch, M. (2003). *Demokratie per Mausklick. Neue Informationstechnologien und ihre Auswirkungen auf Demokratietheorie*. Stuttgart: Ibidem-Verlag.

Schmidt, E. C. (2014). Die Frauenbewegung zwischen Vereinnahmung und Opposition. *Inamo*, pp. 20-24.

Schwab, K. e. (2007). *The Global Competitiveness Report 2006–2007*. World Economic Forum. New York: Palgrave Macmillan.

Seghaier, R. (2018). Policing Women's Sexualities and Getting Credit for It: Sex Work and the Tunisian State. In *Koh A Journal for Body and Gender Researchl*. 4 (1). Retrieved October 28 2018, from https://kohljournal.press/sex-work-and-the-tunisian-state

Sharma, A. & Gupta, A. (eds.). (2006). *The Anthropology of the State: A Reader*. Oxford: Blackwell Publishing.

Shevchenko, I. (2013). We are Femen, the naked shock troops of feminism. *The Guardian*. Retrieved February 12, 2016, from http://www.theguardian.com/commentisfree/2013/apr/10/femen-naked-shock-troops-of-feminism?INTCMP=SRCH

Shirky, C. (2011): "The political power of social media: Technology, the public sphere and political change", Retrieved 18 November 2016, from https://www.foreignaffairs.com/articles/2010-12-20/political-power-social-media. *Foreign Affairs*

Sholkamy, H. (2012). Women Are Also Part of this Revolution. In R. El-Mahdi (Ed.), *Arab Spring in Egypt. Revolution and Beyond* (pp. 153-174). New York, Cairo: American Univesrity in Cairo Press

Silva, N. (2013). Bouleversements dans le milieu prostitutionnel : De l'évolution des interactions entre policiers et prostituées pendant le processus révolutionnaire tunisien. Unpublished Master Thesis. *Université Panthéon-Sorbonne. UFR 11. Etudes Africains.Paris*

Silva, N., & Mahdhaoui, K. (2016). Human. *Gender, Sexuality and Social Justice: What's Law got to do with it?*, 98-102. (K. Lalor, E. Mills, A. S. Garcia, & P. Haste, Ed.) Sussex: Institute of Development Studies, University of Sussex.

Skalli, L. H. (2006, Spring). Communicating Gender in the Public Sphere: Women and Information Technologies in the MENA. *Journal of Middle East Women's Studies*(2), pp. 35-59.

Skandrani, F. (2012, December). L'Histoire du Mouvement Féministe Tunisien. *Journal des Alternatives*.

Smati, N. (2009). Un paysage audiovisuel tunisien en mutation. *Confluences Méditerranée*(69), pp. 87-97.

Smith, B. (1982). Toward a Black Feminist Criticism. In *All Women are White, all Blacks are Male, but Some of Us are Brave* (pp. 156-175).

Société Tunisienne de Sexologie Clinique. (2015, October 1). Communiqué de la Société Tunisienne de Sexologie Clinique à propos du citoyen condamné pour homosexualité. Retrieved 13 January 2017, from http://www.jomhouria.com/art40155_Communiqu%C3%A9%20de%20la%20Soci%C3%A9t%C3%A9%20Tunisienne%20de%20Sexologie%20Clinique%20%C3%A0%20propos%20du%20citoyen%20condamn%C3%A9%20pour%20homosexualit%C3%A9. *Joumhouria*.

Sorkin, J. (2001). The Tunisian Model. *Middle East Quarterly*, pp. 25-29. Retrieved November 2, 2015, from http://www.meforum.org/107/the-tunisian-model

Soubai, S. (2012, September 29). La pilule Microgynon bientôt de retour en Tunisie ? *Nawaat*. Retrieved from tp://nawaat.org/portail/2012/09/29/la-pilule-microgynon-bientot-de-retour-en-tunisie/

Soudani, S. (2014). La Tunisie a-t-elle raté son entrée dans le pluralisme politique ? Retrieved February 11, 2016, from http://nawaat.org/portail/2015/01/04/la-tunisie-a-t-elle-rate-son-entree-dans-le-pluralisme-politique/. *Nawaat*.

Spiegel, A. (2010). *Contested Public Spheres - Female Activism and Identity Politics in Malaysia*. Wiesbaden: VS Research Verlag für Sozialwissenschaften.

Spivak, Gayatri Chakravorty, 2007: „Feminism and Human Rights". In: Shaikh, Nermeen (Ed.): The Present as History: Critical Perspectives on Global Power. New York, pp. 172-201.

Statista.com. (2016). Aktuelle Statistiken und Informationen zu Facebook. Retrieved November 26, 2015, from http://www.statista.com/statistics/272014/global-social-networks-ranked-by-number-of-users/. *Statistica.com*

Strickland, P. O., & Verghese, N. (2014, November 10). Tunisia's Nidaa Tounes: Nostaligia for a Past that never was? *MiddleEastEye*. Retrieved February 11, 2016, from http://www.middleeasteye.net/news/tunisia-s-nidaa-tounes-nostalgia-past-never-was-313445692.

Stromquist, N. P. (2007). *Feminist Organisations and Social Transformation in Latin America*. Colorado: Paradigm Publishers.

Syndicat National des Journalistes Tunisiens (2009): Syndicat National des Journalistes Tunisiens : Chronique d'une conspiration programmée. Statement by the Executive Board of the SNJT. Retrieved 6 February 2017, from https://nawaat.org/portail/2009/08/16/syndicat-national-des-journalistes-tunisiens-chronique-dune-conspiration-programmee/. *Nawaat.org*

Tamaru, N., Holt-Ivry, O., & O'Reilly, M. (2018). Beyond Revolution: How Women Influenced Constitution Making In Tunisia. Inclusive security. Retrieved on 2 August 2018 from https://www.inclusivesecurity.org/publication/beyond-revolution-women-influenced-constitution-making-tunisia/

Taylor, V. (1998). Feminist Methodology in Social Movements Research. *Qualitative Sociology,, 21*(4), pp. 357 -379.

Thussu, D. (2010). Contra-flow in Global Media. In d. Thussu (Ed.), *International Communication. A Reader.* London: Routledge.

Touhami, H. (2. February 2012). Disparités Sociales et Régionales et Chômage des Diplômés du Supérieur. Retrieved 20 January 2016, from http://www.leaders.com.tn/article/9988-disparites-sociales-et-regionales-et-chomage-des-diplomes-du-superieur *Leaders* .

Tripp, C. (2015). Battlefields of the Republic: The Struggle for Public Space in Tunisia. *LSE Middle East Centre Paper Series (13)* . (L. M. Series, Ed.)

Tsotsis, A. (2011, January 16). A Twitter Snapshot Of The Tunisian Revolution: Over 196K Mentions Of Tunisia, Reaching Over 26M Users. Retrieved

18 december 2016, from https://techcrunch.com/2011/01/16/tunisia-2/ *Techchrunch* .

Tsourapas, G. (2013). The Other Side of a Neoliberal Miracle: Economic Reform and Political De-Liberalization in Ben Ali's Tunisia. *Mediterranean Politics*, pp. 23-41.

Tunisian Ministry of Employment and Qualifications & National Observatory on Employment and Qualification. (2013). *Rapport Annuel sur: Le marché du Travail en Tunisie*.

Tuniscope.com (11 April 2015): *Défilé de Ayoub Moumene - Fête de la Mode 2015*. [Video file]. Retrieved 16 March 2017, from https://www.youtube.com/watch?v=kJS5bhnGeOs

United Nations (1995): Tunisia's Message to the Fourth World Conference on Women Beijing 4 - 15 September 1995. Retrieved 15 February 2017, from   http://www.un.org/esa/gopher-data/conf/fwcw/conf/gov/950905171419.txt

United Nations Population Fund. (2010). In e. d. Réunion régionale des partenaires d'Afrique subsaharienne (Ed.), *L'Expérience Tunisienne et l'évolution des services de l'avortement et PF depuis 1965*.

United Nations (23 April 2014) CEDAW. NEW YORK, 18 DECEMBER 1979. Tunisia. Withdrawal of the declaration with regard to article 15(4) and of the reservations to articles 9(2), 16 (C), (D), (F), (G), (H) AND 29(1) Made upon ratification. Retrieved on 1 August from https://treaties.un.org/doc/Publication/CN/2014/CN.220.2014-Eng.pdf

UN Women (2009): Declarations, Reservations and Objections to CEDAW retrieved on 1 August from http://www.un.org/womenwatch/daw/cedaw/reservations-country.htm

Voorhoeve, M. 1. (2014, March 11). Women's rights in the new Tunisian constitution.   *Open   Democracy*.   Retrieved   from https://www.opendemocracy.net/arab-awakening/maaike-voorhoeve/women%e2%80%99s-rights-in-new-tunisian-constitution

- (2015). "Women's Rights in Tunisia and the Democratic Renegotiation of an Authoritarian Legacy. *New Middle Eastern Studies*(5).

- (26. October 2015). The Struggle for Greater LGBT Rights in Tunisia Is Still an Uphill Battle. Retrieved 8 November 2015, from http://muftah.org/the-struggle-for-greater-lgbt-rights-in-tunisia-is-still-an-uphill-battle/. *Muftah.org*.

Wahba, D. (2016). Gendering the Egyptian Revolution. In: F. Sadiqi (Ed.), *Women's Movements in Post-"Arab Spring" North Africa*. New York: Palgrave MacMillan. pp. 61-77.

Walker, R. (1992). Becoming the Third Wave. *Ms. Magazine , 11* (2), 39–41.

Webb, E. (2014). *Media in Egypt and Tunisia: From Control to Transition?* New York: Palgrave Macmillan.

Weber, A. F. (2001). *Staatsfeminismus und autonome Frauenbewegungen in Tunesien* (Vol. Bd. 62). (D. O. Institut, Ed.) Hamburg.

Weber, M. (1919). Politics as a Vocation. *Weber's Rationalism and Modern Society(2014)*. (D. Waters, B. Elbers, & T. Waters, Trans.) Palgrave.

Wei, B. (2008). Girl's Issues, Gender and the Media: Feminist activism in China. In K. Drotner, & S. Livingstone (Eds.), *The International Handbook of Children, Media and Culture*. London: Sage.

Wengraf, T. (2001). *Qualitative Research Interviewing*. London: Sage Publications.

Wheeler, D. L. (2004). Blessings and Cursses: Women and the Internet Revolution in the Arab World. In N. Sakr (Ed.), *Women and Media in the Middle East - Power through Self-Expression* (pp. 138-162). London/New York: I.B. Tauris.

Wimmer, J. (2007). *(Gegen-)Öffentlichkeit in der Mediengesellschaft Analyse eines medialen Spannungsverhältnisses*. Wiesbaden: VS Verlag.

Wong, J. C. (9. September 2016). Zuckerberg accused of censorship after Facebook deletes 'napalm girl'. (https://www.theguardian.com/technology/2016/sep/08/facebook-mark-zuckerberg-napalm-girl-photo-vietnam-war, Ed.) *The Guardian*.

Yousif, E.-I. (2002). *Les chroniqueurs syriaques*. Paris: L'Harmattan.

Yuval-Davis, N. (1997). *Gender and Nation*. London: Sage Publications.

Zaki, H. A. (11. April 2016). Tunisia Uncovered a History of State Sexual Violence. Can it do anything? Retrieved on 5 January 2017, from https://www.washingtonpost.com/news/monkey-cage/wp/2016/04/11/tunisia-uncovered-a-history-of-state-sexual-violence-can-it-do-anything/. *The Washington Post*.

Zayani, M. (2015). *Networked Publics and Digital Contention: The Politics of Everyday Life in Tunisia*. Oxford: Oxford University Press.

Zlitni, S., & Touati, Z. (2012). Social Networks and Women's Mobilization in Tunisia. *Journal of International Women's Studies, 13*(5), pp. 46-58.

Zwingel, S. (2005, September). From Intergouvernemental Negotiations to (Sub)natinal Change: A Transnational Perspective on the Impact of CEDAW. *International Feminist Journal of Politics*(7:3), pp. 400-427.

Druck:
Canon Deutschland Business Services GmbH
im Auftrag der KNV-Gruppe
Ferdinand-Jühlke-Str. 7
99095 Erfurt